THE RENAISSANCE

This volume introduces the most recent scholarship on the history of the Renaissance. It considers not only humanists and artists, but looks at people from all classes, men and women alike. The themes covered in this collection include politics and society, identity and gender, and religion and science. The focus is on Italian developments, but aspects of the Renaissance in Germany, France and England are also covered.

The contributors to *The Renaissance* are among the most highly regarded scholars in the field. Their work has opened up new ways of thinking about the period from a variety of perspectives: from the history of the body to new ways of thinking about the relation of culture to power. Clearly, the Renaissance remains a vital area of research, even as scholars grow increasingly sceptical about their ability to trace the origins of their own world back to this era in European history. It helped to shape modernity, but, as Martin argues in his provocative introduction, we are now looking back to the Renaissance from a postmodern perspective.

The Renaissance: Italy and Abroad presents a thorough introduction to the major debates in Renaissance studies for students at all levels.

John Jeffries Martin is Professor of History at Trinity University. He is the author of *Venice's Hidden Enemies: Italian Heretics in a Renaissance City* (1993) and co-editor of *Venice Reconsidered: The History and Civilization of an Italian City-state, 1297–1797* (2000).

Series editor **Jack R. Censer** is Professor of History at George Mason University.

REWRITING HISTORIES
Series editor: Jack R. Censer

THE RENAISSANCE
Italy and Abroad
Edited by John Jeffries Martin

THE REVOLUTIONS OF 1989
Edited by Vladimir Tismaneanu

SEGREGATION AND APARTHEID IN TWENTIETH-CENTURY
SOUTH AFRICA
Edited by William Beinart and Saul Dubow

SOCIETY AND CULTURE IN THE SLAVE SOUTH
Edited by J. William Harris

STALINISM
New Directions
Edited by Sheila Fitzpatrick

TWENTIETH-CENTURY CHINA
New Approaches
Edited by Jeffrey N. Wasserstrom

THE RENAISSANCE

Italy and Abroad

Edited by
John Jeffries Martin

LONDON AND NEW YORK

2003

First published 2003
by Routledge
11 New Fetter Lane, London EC4P 4EE

Simultaneously published in the USA and Canada
by Routledge
29 West 35th Street, New York, NY 10001

Routledge is an imprint of the Taylor & Francis Group

Typeset in Palatino by Taylor & Francis Books Ltd
Printed and bound in Great Britain by T J International Ltd, Padstow,
Cornwall

British Library Cataloguing in Publication Data
A catalogue record for this book is available from the British Library

Library of Congress Cataloging-in-Publication Data
Martin, John Jeffries, 1951–
The Renaissance: Italy and abroad/John Jeffries Martin.
p.   cm. — (Rewriting histories)
Includes bibliographical references and index.
1. Renaissance — Italy. 2. Italy—Civilization—1268–1559.
3. Renaissance. I. Title. II. Re-writing histories.

DG445 .M37 2002
945′.05—dc21

2002009261

ISBN 0–415–26062–0 (hbk)
ISBN 0–415–26063–9 (pbk)

CONTENTS

CONTENTS

ILLUSTRATIONS

Figures

PREFACE

It is the design of this book to introduce readers to current controversies and debates in the study of Renaissance history. The Introduction attempts to provide an overview of the historiography of the field and to explain how it has changed since Jacob Burckhardt published his celebrated *The History of the Renaissance in Italy* (1860). The essays that follow, each by a leading scholar, present some of the most stimulating current writings on various aspects of the Renaissance. You will read in this volume not only about artists and humanists but also about power and politics, identities and gender, religion and science. You will have an opportunity to explore aspects of the Renaissance in Italy in depth while nonetheless examining some of its most important repercussions in France, England and Germany. I include selections that bring together two approaches to this fascinating era – intellectual and social history – approaches that have tended, to the detriment of each, to develop in isolation from one another. Finally, both the introduction and the selected essays are intended to convey a sense of the state of the field today, as we enter the twenty-first century. It is my view that the study of Europe from roughly 1350 to roughly 1650 remains essential to our understanding of the modern world. To be sure, the Renaissance may seem more distant to us than it did to previous generations of scholars; it may seem more complex and less coherent; it might even seem a somewhat more elusive concept; but we must come to terms with it if we are to make sense of the way in which Europe became integrated into an increasingly global setting at the very time that its elites – artists, intellectuals, magistrates and courtiers – were reshaping the understanding of the past and refashioning their own political, religious, scientific, moral and aesthetic values.

I owe a special debt of gratitude to the authors of the essays reprinted in this anthology. Each was gracious in responding to my requests and queries; several permitted me to abridge their works; and some played an active role in helping me rethink how to present their articles to a larger audience. I am also grateful to Jack Censer for his invitation to contribute to this series; and to Routledge for making it possible to reproduce the essays with the notes included. Footnotes are, after all, not only important for scholars; students too should immerse themselves in them, to understand better how the historian's art is connected – as one of the contributors to this volume has written in his lively book on the history of the footnote – not only to archival and manuscript sources but also to shifting conventions in the collection and evaluation of evidence. The works cited in the notes, moreover, allow for a more expansive view of the issues than the bodies of the essays alone can offer. Finally, my students have been thoughtful readers and listeners as I have struggled to make sense of the shape of the field in which I have done most of my work. Since it isn't always easy, when in the woods, to see the forest for the trees, their perspectives have jarred me into what I hope is a reasonable portrait of the Renaissance, both in the introduction and in the essays that I have selected.

The History Department at Trinity University has offered not only friendship and intellectual stimulation but also logistical support. On this front, Eunice Herrington has once again proven indispensable not only on technical matters relating to the production of the manuscript but, more decisively, in her own enthusiasm for and broad knowledge of history. She worked magic in scanning these essays; and she, together with Sherea Norris, Heath Hamrick and Kati Hobbs, helped proofread the articles, the latter two with financial support from the department's Joullian Fund. Antonio Calabria and Alida Metcalf, my friends and colleagues, offered incisive readings of the first draft of the introduction. I owe much as well to on-going conversations about the state of Renaissance studies with many colleagues, especially Kenneth Gouwens, Edward Muir and Dennis Romano. Above all, I thank my wife and best friend Mary Ellen, as well as our children Margaret and Junius, for their love, encouragement and humour.

I dedicate this volume to the memory of Junius Jeffries Martin. It was his thin, single-volume copy of *The Civilization of the Renaissance in Italy* – a work I found one summer day high up on a bookcase in his study – which first introduced me to the Renaissance and cultural history. I still have this volume; he had purchased it in 1945, just at the end of the Second World War. One of his marginal notations seems to me significant. It points to Burckhardt's passage on moral courage. 'This is that enigmatic mixture of conscience and egotism which often survives in modern man', Burckhardt wrote, 'after he has lost, whether by his own fault or not, faith, love, and hope'. In the middle of the 1940s, as history seemed to have passed the worst moments of one its darkest hours, these words must have offered many readers some hope that the individual could play a role in making the world better. It may not be an exaggeration to say that this brief passage also had a part in shaping my father's commitments and character.

John Jeffries Martin

ACKNOWLEDGEMENTS

The editor and the publishers wish to thank the following for their permission to reproduce copyright material:

William James Bouwsma for permission to abridge and reproduce 'The Renaissance and the Drama of Western History', from *The American Historical Review* 84(1979): 1–15, reprinted by permission of the American Historical Association. John M. Najemy for permission to abridge and reproduce 'The Dialogue of Power in Florentine Politics', from *City- States in Classical Antiquity and Medieval Italy*, eds Anthony Molho, Kurt Raaflaub and Julia Emlen (Ann Arbor, 1991): 269–88, reprinted by permission of Franz Steiner Verlag. James Hankins for permission to abridge and reproduce his essay 'The "Baron Thesis" after Forty Years and Some Recent Studies of Leonardo Bruni', from *The Journal of the History of Ideas* 56(1995): 309–38, © Journal of the History of Ideas, Inc., reprinted by permission of the Johns Hopkins University Press. Elena Fasano Guarini for permission to abridge and revise her essay 'Center and Periphery', from *The Origins of the State in Italy, 1300–1600*, ed. Julius Kirshner (Chicago, 1995): 74–96, reprinted by permission of the University of Chicago Press. Samuel K. Cohn, Jr. for permission to reproduce his essay 'Burckhardt Revisited from Social History', from *Language and Images of Renaissance Italy*, ed. Alison Brown (Oxford, 1995): 217–34, reprinted by permission of Oxford University Press. Stephen Greenblatt for the use of his essay 'Psychoanalysis and Renaissance Culture', from 'Psychoanalysis and Renaissance Culture', in *Literary Theory/Renaissance Texts*, eds Patricia Parker and David Quint (Baltimore, 1986): 210–24, © 1986 Johns Hopkins University Press, reprinted by permission of the Johns Hopkins University Press; this essay also appeared in Greenblatt, *Learning to Curse: Essays in Early Modern Culture* (London, 1990): 131–45, and is reprinted here by permission of Routledge, Inc., part of the Taylor and Francis Group. Michael Rocke for permission to reproduce 'Gender and Sexual Culture in Early Modern Italy', from *Gender and Society in Renaissance Italy*, eds Judith C. Brown and Robert C. Davis (New York: Longman, 1998): 150–70, © Addison Wesley Longman Ltd 1998, reprinted by permission of Pearson Education Publishing. Virginia Cox for permission to abridge and reproduce her essay 'The Single Self: Feminist Thought and the Marriage Market in Early Modern Venice', from *Renaissance Quarterly* 48(1995): 513–81, reprinted by permission of the Renaissance Society of America. Anthony Grafton for permission to reproduce, with the notes abridged, '*Historia* and *Istoria*: Alberti's Terminology in Context', from *I Tatti Studies: Essays in the Renaissance*, 8(1999): 37–68, reprinted by permission of *I Tatti Studies* and the Villa I Tatti in Florence. Katharine Park for permission to reproduce, with the notes abridged, 'The Criminal and the Saintly Body: Autopsy and Dissection in Renaissance Italy', from *Renaissance Quarterly* 47(1994): 1–33, reprinted by permission of the Renaissance Society of America. David Wootton for permission to reproduce 'Friendship Portrayed: A New Account of *Utopia*', from *History Workshop Journal* 45(1998): 29–47, reprinted by permission of Oxford University Press. Edward Muir for permission to reproduce his 'The Virgin on the Street Corner: The Place of the Sacred in Italian Cities', from *Religion and Culture in the Renaissance and the Reformation*, ed. Steven Ozment (Kirksville MO, 1988) © 1989 Truman State University Press; reproduced by permission of Truman State University Press in the format Textbook via Copyright Clearance Center. Euan Cameron for permission to reproduce his 'Civilized Religion: From Renaissance to Reformation and Counter-Reformation', from *Civil Histories: Essays in Honour of Sir Keith Thomas* eds Peter Burke, Brian Harrison and Paul Slack (Oxford, 2000), reprinted by permission of Oxford University Press.

Every effort has been made to notify copyright holders. Any omissions or errors will be rectified in any subsequent printings if notice is given to the publishers.

A RENAISSANCE
CHRONOLOGY

There is no general consensus among historians about the chronological boundaries of the Renaissance, though most scholars would agree that by about 1350 it had taken root in Italy and that it lasted in Italy and Western Europe as a whole down to the mid-seventeenth century. I have, however, in the highly selected chronology that follows, included some events that predate and a few that postdate the Renaissance. This more expansive timeline is meant to help readers place the history of this period in a larger framework.

Late 1200s   Florentine writers begin to experiment with a vernacular poetry that comes to be called the 'dolce stil nuovo'. Drawing on and transforming this tradition, Dante Alighieri (1265–1321) writes the *Divine Comedy*.

1293   In Florence the Ordinances of Justice bar magnates – especially certain noble families with a reputation for violence – from holding office in the city's guild-based government.

1295   Death of Ottone Visconti; in this same year Marco Polo, a native Venetian, returns from his travels of nearly a quarter century. He has spent many years in China, where he has served the Kublai Khan as an official. His narrative *The Description of the World* offers the first detailed description of Asia to the Europeans.

1297   The *Serrata* (or Closing) of the Great Council in Venice initiates the republican regime of the city. As in Florence, it is the wealthy merchants who now hold the power, though they preserve for themselves the title of nobility. The Venetian Republic will last 500 years, until its fall to Napoleon in 1797.

c.1304   The artist Giotto (c.1267–1337) begins work on the fresco cycle at the Arena Chapel in Padua.

1309   Seat of the papacy relocated to Avignon, where it will remain until 1377 in a period known as the 'Babylonian captivity of the church'.

1315–17	Period of severe famine throughout most of Europe.
1337	The English king, Edward III, outraged by Philip VI's confiscation of Gascony, declares war on the French king – initiating a period of conflict that will come to be known as the Hundred Years War.
1345	Petrarch's discovery of Cicero's letters to Atticus, Brutus and Quintus in a Carthusian monastery in Verona. Petrarch, the first great humanist of the Renaissance, had been crowned Poet Laureate in Rome in 1341.
1346	Failure of the Bardi and the Peruzzi banks in Florence.
1347–51	The Black Death – this first visitation of bubonic plague or possibly a cluster of other, still imperfectly identified diseases, kills approximately one third of the European population.
1350	Giovanni Boccaccio writes *The Decameron*, a collection of one hundred tales – many of them bawdy, all beautifully rendered. The work opens with a famous description of the devastation of the Black Death in the city of Florence.
1361–2	First (of many) recurrences of the plague.
1378	*Ciompi* Revolt in Florence – an uprising by disenfranchised cloth workers who briefly manage to gain political power. In the same year, the Roman church is confronted by a struggle between rival popes, initiating a period known as the Great Schism, which will be resolved in 1417 with the election of Pope Martin V.
1381	The English Peasants' War, also known as Wat Tyler's Rebellion.
1387	Geoffrey Chaucer begins *The Canterbury Tales*.
1396	The Byzantine scholar Manuel Chrysoloras takes up a position as a professor of Greek in Florence and becomes a key figure in the revival of Greek studies in Western Europe.
1397	Establishment of the Medici bank in Florence.
1401	Lorenzo Ghiberti, whose plans for the doors of the Baptistery of San Giovanni in Florence are selected over the proposals of his rival Filippo Brunelleschi (1377–1446), begins works on the famous bronze doors of the Florentine baptistery. He will complete them in 1452.
c.1402	Leonardo Bruni composes *The Panegyric of the City of Florence*. Bruni will later become Chancellor of Florence; his writings have traditionally been seen as celebrating the emergence of a civic humanism.
1414–18	The Council of Constance – during this council, called to condemn Huss and settle the matter of who was the 'real' pope, ending the Great Schism – Poggio Bracciolini (1380–1459)

makes several of his most significant discoveries of ancient manuscripts, including works by Cicero and lost sections of Quintilian's *On Oratory*.

1415   The English, under Henry V, defeat the French at Agincourt.

1420   Filippo Brunelleschi begins construction of the dome for the Florentine cathedral; the work is completed in 1436.

1430   Death of Christine de Pizan. Born in Venice to the astrologer Tommaso di Benevuto da Pizzano, Christine was raised in Paris at the royal court. Among her writings were works such at the *Book of the City of the Ladies* (1405) which is often seen as one of the first works of feminism.

1434   Cosimo de' Medici assumes power in Florence. For the next sixty years, the Medici family will effectively rule the city behind a façade of republicanism.

1434   Flemish artist Jan van Eyck paints the wedding portrait of Giovanni Arnolfini and his wife.

1435   Leon Battista Alberti (1404–72) publishes the first Latin edition of his work *On Painting*, elevating the craft of painting to a liberal art and laying out a scientific theory of perspective.

1436   Paolo Uccello (1397–1475) prepares and paints his fresco of Sir John Hawkwood, the last of the great *condottieri* or mercenary warriors, in the cathedral in Florence.

1440   Lorenzo Valla (*c*.1407–57) publishes his attack on the *Donation of Constantine*, demonstrating that the document was a 'forgery' – a demonstration that would do much to undermine the claims of the papacy to political power.

1440s   Printing with movable type makes possible the manual reproduction of books; developed in Germany, this new technology spreads rapidly throughout Europe.

1446   Tommaso Parentucelli (1397–1455) is elected Nicholas V; Nicholas, a patron of humanism, plays a key role in the establishment of the Vatican Library.

1447   Establishment of the short-lived Ambrosian Republic in Milan.

1450   The *condottiere* Francesco Sforza seizes control of Milan from the Visconti. The Sforza court becomes a major centre of Renaissance culture.

1453   Constantinople falls to the Ottoman Turks. In the wake of this conquest, many Greeks flee to Italy; their presence there will do much to deepen the understanding of the ancient Greek language among Western European humanists.

1454   The Peace of Lodi establishes a diplomatic framework that regulates relations among the great Italian powers (Milan, Venice, Florence, Rome and Naples) for the next forty years.

1463	Marsilio Ficino (1433–99) begins his project of translating Plato's dialogues from Greek into Latin.
1469	Marriage of Isabella of Castile to Ferdinand of Aragon.
1478	Pazzi conspiracy; Lorenzo the Magnificent escapes assassination and the Medici regime survives.
1478	Establishment of the Spanish Inquisition. This new office turns with special vehemence against Jews and those new Christians suspected of secretly practicing Judaism.
1484	Pope Innocent VIII issues *Summis desiderantes* on 5 December. In this bull the pope expresses his approval for witch-hunting. Two years later, the *Malleus maleficarum* or the *Hammer of Witches* is published. This work lays out the legal procedure for the prosecution of witchcraft.
1485–6	Sandro Botticelli paints *The Birth of Venus* for Lorenzo de' Medici.
1486	Pico della Mirandola composes his *Oration on the Dignity of Man*; William Caxton establishes the first printing press in England.
1487	Bartholomeu Dias rounds the Cape of Good Hope, establishing the sea passage from the Atlantic to the Indian Ocean.
1490	Establishment of the Aldo Manuzios's press in Venice; the Aldine press played a key role in producing the classics in books that were both handsomely produced and affordable.
1492	Christopher Columbus (1451–1506) undertakes his first voyage to the Indies; the continent he discovers will receive the name America, after the Florentine explorer Amerigo Vespucci. The Moors and Jews are expelled from Spain.
1494	The French King Charles VIII invades Italy, initiating a period of violence known as the Wars of Italy. The Medici are driven from power in Florence.
1495	Leonardo da Vinci (1452–1519), the epitome of the 'Renaissance man' begins his painting *The Last Supper* in Milan.
1497	John Cabot – a Venetian sailing for the English crown – reaches Newfoundland.
1498	Execution of Fra Girolamo Savonarola; this Dominican, who had virtually ruled Florence since 1494, is burned on the piazza della Signoria in Florence.
1500	Albrecht Dürer (1471–1528) produces his striking self-portrait in which he closely identifies himself with Christ. Cabral discovers Brazil and claims it for the Portuguese.

1501	Michelangelo (1475–1564) begins the *David*; in 1504 this statue is placed outside the Palazzo della Signoria as a symbol of Florentine liberty.
1504	The Kingdom of Naples becomes a Spanish possession.
1506	The German humanist Johann Reuchlin (1455–1522) publishes *The Rudiments of Hebrew Grammar*; *Laocoön* discovered at Rome.
1509	The Venetian military is defeated at Agnadello; the Republic under siege by the League of Cambrai loses all its mainland territory for the next seven years. In the meantime, in England, Erasmus writes *The Praise of Folly*.
1510	Ferdinand the Catholic, Regent of Castile, approves the shipment of Africans as slaves to the Americas. The use of African slaves had become a major part of the Portuguese trade in the mid-fifteenth century (at the very height of the Renaissance) and would become a fixed feature of the late Renaissance world.
1512	The Medici return to power in Florence, effectively ending the republican regime that had been established after their expulsion eighteen years earlier. In this same year Michelangelo completes his painting of the ceiling of the Sistine Chapel.
1513	Giovanni de' Medici (1475–1521) becomes pope Leo X. In exile, Machiavelli (1469–1527) writes *The Prince*. In this same period, Machiavelli and other Florentine humanists (Francesco Guicciardini, Francesco Vettori, Antonio Brucioli) are engaged in conversations in the Rucellai Gardens – conversations that will go a long way towards laying the foundations of modern republican theory. Machiavelli's *Discourses* is the most famous product of these encounters.
1516	Erasmus' close friend Thomas More (1478–1535) publishes *Utopia*.
1517	The Augustinian canon Martin Luther, a professor of sacred theology at the University of Wittenberg, posts his *Ninety-Five Theses*, denouncing the sale of indulgences, which were being used, in part at least, to help finance the remodelling of St Peter's Basilica in Rome.
1518	Las Casas argues for the use of Africans for slave labour in the New World – traditional date for the start of the African slave trade.
1519	Charles I, King of Spain, becomes Charles V, the Holy Roman Emperor.
1522	Magellan's crew completes the first circumnavigation of the world.
1522	Cortés defeats the Aztecs in Mexico.

1527	Troops of Charles V sack Rome; the Medici are driven from Florence.
1528	Baldassare Castiglione (1478–1529) publishes the first edition of *The Book of the Courtier*.
1530	The Medici return to Florence, destroying its last republican experiment (1527–30); they will soon be known as the Grand Dukes of Tuscany.
1533	Pizarro defeats the Incas in Peru.
1535	Execution of Thomas More, now Lord Chancellor of England, for his refusal to reject papal supremacy and to support King Henry VIII of England; the Duchy of Milan becomes a Spanish possession.
1536	John Calvin publishes the first edition of *The Institution of the Christian Religion* in Basel and dedicates it to King Francis I of France.
1540	Ignatius of Loyola obtains papal approval for the Society of Jesus.
1542	In the bull *Licet ab initio* Pope Paul III centralizes the church's inquisitorial courts under the authority of the Congregation of the Inquisition in Rome.
1543	Vesalius (1514–64) publishes the first edition of his *On the Fabric of the Human Body*; in this same year, Copernicus (1473–1543) publishes *On the Revolution of the Celestial Spheres*.
1545	First Session of the Council of Trent convenes to condemn Protestant doctrine and to redefine Catholic orthodoxy. The Council will meet on and off for the next eighteen years, holding its last session in 1563.
1550	Giorgio Vasari (1511–74) publishes the first edition of his *Lives of the Most Excellent Painters, Sculptors and Architects*.
1555	Peace of Augsburg – religious settlement in the Holy Roman Empire between the Catholics and Lutherans.
1558	Elizabeth I becomes Queen of England. Benvenuto Cellini (1500–71) begins work on his *Autobiography*.
1559	Peace of Cateau-Cambrésis recognizes Spain as the dominant power on the Italian peninsula.
1561	Sir Thomas Hoby's English translation of Castiglione's *The Book of the Courtier* is published.
1564	Death of Michelangelo.
1565	St Augustine, Florida settled by the Spanish.
1569	The Mercator map includes latitudes and longitudes.
1571	Battle of Lepanto – major naval battle that ends with the defeat of the Ottoman fleet.
1572	Massacre of St Bartholomew – some 3,000 Huguenots (Protestants) killed in Paris alone.

1573	The artist Paolo Veronese is tried before the Venetian Inquisition.
1576	Tycho Brahe constructs his observatory on Ven, an island between Sweden and Denmark.
1580	Montaigne publishes the first two volumes of his *Essays*; the complete work appears in 1595.
1582	Calendar reform: in Catholic countries the Gregorian replaces the Julian calendar. In these lands, those who went to bed on 4 October 1582 woke up on 15 October.
1585	Establishment of Roanoke, first English colony in America.
1588	English navy defeats the Spanish Armada.
1599	The Globe theatre opens in London.
1600	Posthumous publication of *The Worth of Women* by Moderata Fonte; Giordano Bruno burned at the stake on the campo dei Fiori in Rome.
1601	First production of Shakespeare's *Hamlet*.
1602	The Bodleian Library opens in Oxford; it is the first public library in Europe.
1603	John Florio's translation of Montaigne's *Essays*.
1607	14 May: Colony of Jamestown founded in Virginia by John Smith.
1609	Galileo turns a telescope on the heavens and forever changes the way we see ourselves in the universe.
1611	King James' Version of the Bible published in England.
1620	Francis Bacon publishes the *Novum Organum*; the *Mayflower* sails to New England.
1621	Robert Burton publishes his *Anatomy of Melancholy*.
1628	William Harvey publishes *On the Motions of the Heart and Blood*.
1633	The Roman Inquisition finds Galileo guilty of upholding the views of Copernicus and condemns him to house arrest at Arcetri, his estate just outside Florence.
1636	Establishment of Harvard College.
1637	Descartes publishes his *Discourse on Method*.
1642	The Puritans force the closure of the Globe theatre.
1648	The Peace of Westphalia brings an end to the Thirty Years War.
1653	Rembrandt paints his *Aristotle Contemplating the Bust of Homer*.
1664–6	The Great Plague of London kills some 70,000 people in the capital city. This was one of the last great outbreaks of bubonic plague in Europe.
1667	John Milton (1608–74) publishes the first edition of *Paradise Lost*. It is likely that Milton had met Galileo on his estate at Arcetri in 1638.

1

INTRODUCTION

The Renaissance: between myth and history

John Jeffries Martin

Few readers of this anthology – whether students or the merely curious – will come to it without some knowledge of the Renaissance. Its leading figures, after all, have become cultural icons; and their names – especially those of such luminaries as Petrarch, Machiavelli, Dürer, Michelangelo, Erasmus and Shakespeare – are well known. Readers of this book will likely know something too of the magnificent buildings of this period: of the dome of the cathedral in Florence or of the Basilica of St Peter's in Rome. Indeed, if you have travelled to Italy, you have *seen* the Renaissance: in the Sistine Chapel at the Vatican, in the Uffizi Gallery in Florence, in the many churches and museums of Venice. Renaissance paintings and sculptures form important parts if not the core of the collections of museums in Vienna, Paris, London, Boston, New York, Washington and Los Angeles. Travel can bring this era to life – especially in the great museum cities of Italy, where something of the human scale of the towns and cities as they appeared 500 years ago is preserved. This tangible, physical survival of so many important works of art and architecture has invested the Renaissance with a palpable reality, reinforcing the apparent centrality of this epoch in the grand sweep of Western history.

Indeed, the Renaissance – especially as it is presented in the popular media of textbooks, films, bestselling books and study tours – continues to occupy pride of place as a major turning point in European, if not world history. This was an era of overseas exploration, of the discovery of new worlds, of new models of the universe, even of new understandings of the inner workings of the human body. It was also an age of stunning artistic and literary achievements. From the early fourteenth to the early seventeenth century, at first in Italy and then throughout Europe, painters and sculptors began to invest the human form with a robust three-dimensionality, while humanists, poets and playwrights explored and represented the inner landscapes of the human person with a new self-consciousness. The Renaissance was not only an era of grand cultural achievements; it was also a period that witnessed an intensified sense of identity and individuality, at least among European elites.

The fact that the humanists and artists of this age saw themselves engaged in an effort to bring the glories of antiquity back to life has given the period its name; the French word 'renaissance' means 'rebirth'. From Petrarch's discovery of Cicero's personal and rumour-laden letters in a monastic library in northern Italy in the 1340s – a discovery that led to a fundamental rethinking of the problem of personality as well as to a new sense of historical time – to the excitement provoked in Rome on 14 January 1506 by the accidental uncovering of the *Laocoön* – a statue known until that moment only from its description in Greek and Latin sources – artists, intellectuals and their patrons remained fascinated by the ancient world.[1] Occasionally the fascination seemed to exceed all bounds of rationality. When in April 1485, for example, workmen in Rome uncovered the well-preserved remains of a young girl identified by her sarcophagus as 'Julia, the daughter of Claudius', her body was put on display on the Capitoline and thousands of the city's inhabitants came to see this girl whose beauty, they believed, far exceeded that of any of their contemporaries.[2] At other times, the relation of Renaissance men to the past was intensely deliberative. The enigmatic Florentine writer Niccolò Machiavelli, author of *The Prince*, changed into the clothes of a courtier to study the writings of the Roman historian Livy and other ancient authors, while the prudent Frenchman Michel de Montaigne developed as a great writer, the creator of the 'essay', in part because of the fancy of his father to make Latin his son's first language. Others would make antiquity into a weapon: Lorenzo Valla, in his celebrated attack on the *Donation of Constantine*, proved this work a 'forgery' and thereby undermined one of the central claims of the papacy to its power, while the Dutch humanist Desiderius Erasmus published the first scholarly edition of the Greek *New Testament* and challenged many of the traditional interpretations of the medieval theologians. In a similar vein, the Italian humanists Angelo Poliziano and Leon Battista Alberti turned to the ancients to establish new rules of philology and of scientific scholarship, while Poggio Bracciolini and Niccolò Niccoli did much to recover many of the lost texts by ancient authors. But texts were only one avenue into the study of Antiquity. Humanists clambered among ruins and tried to make sense not only of inscriptions from Italy and Greece but also of hieroglyphs and obelisks from Egypt. They examined engineering practices from the ages of the emperors Augustus and Hadrian; and they collaborated with the artists, engineers and scientists of their own time. To be sure, the ancient world had long been a subject of fascination to those living in the Middle Ages, but never with the intensity of the artists and humanists of the period running from the fourteenth to the early seventeenth century that has made the term 'Renaissance' a not entirely unfitting one for this era of European history.

In the economic and social spheres, changes were equally far-reaching. Economic life quickened with new trades and industries. The prominent Medici family of Florence, like their counterparts the Fugger of Augsburg, built their fortunes, in part at least, on international banking. To be sure, Europe in general had entered a period of economic expansion before, in the eleventh and twelfth centuries, and in Italy and the Low Countries in particular this shift had brought about a revival of urban life, of craft, even of industries, from the manufacture of textiles and armaments to shipbuilding. At roughly the same time the Crusades had begun to bring Europeans face-to-face with other civilizations; and, over time, an intense competition developed among various states for the control of the spice markets – a competition that played a major role in spurring overseas exploration. But the economic take-off that had begun shortly after the year 1000 stagnated in the fourteenth century, even before the catastrophic visitation of the Black Death in 1347–51. This and subsequent plagues disrupted pre-existing social patterns and, in the long run, led to a more rapidly changing economy, sustained by new forms of risk-taking, investment and competition – business strategies that themselves intensified as the Europeans began to exploit the riches of the New World. Technological change was also important. New weapons and, in particular, the use of gunpowder gradually transformed the nature of warfare, rendering infantrymen, now armed with arquebuses and muskets, more powerful than the traditional cavalrymen and knights. But the most consequential invention of the period was the printing press. First used in Germany in the mid-fifteenth century, the press rapidly restructured the ways in which Europeans communicated with one another, brought down the costs of books, and eventually led to a higher and higher literacy rate, particularly in the towns.

As an age of emergent capitalism, finally, the Renaissance witnessed the development of increasingly modern political structures, as merchants and entrepreneurs elbowed their ways up the social hierarchy and either worked alongside or displaced many of Europe's traditional aristocracy. Often, especially in Italy, the heightened status of these 'new men' led to the greater participation of merchants and tradesmen in town councils and judicial courts. Florentine citizens and Venetian noblemen created institutions that they self-consciously modelled on ancient republics, and rule was shared by relatively large numbers of individuals in each city. Other states such as Milan and Mantua developed along more traditional monarchical lines, but monarchy too was changing in this era, as princes north and south of the Alps (including the popes) sought to establish greater and greater authority over the territories they ruled, and were often able, through the large-scale recruitment of infantrymen, to free themselves from the influence of the nobility. Not surprisingly, both urban magistrates and princely courts became powerful patrons of the arts. Paradoxically, in commissioning works of art, wealthy merchants appropriated for themselves many attributes of the nobility they had struggled to dislodge from power, while kings and their courtiers used patronage as propaganda for their own standing, often at the expense of regional aristocracies. Indeed, many of the most notable works of the Renaissance were originally created to glorify a particular ruler or his family. This was an age of restored monumentality and a new sense of proportionality. The sculptors and architects of the period imagined and constructed vistas, buildings, urban spaces, sculptures and gardens that imitated and exceeded the grandeur of their Greek and Roman models.

Until recently many scholars in Europe and the United States turned to the study of the Renaissance in order to understand the origins of their own world. They argued that the Renaissance – with the growth of commerce and its emerging capitalist economy; the emphasis on individualism and republicanism; the unfolding of humanism and secularism; and the development of realism in art and politics – explained the values and the culture of the world in which they lived. In Western democracies especially, this period came to be perceived as the foundational epoch in the shaping of democratic, secular and capitalist institutions. When I first studied the Renaissance as a student at Harvard in the early 1970s, for example, I learned European history more or less along these lines. My professors assigned a series of canonical texts in which we were expected to see the origins of our own culture and society. But over the last twenty-five years historians, as we shall see, have largely abandoned this interpretation and have begun to rethink the very categories under which previous generations were once accustomed to approach this epoch. This volume is meant to convey some sense of the questioning that has begun to take place, as well as some of the central debates within the field at the beginning of the twenty-first century.

The pivotal figure in the making of the modern interpretation of the Renaissance was Jacob Burckhardt (1818–97), a Swiss historian who taught at the University of Basel in the mid-nineteenth century. In 1860 he published *The Civilization of the Renaissance in Italy: An Essay*. The work was remarkable not only for its erudition and the eloquence with which Burckhardt described the political and cultural history of Italy in the fourteenth and fifteenth centuries, but also for its approach. Not only did Burckhardt offer a fresh perspective on the history of the Italian Renaissance, he also presented a new way of conceptualizing the history of culture. Burckhardt, that is, was not interested exclusively in the political history of the Italian states – though he did devote the first section of his book to a discussion of what he called 'The State as a

Work of Art'. Rather he was intrigued above all by the worldviews, the assumptions and the spirit of a particular period – a form of historical study that the Germans came to know as *Kulturgeschichte* ('the history of civilization' or perhaps 'cultural history'). Equally important, Burckhardt's portrait of the Renaissance assumed that it was a pivotal period in the transition from the medieval to the modern world. His work, therefore, reflected the interest of many other nineteenth-century thinkers who, also impressed by the rapid pace of social and economic change in their own day, sought to explain the sources of an increasingly capitalistic, industrialized, democratic and individualized modernity. The most notable of these other intellectuals was Karl Marx (1818–83), whose student days at the University of Berlin had overlapped in part with those of Burckhardt. Marx, especially in the wake of the revolutions of 1848, was intent on uncovering the laws of historical development, though, in sharp contrast to his Swiss contemporary, his emphasis fell on material or economic rather than cultural forces as the wellsprings of historical change and modernization.[3]

To be sure, Burckhardt was not the first writer to look to the Italy of the Renaissance as an exceptionally creative era. Many of the Italian humanists and artists, as early as the fourteenth century, were themselves self-conscious about their endeavours to recover and even bring back to life the world of antiquity. The humanists spoke more often of a *renovatio* (or a renewal) than of a rebirth (a re-naissance); and it was they who first used the term *medium aevum* ('the Middle Ages') to describe the long stretch of time that reached from the world of ancient Greece and Rome down to their own day. By the mid-sixteenth century this self-consciousness achieved its most powerful expression in Giorgio Vasari's *Lives of the Artists*. To Vasari, looking back over the previous three centuries of artistic achievement, it seemed clear that his own age was one of *rinascità*, or re-birth. He viewed the Renaissance, moreover, in stages. To Vasari, the early Renaissance had been characterized by the ability of its artists (especially Giotto) to restore the skills of the ancients, while the late Renaissance was defined by the ability of the artists of his own day (especially the 'divine' Michelangelo) to surpass the sculptors and painters of antiquity in creative virtuosity.[4]

Burckhardt's ideas did not catch on quickly. He himself complained about how slowly his book was selling. Indeed, at first, it was from the picturesque writings of the British scholars John Addington Symonds (1840–93) and the psychologically and aesthetically astute essays of Walter Pater (1839–94) that the educated public learned to view the Renaissance as a largely secular and relatively socially-tolerant era.[5] But gradually Burckhardt's work acquired a following; it was translated into Italian in 1876; into English in 1878; and into French in 1885.[6] And it was on Burckhardtian foundations that the modern historiography of the

Renaissance would develop, though not without some resistance from within the academic world, especially from medievalists who viewed Burckhardt's claims for the originality of the Renaissance with skepticism. The Harvard historian Charles Homer Haskins had Burckhardt in mind when, in 1927, he entitled his own influential study of medieval humanism *The Renaissance of the Twelfth Century*.[7]

Nonetheless, by the mid-twentieth century, the Renaissance had emerged as a major field of study. While individual scholars had, prior to the 1940s, explored and illuminated various aspects of the Renaissance, it was the impact of the events immediately preceding and following the Second World War that explains the context for the prestigious place that this field of study came to occupy in departments of history, art history and literature, especially in Great Britain and the United States. Indeed, looking back, it is increasingly clear that the growing emphasis on the study of Renaissance in these years functioned in part as a liberal response to the tyrannies of National Socialism, fascism and communism. A heady generation of American and British scholars discovered in the Italy of the fourteenth to sixteenth centuries – largely because of the persuasive power of Burckhardt's book – a compelling narrative of progress that appeared to offer an explanation for the emergence of the very values that they saw as necessary to the preservation of British or American ideals. In the years immediately following the Second World War, that is, Burckhardt's idea of the Renaissance became the reigning interpretative orthodoxy. His 'Renaissance', in short, turned out to be perfectly suited to a triumphant United States (and to some degree a triumphant Western Europe) in the first decades of the Cold War.

But the success of Burckhardt's interpretation was not merely because of the ways in which his ideas came to fit in with liberal, democratic ideologies in Europe. The rise of the Nazis to power in the 1930s had forced many scholars of Jewish origin in Germany and Austria to emigrate. Among these were a remarkably talented group of historians and art historians, whose own impeccable humanistic educations and mastery of classical languages nurtured a high level of scholarship in the field. The arrival in the United States of Felix Gilbert (1905–91) and Erwin Panofsky (1892–1968), both of whom would eventually enjoy prestigious appointments at the Institute for Advanced Study at Princeton, as well as that of Ernst Gombrich (1909–2001) and Nicolai Rubinstein (1911–2002) in London, contributed significantly to the development of Renaissance studies on both sides of the Atlantic.[8]

In historical studies, the most influential of these émigrés from Germany were Paul Oskar Kristeller (1905–99) and Hans Baron (1900–88). As a student Kristeller had written his *Habilitationschrift* (an advanced doctoral thesis) on Marsilio Ficino, the eminent neo-Platonic philosopher in the circle of Lorenzo the Magnificent in late fifteenth-century Florence.[9] Kristeller, who after his flight from Europe obtained a position at Columbia University, was a scholar's scholar. Not only did he publish a large number of highly influential essays that illuminated the methods and assumptions of Renaissance humanists and philosophers, he also undertook extensive research in Italian and other European libraries and archives, bringing to light and cataloging thousands of manuscripts, and thereby significantly expanding our knowledge of the intellectual activity of the period.[10] Baron's work, by contrast, was more explicitly concerned with illuminating the values rather than the methods of the humanists. Like Kristeller, Baron was a gifted intellectual historian; and he was able to move with ease through the Latin writings of Renaissance authors. But his key contribution lay in his effort to map out the connections between humanist thought and the political developments of the early fifteenth century. In his most influential book, *The Crisis of the Early Italian Renaissance*, he attributed the emergence of republican ideology and civic humanism to the response of the Florentine humanists to the siege of their city (a republic) by Milan (a despotism) in 1402. It is difficult not to see in his interpretation of the period a veiled commentary on his own world, with Milan cast in the role of Germany and Florence in the role of a besieged Britain in the Second World War.[11]

Yet the study of the Renaissance was animated not only by émigré German scholars whose emphasis lay either in art history, the history of ideas or political history; it also became a field of great interest to economic historians. Even before the Second World War, several historians had begun systematic studies of aspects of the economic history of the Renaissance. Alfred Doren and Armando Sapori were among the most influential historians who, prior to the war, illuminated aspects of the economic history of Italy in this period.[12] Nonetheless, the take-off of Renaissance economic history was largely spurred by the work of Robert S. Lopez (1910–87), who had fled Italy after the promulgation of Mussolini's anti-Semitic laws and soon took up a faculty position at Yale. Lopez's understanding of the craft of economic history was greatly influenced by the Great Depression, an event that forced economic historians, like economists in general, to recognize the fundamental importance of statistical analysis as well as the cyclical nature of economies.[13] Lopez's contribution lay in his ability to extend this approach to a pre-modern period. His findings were astounding. While earlier generations of economic historians had largely viewed the history of economic development in the West as one of continuous growth, Lopez's work, together with that of many of his contemporaries, overturned this assumption. Far from being a period of economic prosperity, the economy of late medieval or Renaissance Europe, Lopez argued, had entered a period of crisis and stagnation. The flowering of Renaissance art occurred, he argued, not because of the expansion of wealth in this period, but rather because 'hard times' led the wealthy to 'invest in culture' as commercial opportunities dried up.[14]

Lopez's ideas were controversial when first presented, and they remain a matter of debate even today, but their significance cannot be exaggerated. From Burckhardt on, scholars of the Renaissance had assumed that economic prosperity underpinned the cultural flowering of the period. And this interpretation lasted well into the twentieth century. In 1930s, for example, the art historians Frederick Antal and Martin Wackernagel both stressed social and economic factors that contributed to the development of Renaissance art.[15] In his *Sociology of the Renaissance*, Alfred von Martin, also writing in this decade, popularized the theory that the Renaissance was largely the outgrowth of an expanding, bourgeois economy.[16] Though Marxist, von Martin's arguments fitted in comfortably with the views of non-Marxist scholars who celebrated the capitalist energies his work described.

Yet Lopez's work had undermined the simple assumption that economic prosperity provided the key to understanding the culture of the Renaissance. His contribution inspired a new generation of scholars, both in the United States and Britain, who began to explore the history of Italy with the optimistic view that archival research (increasingly supported by grants from Western governments and private foundations) could disclose the nature of the connections between the social and cultural history of the period. To be sure, the Renaissance had always been a field in which scholars had struggled to relate art or literature to the broader culture or to politics. This had, for example, been a topic of interest to Aby Warburg in the early 1900s.[17] But it was only in the wake of Lopez's work that the social and economic contexts were approached in a systematic, scientific fashion.

Other historical models, largely imported from France, also played a key role in refashioning the way in which British and American scholars approached the period. Fernand Braudel's magisterial study, *The Mediterranean and the Mediterranean World in the Age of Philip II*, first published in 1949, offered an entirely new perspective on history. Rather than concentrating on the rarified atmosphere occupied by great men or on major events, Braudel (1902–85) developed an ambitious model of historical analysis. Working within the framework of the *Annales* school – a group of French historians who, in reaction to the largely event-driven history of their predecessors, began to draw on the insights of anthropology, sociology, economics and geography – Braudel constructed a history of latent structural forces. He cared less about 'headlines', that is, than the deep-seated geological, climatic, demographic, economic and social realities that underlay and, in his view, bore on their crest events that had been the subject of more traditional works of history.[18] This new model, along with other forms of social and economic history, seemed to offer scholars the keys to unlocking the secrets of the past – the promise of excavating the layers of economic, demographic and social changes that would have escaped the notice of contemporaries. Perhaps social science could solve the Renaissance problem – find an explanation, that is, for the remarkable flourishing of artistic, humanistic and political creativity in this period.

Many eminent scholars attempted to connect the social history of the Renaissance with the political and intellectual developments of the period. In a precocious and influential study, Lauro Martines placed the humanist culture of Florence in its social context, while Richard Goldthwaite turned his attention to the problem that Lopez had raised, demonstrating in a number of important books, the first of which appeared in 1969, how patterns of wealth and consumption played a significant role in the development of Renaissance culture.[19] And in 1972 the British historian Peter Burke offered an intriguing set of hypotheses on the social factors (general and particular) that enabled the emergence of a 'creative elite' in northern Italy in this era.[20] But perhaps the most notable historian in this respect is Gene Brucker (b. 1924), whose writings, though rooted in an effort to identify the social foundations of Renaissance politics, have always moved easily among the different discourses of Renaissance studies.[21] Brucker, who has remained committed to offering a coherent understanding of the period, inspired an entire generation of historians, with some of his students focusing on questions closely tied to the problem of the Renaissance, while others have broken away from this paradigm almost entirely, attending instead to problems in economic, fiscal and social history with little attention to the intellectual or cultural aspects of the period.

Social historians also came to focus on various groups whom the traditional narratives of Renaissance history had relegated to the shadows. The political turmoil of the late 1960s and early 1970s fostered a climate on university campuses that was especially receptive to the exploration of the experience of 'marginal' groups, the functional antecedents to members of repressed groups (women, blacks, the poor) in both Europe and America. Natalie Zemon Davis' work on journeymen printers in sixteenth-century France; Brian Pullan's study of the poor in late Renaissance Venice; and Samuel Cohn's analysis of the social world of Florentine workers in the fourteenth and early fifteenth centuries were all path-breaking works in this new intellectual climate.[22] Drawing on Marxist, *Annaliste* and social scientific models, these historians made it clear that most Europeans, in this age of splendour, not only lived in appalling circumstances – their lives inevitably threatened by famine or disease – but also found ways to express their discontent, at times through political organization. The great forces of history, the new social historians argued, were not ideas but rather the transformations in the structure of agrarian regimes or in the availability of basic resources that affected daily life. Then in the 1970s, the emergence of feminist scholarship had a similarly unsettling affect, as research into the history of women (much of it ignited by the brilliantly polemical title of Joan Kelly-Gadol's famous article 'Did Women Have a Renaissance?') challenged and at times seemed to undercut a paradigm of European history that had been based almost exclusively on the study of men.[23] Finally, several scholars, most notably Carlo Ginzburg – in works influenced not by new trends in social history but rather by radical concepts of the relation of culture to power that had emerged in part out of the work of the Italian social theorist Antonio Gramsci (1891–1937) – argued that oral and folk traditions were as important, if not more so, in shaping the worldviews of men and women in this era than were the ideas of the great humanists and philosophers.[24] It was only a matter of time before many of the historians working in these newer traditions would come to conceptualize the origins of the modern world not as a result of humanism and the revival of antiquity, but rather as a result of fundamental transformations in the social and economic structures of Western Europe. Within this framework, the Black Death, the catastrophic pandemic that killed approximately a third of the European population in the middle of the fourteenth century, emerged, paradoxically, as an attractive explanation for the development of modern Europe.[25] Not surprisingly, in this context, the idea of the Renaissance seemed to have lost much of its explanatory power. Many social historians, for example, began to view the Renaissance less and less as a period, holding instead that it was more accurate to view it as a movement, and an elitist movement at that, within the broader context of late medieval and early modern Europe. Curiously, it was the art historian Ernst Gombrich who presented the most compelling argument that the Renaissance is better interpreted as a movement rather than a period. Yet, in my view, the metaphor of a movement tends to be even more elitist than the metaphor of a period, since, in the case of Renaissance studies, the movement involved only the cultural and political elites. By contrast, to think of the Renaissance as a period invites us to study the history of everyone, rich and poor, male and female, young and old.[26]

For a season, social history appeared as though it would not only undermine the traditional assumptions of Renaissance history but even overthrow the field entirely. And both ideological and philosophical developments also seemed to conspire against the significance of the Renaissance. From an ideological perspective, after all, the whole conception of the Renaissance began to appear, to many scholars, as little more than a construct that had legitimized the political and economic arrangements of the ruling classes in Europe and the United States in the latter half of the nineteenth century and throughout the twentieth century. Moreover, the very values that scholars once celebrated – humanism and secularism, individualism and capitalism – had proven less progressive than once thought. Fascism, communism and Nazism all had roots, in part at least, in secular, capitalist cultures, and all were great failures, with inexcusably devastating human consequences. From this vantage point, the Renaissance hardly seemed like something worth celebrating. Finally, from a philosophical perspective, the Renaissance also seemed a candidate for the endangered species list. At the end of the twentieth century, several influential thinkers (Jacques Derrida, François Lyotard, Michel Foucault) sought to deny the explanatory power of grand narratives, demonstrated a healthy scepticism towards finding the foundations of one period in the practices of another, and called into question most efforts to offer a coherent portrait of an age or a movement.[27] Writing about this trend, Edward Muir (b. 1946) has noted that, as the traditional narrative of Western history collapses, 'the Renaissance becomes a playground for postmodernists, a mental world of signs disconnected from their signification: a social space of ambiguous, disharmonious practices; and a time of oligarchs and princes whose authority derived solely from their self-representations'.[28] In such a playground, one wonders, would historians have any place at all?

Yet it is not only premature to pronounce the Renaissance 'extinct' – the field as a whole has emerged from these controversies stronger than ever, though, as I shall argue below, the relationship of historians to the study of the Renaissance has been radically reconfigured over the course of the last twenty-five years. In closing this essay, therefore, I wish to point to three new directions in Renaissance studies: (1) a convergence between the practices of social and intellectual historians, a convergence that has the possibility – should the practitioners in each of these two sub-fields begin reading one another – of raising entirely new questions about the constantly shifting relation between society and culture; (2) a heightened awareness that Renaissance culture was different from our own and needs to be approached on its own terms; and (3) a growing recognition that the Renaissance, while perhaps the inaugural chapter in the history of the early modern if not the modern world, was not the foundation of our own postmodern culture. This perspective has significant implications for the periodization of Western history, and is connected to what I call 'the death of the myth of the Renaissance'.

First, the convergence between social and intellectual history. To a large degree, this development is a result of a mutually beneficial broadening of both approaches. Social history, for instance, scored some of its first major victories in the study of the family, transforming our under-standing of household structures and gender roles.[29] And kinship studies have also gone a long way to elucidating how marital strategies and alliances under-girded the influence of some of the most powerful fami-lies of the era: the Medici and Rucellai in Florence; the Priuli and Mocenigo in Venice; the Fugger in Germany; and the Tudors and the Lisles in England. In addition, social history has focused attention on a new array of forces. The work on the making and use of urban space, as well as studies of artisans, workers, servants, peasants, prostitutes, women, the poor and other 'marginal' groups such as Jews and Muslims – not to mention such relatively fresh topics as daily life, violence, crimi-nality, witchcraft, magic, the body, gender, sexuality, madness, ritual, charity and religious dissent – have opened up entirely new areas of Renaissance Europe to study.[30]

From the perspective of an earlier generation of scholars, these issues may at first seem almost entirely unrelated to the traditional problems of the Renaissance, but this turns out not to be the case. On a number of fronts, the new social history of the period has made it possible for scholars to discern significant connections between the cultural life of the period and the experience of individuals and social groups whom previous generations of scholars had ignored altogether. A number of studies on Venetian guildsmen, for example, make explicit their roles in shaping the political, artistic and religious history of the city.[31] In a similar fashion, feminist art historians have done much to disclose the powerful influence that noble women had in the patronage of art and architecture in this period.[32] Recently, peasant communities also have emerged as having played a decisive role in the formation of the Renaissance state.[33]

Intellectual and cultural historians have also expanded their inter-ests.[34] Unlike scholars in previous generations, they are less and less likely to view the works of great artists and humanists as the master-pieces of geniuses working in isolation from their broader culture and society. To the contrary, they now tend to view these works as cultural artefacts emerging, on the one hand, from the culture of the artists' ateliers, and, on the other, from those communities of scholars who were often more than willing to share ideas, to critique one another's work (at times in biting Lucianic satires), or to find a copy of a rare classical text for a friend. Intellectual historians today, moreover, have also begun to look at the ways in which social and political pressures – manifest in patronage patterns as well as evolving humanistic practices – came to condition texts, paintings, sculptures and buildings. Humanism was not the expression of a set of clearly identifiable values that would shape modern ethics. Rather, as several scholars, perhaps most notably Anthony Grafton (b. 1950), have demonstrated, we do better to view humanism as a set of interdisciplinary practices that were by no means restricted to the study of classical texts, though this is the arena in which most great humanists cut their teeth. Rather, humanism spilled over into the study of art, archeology, numismatics, chronology, demonology, engineering, hydrologics, medicine, philosophy and theology. It is therefore possible to view humanism as a set of practices which, first elaborated in the Renaissance, would continue to reverberate throughout the early modern period, animating reforms in theology (the Reformation and Counter-Reformation), scholarship (the new antiquarianism), and science (the Scientific Revolution) down to the eighteenth century (the Enlightenment).[35] Finally, by approaching intellectual history with an emphasis on scholarly practices and communities of artists, engineers and humanists in which fifteenth-century thinkers were embedded, it becomes increasingly difficult to view intellectual and social history as separate fields.

Second, the broadening of the field of inquiry has opened up a gap between the Renaissance and our own times. No longer tied to a narrative that views the Renaissance as a foundation for our own culture, contemporary scholarship – informed not only by recently developed methods in social and intellectual history but also by feminism, gender studies, discourse theory and structuralism – focuses less on the modernity of the Renaissance than on the specific ways in which Renaissance men and women approached the world and nature on their own terms. Historians, in particular, have shown a growing interest in the particular vocabularies and codes within which Renaissance men and women, rich and poor, viewed their world. Thus, while scholars continue to view the Renaissance as a period in which many of the members of the cultural elite saw themselves as engaged in a dialogue with antiquity, they no longer believe that this dialogue laid the foundations for the world we live in today. To the contrary, the Renaissance they study has emerged as a less familiar, darker, more superstitious, messier and less rational place than once believed. Alongside a secular and rational Renaissance, then, we now have portraits of a more textured age in which religion, magic, witchcraft, demonology and alchemy were equally defining features – without, it should be added, labelling these latter elements 'medieval' in contradistinction to the more 'modern', rational elements of the period.[36] To the contrary, scholars today view both facets of the Renaissance as integral to its culture. Thus, for example, these two seemingly contradictory aspects of the era are now as visible in the anxieties of great humanists and artists as they are in the often-frayed social fabric of Renaissance cities. And perhaps these anxieties, evidently rooted in the acceleration of social change, go some way in explaining the new ways in which Renaissance princes, magistrates and prelates sought to tame and control the larger social world of which they were a part. The evidence for this – in the elaboration of new rules of civility, in the codification of the rule of etiquette and ritual at court, and in the radical transformation of religious beliefs and practices, with a proliferation of new devotional practices – is extensive.[37]

Finally and most significantly, both these developments in the historiography have tended, in turn, to reconfigure the place of the Renaissance in relation to the *longue durée* of Western history. No longer, that is, do scholars view the Renaissance as the inaugural chapter in the history that leads down to our own time, a view of history – still the orthodoxy in most textbooks and university course catalogues – that we might represent diagrammatically as follows:

To the contrary historians have come to see the Renaissance as a period that stood at the origins of early or perhaps even late modernity, that is, the period running from the fifteenth to the mid-twentieth century, a 500-year era from which, for reasons that I shall explain shortly, we seem to be increasingly severed. The diagrammatic representation of this view of history, now focusing on the period running only from the late Middle Ages to the present, would look something like this:

Hints of this new periodization – in which I deliberately stress the continuities between early modern and late modern history in what is admittedly an overly linear and Eurocentric representation of history – have emerged in reflections on both ends of the early modern/modern period.[38] In studying the emergence of early modern culture, Grafton, as we have seen, has interpreted Renaissance humanism as a movement that laid the foundations for early modern modes of intellectual inquiry in such varied fields as science, history, antiquarianism, numismatics and chronology.[39] Examining the other end of the spectrum, namely the recent crisis in modernity, William James Bouwsma, in the essay reproduced in Chapter 2 of this volume, argues that the traditional narrative of Western history, represented in the first of the two diagrams above, is no longer meaningful. As Bouwsma poignantly observes, 'the argument that attached the Renaissance to the modern world was based on two assumptions: that the modern world does, in fact, constitute some kind of intelligible entity, and that modernity has emerged by way of a single linear process', quickly adding that 'neither of these assumptions is … self-evident'.[40] Bouwsma himself notes that postmodernism has made us increasingly sceptical of the view that we can explain our own world in any coherent fashion.[41]

Following the lead of Grafton, Bouwsma and other scholars, therefore, we would do well to abandon the view that the Renaissance explains our current reality, while nonetheless granting that it did shape many of the artistic, cultural and literary practices for some two to three hundred years, if not, despite the intervention of the Enlightenment and the French Revolution, the next four to five hundred years. The Renaissance, in short, did inaugurate modernity – understood here as the period that emerged in the time of Alberti and that remained familiar not only to Burckhardt and his contemporaries in the nineteenth but even to historians in the early and mid-twentieth century. *But we are no longer modern!* We must recognize, or rather we are forced to recognize, that is, that recent political, cultural and technological changes have so altered our world (and altered it so quickly) that it is difficult, if not impossible to discern continuities, not only between the world of the Renaissance and our own, but also between the modern era and our own.[42]

Specific examples are helpful here. In the fifteenth century the Florentine humanist and polymath Leon Battista Alberti disclosed the underlying mathematical science of perspective that enabled artists to represent a three-dimensional world on a two dimensional surface – a technique that would inform the work of most painters for the next 400 years – while Alberti's German contemporary Johannes Gutenberg developed a technology that led to the rise of print culture.[43] And artistic realism and the widespread use of books in the making of culture, science and religion would become, in fact, defining traits of modernity. Other features of the early modern and modern world also developed in the Renaissance: the development of the new monarchies and the nation state; the growing reliance of increasingly centralized governments on infantrymen and ground-based artillery to protect or expand their territories; the gradual acceptance of the Copernican or Galilean model of a sun-centred rather than an earth-centred universe; the construction of the 'author' as an individual voice, capable of original ideas; and an interest in the individual that would manifest itself in the proliferation of biographies and autobiographies as well as portraits and self-portraits.

Yet each of these features of the 500-year period running from the mid-fifteenth to the mid-twentieth century are less and less central to our own increasingly chaotic and de-centered postmodern world. Einstein's relativity theory and the turn to abstract art disrupted both Galilean physics and Albertian perspective, while more recent developments such as television, the use of the internet, hypertext and new forms of electronic data-storage have dislodged the printed book from its central role in the production and reproduction of culture. The postmodern is manifest in other defining features of life as well, as the organization of economic activity within and by nation–states gives way to incipient forms of corporate nationalism and the emergence of highly organized transnational trading blocks such as the EEC and NAFTA; as states move from a reliance on armies and the massive deployment of soldiers to high-tech forms of warfare that, while undoubtedly still horrific and deadly, resemble nothing so much as video-games; as the very notion of authorship and authorial intent are challenged; and as early robust forms of individualism are replaced by increasingly fragile and unstable representations of the self, with psychotropic medications, cyborgs and the possibility of cloning a human being all making Burckhardt's 'individual' look more and more like a strange, even quaint artefact from a forgotten era.[44]

In our own times, that is, it is no longer possible to look to the Renaissance, as Burckhardt and as many of his followers for the next 100 years or so did, to explain ourselves and our values. In this sense, the myth of the Renaissance – that is the view of the Renaissance as the foundational story for the making of *our* world – is dead. This is not to say that such a myth was not part of the social, political and cultural life of Europeans from the age of Alberti to that of Burckhardt. Burckhardt doubtless saw in the historical changes of late medieval Italy the emergence of cultural and political values that remained central to the experience of Europeans down to his own day. Fifteenth-century Florence was, in many ways, an anticipation of nineteenth-century Basel, and Burckhardt's education a reflection of educational ideals that the Italian humanists had elaborated 400 years earlier.[45] *But the myth is dead for us.* When scholars study the Renaissance from the perspective of the present, that is, they approach it as a historical period whose ties to the contemporary, postmodern world are tenuous at best. Suddenly at sea, we can now only look back on the modern world as the receding shoreline of a continent to which we are unlikely to return.

The essays that follow illuminate, in various ways, these recent developments in Renaissance studies. First, most of the essays point to the convergence between social and cultural history. Samuel Cohn's analysis of Renaissance individualism ties the late medieval search for fame and glory not to the new ideas of humanists and the encounter with ancient texts, but rather to the strategies of lineages, at a time of plague, to preserve their identities; John Najemy's essay makes it plain that

16

economic, political and intellectual life were profoundly interconnected in the shaping of the Florentine republic; and Virginia Cox opens up an entirely new way of understanding the relationship of new feminist ideas to particular economic developments and marital strategies in late Renaissance Venice.

But even those historians who are less explicit about the connection between social and cultural life nonetheless underscore the ways in which various symbolic languages – religious, iconic, artistic, medical, imaginative and ethical – shaped social experience (and vice versa), as we see in the contributions below by Michael Rocke, Edward Muir, Anthony Grafton, Katharine Park, David Wootton and Euan Cameron. The emphasis, moreover, that recent historians such as Grafton and James Hankins have placed on rhetoric as a way of understanding the active role of language in the construction of social life as well as the development of new models of literary analysis (especially the work of Stephen Greenblatt and other exponents of literary history that has come to be called 'New Historicism') have also tended to collapse the traditional distinction between cultural and social history.[46] Renaissance historians today, that is, are more likely than their predecessors to view culture (high culture included) as a set of practices and values that played a constitutive or active role in the making of social and even economic life. Humanists were not ivory-tower intellectuals, and artists were not romantic geniuses secreted away in their garrets, entirely cut off from the world they inhabited. Rather, both humanists and artists responded to events and trends around them: to visitations of the plague; to war and reports of war; and to the early accounts of the Americas. They created imaginative and compelling works of art, literature, philosophy and theology that influenced political institutions and religious reforms. School teachers, priests, friars and itinerant intellectuals, as well as manuscripts, books, broadsheets and numerous forms of art, popular and elite, intersected in complex ways with various sectors of Renaissance society, not merely with the rich but also with workers, women, artisans and other groups, urban and rural. For these and other reasons, the traditional divide between social and cultural history appears to be more a function of academic convention than of the lived experience of men and women in the past. As Marc Bloch, one of the founders of the *Annales* school, observed, 'though the artificial conception of man's activities which prompts us to carve up the creature of flesh and blood into the phantoms *homo oeconomicus, philosophicus, juridicus* is doubtless necessary, it is tolerable only if we refuse to be deceived by it'.[47]

Many of the contributions here also show the degree to which current scholarship has stressed the distance between our own world and that of the Renaissance, rather the continuities between the Renaissance and modern culture that historians down to the time of Burckhardt and beyond traditionally emphasized. In this respect, Michael Rocke's evocation of Renaissance notions of gender and sexuality is the most compelling example. But we also see a similar emphasis on the Renaissance as a profoundly unfamiliar world in other works as well: in Hankins' analysis of the rhetorical culture of the humanist Leonardo Bruni; in Park's discussion of Renaissance attitudes towards the opening up of dead bodies; in Muir's anthropologically informed presentation of the function of street-corner shrines; and in Cohn's and Cox's studies of family and marital strategies. Each of these scholars, in short, examines Renaissance culture and society on its own terms; each writes of it not because it is familiar but rather because it is unfamiliar, if not, at times, remarkably strange.

Finally, as I have argued above, while contemporary scholarship is far less likely than that of previous generations to view the Renaissance as the origins of our own (postmodern) world, historians have by no means given up on the idea of the importance of the Renaissance. First, the Renaissance was no doubt a period of rapid and complex change resulting from the convergence, on the one hand, of a new set of social, economic and technological forces (increased urbanization; commercialization; overseas exploration and conquests; dislocations due to plague; and various inventions, from the fork and the flat, mercury-backed mirror to gunpowder and the printing press) with, on the other, a cluster of interrelated practices (in painting, sculpture, architecture, poetry, humanism and science) in which many of the era's cultural elites – often with an eye to antiquity as a model for their pursuits – creatively and self-consciously engaged. Out of this convergence, the Renaissance played a key role in laying the foundations of many aspects of the modern world, certainly down to the eighteenth century and, in some respects, down to the twentieth. Thus Grafton's study of Alberti makes it clear that his language and understanding of art and history set the tone for both disciplines in much of the early modern if not the modern world; Park demonstrates the ways in which the Renaissance witnessed a fundamental shift in the understanding of anatomical science (which she nicely connects to long-standing religious and academic practices in the Middle Ages) that would play a revolutionary role in the shaping of modern medicine; and Greenblatt offers a provocative argument about Renaissance constructions of identity – constructions that, largely based on one's economic and social function, gradually laid the foundations of a modern form of selfhood to which Freudian psychoanalysis would eventually claim privileged access. In a similar fashion, Elena Fasano Guarini underscores the significance of the development of the regional state in this period; and David Wootton connects one of the most imaginative works of the Renaissance – namely Thomas More's *Utopia* – not only to its humanist context but also to an early vision of communism. But while each of these scholars, explicitly or implicitly, points to salient ways in which Renaissance developments shaped early modern or even late modern culture, they each stop short of claiming that the Renaissance explains *our* world. After all, recent shifts in the understanding of art, history, politics, medicine and notions of identity, as well as the collapse of communism, have not only weakened the connection between the Renaissance and our own world – they have called into question whether there is any connection at all.

As I have tried to show in this brief introduction to the history of the *history* of the Renaissance, each generation of scholars is likely to view this particular epoch or movement in different ways. As our world continues to change, moreover, we will continue to adjust, redefine and perhaps even radically reconfigure our perspectives on this and on other historical periods. Herein lies the value of the study of historiography, a field that is perhaps especially important at a time when one's own culture is undergoing such rapid and profound shifts. It is an old scholarly conviction that we will see farther and better if we know how those who came before us looked at the past. But perhaps we should be more modest – Burckhardt certainly was in calling his work 'an essay'. Tellingly, in the first chapter of Part I of his book, he observes that

> to each eye, perhaps, the outlines of a given civilization present a different picture; and in treating of a civilization which is the mother of our own, and whose influence is still at work among us, it is unavoidable that individual judgement and feeling should tell every moment both on the writer and on the reader.[48]

Burckhardt's observation seems remarkably fresh and, in certain respects, oddly postmodern – though none of us would, I suspect, share his view that the civilization of the Renaissance is 'the mother of our own'.

Notes

1 For the broader contexts in which these discoveries took place, see Ronald Witt, 'Medieval "Ars Dictaminis" and the Beginnings of Humanism: A New Construction of the Problem', *Renaissance Quarterly* 35(1982): 1–35; and Leonard Barkan, *Unearthing the Past: Archeology and Aesthetics in the Making of the Renaissance* (New Haven, 1999).
2 Jacob Burckhardt, *The Civilization of the Renaissance in Italy: An Essay*, trans. S. G. C. Middlemore (London, 1944), 112.
3 The literature on Burckhardt is an ocean, but see Felix Gilbert, *History: Politics or Culture?: Reflections on Ranke and Burckhardt* (Princeton, 1990). For an earlier assessment of Burckhardt's influence and some of his early critics, see Wallace K. Ferguson, *The Renaissance in Historical Thought* (Boston MA, 1948).

4 Giorgio Vasari, *The Lives of the Most Eminent Painters, Sculptors, and Architects*, trans. Gasto du C. de Vere, 10 vols (London, 1912–15). On other anticipations of Burckhardt's ideas, see Johan Huizinga, 'The Problem of the Renaissance', in his *Men and Ideas: History, the Middle Ages, the Renaissance*, trans. James S. Holmes and Hans van Marle (Princeton, 1984). The original Dutch version of this essay was first published in 1920.

5 John Addington Symonds, *The Renaissance in Italy*, 7 vols (London, 1875–86) and Walter Pater, *The Renaissance: Studies in Art and Poetry* (London, 1873). Burckhardt's interpretation did influence Symonds' work in particular.

6 The original German edition appeared as *Die Cultur der Renaissance in Italien: Ein Versuch* (Basel, 1860), with the following early translations: *La civiltà [del secolo] del Rinascimento in Italia*, trans. D. Valbusa (Florence, 1876); *The Civilization of the [Period of the] Renaissance in Italy*, trans. S. G. C. Middlemore (London, 1878); *La civilisation en Italie au temps de la Renaissance*, trans. M. Schmitt (Paris, 1885).

7 On the continuing vitality of Haskin's work, see *Renaissance and Renewal in the Twelfth Century*, eds Robert L. Benson and Giles Constable (Cambridge MA, 1982).

8 For a general orientation to this migration and a sense of some of the ways in which it stimulated the scholarship in the United States, see *The Intellectual Migration: Europe and America*, eds Donald Fleming and Bernard Bailyn (Cambridge MA, 1969) and H. Stuart Hughes, *The Sea Change: The Migration of Social Thought, 1930–1965* (New York, 1975). On Gilbert's memories of Berlin before the Second World War, see his *A European Past: Memoirs, 1905–1945* (New York, 1988). The major works of the émigrés are too extensive to cite here, but for a sampling, see Gilbert, *History: Choice and Commitment* (Cambridge MA, 1977); Panofsky, *Renascences and Renaissances in Western Art* (New York, 1969); Gombrich, *Norm and Form: Studies in the Art of the Renaissance* (London, 1966); and Rubinstein, *The Government of Florence under the Medici (1434 to 1494)* (Oxford, 1966).

9 The English translation of this work, first published in German in 1937, was published as *The Philosophy of Marsilio Ficino* (New York: Columbia University Press, 1943).

10 Among Kristeller's best-known publications, see *Renaissance Thought: The Classic, Scholastic and Humanist Strains* (New York, 1961); *Renaissance Thought II: Papers on Humanism and the Arts* (New York, 1965); and *Eight Philosophers of the Italian Renaissance* (New York, 1964). His greatest achievement was, however, undoubtedly his finding list of uncatalogued or incompletely catalogued Renaissance manuscripts, the *Iter Italicum*, 6 vols (Leiden, 1963–92), now available on CD-ROM (Leiden, 1995). For Kristeller's intellectual formative years in Germany and Italy and his eventual flight to the United States, see his poignant recollections, edited by Margaret L. King, 'Iter Kristellerianum: The European Journey', *Renaissance Quarterly* 47(1994): 907–29.

11 Hans Baron, *The Crisis of the Early Italian Renaissance: Civic Humanism and Republican Liberty in an Age of Classicism and Tyranny*, 2 vols (Princeton, 1955). On the Baron thesis, see the essay by James Hankins below (Chapter 4).

12 Many of the early studies of these scholars are published in collections of their works: Alfred Doren, *Le arti fiorentine*, trans. G. B. Klein, 2 vols (Florence, 1940–8) and Armando Sapori, *Studi di storia economica*, 3 vols (Florence, 1955).

13 These remarks about the impact of the Great Depression on the practice of economic history have been informed by conversations with colleagues William Breit and John J. McCusker Jr.

14 Roberto S. Lopez, 'Hard Times and the Investment in Culture', *The Renaissance: A Symposium* (New York, 1953), 19–32.

15 Frederick Antal, *Florentine Painting and its Social Background* (London, 1947) and Martin Wackernagel, *The World of the Florentine Renaissance Artists: Patronage, Workshop and the Art Market* (Princeton, 1938; original German edition also 1938).

16 Alfred von Martin, *Sociology of the Renaissance* (Oxford, 1944; original German edition, 1932).

17 Ernst Gombrich, *Aby Warburg: An Intellectual Biography* (London, 1970); cf. Felix Gilbert, 'From Art History to the History of Civilization: Aby Warburg', in Gilbert, *History: Choice and Commitment*, 423–39.

18 Fernand Braudel, *The Mediterranean and the Mediterranean World in the Age of Philip II*, trans. S. Reynolds, 2 vols (New York, 1974; revised French edition, 1966). On the *Annales* School and its influence, see Peter Burke, *The French Historical Revolution: the* Annales *School, 1929–1989* (Stanford, 1990).

19 Lauro Martines, *The Social World of the Florentine Humanists* (London, 1963); Richard Goldthwaite, *Private Wealth in Renaissance Florence* (Princeton, 1969), *The Building of Renaissance Florence: An Economic and Social History* (Baltimore, 1980), and *Wealth and the Demand for Art in Italy* (Baltimore, 1993). Lisa Jardine has popularized many of Goldthwaite's ideas in her *Worldly Goods: A New History of the Renaissance* (London, 1996).

20 Peter Burke, *Culture and Society in Renaissance Italy, 1420–1540* (New York, 1972). The creative elite Burke describes included 313 painters and sculptors, 88 writers, 50 musicians, 55 scientists and 74 humanists.

21 Gene Brucker, *Florentine Politics and Society, 1343–1378* (Princeton, 1963), *The Civic World of Early Renaissance Florence* (Princeton, 1977) and, for a more synthetic statement, *Renaissance Florence* (New York, 1969).

22 Natalie Zemon Davis, 'Strikes and Salvation at Lyon', in Davis, *Society and Culture in Early Modern France* (Stanford, 1965), 1–16, as well as many of the other essays in her volume; Brian Pullan, *Rich and Poor in Renaissance Venice: The Social Institutions of a Catholic State, to 1620* (Cambridge MA, 1971); and Samuel K. Cohn, *The Laboring Classes in Renaissance Florence* (New York, 1980).

23 The feminist historiography of the Renaissance begins with the still influential article of Joan Kelly-Gadol, 'Did Women Have a Renaissance?', in *Becoming Visible: Women in European History*, eds Renate Blumenthal and Claudia Koonz (Boston, 1977) [though now see Christiane Klapisch-Zuber, *Women, Family, and Ritual in Renaissance Italy*, trans. Lydia Cochrane (Chicago, 1985) and Margaret L. King, *Women of the Renaissance* (Chicago, 1991) as well as the exciting series of volumes published by the University of Chicago Press on women's history, under the general editorship of Margaret L. King and Albert Rabil Jr, entitled *The Other Voice in Early Modern Europe*].

24 Carlo Ginzburg, *The Nightbattles: Witchcraft and Agrarian Cults in the Sixteenth and Seventeenth Centuries*, trans. John and Anne Tedeschi (Baltimore, 1983; original Italian edition, 1966) and *The Cheese and the Worms: The Cosmos of a Sixteenth-century Miller*, trans. John and Anne Tedeschi (Baltimore, 1980; original Italian edition, 1976). For two other important scholars who emphasize the importance of folklore in the interpretation of culture, see Gustav Henningsen, *The Witches' Advocate: Basque Witchcraft and the Spanish Inquisition* (Reno NV, 1980) and Piero Camporesi, *Bread of Dreams: Food and Fantasy in Early Modern Europe*, trans. David Gentilcore (Chicago, 1989).

25 David Herlihy, *The Black Death and the Transformation of the West*, ed. with an introduction by Samuel K. Cohn (Cambridge MA, 1997) and Samuel K. Cohn, *The Black Death Transformed: Disease and Culture in Renaissance Europe* (London, 2002).

26 Ernst Gombrich, 'The Renaissance – Period or Movement?', in *Background to the English Renaissance*, ed. A. G. Dickens (London, 1974), 9–30. The term 'early modern', while beneficial in enabling studies of broader social and cultural concern, is still explicitly teleological. In this sense, this newer term fails as a useful replacement of the word 'Renaissance', at least for those who wish to deconstruct this period as an age of transition from the medieval to the modern world. On some of the limits of 'early modern' as a category, see Lorraine Daston, 'The Nature of Nature in Early Modern Europe', *Configurations* 6(1998): 149–72. We do well, however, to remember that words such as 'period', expressing a fixed moment in time, and 'movement', expressing a process, are metaphors. On the use of metaphors in social thought, see Daniel Rigney, *The Metaphorical Society: An Invitation to Social Theory* (Lanham MD, 2001).

27 Yet certain tensions in the postmodern project were inevitable. Foucault's theories were profoundly historical, offering new ways of interpreting various 'periods' in Western history; and even Lyotard's work seemed to endorse the idea that the postmodern is itself an epoch.

28 Edward Muir, 'The Italian Renaissance in America', *American Historical Review* 100(1995): 1096.

29 Francis William Kent, *Household and Lineage in Renaissance Florence: The Family Life of the Capponi, Ginori and Rucellai* (Princeton, 1977) and Stanley Chojnacki, *Women and Men in Renaissance Venice: Twelve Essays on Patrician Society* (Baltimore, 2000) offer subtle analyses of family life in Renaissance Florence and Venice. But see also the pioneering work of David Herlihy and Christiane Klapisch Zuber, *Les toscans et leurs familles: une étude du Catasto florentin de 1427* (Paris, 1978).

30 Muir, 'The Italian Renaissance in America', provides references to many of the most important works in Renaissance social and political history in his footnotes.

31 The study of the relationship of artisans and guildsmen to various aspects of Renaissance culture has been especially important in Venice: see Pullan, *Rich and Poor in Renaissance Venice*; Patricia Fortini Brown, *Venetian Narrative Painting in the Age of Carpaccio* (New Haven, 1988); and my *Venice's Hidden Enemies: Italian Heretics in a Renaissance City* (Berkeley, 1993).

32 See, among her many groundbreaking essays, Carolyn Valone, 'Women on the Quirinal Hill: Patronage in Rome, 1560–1630', *Art Bulletin* 76(1994): 129–46 and Sheryl E. Reiss and David G. Wilkins (eds) *Beyond Isabella: Secular Women Patrons of Art in Renaissance Italy* (Kirksville MO, 2001).

33 Samuel K. Cohn, *Creating the Florentine State: Peasants and Rebellion, 1348–1434* (Cambridge, 1999).

34 Kenneth Gouwens, 'Perceiving the Renaissance: Renaissance Humanism after the "Cognitive Turn"', *American Historical Review* 103(1998): 55–82. This essay was published along with Paula Findlen, 'Preserving the Past: The Material World of the Italian Renaissance' (83–114) as part of an *AHR Forum* that also includes a jointly authored introduction, 'The Persistence of the Renaissance' (51–4) together with responses to the essays by William J. Bouwsma, Anthony Grafton and Randolph Starn. Gouwen's and Findlen's footnotes provide references to many of the most significant works in Renaissance cultural and intellectual history.

35 Anthony Grafton, *Defenders of the Texts: The Traditions of Scholarship in an Age of Science, 1450–1800* (Cambridge MA, 1991).

36 The literature on these and related aspects of the Renaissance is enormous, but see Charles Trinkaus, *In Our Image and Likeness: Humanity and Divinity in Italian Humanist Thought*, 2 vols (Chicago, 1970), D. P. Walker, *Spiritual and Demonic Magic from Ficino to Campanella* (Nendeln, 1969), Frances Yates, *Giordano Bruno and the Hermetic Tradition* (Chicago, 1964), and Guido Ruggiero, *Binding Passions: Tales of Magic, Marriage and Power at the End of the Renaissance* (Oxford, 1993).

37 John R. Hale, *The Civilization of Europe in the Renaissance* (New York, 1995), the most compelling recent synthetic study of the period, stresses the new ways in which Renaissance culture sought to control or tame human nature.

38 The growing integration of cultures requires a more global perspective on historical change, a process that itself accelerated in the Renaissance with the conquest of the Americas, explorations along the African coast, and new sea routes to Asia. The diagram provided here represents a radical reduction of historical complexity; I present it as a contrast to the dominant notion of peri-odization *within* European history, but not as a representation of historical processes which, clearly, are far more multi-dimensional.

39 Grafton, *Defenders of the Text* and *Bring Out Your Dead: The Past as Revelation* (Cambridge MA, 2001).

40 William James Bouwsma, 'The Renaissance and the Drama of Western History', *American Historical Review* 84(1979): 1–15, reprinted as Chapter 2 of this volume.

41 Bouwsma, 'The Renaissance', 5.

42 I am influenced here and in what follows by the suggestive comments of David Harvey, *The Condition of Postmodernism* (Oxford, 1990), 244 esp. I thank my colleague David Spener for referring me to Harvey's book. See also John Lukacs, *At the End of an Age* (New Haven, 2002).

43 For the broader and rather problematic contexts of Alberti's and Gutenberg's innovations, see Grafton, 'Panofsky, Alberti, and the Ancient World', in *Meaning in the Visual Arts: Views from the Outside: A Centennial Commemoration of Erwin Panofsky*, ed. Irving Lavin (Princeton, 1955), 123–30, now reprinted in Grafton, *Bring Out Your Dead*, 19–30; and Adrian Johns, *The Nature of the Book: Print and Knowledge in the Making* (Chicago, 1998), 324–79.

44 See Francis Fukuyama, *Our Posthuman Future: Consequences of the Biotechnology Revolution* (New York, 2002).

45 As my remarks here indicate, postmodernism does not, *pace* Lyotard, require that we abandon all narratives or even meta-narratives – only that we recog-nize their inevitably provisional character. For an important reading of the anxieties, ambivalences and stoicism in Burckhardt's *The Civilization of the Renaissance in Italy*, see Lionel Grossman, *Basel in the Age of Burckhardt: A Study in Unseasonable Ideas* (Chicago, 2000), esp. 251–95.

46 Stephen J. Greenblatt, *Renaissance Self-Fashioning: More to Shakespeare* (Chicago, 1980) inaugurated New Historicism as an important historical-critical approach to literature. For a general introduction to the significance of this approach, see H. Aram Veeser, *The New Historicism* (New York, 1989).

47 Marc Bloch, *Feudal Society*, trans. L. A . Manyon, 2 vols (Chicago, 1961; orig-inal French edition, 1940), 59.

48 Burckhardt, *The Civilization of the Renaissance in Italy*, 1.

Part I

THE RENAISSANCE
PARADIGM IN CRISIS?

*It is the most serious difficulty of the history of civilization that a
great civilization must be broken up into single, and often into what
seem arbitrary categories in order to be in any way intelligible.*
                                                                    Burckhardt

*The essay in this section – William James Bouwsma's 'The Renaissance and the
Drama of Western History' – offers readers a crucial point of departure for the
exploration of the field of Renaissance studies. Bouwsma's article raises several
major questions not only about the very category of the 'Renaissance' but also
about the roles of narrative and drama in the presentation of the history of the
European past. Is a dramatic narrative of Western history necessary? Why has
the Renaissance occupied such a privileged place in this narrative? In what
ways does Bouwsma attempt to preserve the significance of the Renaissance?
Finally, how do his solutions differ from those suggested by the editor in the
introduction to this volume?*

*Readers should also consider, in their study of Bouwsma's essay, why scholars
in the field of Renaissance history are so concerned with issues of periodization
and interpretative categories. How the Renaissance is defined as a period is one of
the most vexing issues in the field. But equally vexing is the use of the term
'Renaissance'. Many scholars have come to prefer the terms 'late medieval' and
'early modern', both of which overlap extensively with the period generally
thought of as the Renaissance. These differences are significant and, for this very
reason, it is crucial to attend carefully to the terms and categories scholars adopt
in their histories of this period.*

25

2

THE RENAISSANCE AND THE DRAMA OF WESTERN HISTORY

William James Bouwsma

In this essay, first delivered as the presidential address of the American Historical Association in 1978, William J. Bouwsma confronted an emerging crisis in Renaissance studies. The consensus view of the 1950s that it was possible to locate the origins of the modern Western world in the Renaissance was beginning to break down. The source of this collapse of an earlier orthodoxy was, Bouwsma admitted, multifaceted, but he placed special emphasis on the emergence of the new social history. In the wake of the political upheavals of the late 1960s, scholars had begun to ask new questions about the past. On the one hand, they expressed an unprecedented interest in ordinary men and women – artisans, workers, peasants and the poor – and, thereby, shifted the study of history away from the political, intellectual and artistic elites whose work and ideas had been the traditional focus of Renaissance studies. On the other hand, social history offered the promise of new periodizations. Here the work of French scholars associated with the Annales *school was particularly influential. One of France's most prominent historians, Emmanuel Le Roy Ladurie, offered an especially compelling critique of the concept of the Renaissance (and other historical periods that were organized around the activities of elites) in a celebrated article entitled 'Motionless History'. From Le Roy Ladurie's perspective, the overwhelming mass of Europeans had witnessed virtually no change in the period running from the eleventh to the nineteenth century. Movements such as the Renaissance (or the Scientific Revolution or the Enlightenment) were reduced to little significance. As a result the Renaissance was in danger, according to Bouwsma, of losing its pivotal role in what he called 'the drama of Western history'.*

While Bouwsma himself offered some thoughtful ways of reconceptualizing the significance of the Renaissance in the later part of his address, most historians now recognize this essay as an early expression of what has proven to be a long period of doubt about the very category of the Renaissance.

But not everyone has been so convinced. In 1998 The American Historical Review *revisited Bouwsma's essay in an important forum on its impact. The two major essays on this issue (written by Kenneth Gouwens and by Paula Findlen) argued that the demise of the Renaissance had been much exaggerated, and they*

27

wrote energetic articles in its defence – offering new perspectives, drawn above all from recent developments in cultural and intellectual history that, in their view, have done much to revitalize the field. Among the respondents to their essays was Bouwsma himself. If anything his doubts had intensified over the twenty years since he had given his address. 'I am increasingly doubtful that the Renaissance was the beginning of the "modern" world', he wrote. One may disagree with either Bouwsma's doubts or Gouwen's and Findlen's renewed confidence in the value of the Renaissance as an organizing principle for making sense of the past. But there is no question that the orthodoxy of the 1950s, a notion largely Burckhardtian in inspiration, no longer exists.

The essay below is a slightly abridged version of Bouwsma's address which appeared originally in the American Historical Review *84(1979): 1–15 (reprinted in Bouwsma (ed.)* A Usable Past: Essays in European Cultural History *[Berkeley, 1990], 348–65). For the forum 'The Persistence of the Renaissance', see* American Historical Review *103(1998): 51–124.*

* * *

I should like to discuss a remarkable historiographical event – an event so recent that it may have escaped general notice, yet of considerable importance both for historians and for the larger culture of which we are a part. This event is the collapse of the traditional dramatic organization of Western history.

Nothing seemed less likely than this development when I entered the profession some thirty years ago or, indeed, before the last two decades. Earlier in this century, the Burckhardtian vision of the importance of the Renaissance for the formation of the modern world had been under attack in the 'revolt of the medievalists'; and in 1940 Wallace K. Ferguson had described the Renaissance as 'the most intractable problem child of historiography'.[1] But Ferguson had himself never been without hope for straightening out his problem child; and less than a decade later, after studying the history of the case from many directions, he predicted for it a tranquil and prosperous maturity. The time was ripe, he declared, for 'a new and more comprehensive synthesis'.[2] The revolt of the medievalists had apparently been beaten back; indeed, by teaching us greater care in distinguishing the new from the old, they seemed only to have strengthened our sense of the originality and modernity of the Renaissance. In the years after the war a group of unusually distinguished scholars brought new excitement to Renaissance studies; the concreteness and depth of their learning seemed to confirm Ferguson's expectations.[3]

During the 1950s, therefore, it was common for Renaissance specialists from various disciplines to celebrate, by reading papers to each other, their triumph over the medievalists and the world-historical significance of the Renaissance. Our agreement was remarkable. The editor of one volume of such papers noted with satisfaction 'the virtual disappearance of the disposition to deny that there was a Renaissance'. And he ventured to predict, obviously recalling controversies now happily over, 'that future soldier scholars will beat their swords into ploughshares and that what has long been the Renaissance battleground will be transformed into a plain of peace and plenty'. On the other hand, he also hinted that the occasion evoking these papers was a bit dull. 'The atmosphere of charitable catholicity was so all pervading during the symposium', he remarked, 'that even the moderators' valiant efforts to provoke controversy were largely futile'.[4] That the Renaissance was the critical episode in a dramatic process that would culminate in ourselves had become an orthodoxy that few cared – or dared – to question.

The notion of an abiding consensus among historians of any complex subject may now seem rather surprising, and this agreeable situation was probably in part a reflection of the general consensus of the Eisenhower years, when we were all beating our swords into ploughshares. That same ironic mood, that same amiable but slightly complacent consensus, also left its mark on other fields of history. The gentle complaint of our editor, disappointed in his hopes for a little fun at a scholarly symposium, hinted at the charge of dullness brought by bored professors against their boring students of the silent generation – upon which we would soon enough be looking back with a degree of nostalgia. For since the 1960s the world around us has dramatically changed, and with it historiography.

These two sets of changes are not unrelated, and the result for the Renaissance has been rather different from what Ferguson foresaw. In his vision the Renaissance was to retain its pivotal position in the old scenario, but our knowledge of it would be better pulled together. But this has not occurred. Although the consensus of the golden 1950s has not been seriously challenged, we are now remarkably indifferent to the world-historical importance of the Renaissance.[5] We go about our particular investigations as though the Renaissance problem had evaporated; we neither affirm nor bother to deny that there was a Renaissance. And the venerable 'Renaissance' label has become little more than an administrative convenience, a kind of blanket under which we huddle together less out of mutual attraction than because, for certain purposes, we have nowhere else to go.[6]

I do not mean to exaggerate the abruptness of this development. In retrospect we can see that the role of historians in the postwar rehabilitation of the Renaissance was always somewhat ambiguous. We accepted what was said in praise of the Renaissance by representatives of other humanistic disciplines; the importance of the Renaissance for them enhanced our own importance. But, like Garrett B. Mattingly on one such occasion, we were sometimes 'puzzled' about what we might contribute to a Renaissance symposium.[7] The normal scepticism of a professional historian in the presence of large views has now given way, however, to agnosticism and even indifference about what was once the central claim of Renaissance scholarship.

Historians of the Renaissance have responded to these pressures in two ways. First, we began to distinguish more and more clearly between the 'Renaissance' itself, a cluster of cultural movements pregnant with the future, and the 'age of the Renaissance', the more general context within which we encountered these movements. The 'age of the Renaissance' was invoked to accommodate, in some unstable tension with the novelty and modernity of Renaissance culture, whatever seemed inconsistent or in tension with it. But we tended at first to regard these anomalies as so many medieval residues, destined to yield ineluctably, in the long run, to its modernizing forces. This approach was hardly the method of synthesis.

But at the same time we were increasingly uncomfortable with the rather mechanical work of sorting out data into two heaps, one marked 'continuities', the other 'innovations'. This discomfort led to a second move that seems on the surface to have brought us closer to synthesis: we began to describe the age of the Renaissance as the age of transition *to* the modern world. And this formula, which now appears with some regularity in our textbooks, has provoked little dissent. Indeed, the formula appears to exclude the possibility of dissent, for it is nicely calculated to accommodate every anomaly and at the same time to protect the significance of the Renaissance. This, of course, is its purpose. To the objection that every past age might equally be represented as transitional, we can reply that this one was *unusually* transitional, that it was an age of *accelerated* transition.[8] This position now gives a semblance of agreement to Renaissance scholarship, enabling us to engage in a wide variety of tasks, comfortable in the belief that our larger claims are secure – and effectively indifferent to them.

Nevertheless, there are difficulties in this apparently unexceptionable strategy. For one thing, it neglects to state the criteria by which one age can be considered more transitional than another; by begging this question, which was at the heart of our controversy with the medievalists, it invites a new revolt from that direction as well as protests from other quarters. The strategy also seems to me conceptually confused, a reflection of the chronic temptation of the historian to identify 'history' as the actuality of the past with 'history' as the construction he makes of its records. For history as actuality, an 'age' is simply a considerable span of time; for history as construction, an 'age' is a segment of the past on which he can impose some intelligibility. The notion of an 'age of transition' thus exploits what is essentially a structural conception to assert for the Renaissance a continuing significance that actually derives from its place in a process.

This confusion points to a further problem, since the notion of a transitional age depends on the intelligibility of the 'ages' it supposedly connects. The Renaissance as 'transition' suggests something like an unsteady bridge between two granitic headlands, clearly identifiable as the Middle Ages and the modern (or, at least, the early modern) world. As a Renaissance specialist, I am reluctant to commit myself about the present stability of these two adjacent historiographical promontories. But my impression is that neither medieval nor early modern historians would be altogether comfortable with the image.[9] And as an inhabitant of the modern world, I find it rather too amorphous, unintelligible and contradictory, at least as a whole, to provide any stable mooring for such a bridge. I am, in short, doubtful whether we are yet in any position to represent our own time as an intelligible age.

But a reflection of this kind takes us beyond internal historiographical pressures to the impact of contemporary experience on historiography. And such experience may, in the end, be the major cause for the present disarray of Renaissance scholarship: since we are baffled by the modern world, we are hardly in a position to argue for the relevance to it, at least in the traditional way, of the Renaissance.[10] For the argument that attached the Renaissance to the modern world was based on two assumptions: that the modern world does, in fact, constitute some kind of intelligible entity, and that modernity has emerged by way of a single linear process. Neither of these assumptions is, at least for me, self-evident. To be a competent historian of the Renaissance is, of course, hard enough, even without engaging in extracurricular ventures of this kind; but my efforts to sample the work of those scholars who have struggled to define the modern condition leave me as uncertain as the modern world itself.[11] And I am further bewildered by the suggestion that we have now entered into a 'postmodern' age. Meanwhile, the collapse of the idea of progress has profoundly subverted our sense of the direction of history. We can agree, perhaps, only that the present is the complex product of a remarkably tangled past.

Other pressures from the surrounding world have also weakened the ability of the historian of the Renaissance to defend the old dramatic organization of Western history and have at the same time promoted an alternative. Brought into focus by the social and cultural ferment of the 1960s, so stimulating to historiography in other areas, these pressures have left the Renaissance in a partial eclipse. They pose a radical challenge – one that we have largely ignored – to our own doubtful compromise between process and structure.[12]

This challenge is related to a generous concern with the historiographically neglected and suffering majority of mankind that has diverted attention from those elites whose achievements have been the mainstay of claims for the Renaissance. From this standpoint, historical significance tends to be defined largely as a function of numbers, of mass, and, hence, of the masses; this interest in the masses may suggest an ideological and even sentimental content in the supposedly cold and scientific impulse towards quantification. But 'mass' also suggests 'matter' and, therefore, points to the material basis of human existence, with a concomitant tendency to rely on the architectural model – so disruptive of traditional historiography – of superstructure and infrastructure, against the idealism often implicit in the preoccupation of historians of the Renaissance with high culture. A further consequence of this interest has been an emphasis on the more inert aspects of the past, with reduced attention to what had traditionally been seen as the source of the most dynamic forces in modern history. Meanwhile, the peculiar insecurity of the last two decades seems to have intensified the occasional yearning of the historian to regard or himself as a scientist; and the methods recently devised to promote this aspiration and to open up new social groups to investigation have not been suited to the ways of Renaissance study, which has depended, chiefly, on the cultivated judgment and creative imagination of the individual historian.

These impulses have conspicuously been at work in the new social history, which has produced results of great interest, if chiefly for a later period, and which seems to me itself a remarkable feat of the historical imagination. This much is, I think, indisputable, however sceptical one may be of its scientific pretensions[13] and of the claims of some of its practitioners to have overcome at last the distinction between history as actuality and history as construction. And it is particularly instructive from the standpoint of our present difficulties with the Renaissance, because it displays the results of a deliberate and wholehearted acceptance of that notion of an 'age' with which historians of the Renaissance have dealt so gingerly. It may also help to explain why they have preferred compromise.

I am referring to the concept of the *longue durée*, the intelligible age *par excellence*, whose implications for the Renaissance emerge with special clarity in a recent essay by Emmanuel Le Roy Ladurie.[14] This piece offers a general interpretation of the extended period between about the eleventh and the nineteenth century. Situated between two intervals of innovation and expansion, this true age is, for Le Roy Ladurie, an intelligible unity, given fundamental coherence by a kind of grim Malthusian balance. The productivity of agriculture was limited, population was limited by it, and the material conditions of life for the vast majority were virtually unchangeable. By the democratic criterion of numbers, this long period was, except in insignificant detail, changeless; Le Roy Ladurie has accordingly described it as 'motionless'.

From this standpoint the period of the Renaissance appears as little more than, in a double sense, the dead centre of a much longer age in which the conventional distinction between medieval and early modern Europe has been obliterated. At most, the Renaissance is a *conjoncture* that is intelligible only in a far larger temporal context. But the full implications of the argument emerge only in Le Roy Ladurie's reply to the objections that might be raised against it by more traditional historians:

> One might object to this conception of motionless history ... because it is a little too negligent of such fundamental innovations of the period as Pascal's divine revelation, Papin's steam engine and the growth of a very great city like Paris, or the progress of civility among the upper classes as symbolized by the introduction of the dinner fork. Far be it from me to question the radically new character of these episodes. But what interests me is the *becoming*, or rather the *non-becoming* of the faceless mass of people. The accomplishments of the elite are situated on a higher and more isolated plane and are not really significant except from the point of view of a noisy minority, carriers of progress without doubt, but as yet incapable of mobilizing the enormous mass of rural humanity enmeshed in its Ricardian feedback.[15]

One has only to substitute – for Pascal, Papin, Paris and the dinner fork – any random set of Renaissance accomplishments – Petrarch's historical consciousness, the Copernican Revolution, the Florentine city-state with its civic rhetoric, and double-entry bookkeeping, for example – to appreciate the mordant implications here for the Renaissance.

Although the plausibility of this argument, which appears to illustrate the consequences of a thoroughgoing 'synthesis', has perhaps been one element in the present disarray of Renaissance historiography, its approach also has limitations (as I am hardly the first to point out)[16] that make it less decisive for the Renaissance than it may first appear. Largely an adaptation of French structuralism, Le Roy Ladurie's thesis carries with it the antihistorical bias of that movement: structuralist analysis of the past has never been well adapted to deal with change. The consequences are apparent when Le Roy Ladurie, too good a historian to ignore this problem, must account for the end of his *longue durée*, when motion was finally restored to human affairs, the constraints on agriculture loosened, the old Malthusian cycle was broken, the migration from field to factory could begin, and the masses were at last expelled from the traditional world into, presumably, a new age.

At this point Le Roy Ladurie's rich ironies seem to serve chiefly as a rhetorical justification for the limitation of his vision to what, as he so disarmingly puts it, 'interests' him. Here we become aware of a difference in both strategy and tone. Since the masses were helpless to bring about this ambiguous denouement, that ridiculous noisy minority becomes unexpectedly important. Now it represents 'forces of elitist renovation which had been building up slowly over the course of centuries' and which finally succeeded, after about 1720, in 'setting off an avalanche'.[17] This 'build-up of forces' might suggest that Paris and the steam engine – and even, more obscurely, Pascal and the fork – are after all, if one is interested in that 'avalanche', worth some attention. And behind them lies the Renaissance – not, perhaps, as an 'age' but (in the terms of its traditional interpretation) as a critical moment in a process that would in the long run significantly transform the world. The impulses not altogether arbitrarily associated with the Renaissance – its individualism and its practical and empirical rationality – were, though immediately limited to a statistically insignificant minority, destined for some importance even from the standpoint of the majority.[18] I do not mean to deny the value of structural description; indeed, it provides essential safeguards against anachronism for the historian primarily interested in process.[19] But structures can hardly exhaust the concern of the historian; the past is not simply a world we have lost.

The inability of a history of structures to deal with change has, however, a further consequence. Its neglect of the continuities that link the past with the present and one 'age' to the next opens the way to an interpretation of change as cataclysm, with the implication that the modern world is genetically related to the past only remotely. Our own time thus appears as something like a biological mutation, whose survival value remains an open question. For the structural approach to the past may ignore but cannot, after all, repudiate process altogether. One set of structures obviously does, somehow, give way to another. The effect of this approach is to promote, however inadvertently, a discontinuous concept of process. Thus, for the myth of continuity with the Renaissance, it substitutes what I will call the myth of apocalyptic modernization. In calling this a myth, I mean nothing pejorative.[20] A myth is, for the historian, the dynamic equivalent of a model in the social sciences, and we can hardly do without it. The crucial transition from chronicle to history depended on the application of some principle of mythical organization to previously discrete data: the myth of the hero, the myth of collective advance, the myth of decline. That the weakening of one mythical pattern should have left a kind of vacuum for another myth to fill is hardly surprising.

So the apocalyptic myth – a product partly of our own self-importance and partly of the mingled hopes and anxieties generated by recent experience – has emerged, though it is not itself peculiarly modern. A modification of the basic Western myth of linear time of a type periodically recurrent under conditions of stress, the apocalyptic myth provides an alternative to the idea of continuous development, with which it can be variously combined. Indeed, it is not altogether different from the Renaissance notion of radical discontinuity with the Middle Ages. In discussing it critically, I am aware of a certain analogy with the medievalists' protests against the idea of the Renaissance.

Largely as a result of those protests, historians of the Renaissance generally gave up the apocalyptic dimension of the original Renaissance myth, at least as it related to the past. Without renouncing the novelties of the Renaissance, they recognized its continuities with the Middle Ages, themselves increasingly seen as complex. In other words, they made distinctions, within both periods, among contrary tendencies. But these careful distinctions took care of only half of the Renaissance problem. Thus, if we are still in disarray, the explanation may ultimately be that we have failed to modify in the same way that element in the Renaissance myth that pointed to the future: its perception of the modern world – the goal of the historical process – as a coherent entity. Since we can no longer support our claims for the Renaissance origins of the modern world so conceived, we have fallen silent. If this is true, the full solution to the Renaissance problem would thus depend on our giving as much attention to the complexities and contradictions of our own time as we have given to those of the Middle Ages and the Renaissance and on being equally selective about the relation of the Renaissance to the modern world. Among its other advantages, this solution might enable us to put the apocalyptic myth itself in some perspective; we might then notice that some reaction against it is already under way in the social sciences.[21]

Such selectivity might enable us to claim for the Renaissance a substantial role in the formation of those tendencies in our own world that perhaps have a better claim to modernity than does the present apocalyptic mood: the sceptical, relativistic and pragmatic strains in contemporary culture.[22] These strains would suggest, in place of the apocalyptic myth, something like the myth of Prometheus, itself of some interest to Renaissance thought[23] – Prometheus who, by tricking Zeus and stealing the fire that made possible the arts, endowed man with the power to create a world in which he could survive alone. Such a myth might be interpreted to mean that the world man inhabits is formed, not through some transcendent and ineluctable process – whether cataclysmic or uniform – but only out of his own shifting needs and unpredictable inventiveness. From this standpoint, the basic peculiarity of the modern world might be seen as the present consciousness of human beings of their power to shape the world they inhabit, including the social world and, by extension, themselves. A (for us) poignant reflection of this situation might be the unique predicament of the modern historian, who is in a position to choose, among various possibilities, the myth most useful to impose dramatic organization on his data – a problem of which previous historians were largely unaware. In modern culture, then, the determinism and helplessness implicit in the apocalyptic myth are opposed by a still lively belief in human freedom.

The modern sense of the creative freedom of mankind now finds stimulating expression in a concept of culture that underlies the work of a group of distinguished contemporary anthropologists.[24] According to this view of the human condition, the universe man inhabits is essentially a complex of meanings of his own devising; man, as Max Weber perceived him, is 'an animal suspended in webs of significance he himself has spun'.[25] These webs make up his culture or, more exactly, since they are utterly various, his cultures. Furthermore, as philosophers and linguists have made increasingly clear, he spins these webs from language. Through language man orders the chaos of data impinging on his sensorium from, in a singularly mysterious and problematic sense, 'out there', organizing them into categories and so making them intelligible, manageable and useful. The human world might, therefore, be described as a vast rhetorical production, for the operations that bring it into existence are comparable to such basic rhetorical transactions as division and comparison, or metonymy and metaphor.[26] This concept denies not that an objective universe exists, but only that man has direct access to it or can know what it is apart from what he makes of it, out of his own limited perceptual and intellectual resources and for his own purposes, whatever these might be.[27]

The epistemological decisions embedded in language are thus the precondition of human apprehension of an external world; culture in this sense is prior to both materialism and idealism, which represent contrary efforts to assign ontological status to – in the language of sociology, to legitimize – a world whose actual source in the creativity of man violates the all-too-human need for transcendence.[28] From this standpoint history presents itself not as a single process but as a complex of processes, which interests us insofar as we are interested in the almost infinite possibilities of human existence. Beyond this, history as construction often tends to be a misleading and sometimes pernicious reification.

Here, I am only advancing on an old position in the historiography of the Renaissance from a somewhat new direction. For the kind of history this approach suggests was very much that of the most distinguished historians of the Renaissance of the last hundred years, Jacob Burckhardt and Johan Huizinga, notable pioneers in what both called cultural history. Misled by their concentration on evidence drawn from the culture of elites, we have tended to see in their work no more than the study of 'superstructure', losing sight of the generous conception of culture underlying their work. For Burckhardt, the proper subject of

Kulturgeschichte was not simply the arts, which were relatively neglected in his account of the Renaissance, but 'what moves the world and what is of penetrating influence ... the indispensable'.[29] For Huizinga, cultural history required the identification of 'deeper, general themes' and 'the patterns of life, thought, and art taken all together', which he was prepared to pursue in every dimension of human experience.[30] And both had such reservations about the modern world that neither would have found much satisfaction in representing it as the goal of history.

This conception of culture is perhaps the contemporary world's most general legacy from the Renaissance: the recognition that culture is a product of the creative adjustment of the human race to its varying historical circumstances rather than a function of universal and changeless nature, and the perception that culture accordingly differs from time to time and group to group. This insight of the Renaissance suggested that mankind, by its own initiatives, could, for better or worse, shape its own earthly condition. Hints of this idea can be found earlier, of course, both in antiquity and in the Middle Ages; and even in the Renaissance the idea was limited to certain groups in which it only occasionally became explicit – as it did for Petrarch and Nicholas of Cusa (though only at certain moments), for Sir Philip Sidney, and for Montaigne. But this shocking view of the human condition made its first durable impression on the Western consciousness then, and has since continued to shape our world.

The high culture of the Renaissance immediately revealed some of the implications of the new conception of culture. Scholars became aware of the distinct, historically contingent cultures of antiquity, while the voyages of exploration discovered the varieties of contemporary culture in America and the Orient. Although the first European responses to these revelations tended to be ethnocentric, the relativism of Montaigne suggested that another kind of reaction was already possible. Meanwhile, cultural expression was being conceived, more modestly, not as a total and authoritative reflection of external reality but as a particular human insight, conveyed by isolated proverbs, *pensées*, familiar essays, small areas of practical or aesthetic order, of which the autonomous painting of Renaissance art provides a nice symbol.

Perhaps the most profound indication that a radical shift in the understanding of culture was taking place – and hence a shift in the sense of man's relation to the world and to himself – can be seen in the Renaissance crisis of language, that basic instrument in the formation of culture.[31] The first sign of that crisis was a growing uneasiness, at first among the most abstract thinkers but then more broadly, that the human vocabulary was failing to mirror the objective world. *Words*, it was widely lamented, no longer corresponded to *things*. This lament was often taken to mean that the vocabulary should be reformed so that this traditional identity could be restored: a demand, in effect, for a return to the dependence of culture upon external nature. But then an alternative solution to the problem began to unfold. Scepticism about the capacity of the human mind to grasp the structures of nature led directly to growing doubt about the possibility of such an identity, to a recognition of the conventionality of language and its susceptibility to change, to the perception of language as a human creation, and eventually to the conclusion that, as the creator of language, man also shapes through language the only world he can know directly, including even himself.

This insight was a major impulse behind the brilliant imaginative literature of the Renaissance, which was one channel for the diffusion of this new concept of language. So was the steady displacement of Latin, the language of absolute truths both sacred and profane, by the European vernaculars, not only in literature but in law and administration. The variety of the vernaculars suggested that language was based on the consensus of particular peoples, arrived at by the processes of history; and the growing expressiveness of the various languages of Europe appeared to demonstrate that linguistic change signified not that the primordial identity of language with the real world was being corrupted – the traditional view propounded by Socrates in the *Cratylus* – but that language is a flexible tool. The rich elaboration of vernacular languages was not only the deliberate project of elites, but a spontaneous and increasingly popular eruption to meet the shifting requirements of existence.

There was thus nothing ethereal about this portentous cultural shift. If a common culture is the foundation of community and limits the possible modes of social organization and social action, it is also responsive to changing social needs, themselves culturally defined. And, like other historical phenomena, the subtle and reciprocal dialogue between culture and society is open to investigation.[32] The expanding linguistic resources of Renaissance culture simultaneously facilitated and reflected the development of a more complex urban and monarchical society. The sense that language does not simply mirror, passively, the structures of external nature, but functions as a tool to serve the practical needs of social existence, eventually stimulated reflection about the uses and creative possibilities of language. And we can see in those reflections the germ of a new vision of human culture.

Whether given practical expression in the creative modification of language or, at another level, in the Renaissance idea of self-fashioning,[33] the notion of man as creator of himself and the world was heady stuff. It found expression in the modern expectation that government, the economy and education should constantly reconstruct society, the environment, and man himself in accordance with the constantly changing expectations of mankind. There are doubtless limits to such an enterprise, both in the malleability of physical and biological reality and in man's own moral capacities,[34] that this aspiration tends to overlook. These limits and the attempts to exceed them help to explain a perennial impulse since the Renaissance to react against the creativity and freedom of Renaissance culture toward various types of philosophical and scientific determinism and, thus, also to explain the contradictions of the modern world. Perhaps the Renaissance vision of man, with its vast practical consequences, has needed, from time to time, to be chastened in this way. But it has so far survived as the major resource with which to oppose the temptation to escape from the anxieties of the human condition into new versions of authoritarianism.

I began these remarks by announcing the collapse of the dramatic scheme that has long organized our vision of the general career of Western history. Since I think that drama is vital to historiography, because it enables us to impose form on the processes of history and so to make them intelligible, this seems to me an ominous development, especially since it has invited the substitution of another dramatic scheme that would deprive us of our roots in the past. But, although I have argued for the continuing significance of the Renaissance, I have not tried simply to defend the traditional pattern, which seems to me seriously defective, in ways that the legacy of Renaissance culture also helps us understand. The old dramatic pattern, with its concept of linear history moving the human race ineluctably to its goal in the modern world, depended on concealed principles of transcendence inappropriate to the human understanding of human affairs. The trinity of acts composing the great drama of human history and its concept of the modern epoch as not just the latest but the last act of the play, bears witness to its eschatological origins,[35] and such notions seem to me peculiarly inappropriate to so human an enterprise as that of the historian. But I also find the traditional scheme unsatisfactory because it is not dramatic enough. It fails to accommodate the sense of contingency and, therefore, suspense – the sense that the drama might have turned out otherwise – that belongs to all human temporal experience. Though it has survived for over five centuries, for example, I see no reason to assume that the anthropological vision we owe to the Renaissance is destined to triumph forever over the forces arrayed against it, and much in the modern world suggests the contrary.

But the more human concept of the drama of history that had its effective origins in the Renaissance understanding of culture overcomes these various disadvantages. Its pluralism implies the possibility of a multiplicity of historical dramas, both simultaneous and successive; and so it relieves us of the embarrassment, inherent in a linear and eschatological vision of time, of repeatedly having to reclassify in other terms what for a previous generation seemed modern. Since it perceives history as a part of culture and also, therefore, a human creation, it permits us constantly to reconstruct the dramas of history and so to see the past in fresh relation to ourselves. Above all, since it insists on no particular outcome for the dramas of history, it leaves the future open.

Notes

1 Wallace K. Ferguson, *The Renaissance* (New York, 1940), 2.
2 Ferguson, *The Renaissance in Historical Thought* (Boston, 1948), 389.
3 For some of the works that particularly influenced me at this time, in addition to those of Ferguson, see Paul Oskar Kristeller, *The Classics and Renaissance Thought* (Cambridge MA, 1955); Hans Baron, *The Crisis of the Early Italian Renaissance: Civic Humanism and Republican Liberty in an Age of Classicism and Tyranny*, 2 vols (Princeton, 1955); Eugenio Garin, *L'umanesimo italiano* (Bari, 1958); and the various essays of Erwin Panofsky, especially 'Renaissance and Renascences', *Kenyon Review* 6(1944): 201–36.
4 Tinsley Helton (ed.) *The Renaissance: A Reconsideration of the Theories and Interpretations of the Age* (Madison WI, 1961), xi–xii. The papers in this volume were presented at a symposium at the University of Wisconsin, Milwaukee, in 1959. For other symposia, see *The Renaissance: A Symposium* (New York, 1953); and Bernard O'Kelly (ed.) *The Renaissance Image of Man and the World* (Columbus OH, 1966).
5 Randolph Starn has called attention to this; see his review of Nicolai Rubinstein (ed.) *Florentine Studies: Politics and Society in Renaissance Italy* (London, 1968), in *Bibliothèque d'humanisme et Renaissance* 32(1970): 682–3. Also see his 'Historians and "Crisis"', *Past and Present* 52(1971): 19.
6 For explicit recognition that the term functions chiefly as an administrative convenience, see Brian Pullan, *A History of Early Renaissance Italy from the Mid-thirteenth to the Mid-fifteenth Century* (London, 1973), 11.
7 Mattingly, 'Some Revisions of the Political History of the Renaissance', in Helton, *The Renaissance: A Reconsideration*, 3.
8 In his *Renaissance in Historical Thought*, Ferguson tied the notion of transition to synthesis; he combined the two strategies in *Europe in Transition, 1300–1520* (Boston MA, 1962), the first large-scale presentation of the period in these terms, though this project was already foreshadowed in his 'The Interpretation of the Renaissance: Suggestions for a Synthesis', *Journal of the History of Ideas* 12(1951): 483–95. For other works that rely on the idea of transition, see Eugene F. Rice Jr, *The Foundations of Early Modern Europe, 1460–1559* (New York, 1970), ix; Lewis W. Spitz, *The Renaissance and Reformation Movements* (Chicago, 1971), vii, 3; and Pullan, *Early Renaissance Italy*, 11. The widespread assumption that textbooks such as these are no part of our 'serious' work seems to me both troubling and mistaken.
9 It may be noted that medievalists who write about the Renaissance tend to see it not as a 'transition' but as having a distinct identity of its own. See, for example, Denys Hay, *The Italian Renaissance in Its Historical Background* (Cambridge, 1961), 14–25; and Robert S. Lopez, *The Three Ages of the Italian Renaissance* (Charlottesville VA, 1970), 73.
10 For a work that is especially sensitive to this problem, see Rice, *Foundations of Early Modern Europe*, x.
11 I have been helped to see the complexity of this problem by Richard D. Brown's work; see his *Modernization: The Transformation of American Life, 1600–1865* (New York, 1976), 3–22.

12 For a stimulating exception, see John Hale, *Renaissance Europe: The Individual and Society, 1480–1520* (London, 1971). But its short time-span excuses it from the need to deal with larger processes, and in spite of Hale's attempt to write 'majority' history, much of his detail is drawn – inevitably – from 'minority' sources.

13 This issue is muddied by the ambiguity of the term 'science'. For a useful discussion of its somewhat different meanings in French and English usage, see J. H. Hexter, 'Fernand Braudel and the *Monde Braudellien* ... ', *Journal of Modern History* 44(1972): 500.

14 Le Roy Ladurie, 'Motionless History', *Social Science History* 1(1977): 115–36. Clyde Griffen kindly called this article to my attention.

15 Le Roy Ladurie, 'Motionless History', 133–4.

16 For a notable critique, see Hexter, 'Fernand Braudel and the *Monde Braudellien* ... , 480–539. Also see, for a criticism of the neglect of process in much of the new social history, Eugene and Elizabeth Fox Genovese, 'The Political Crisis of Social History: A Marxian Perspective', *Journal of Social History* 10(1976): 215. As Robert M. Berdahl points out, many non-Marxists can agree with this; see his 'Anthropologie und Geschichte: einige theo-retische Perspektiven und ein Beispiel aus der preussisch-deutschen Geschichte', in Robert M. Berdahl, Alf Lüdtke and Hans Medick (eds) *Klassen und Kultur* (Frankfurt, 1982), 263–87.

17 Le Roy Ladurie, 'Motionless History', 134.

18 The long-range significance of these tendencies of the Renaissance is still recognized, however, in some recent work. See Jean Delumeau, 'Le développement de l'esprit d'organisation et de la pensée méthodique dans la mentalité occidentale à l'époque de la Renaissance', in Thirteenth International Congress of Historical Sciences, Moscow 1970, *Doklady Kongressa*, 1, part 5 (Moscow, 1973): 139–50; and Peter Burke, *Culture and Society in Renaissance Italy, 1420–1540* (London, 1972), 225.

19 The very real danger of anachronism seems to have led Charles Trinkaus to renounce the 'traditional genetic-modernist bias', i.e. the scrutiny of the past in the interest of understanding the present; Trinkaus, 'Humanism, Religion, Society: Concepts and Motivations of Some Recent Studies', *Renaissance Quarterly* 29(1976): 677, 685–6. Though I agree that it is subject to abuse, I see nothing illegitimate in principle in genetic explanation, and I am quite sure that its abandonment by historians would only leave it to others less sensitive to its difficulties.

20 For this complex word, see Raymond Williams, *Keywords: A Vocabulary of Culture and Society* (New York, 1976), 176–8. For a generally instructive work on the role of myth in historiography, see Hayden White, *Metahistory: The Historical Imagination in Nineteenth-Century Europe* (Baltimore, 1973).

21 See Shmuel N. Eisenstadt, 'Sociological Theory and an Analysis of the Dynamics of Civilizations and Revolutions', *Daedalus* 106(1977): esp. 61–3.

22 Isaiah Berlin has helped me bring these strains into focus; see his *Vico and Herder: Two Studies in the History of Ideas* (New York, 1976).

23 See Charles Trinkaus, *In Our Image and Likeness: Humanity and Divinity in Italian Humanist Thought*, I (Chicago, 1970), 244–5. Also see, for a significant and more recent application of this myth, Donald R. Kelley, 'The Metaphysics of Law: An Essay on the Very Young Marx', *American Historical Review* 83(1978): 350.

24 For studies that reflect this concept of culture, see Pierre Bourdieu, *Outline of a Theory of Practice*, trans. Richard Nice (Cambridge, 1977); Mary Douglas, *Purity and Danger: An Analysis of Concepts of Pollution and Taboo* (London,

1966), *Natural Symbols* (London, 1970) and *Implicit Meanings: Essays in Anthropology* (London, 1975); Louis Dumont, *From Mandeville to Marx: The Genesis and Triumph of Economic Ideology* (Chicago, 1977); Clifford Geertz, *The Interpretation of Cultures* (New York, 1973); Marshall Sahlins, *Culture and Practical Reason* (Chicago, 1976); Victor Turner, *The Ritual Process: Structure and Anti-Structure* (Ithaca NY, 1969); and, seminal for the role of language in culture, Edward Sapir, *Culture, Language, and Personality: Selected Essays*, ed. David G. Mandelbaum (Berkeley and Los Angeles, 1949).

25 Geertz, *Interpretation of Cultures*, 5.

26 The historian's creation of the world of the past out of language provides a close analogy.

27 For much of this I am indebted to the theoretical essays of Harry Berger Jr. See, in particular, his 'Outline of a General Theory of Cultural Change', *Clio* 2(1972): 49–63, and 'Naive Consciousness', *Papers on Language and Literature* 8(1973): 1–44.

28 See Sahlins, *Culture and Practical Reason*, esp. ix–x.

29 As quoted in Karl J. Weintraub, *Visions of Culture: Voltaire, Guizot, Burckhardt, Lamprecht, Huizinga, Ortega y Gasset* (Chicago, 1966), 138.

30 Huizinga, *Men and Ideas: History, the Middle Ages, and the Renaissance*, trans. James S. Holmes and Hans van Marle (New York, 1959), 28. Also see Weintraub, *Visions of Culture*, 230–1.

31 For a general discussion of Renaissance views of language, see Karl-Otto Apel, *Die Idee der Sprache in der Tradition des Humanismus von Dante bis Vico*, Archiv für Begriffsgeschichte, no. 8 (Bonn, 1963). For some of the studies that have influenced my own understanding of these matters, see Michael Baxandall, *Giotto and the Orators: Humanist Observers of Painting in Italy and the Discovery of Pictorial Composition, 1350–1450* (Oxford, 1971); Salvatore I. Camporeale, *Lorenzo Valla: Umanesimo e teologia* (Florence, 1972); Thomas M. Greene, 'Petrarch and the Humanist Hermaneutic', in K. Atchity and G. Rimanelli (eds) *Italian Literature: Roots and Branches* (New Haven, 1976), 201–24; Gordon Leff, *William of Ockham: The Metamorphosis of Scholastic Discourse* (Manchester, 1975), esp. 124–237; J. G. A. Pocock, *Politics, Language, and Time: Essays on Political Thought and History* (New York, 1971); and Nancy S. Struever, *The Language of History in the Renaissance: Rhetoric and Historical Consciousness in Florentine Humanism* (Princeton, 1970). It is increasingly apparent that those self-conscious antagonists, Renaissance humanists and later Scholastics, in fact collaborated in this development.

32 For an especially useful discussion of this relationship, see Bourdieu, *Outline of a Theory of Practice*, esp. 72–95.

33 On this radical application of the Renaissance concept of human creativity, see A. Bartlett Giamatti, 'Proteus Unbound: Some Versions of the Sea God in the Renaissance', in Peter Demetz (ed.) *The Disciplines of Criticism* (New Haven, 1968), 431–75; and Stephen J. Greenblatt, 'Marlowe and Renaissance Self-Fashioning', in Alvin Kernan (ed.) *Two Renaissance Mythmakers: Christopher Marlowe and Ben Jonson* (Baltimore, 1977), 41–69.

34 Hence the condemnation of the Renaissance in Protestant neo-orthodoxy; see Herbert Weisinger, 'The Attack on the Renaissance in Theology Today', *Studies in the Renaissance* 2(1955): 176–89. This hostility continues to inhibit recognition of the filiation between the Reformation and the Renaissance.

35 The structural principle of the conventional ancient/medieval/modern division seems to persist in more recent trinitarian schemes – i.e. primitive-traditional-modern and aristocrat-bourgeois-proletarian.

Part II

POLITICS, LANGUAGE AND POWER

... a new fact appears in history – the state as the outcome of reflection and calculation, the state as a work of art.

Burckhardt

In this section, three leading historians offer new perspectives on the history of republicanism, civic humanism, and the state in Renaissance and early modern Italy.

The first two essays focus on Florence and in particular on the political vocabulary of the Florentines, though the authors approach the subject from different angles and reach fundamentally different conclusions. Najemy's essay is an attempt to show how the struggles and the language of the popolo *played a major role in shaping a republican ethos in the city even after the Medici came to power in the early fifteenth century, while Hankins' article calls into question the sincerity of Leonardo Bruni, long considered one of the chief architects of republican thought and the ideals of civic humanism, and shows him instead to have been a rhetorician who served as a propagandist for the state. Readers will find it useful to compare and contrast the methods of Hankins and Najemy, to consider why both make language so central to their analyses, and how their focus on different milieu may affect the differences in their interpretations of Florentine politics, especially in their understanding of the nature of republican discourse in this Renaissance city-state.*

The third essay by Elena Fasano Guarini serves as a counterpoint to both Najemy and Hankins. Unlike her American colleagues, Fasano Guarini does not privilege language and rhetoric but rather offers a detailed examination of the relation of power to state politics in early modern Italy. Accordingly she moves us away from both the rulers and humanists of the major cities to the economic, social and institutional forces that defined and limited the exercise of power, in the towns and villages of the provinces or outlying areas of the early modern state. From her vantage point, the traditional distinction between republics, on the one hand, and despotisms and/or monarchies, on the other, seems virtually insignificant.

3

THE DIALOGUE OF POWER IN FLORENTINE POLITICS

John M. Najemy

The political history of Florence has long been a subject of fascination to historians. It is, after all, a story of class struggle and factionalism, of conspiracy and revolution, of murder, exile and dramatic executions – and, ultimately, of the emergence of one family, the Medici, as the rulers of the city and the territories it had gradually conquered. It is no accident that this was the world that produced Niccolò Machiavelli, along with several other seminal historians and political theorists, from the age of Dante (d. 1321) to that of Francesco Guicciardini (d. 1540). And it is no surprise that many of the greatest historians of the Renaissance – from Burckhardt and Baron to Rubinstein and Brucker – have seen the history of this city-state as a cauldron in which modern political ideas, institutions and theories first emerged.

But how one should frame this political history is a contentious matter. On the one hand, many scholars – especially in recent years – have tended to take an increasingly elitist or top-down view of the history of this city-state. Historians such as Sergio Bertelli and Dale Kent, for example, have shown how great families used patronage networks and marriage strategies to consolidate their power. These scholars tend to view the popolo *(the workers, artisans and guildsmen of the city) as a largely passive group, rather easily manipulated by the oligarchs. On the other hand, scholars such as Samuel K. Cohn and John M. Najemy have provided a far different perspective, stressing the role of the people (both in the city and the countryside) in the shaping of Florentine political institutions and ideas. To these latter two historians, the earlier model succumbs too easily to the myth of the Renaissance and tends to privilege the actions of the great families, in part because of their role in underwriting the artistic and humanist culture of the age. In place of this model, they underscore the contested and negotiated nature of Florentine political history, giving class struggle a prominent place in the compelling accounts they have provided.*

Najemy's essay, which reprises many of the arguments he presented in Corporatism and Consensus in Florentine Electoral Politics, 1280–1400 *(Chapel Hill, 1982), first lays out the contours of this debate and then argues forcefully for a more inclusive or expansive view of the political culture of this Renaissance city-state. Of special interest is his model of the 'dialogic' nature of Florentine politics. He does not wish to deny the fact that the elites did in fact*

45

co-opt and exploit the popolo *to their own ends, but he also wishes to give the latter a role in shaping the political vocabulary and behaviours of the city's great families. In Najemy's view, the* popolo *and the memory of popular governments continued to influence Florentine political life well into the sixteenth century. Popular governments in the thirteenth and fourteenth centuries had established patterns and expectations for guild representation and electoral politics, and had created a wide array of republican institutions that the oligarchs in Florence, even in the fifteenth century, could not ignore.*

Readers should keep in mind that the debate is to some degree determined by the period upon which particular scholars focus. Najemy's work has largely developed out of his interest in the early Renaissance – a period in which popular guild-based governments did indeed hold power, most famously in the aftermath of the Ciompi Revolt of 1378. Dale Kent, by contrast, has been more interested in the political history of the later Renaissance, a theme she eloquently explored in The Rise of the Medici: Faction in Florence, 1426–1434 *(Oxford, 1978). Nonetheless, while it is true that the Medici exercised much control over Florence throughout the better part of the fifteenth century and then definitively after their restoration in 1530, eventually becoming the Grand Dukes of Tuscany, it is equally true that republican ideas and ideologies had a rich after-life in the city, especially in the period following the French invasion of Italy in 1494 and in the writings of Machiavelli in the early sixteenth century.*

The essay 'The Dialogue of Power in Florentine Politics' originally appeared in City-States in Classical Antiquity and Medieval Italy, *eds Anthony Molhor, Kurt Raaflaub and Julia Emlen (Ann Arbor, 1991), 269–88, and is reproduced here in an abridged form. The literature on Renaissance Florentine politics is vast, but the works I have cited on this theme in this volume's intro-duction will provide a useful starting point, as will the essay on the Baron thesis by James Hankins in Chapter 4 below.*

* * *

Modern historiography on medieval and Renaissance Florence is nearly unanimous in emphasizing the continuous and decisive role in the city's political life of an elite or oligarchy or patriciate, usually identified with the republic's great families. The terminology varies and can indeed be tricky, criss-crossed as it is by hidden polemics and ideological subtexts. For some this elite was a ruling class and for others a dominant class. Still others avoid the notion of class altogether and prefer Nicola Ottokar's 'ceto dirigente'. One can always use the terms employed by contemporaries (*grandi, ottimati,* or even just *famiglie*). Despite these differences and nuances of language, the standard wisdom among histo-rians of republican Florence now sees a continuity of elite power over several centuries, and over and beyond the formal configuration or rhetorical proclamations of particular regimes. According to this view, governments, revolutions, institutions and even new classes and *gente nuova* came and went, but the great families (indeed some would stress the extent to which they were the *same* great families) always remained as a controlling force in political life, even if not always in positions of official power.[1]

More recently, however, certain claims for the power of elites in Florence and other Italian city-states have gone beyond the views summarized here to assume a degree of aristocratic hegemony so enduring and so complete as to constitute in effect a permanent and immovable structure. It is now asserted that the Florentine elite enjoyed a virtual monopoly of power, and indeed that politics itself was always and inevitably an affair of the elite. According to Dale Kent, 'almost all politically effective activity took place within the confines of a single class – the patriciate'.[2] In her discussion of 'the three major entities involved in the political process' in the Florence of the 1430s, Kent defines the largest of these entities as 'that group of several hundred families' with a long tradition of participation in the chief offices of government, a group that she calls the 'traditional *classe dirigente*'.[3] Within this group she finds the other two entities: a more restricted group of families (or of individuals from families) that held important offices with great frequency, and – at the centre, after 1434 at least – the Medici party. But the important point here is that, according to Kent, the outer perimeter of the Florentine 'political process' introduces us to no more than a few hundred families. Roslyn Pesman Cooper, viewing the matter from the vantage point of her study of the office-holding cadres of the republic of 1494–1512, begins a recent summary of her findings by claiming that 'contemporaries and later historians concur in the view that always in Florence effective power rested in the hands of a small elite'.[4] A similar assumption underlies George Holmes' assertion that 'political division within Florence [in the late thirteenth and early fourteenth centuries] was primarily a matter of family feud', it being understood that the families in question were those of the elite.[5]

Perhaps the most radical statement of the view that politics, let alone power, belonged entirely to the elites of the Italian cities comes from Sergio Bertelli, who declares that 'the extreme narrowness of its political nucleus was a constant characteristic of the medieval and Renaissance city'. 'The constitutional edifice of the city-state', continues Bertelli, 'was such that it impeded – contrary to the idealizations of nineteenth-century historiography – any democratic participation in political life'. Bertelli obviously oversimplifies the problem by implying that the alternatives were narrow oligarchy and participatory democracy: if the city-states did not allow for the latter, he seems to be saying, then they must have been characterized by the former. Thus, a judgment that no one would dispute – namely the inappropriateness of any notion of participatory democracy for these cities – becomes the basis for asserting that

> political struggle in the city-state takes place exclusively in the very restricted world of the *cives optimo jure*. Outside this world there is nothing, the nihilism of the *jacqueries*. ... Whenever the lower classes (*le classi subalterne*) burst into the political theatre ... this happens because a part of the oligarchy appeals to the masses, breaks with the constitutional framework, and makes use of the masses in order to settle differences that could not be resolved within the world of the *cives*.

Here too we have city-states reduced to just two components: on the one hand the oligarchy, and on the other the masses, who can only 'burst into' the oligarchy's 'political theatre' when provoked to do so by the oligarchy itself. The argument depends, of course, not only on a dismissive view of the so-called masses, but also on suppressing the notion that between these masses and the oligarchy there existed a class (or coalition of groups) with purposes, policies, organization, discourse – in sum, a politics of its own. And, in fact, Bertelli declares that the *popolo* was not a class but a party, and that in the movements that go under this name 'what is happening, in reality, is a redistribution of power inside the oligarchic group which manages its own [otherwise] irresolvable differences with an appeal outside itself, involving the *cives* never admitted to power in the oligarchy's own struggles'. According to Bertelli, 'it was not even a case of certain nobles detaching themselves from their own class [as another historian hypothesizes], but rather a rearrangement among themselves [*un diverso porsi di essi*]'.[6] Exactly the same formula – oligarchs manipulating other groups in order to settle their own quarrels – is invoked for both the 'masses' and the *popolo* in order to safeguard the notion that all politics originated with the oligarchy/nobility, even when it was not in fact limited to that class.

The recent tendency to emphasize and indeed to insist on the elite's virtual monopoly of both power and the very terrain of politics has generally been accompanied by a particular view of how this elite exercised power. Grounded in the assumption that the politics of late medieval city-states was fundamentally personal, local and immediate, this view holds that power was generated, accumulated and exercised through personal and family bonds of blood, marriage and friendship, through ties of patronage, obligation, dependence and protection; and in neighbourhood and factional networks that organized these various links into recognizable groups with the capacity to influence or modify the behaviour of both their own 'members' and those of other groups.

Dale Kent articulates the underlying assumption of this approach to Florentine politics: 'The actions – whether public or private, political or personal – of the majority of Florentines were broadly governed by considerations of personal interest and of obligation toward that group of associates to which they constantly refer: "relatives, neighbors, and friends"'. If the behaviour of the 'majority of Florentines' was 'governed' by such considerations, on what grounds can it be claimed that the 'political process' or politics was confined to an elite of no more than a few hundred families? The answer, presumably, is that only upper-class families were large enough to have a quantity of links, bonds, and connections sufficient to contribute to the formation of a network or visible group. Implicitly, the raw material of politics – personal bonds and obligations – was everywhere, but only the large and wealthy families of the elite had the resources to convert that potential into power by organizing and managing those ties. Kent summarizes her authoritative analysis of the rise of the Medici in Florence as follows:

> Leaving aside the importance of their wealth and the influence that came to the Medici family from abroad as a result of the bank, I believe that a crucial factor in their triumph in 1434 was the particular nature of their patronage network. The personal ties that linked the Medici and their supporters had been systematically created or consolidated by the family's leaders from about 1400, with the precise purpose of increasing their political influence and the representation of their supporters in important positions.[7]

The Medici were thus more skillful, systematic and purposeful than their rivals, but in a kind of contest that by its very nature (as defined by Kent) admitted as contenders only upper-class families of a certain size and tradition. This is not to disagree, even minimally, with Kent's explanation of Medici success. It is only to point out that to restrict the notion of politics to that particular contest (and the idea of power to success in that contest) makes it not only possible but necessary to claim that 'almost all politically effective activity took place within the confines' of the patriciate. The view of politics as fundamentally a matter of patronage networks thus entails, almost as a matter of definition, the elite's monopoly of the very activity of politics (when that elite is defined – as it usually is – in terms of great families). Not surprisingly, therefore, the more one wishes to argue for a structural view of oligarchic supremacy, the more appealing the definition of politics as patronage will seem. If one adds the wish to avoid notions of class and class conflict, the combination of elites as ineluctable structures and politics as patronage may become irresistible.

49

This cluster of views and assumptions has lately become something of an orthodoxy, according to which only the study of patronage, neighbourhoods, personal ties, the informal distribution of favours and patterns of influence can give us the inner workings of Florentine politics where it really – and exclusively – took place. Just how quickly a valuable hypothesis about the behaviour of the elite can become an allegedly exclusive truth about the nature of Florentine politics emerges from a recent essay by Bertelli. Summarizing the significance for political history of the studies of social networks and neighbourhood ties by Dale Kent, Francis William Kent, Christiane Klapisch-Zuber and Ronald Weissman,[8] Bertelli concludes that 'neighbourhood ties would seem to be, then, within the patriciate, the true mainspring for the control of political power in the fourteenth and fifteenth centuries'. But within two paragraphs even the hint of caution ('would seem to be') falls away as, suddenly, a whole theory of city-state politics is assumed on the basis of the hypothesis about neighbourhood networks:

> At this point it remains to be asked: how long did this network of territorial relationships remain at *the foundation of the city's political life*? Did neighborhood links still *govern the Florentine political system* after the overthrow of Piero [de' Medici in 1494]?[9]

The point of the emphases added to these sentences is to show the ease with which Bertelli equates neighbourhood social networks with the 'city's political life' and the 'Florentine political system'. For him the question is no longer whether it was so, but for how long it remained so. In fact, however, no one has demonstrated any such thing for the fourteenth century, and even for the fifteenth century it remains at the level of an intriguing hypothesis.

Orthodoxies, even new ones, usually limit vision, and in this essay I explore some of what seem to me the limitations of the currently fashionable approach to Florentine politics that I have outlined. I should say at the outset that I do not for a moment doubt that there was an elite of great families in Florence, that it was both resilient and powerful, and that it (or some part of it) did indeed function as a ruling class or oligarchy for much of the republic's history. Nor do I doubt that the study of patronage and neighbourhood networks tells us many important things about how these families extended their influence and built factions that played a major role in city politics. What I do doubt is the usefulness or accuracy of thinking of elites and their networks of patronage as the sum and substance or as the 'governing' structures, foundations, or underlying 'realities' of Florentine politics.

The first of the limitations imposed by such interpretations is the loss of any sense of the historical alternative or alternatives against which the Florentine elite established its power as a ruling, and sometimes as a dominant, class. If the political supremacy of the elite is accepted as inevitable and permanent, then obviously there can have been no alternatives. But, in fact, throughout the thirteenth and fourteenth centuries, the relationship between the elite of great families and the rest of Florentine society was always turbulent and frequently one of open confrontation. Until about 1400 the elite faced repeated challenges to its power, and at certain times it even ceased to be a ruling class at all – in the sense that it occasionally lost its leadership role and had to endure the control of government by popular movements that defined themselves explicitly in terms of their antagonism to (and determination to do something about) what they saw as the intolerable privileges, propensity for violence, contempt for law, exploitation of the communal fisc, and the general arrogance and *prepotenza* of the class they called the 'grandi'.[10] Historians who see only aristocratic hegemony in Florence will insist that these challenges from the *popolo* were brief and unstable. This is certainly true of the separate periods of actual popular government, but not of the movement as a whole, once its resilience and consistency over a century and a half come into focus.

Popular governments came to power and stayed there for some years on four different occasions between the middle of the thirteenth century and the end of the fourteenth century, and each of these governments attacked elite power and privilege in ways that the great families never forgot or forgave.[11] The *primo popolo* of 1250–60 upset the rationale of an entire generation of upper-class politics by declaring a neutral course between Guelfs and Ghibellines. If in the end the regime was unable to maintain such a course in foreign policy, in domestic politics it did so with a vengeance by destroying or limiting the height of the towers of aristocratic houses, by keeping the representation in offices of members of the Guelf and Ghibelline parties roughly even and at low levels, by abolishing the association of knights (the *universitas militum*) that had been a part of the structure of government before 1250, and by promulgating a new constitution in which representatives of the military and professional associations of the *popolo* elected the commune's chief magistrates. After two brief attempts to reorganize communal government along essentially similar lines in 1266–7 and again in 1282–3 – attempts that failed in their larger purposes but that left important legacies in terms of strengthened guilds and the new magistracy, continuous after 1282, of the priorate of the guilds – the second *popolo* came to power at the end of 1292 and the beginning of 1293 with a more radical programme, enunciated in the Ordinances of Justice, for the containment of upper-class violence. This government designated first thirty-eight and later seventy-two families of the elite, for a total of perhaps 1,500 males, both Guelf and Ghibelline, as magnates and inflicted special penalties on all the members of a magnate house in the event of a crime committed by any one of their number against a *popolano*. It entrusted the election of the priorate to representatives of the guilds and barred the magnates from the councils of the *popolo*, the consulates of the guilds, and, most important, the priorate. In 1343 another popular government symbolically reissued the Ordinances of Justice and instituted new electoral procedures that brought more minor guildsmen and non-elite major guildsmen into office while sharply limiting the representation of great families in the priorate until 1348. This regime supplanted its oligarchic predecessor of the 1330s largely because the latter proved itself incapable of dealing with the looming crisis in communal finances and with the potentially disastrous bankruptcies of some of the largest merchant and banking companies. The popular government directly contributed to the collapse of much of the old economic elite by forcing the banks to satisfy their creditors from the liquidation of landed assets, by halting the repayment to communal creditors (prominent among them the same threatened banking companies) of loans to the government, and by limiting interest payments (after the debt was funded in 1345) to only 5 per cent, instead of the 10 or even 15 per cent for which many loans had been contracted in the 1330s. A significant portion of the elite never recovered either its former economic might or the political power that had accompanied that wealth. The last popular government (1378–82) again reissued the Ordinances, reformed the electoral procedures, drastically limited the presence of elite families in high office, brought a new wave of non-elite major guildsmen and minor guildsmen to the priorate, and reduced interest payments on the debt once again to 5 per cent. But in addition, this regime undermined the traditional structure of the woolen cloth industry by permitting, even after the defeat of the Ciompi, the existence of two independent guilds of skilled artisans formerly subject to the jurisdiction and regulation of the wool guild.

These events are well known to historians of Florence and late medieval Italy, but there is a curious tendency to minimize their import: either to diminish their novelty and impact by claiming that these governments never intended anything very radical, and by observing that in many cases such policies had precedents; or by arguing that, whatever the intentions or degree of originality, the actions of popular governments never really changed things very much.[12] Both arguments have been used to support the thesis of permanent, structural oligarchic supremacy, and I believe both are wrong. Certainly the elite believed that these governments were very real threats to its survival as a ruling class of wealth and power. The hostility of the great families towards the popular regimes, their guild-based constitutions, and the waves of 'new men' that they promoted into office emerges forcefully from a variety of sources: from literary evidence (for example, Compagni's account of assaults on the guild consuls by magnates and *grandi* in the 1290s, Dante's derision of the institutions and discourse of the *popolo*, Villani's angry denunciation of the government of the mid-1340s, Giovanni Cavalcanti's report of Rinaldo degli Albizzi's harangue – nearly fifty years after the events in question – against 'those forty damned months' from September 1378 to January 1382 when the guilds and their consuls 'kept this people in bondage');[13] and from legislation and other political responses through which the elite sought to undermine the power of these popular governments (for example, the so-called anti-foreigner laws of 1346 and 1379 that challenged the eligibility of 'new men' for communal offices, the temporary halving of the number of minor guilds by the *balìa* of 1348, and the gradual but systematic elimination of the electoral autonomy of the guilds by the *balìe* of the 1380s and 1390s).[14] We may legitimately doubt that Piero degli Albizzi and the other conspirators against the popular regime in 1379 actually intended to destroy the guilds, as Coluccio Salutati accused them of planning to do in the letter he sent in 1380 to the pope explaining why his government executed the conspirators; but, even if it was a political and rhetorical exaggeration on Salutati's part, its force must have rested on its verisimilitude – on the apparent likelihood that angry elements of the elite of great families, given what the government of the guilds meant for them, would indeed have wished to destroy the institutions that stood at the base of that whole alternative conception of Florentine politics. The alternative was real and sufficiently threatening to the Florentine elite to make Salutati's accusation believable.[15]

The second weakness of the current conventional wisdom on Florentine politics flows inevitably from the first: lacking any sense of the durable alternative with which elite power contended, it obviously misses the extent to which the elite was shaped and even transformed by that regular and almost permanent conflict. Is it conceivable that a century and a half of sustained rivalry and confrontation with so tenacious a competing class would not have left a profound imprint on the elite? That the long encounter with the *popolo*'s institutions and discourse of politics, its vision of the republic and its reading of history, and most of all its formidable critique of oligarchic power and misrule would not have conditioned the ways in which the elite sought to protect and exercise its power? The elites-and-patronage view of Florentine politics has little room for such notions; insofar as this view stresses one particular mode of the political behaviour of the elite and then, typically, argues that this mode reflects the structures of clientage and patronage found throughout Florentine, communal, Italian, or even Mediterranean society, it tends to promote a static picture of the elite and its politics. In fact, the Florentine elite underwent a veritable metamorphosis between, roughly, 1250 and 1450. At the beginning of this period it was a warrior class of wealthy families (its two most prominent institutional faces until 1250 were the associations of knights and of Calimala merchants) who frequently fought among themselves and used the city and its streets as their battleground. Chronicles and diaries abound with tales of violence and vendetta; whatever the literal truth of the legendary Buondelmonti murder, here again we can say that the story's popularity and force surely rested in its verisimilitude. Insofar as we have any sense of the political style of the great families in the thirteenth century, of the ways in which their members normally expected to exercise power, two notions prevail: the politics of intimidation and *grandigia* of a Corso Donati; and the uncomplicated elitism according to which decisions in family, party, and commune could safely be entrusted to a few prestigious elders.[16]

By the early fourteenth century, the elite's image had taken an economic turn. Powerful men from great families were now more likely to be, and to be seen as, influential bankers and merchants, as heads of family firms rather than family armies. The change was, to be sure, one of perspective and perception, for upper-class families had been involved in business and trade for a long time before the fourteenth century. But now, under the influence of the idea, whose origins lay with the *popolo* and the guild community, that good citizens were successful merchants and that successful participation in some business or trade ought to be a prerequisite for political office, members of the elite too began to present themselves more as prudent merchants than as valiant fighters. Giovanni Villani's celebrated description of Florence in the 1330s was in part a justification of the city's great wealth and the elite's economic leadership. He praised all this wealth because, as he saw things (or wanted to see them), it was widely distributed to the benefit of workers and consumers. Good merchants, he implies, were those who put their wealth to work for the whole city; those who used their money for their own conspicuous consumption – the example he gives is that of wealthy families building sumptuous houses on the hills overlooking the city – were 'committing sin'. In essence, Villani was providing a rationalization for the elite's wealth in terms of what we might call the moral economy of the *popolo*.[17]

The shift in self-perception generated modifications in behaviour as well. Although the great families remained hostile to the notion of guild government, and especially to any increase in political influence for the minor guilds or for the non-elite elements of the major guilds, the members of such families nonetheless joined guilds, partly because they wanted and needed to exert influence within these associations, but also because they themselves came under the influence of ideas that emerged from the guild community. By joining guilds and seeing themselves as part of a community of merchants and guildsmen, even as they and everyone else knew perfectly well that vast differences in wealth and power and in the nature of their economic activities and interests separated them from the other guildsmen, the elite families joined a system of discourse that changed them as they changed it. By the end of the fourteenth century, they had deprived the guilds of their former political autonomy and eliminated even the fiction, quite useful to popular governments, of the equality of the guilds. But in the process the elite had also come to accept as normal and normative the notions – all derived from the long political experience of the guilds as *universitates* – of consent and representation as the foundation of legitimate republican government, of office-holding as a public trust, of the supremacy of law, and of the delegated quality of all formal power: fictions all, to be sure, but ones that deeply affected the political style of the Florentine elite, modifying the means and forms of its power. To deny the influence on the elite of these elements of the political discourse of the *popolo* and the guilds is to miss the universe of difference between the way Corso Donati exercised power in the age of Dante and the way Rinaldo degli Albizzi and Cosimo de' Medici did so in the age of civic humanism.

This is not to say or even to imply that the great families of Florence naively converted to the ennobling myths of civic humanism, or that they actually exercised power according to its standards of good government. The power of the Florentine elite, especially in the fifteenth century, was to a considerable extent grounded in the systematic manipulation and behind-the-scenes control of the institutions of government and society: the guilds themselves; the electoral system; the *pratiche*, or advisory sessions; and the fiscal system. In each case the measure of oligarchic power is the distance between the official ideology of how things were meant to work and the way they in fact did work, between – to take the example of electoral politics – the official ideology of universal eligibility among guildsmen, the equal hope of attaining high office, and the levelling effect of sortition, and the reality of preferential treatment for an inner elite, weighted appointment of the scrutiny committees, and the power of the *accoppiatori* to shift, exclude, and add name tickets to and from the pouches. But the very fact that elite power now had to go through the complex institutions of elections and scrutinies, of guild councils and courts, and of systems of consultation and representation, demonstrates how far the political practice of the *popolo* had transformed the means and mechanisms of upper-class political power. It was owing to the *popolo* that those institutions became part of government, avenues and necessary instruments of power. And, precisely because power resided in the distance between ideology and practice, the elite could hardly pretend that the ideology was irrelevant or nonexistent, as many modern historians do. Its power depended on taking that normative ideology seriously, on getting the rest of Florentine society – but especially the rest of the guild community – to believe that they, the members of elite families, believed that the legitimacy of their own power rested on the mechanisms of elections, consent and representation of the popular will, to believe that Florentine institutions worked to guarantee, as Bruni wrote in the *Laudatio*, that 'in Florence it has always happened that the majority view has been identical with the best citizens'.[18] As Gene Brucker has shown, two generations of Florentines from the 1380s to the 1420s believed as much, enough of them at least to make possible the coexistence of elite power and civic humanism and to give the elite the kind of broad-based support that it had lacked in the fourteenth century.[19] No doubt aware of the irony, the oligarchy cultivated that support by admitting large numbers of non-elite guildsmen into office, by making the consultation of citizens a regular part of the ritual of decision making, and by proclaiming, as the *balìa* of 1382 did, that the legitimate exercise of power derived from 'the full, free, total, and absolute power and authority of the whole Florentine people'.[20] When members of great families, now close to the power of a true oligarchy, began to use notions of popular sovereignty to affirm and legitimate their authority, two things happened: on the one hand, the *popolo* lost control of its political language, which oligarchs were now using for their own purposes and, indeed, as a way of controlling the *popolo*; on the other hand, the two-century challenge of the *popolo* forced the elite to speak, behave, and govern in ways that were closer to the *popolo*'s conception of politics than to the elite's own original governing style. The *popolo* never succeeded in taking power away from the elite (or at least not for very long), and it was never able to diminish the elite's social prestige. But it did change the elite's political style and its mode of exercising power.

The long competition between these two political cultures thus produced some curious results. Each class modified the behaviour of the other and can thus be said to have exercised power *vis-à-vis* the other. The competition was a dialogue in which both interlocutors acted and were acted upon. By 1400 the *popolo* had acquiesced in the elite's leadership and emerging dominance; after this point organized challenges from the guild community no longer materialized. But the other side of the coin is that this now dominant elite ruled and governed to a great extent in the image (and language) of the *popolo*. There is no need to exaggerate the point by claiming too much: no one was likely to miss the enormous difference between a Maso degli Albizzi and a Giovanni Morelli, between a Buonaccorso Pitti and a Gregorio Dati, between a Benedetto Alberti and a Filippo Bastari, or between a Palla Strozzi and a Matteo Palmieri. But when Maso degli Albizzi found, to his surprise, that knighthood and foreign military adventures provoked suspicion and even hostility in the Florence of the late 1380s, even among fellow members of great families; when Buonaccorso Pitti abandoned the gambling, horse trading, and risky wheeling and dealing that kept him abroad until the early 1390s and settled down to a career as a cloth manufacturer and regular officeholder in the communal government; when Benedetto Alberti discovered, to his dismay, that the magnificence and splendor of the Alberti family's 'private' celebrations of Charles of Durazzo's coronation as king of Hungary in 1386 aroused the resentment of many members of the ruling elite who thought that a single family ought not to rival the commune's ritual pageantry – a resentment that no doubt made it easier for the enemies of the Alberti to inflict exile on them, beginning in the next year; and when, a generation later, Palla Strozzi refused to lead a rebellion against the newly drawn pro-Medicean signoria of September 1434 and then accepted, with dignified resignation, what many considered an unjust exile – these political leaders from elite families were exhibiting, or experiencing the impact of, standards of political behaviour that one century earlier would have had little or no effect on their class. The normative discourse of politics that emerged within the elite at the end of the fourteenth century became routine in the fifteenth, as the *ottimati* became the most conspicuous defenders of the republican constitution.[21] In fact, both the Medici regime and the opposition it encountered show the imprint of this normative discourse in their respect for constitutional tradition and the limits of formal power. But at the end of the thirteenth century such attitudes were not only exclusively the property of the *popolo*; they were actually the targets of contempt and abuse from the elite families. How did this metamorphosis happen? By what processes did the elite of great families come to tolerate, adapt and appropriate a political style that it had originally repudiated and derided?

I say 'political style' – and not programme or policy – in order to avoid the implication that the elite in any way accepted or acquiesced in the specific objectives promoted by the *popolo*. The decentralized federated republicanism of the popular governments of the 1290s, 1340s and late 1370s, with its notions of the equality and autonomy of all the constituent guilds of the federation, was never tolerable to the elite, for the simple reason that such systems of government neutralized the influence of large families and placed their members in a clear minority *vis-à-vis* the non-elite guildsmen in crucial magistracies and councils. There was never any question that the elite families would accept this constitutional system. But guild republicanism, never powerful or stable enough to supplant the elite altogether, was indeed powerful enough to create certain institutions that endured and slowly transformed the discourse, attitudes and behaviour of those who lived, sometimes reluctantly, in or next to them. The priorate itself (as its full name, *priores artium* – priors of the guilds, tells us) was originally an institution of the *popolo*; created in 1282 by a movement that opposed the hegemonic pretensions of the elite by building political strength in an expanding community of guilds, it soon became the republic's chief magistracy and remained so for two and a half centuries (although by the middle of the fifteenth century its old link to the guilds was largely forgotten as its name was changed from 'priors of the guilds' to 'priors of liberty'). The union of the guilds, first attempted in 1266–7 by those associations later designated as major guilds, and revived in 1293 as a formal federation of twenty-one guilds, all with constitutional rights, also became part of the Florentine political landscape and, like the priorate, so remained in a formal sense (long after the guilds ceased to play any political role) for the duration of the republic. Another institution produced by the popular government of 1293 was the office of the Standard-bearer of Justice, similarly destined for a long life. Both the union of the guilds and the Standard-bearer of Justice came into being with the Ordinances of Justice, the collection of decrees issued by the first priorate of the popular government of 1292–5 that also contained tough laws against the elite families designated as magnates. The Ordinances too remained on the books (except for one brief attempt at abrogation by a particularly reactionary regime in the summer of 1343) until their partial incorporation into the statutes of the commune in 1415. Even the office of the Executor of the Ordinances of Justice and what became the advisory college of the Sixteen Standard-bearers of the militia companies both originated as part of an effort in the early fourteenth century to revive the *popolo*'s anti-magnate policy. Although the effort and the policy failed, the office of the Executor lasted until 1435, and the college of the Sixteen until the republic's demise. Thus much of what came to be thought of as the republic's political constitution – its *ordini* in the sense in which Machiavelli was to use the term – had its origins in the movements of the *popolo* that sought to limit the elite's power and curtail its abuses. And the same can be said of other characteristic Florentine institutions as well: the office of the *Capitano del popolo* and the councils that assembled under his authority, which went back to the *primo popolo* of 1250–60.

Popular regimes lasted only a few years, mainly because of the elite's hostility to their political aims. But the institutions to which they gave birth lasted in many cases for a very long time, and the reasons for this endurance are not, perhaps, quite so obvious. An old and rather odd view of the institutional history of the Italian city-states holds that the communal regimes went on adding new institutions in response to new circumstances and needs without clearing away the old ones, with a resulting haphazard accumulation of offices

that makes it difficult to tell at first sight which institutions were relevant and functioning at any given moment. The notion that institutions can become empty shells is only a step away from a recent
assumption of the elites-and-patronage school of Florentine historiography: namely, that formal institutions and constitutional and legal
arrangements *never* tell us very much about how politics and power
actually worked. Here is the third limitation of the current orthodoxy:
a tendency to dismiss institutions as a kind of façade, with little or no
correspondence to the underlying 'reality' of personal ties and
patronage networks, and to relegate them to the realm of the merely
prescriptive. But this will get us nowhere in trying to understand why
the institutions of the *popolo* proved so durable, despite the long-term
failure of its programme. Florentines did not collect institutions and
keep them on the shelves for show; nor did they just forget to discard
ones that were no longer useful. And, certainly, governments
controlled by the elite had no reason to be overly fond of institutions
that originated in movements that took direct aim at the power of
great families. Yet many of the institutions of the *popolo* survived into
the subsequent periods of elite dominance and became, as it were,
fixtures of the constitution. To explain this, we need a completely
different model of what these institutions were, what they represented,
and how they functioned in the Italian city-states.

The cluster of institutions that emerged from the *popolo*'s contestation of elite power constituted a compelling collective discourse, a way
of talking and thinking about politics that raised and answered questions about the exercise of power that had never even been formulated
in Florence prior to the *popolo*'s challenge. In the agreements by which
some Florentines entered guilds, endowed the consuls, councils and
committees of these guilds with authority and jurisdiction based on the
legal fiction of representation, then extended this practice of associa-
tional authority and representation to groups or federations of guilds
and ultimately – in the Ordinances of Justice – to an alliance of guilds
that claimed itself coterminous with the power of the commune, the
popolo was, for the first time in the commune's history, posing the question of how – by what practice and in what terms – the exercise of
power could be legitimated. That question rarely gets posed unless and
until prevailing power is contested, and it is hardly surprising that it
should be posed first by the challenger. The *popolo*'s answer – in four
words: consent, representation, delegation, accountability – was
embedded in that cluster of agreements and institutions. Implicitly, it
denied that the great families of Florence had *any* answer to the question of how their power could be made – or be made to seem –
legitimate, rational, or just more than arbitrary. The *popolo*'s answer
drew on the prestigious traditions of Roman law and presented striking

affinities to the corporation theory of medieval canon law. And once the theorists of this discourse discovered Aristotle's *Politics*, they appropriated this greatest of philosophical authorities as a kind of unimpeachable underpinning. For a variety of reasons, therefore, the *popolo*'s discourse of politics was compelling, but most of all because, once the question of the legitimacy of power had been posed, it could not be dismissed, forgotten or shoved aside. The Florentine elite, even in those periods in which it retained and consolidated its power, had to offer some answer to the question of legitimacy, either one of its own devising or some version or adaptation of the *popolo*'s answer. In the long run, its answer was mostly the latter: a sanitized version (divorced from the political programme it had once justified) of the idea that power is legitimate because it represents the will of the people. Such a legitimation of the power of the elite would have seemed absurd to Farinata degli Uberti in the mid-thirteenth century; to Corso Donati, around 1300, it was a threat that needed to be met and neutralized; the oligarchy of the 1330s acknowledged it in theory and ignored it in practice; the powerful families of the 1350s and 1360s made compromises with it; after 1382, and certainly after 1400, it became the reigning and sustaining fiction of oligarchic power. And that fiction was in turn sustained by the institutions of the *popolo*.

By the fifteenth century this borrowed and transformed discourse of the *popolo* had become the elite's second nature, just as many of the *popolo*'s formal institutions were absorbed into the constitution of an aristocratic republic. The long, slow metamorphosis of the Florentine elite must be understood in terms of this dialogue between classes, the process by which the elite learned from the *popolo* to speak the language of popular sovereignty, representation and consent as the surest foundation of its own leadership role. The historical phases and mechanisms of this process have yet to be grasped in their relation to the exercise and practice of power and to the evolution of the very notion of power – its origin, purpose, limits, and legitimacy. Power itself had a history in Florence that will become clear only when we take seriously the way in which institutions emerging from the dialogue between the elite families and the *popolo* transformed the discourse and practice of politics. Marvin Becker has interpreted the history of the funded public debt, the *Monte*, in such terms,[22] and my analysis of the commune's electoral institutions also stresses the importance of this dialogue. Both fiscal and electoral institutions emerged repeatedly as focal points of controversy and competition between the elite and the *popolo*; both were objects of reform and counter-reform in that inter-class dialogue; and both, it has been claimed, changed attitudes, assumptions and behaviour within the elite and among the non-elite guildsmen.

The appeal of the elites of both classical and Renaissance city-states has been profound and enduring in scholarly traditions that have frequently admired and even idealized them as the collective architects of ideal spaces, protectors of culture, and, above all, as wielders of benevolent and enlightened power.[23] To imagine that these elites monopolized all real power and politics, and that on the whole they used their power well enough to create much that we still admire, is a favourite combination in recent idealizations of Renaissance elites. The general tendency to see the 'aristocracies' and 'patriciates' in such favourable terms may have emerged from the influences under which these scholarly fields were first constituted, and perhaps also because of subtle interactions between historical scholarship and certain popular myths about these cities and the roles assigned to them in larger stories about 'civilization' and 'the West'. But one wonders whether such idealizations persist, sometimes in new dress, mainly because they neutralize politics and ennoble the very idea of power. Power that is held to be in the very nature or structure of things is power above the fray, beyond struggle, negotiation and contestation, removed from the daily necessity of limitation and compromise. And the perception that such power is well used – exercised with restraint and with beneficent consequences over those who do not share it – consecrates the inevitable with an aura of moral dignity. To the extent that structural interpretations of the inevitability of elite power imply such idealizations, they are themselves implicated in the process of legitimating those elites.

There may be forms of power that fit this model, but political power in republican Florence was not one of them. In this city-state at least, power was more negotiated than exercised; power relationships were a locus of exchange and dialogue in which alternatives were always present and sometimes tested. That is precisely what Dante could not tolerate as he contemplated the fractious instability of Florentine politics (as, for example, in *Purgatorio* 6) and yearned for a source of virtuous and uncontested power: a nobility – in both senses of the word – that Cacciaguida (*Paradiso* 15 and 16) identified with the elite families of old Florence, even as Dante's most famous expression of this notion of ideal power was the fiction of the all powerful and incorruptible emperor of the *Monarchia*. The civic humanists were notoriously reluctant to acknowledge the dialogue of power in Florentine politics. What Dante condemned, they pretended not even to see. But their resistance was itself part of the dialogue: it enhanced the oligarchy's legitimacy by removing any memory that the elite had ever been other than the civic-minded aristocracy it now claimed (and wanted) to be, any notion that the *popolo* or the guilds had dragged a kicking and screaming elite into a new sense of itself. Bruni's interpretation in the *Laudatio* of the role of the Parte Guelfa in Florentine politics makes clear the utility of ignoring the Parte's stormy and disruptive place in the contest between the elite families and the *popolo*.[24] Forgetting certain things made the emerging oligarchy seem even more inevitably anointed in its power and responsibilities.

But a certain thread of Florentine political discourse – from Compagni and some of the other chroniclers of the fourteenth century to Cavalcanti and on to Savonarola and Machiavelli – did acknowledge, and even accept as normal and natural, the notion that Florentine politics was and always had been a contest for power between an elite of *grandi* or *nobili* and a *popolo* of guildsmen: an acknowledgment they were willing to make even when they judged the results of that contest less than good. But it was Machiavelli who put his finger directly on the role of the *popolo* in the metamorphosis of the elite. In the first chapter of the third book of the *Florentine Histories,* he elevated what he called the 'grave and natural enmities between the people [*gli uomini popolari*] and the nobles, caused by the desire of the latter to command and of the former not to obey', into an organizing principle for the interpretation of politics in city-states: these enmities, he wrote, 'are the cause of all the ills that occur in cities'. Machiavelli goes on to say that in Rome this contest actually had beneficial results, whereas in Florence the struggle between the *nobili* and the *popolo* had less happy consequences; but he insists that it was nonetheless decisive for both the city and its 'noble' families. Even though he considered, in this passage at least, the Florentine *popolo*'s aim of excluding the 'nobility' from politics 'damaging and unjust' because it led to more desperate countermeasures from the elite and thus to bloody confrontations and the expulsion of many citizens, Machiavelli argued that the *popolo* emerged victorious from this struggle and transformed the 'nobility' in the process. 'As the *popolo* gained its victory [*vincendo il popolo*]', he wrote, the 'nobles' were deprived of political offices, and if they wished to regain them,

> it was necessary for them not only to be, but to appear, similar to the *popolo* in their governance, their spirit, and their way of life [*era loro necessario, con i governi, con lo animo e con il modo del vivere, simili ai popolani non solamente essere ma parere*]

from which came all the changes in coats of arms and family names that the nobles made 'in order to seem like the *popolo* [*per parere di popolo*]' and which caused the extinction of 'military valour and generosity of spirit' among them.[25] It is important to bear in mind that Machiavelli was not romanticizing the *popolo* in this interpretation, whose governing assumption seems to be that only by demythologizing both the *popolo* and the elite is it possible to hear their dialogue.

Notes

1   Nicola Ottokar, *Il comune di Firenze alla fine del Dugento* (Florence, 1926; reprint ed. Turin: Giulio Einaudi, 1962). In broad agreement with Ottokar is the prosopographical study of the Florentine elite for the period 1260–1300 by Sergio Raveggi, Massimo Tarassi, Daniela Medici and Patrizia Parenti, *Ghibellini, guelfi e popolo grasso: i detentori del potere politico a Firenze nella seconda metà del Dugento* (Florence: La Nuova Italia, 1978). The perception of a fundamental continuity of elite power [also] underlies the work of Dale Kent: see *The Rise of the Medici: Faction in Florence, 1426–1434* (Oxford: Oxford University Press, 1978); also 'The Florentine *Reggimento* in the Fifteenth Century', *Renaissance Quarterly* 28(1975): 575–638; and 'Dinamica del potere e patronato nella Firenze dei Medici', in *I ceti dirigenti nella Toscana del Quattrocento* (Florence: Francesco Papafava, 1987), 49–62. Roslyn Pesman Cooper offers a compatible vision of Florentine politics through the years of the restored republic and the Great Council after 1494 in 'The Prosopography of the "Prima Repubblica"', *ibid.*, 239–55, and in 'The Florentine Ruling Group under the *governo popolare*, 1494–1512', *Studies in Medieval and Renaissance History* 7(1985): 69–181. [On the period running from the late fourteenth to the early sixteenth century] see, Nicolai Rubinstein, *The Government of Florence Under the Medici (1434–1494)* (Oxford: Clarendon Press, 1966); Gene Brucker, *The Civic World of Early Renaissance Florence* (Princeton: Princeton University Press, 1977), a work that nevertheless also acknowledges the 'dialogue' with which this essay is concerned; and H. C. Butters, *Governors and Government in Early Sixteenth-century Florence, 1502–1519* (Oxford: Clarendon Press, 1985). [Finally, for some general interpretations of late medieval Italian history that also emphasize the power of elites] see especially Sergio Bertelli, *Il potere oligarchico nello stato-città medievale* (Florence: La Nuova Italia, 1978), and Philip Jones, 'Economia e società nell'Italia medievale: la leggenda della borghesia', in Ruggiero Romano and Corrado Vivanti (eds) *Storia d'Italia. Annali I: Dal feudalesimo al capitalismo* (Turin: Giulio Einaudi, 1978), 185–372.

2   Kent, *The Rise of the Medici*, 7.

3   Kent, 'Dinamica del potere e patronato', 50 (my translation).

4   Pesman Cooper, 'The Prosopography of the "Prima Repubblica"', 239.

5   George Holmes, *Florence, Rome and the Origins of the Renaissance* (Oxford: Clarendon Press, 1986), 165.

6   Bertelli, Il *potere oligarchico*, 7–8, 168, 63 (my translation). Bertelli has also studied the ways in which the manipulation of consultative committees enabled oligarchies in several cities, including Florence, to compose their differences and establish firm control over the decision-making process; see his 'Il potere nascosto: I consilia sapientum', in *Forme e tecniche del potere nella città (secoli XIV–XVII)* (Perugia: Università di Perugia, Annali della Facoltà di scienze politiche, 1979–80), 11–31.

7   Kent, 'Dinamica del potere e patronato', 50–1 (my translation).

8   In addition to the studies of Dale Kent cited earlier, Bertelli refers to the following: F. W. Kent, *Household and Lineage in Renaissance Florence: The Family Life of the Capponi, Ginori and Rucellai* (Princeton: Princeton University Press, 1977); D. V. and F. W. Kent, *Neighbours and Neighbourhood in Renaissance Florence: The District of the Red Lion in the Fifteenth Century* (Locust Valley NY: J. J. Augustin, 1982); Christiane Klapisch-Zuber, '"Kin, Friends, and Neighbors": The Urban Territory of a Merchant Family in 1400', in her collection of essays *Women, Family and Ritual in Renaissance Italy* (Chicago:

University of Chicago Press, 1985), 68–93; and Ronald F. E. Weissman, *Ritual Brotherhood in Renaissance Florence* (New York: Academic Press, 1982).

9 S. Bertelli, 'Ceti dirigenti e dinamica del potere nel dibattito contemporaneo', in *I ceti dirigenti nella Toscana del Quattrocento*, 41 (my translation).

10 A good place to begin on the wider Italian phenomenon of the *popolo* is Lauro Martines' *Power and Imagination: City-States in Renaissance Italy* (New York: Vintage, 1979), esp. chs. 4 and 5.

11 For the developments summarized in this paragraph, see Gaetano Salvemini, *Magnati e popolani in Firenze dal 1280 al 1295* (Florence, 1899; reprint ed. Milan: Feltrinelli, 1966); Marvin B. Becker, *Florence in Transition*, 2 vols (Baltimore: Johns Hopkins University Press, 1967–8); Armando Sapori, *La crisi delle compagnie mercantili dei Bardi e dei Peruzzi* (Florence: Leo S. Olschki, 1926); Niccolò Rodolico, *La democrazia fiorentina nel suo tramonto, 1378–1382* (Bologna, 1905; reprint ed. Rome: Multigrafica Editrice, 1970); Gene Brucker, *Florentine Politics and Society, 1343–1378* (Princeton: Princeton University Press, 1962), and his *Civic World*, cited in note 1; my *Corporatism and Consensus in Florentine Electoral Politics, 1280–1400* (Chapel Hill: University of North Carolina Press, 1982), and my '*Audiant Omnes Artes*: Corporate Origins of the Ciompi Revolution', in *Il Tumulto dei Ciompi: un momento di storia fiorentina ed europea* (Florence: Leo S. Olschki, 1981), 59–93.

12 See, for example, the views of Philip Jones in the essay cited in note 1.

13 D. Compagni, *Cronica*, I, 21; Dante, *Purgatorio*, VI; G. Villani, *Cronica*, XII, 42; G. Cavalcanti, *Istorie fiorentine*, ed. F. Polidori (Florence, 1838), I, 82, 84–5. A dramatic example of the hostility of the elite families toward the guilds is the murder by the Benelli family in 1377 of a member of the guild of the Medici, Speziali e Merciai, in a dispute over a failed marriage. This episode reveals the powerful persistence of class antagonisms even in the circumstances of a marriage link and all the resulting face-to-face contacts between the two families. On this event, see my '*Audiant Omnes Artes*', 86–91.

14 See *Corporatism and Consensus*, 153–62, 254–6, 263–300.

15 On Salutati's letter, see my 'Guild Republicanism in Trecento Florence: The Successes and Ultimate Failure of Corporate Politics', *American Historical Review* 84(1979): 66–7.

16 Two versions of the Buondelmonti story are in the *Cronica fiorentina compilata nel secolo XIII*, in *Testi fiorentini del Dugento e dei primi del Trecento*, ed. Alfredo Schiaffini (Florence: Sansoni, 1954), 117–19; and in Compagni, *Cronica*, I, 2, where it is used to foreshadow the similar eruption of upper-class violence between Black and White Guelfs in the years around 1300. Compagni's purpose was of course to highlight the almost gratuitous, and in any case irrational, recourse to violence that characterized the elite families. His famous portrait of Corso Donati is in *Cronica*, II, 20. See also the excellent English translation by Daniel E. Bornstein, *Dino Compagni's Chronicle of Florence* (Philadelphia: University of Pennsylvania Press, 1986). For an expression of the thirteenth-century elite's confidence that decision making should be left to a handful of 'prudent men privately consulted', see *Corporatism and Consensus*, 13.

17 G. Villani, *Cronica*, XI, 94.

18 The translation is B. G. Kohl's, in *The Earthly Republic*, eds B. G. Kohl and R. G. Witt (Philadelphia: University of Pennsylvania Press, 1978), 158.

19 Brucker, *Civic World*, esp. ch. 5, 248–318.

20 Quoted in *Corporatism and Consensus*, 268. The *balìa* went on to assert that its authority required the convocation of the 'whole Florentine people in a

general assembly, especially in view of the custom heretofore observed among the Florentine people (*maxime considerato more in populo florentino hactenus observato*)' – an excellent example of the emerging oligarchy's tactic of appealing to the traditions and political principles of the *popolo* (in this case the notion of consent) while implementing reforms that moved in altogether different directions. General assemblies of the 'whole Florentine people' were not, in fact, part of the *popolo*'s vision of the republic as a federation of guilds held together by systems of representation.

21 See especially Rubinstein, *The Government of Florence*, and his 'Florentine Constitutionalism and Medici Ascendancy in the Fifteenth Century', in *Florentine Studies*, ed. N. Rubinstein (London: Northwestern University Press, 1968), 442–62.

22 See Becker's *Florence in Transition*, vols I and II; and 'The Florentine Territorial State and Civic Humanism in the Early Renaissance', in *Florentine Studies*, ed. N. Rubinstein, 109–39.

23 On this tendency and some of the reasons for it, see Roberto S. Lopez, *Intervista sulla città medievale*, ed. Marino Berengo (Bari: Laterza, 1984).

24 In Hans Baron, *From Petrarch to Leonardo Bruni: Studies in Humanistic and Political Literature* (Chicago, 1968) 260–2.

25 Niccolò Machiavelli, *Tutte le opere*, ed. Mario Martelli (Florence: Sansoni, 1971), 690. Christiane Klapisch-Zuber has analysed this phenomenon in 'Ruptures de parenté et changements d'identité chez les magnats florentins du XIVe siècle', *Annales: Economies, Sociétés, Civilisations* (1988): 1205–40.

4

THE 'BARON THESIS'

James Hankins

No twentieth-century interpretation of the cultural and political history of the Italian Renaissance has been more influential than the celebrated 'thesis' of Hans Baron (1900–88). His book Crisis of the Early Italian Renaissance: Civic Humanism and Republican Liberty in an Age of Classicism and Tyranny *(1955) shaped the scholarship of a generation and provided a powerful intellectual framework not only for Renaissance Italian history but also for the study of 'civic humanism' and republican ideals down to the time of the French Revolution. In the essay below, James Hankins, a distinguished scholar of fifteenth-century Florentine intellectual history, first presents a lucid overview of the 'Baron thesis' and then – drawing upon both his own research and the work of several other contemporary scholars – essentially deconstructs Baron's argument.*

Of particular importance in Hankins' essay is the figure of the humanist Leonardo Bruni (1370–1444), who, after serving as papal secretary, returned to Florence where, in 1427, he became chancellor and one of the most prolific scholars of his time, producing important translations of Aristotle, writing history, and contributing decisively to Florentine political thought. To Baron, Bruni's writings provided the cornerstone of his argument. In Bruni's Laudatio Florentinae urbis *[Panegyric of the City of Florence] as well as in many of his other works, Baron found the articulation of the ideal of civic humanism, a commitment to the common good, and a conviction that republican government was superior to monarchy and despotism. Hankins, by contrast, reads Bruni primarily as a rhetorician whose 'political masters' employed him above all 'to produce propaganda for the state'.*

Hankins' argument – it should be noted – is developed in the context of a historiographical essay. From it, readers should be able to derive a sense of the almost dizzying speed at which interpretations of Italian Renaissance history have shifted over the last generation. Hankins, therefore, introduces some of the great controversies in the study of the period: Baron's 'civic humanism' is contrasted with Burckhardtian 'individualism', and Baron's thesis, in turn, is critiqued by such major scholars as Paul Oskar Kristeller (1905–99) and Riccardo Fubini, currently Professor of History at the University of Florence.

With this essay, finally, Hankins too joins the ranks of Baron's most important critics. Clearly, it is no longer possible to link the ideal of civic humanism exclusively with republicanism. Rather, civic humanism becomes, in Hankins' account, a much broader and much more malleable concept. Its origins were Roman, primarily Ciceronian, and its goal was the cultivation of ethical governance, whether this be the governance of the people by a prince or the governance by the people of a republic.

This essay, which originally appeared in the Journal of the History of Ideas *(1995) under the title 'The "Baron Thesis" after Forty Years and Some Recent Studies of Leonardo Bruni', is presented here in an abridged form; it excludes, moreover, Hankins' supplemental bibliography of Bruni studies as well as an appendix in which he both offers a trenchant critique – drawing on the author's extensive knowledge of Bruni's manuscripts – of Paolo Viti's work,* Leonardo Bruni e Firenze: Studi sulle lettere pubbliche e private *[Leonardo Bruni and Florence: Studies on his Public and Private Letters] (Rome, 1982) as well as editions of two of Bruni's previously unpublished short works (a letter and an oration). Specialists and advanced students should, naturally, consult the original version of Hankins' review essay.*

* * *

'It is by now commonplace' (John Najemy has written),

> that what Burckhardt was to nineteenth-century Renaissance historiography, Baron is to its twentieth-century counterpart: each provided his century's most influential, compelling, and debated interpretation of the significance of the cultural developments of Italy between the end of the Middle Ages and the modern era.

And again: 'In recovering Bruni and the civic humanism of the early fifteenth century, Baron did nothing less than recast the entire Renaissance from Petrarch to Machiavelli'.[1] Large claims indeed, yet it is difficult to quarrel with them, especially coming from a scholar of Najemy's authority. Baron was surely one of the three or four most influential interpreters of the Renaissance in the second half of the twentieth century, particularly in Italy and America, and his studies of the history of republicanism sparked a broad revival of interest in this topic among students of early modern history; the term 'civic humanism' is now as widely used among students of eighteenth- as of fifteenth-century politics. His lifelong campaign to interpret literary and philosophical texts in their historical setting – a method still unusual in Baron's youth – is today normal practice (and rightly so) among intellectual historians and historians of political thought.

What is more controversial, however, is another claim made in Najemy's review essay:

> Recent work has by and large confirmed Baron's view that civic humanism successfully promoted a distinctive cultural program and political outlook that reshaped Florentine, Roman, and Italian history, redefined notions of citizenship and liberty, and created new expectations about the role of intellectuals and education in society.

It could be argued – as this essay will argue – that in fact the tendency of recent studies of Florentine intellectual history, and particularly studies of Leonardo Bruni, has been to revise or even undermine Baron's view of the nature and significance of the phenomenon he called 'civic humanism'.

It may be useful for purposes of exposition to recapitulate the genesis and chief features of what has become known as the 'Baron thesis'. Baron's point of departure, by his own account, was Burckhardt's interpretation of the Renaissance, especially his view of the individualism of Renaissance Italians.[2] Burckhardt famously saw the Renaissance as a period when men ceased submerging their identities in collectivities of various kinds and sought like artists to shape themselves into beautiful, powerful, virtuous and wise individuals, using as models idealized versions of their Graeco-Roman forebears. For Burckhardt this implied a loosening of allegiances to family, guild, state and religion, a new willingness to treat these latter not as givens of tradition but as *Menschenwerke*, plastic in the hands of their human makers. It was this more than anything that made Renaissance men 'firstborn among the sons of modern Europe'. For Burckhardt, of course, this was not an unqualified compliment: the individualism of the Renaissance could sometimes issue in an amoral egoism, indifferent to the good of the community and destructive of the moral values necessary to the survival of civilized society.[3]

As is now clear from the brilliant study of Riccardo Fubini, Baron was early in his life a disciple of Ernst Troeltsch, a liberal Protestant theologian who (influenced by Dilthey) wished to reject the dogmatism and soteriological individualism of traditional Christianity, instead interpreting its message as a theology of social action. In the 1920s Baron was also a firm supporter of the Weimar Republic, eager to wean Germany away from its chauvinistic and monarchical past.[4] He felt that the new era of democratic socialism demanded a new kind of education and culture that would produce an active and informed citizenry. He believed Germany's unhealthy political tradition had been aggravated by an entrenched university culture stressing philology and overspecialized historical studies; the effect was to distract attention from larger historical issues and thus to detach scholarship from political commitment. Moreover, against the prevailing chauvinism that tried to make 'the German Spirit' the origin of all worthwhile contributions to civilization, he was anxious to demonstrate that Germany was in fact indebted for valued parts of her culture to other lands; this, he felt, would help make educated Germans readier to look abroad and to the non-German past for models of a healthy political culture. Finally, perhaps above all, Baron wanted to prove that humanistic culture was compatible with political commitment. An obstacle to the latter aim was Burckhardt's identification of humanism with the cultivation of the individual. This was a matter of more than purely academic interest, as Burckhardt's book had acquired something of a cult following among highly educated but politically passive Germans during the 1920s; the George-Kreis, for example, admired the book immoderately. The German elites who admired Burckhardt's great book, however, tended to ignore his message about the dangers of untrammelled individualism and to focus instead on his seductive picture of genius liberated from the claims of traditional morality and social convention.

These concerns prepared the ground for Baron's major discoveries as a Renaissance historian. Sometime in the late 1920s Baron's research began to disclose in fifteenth-century Italy – supposedly the homeland of the detached 'individual' nurtured on classicizing culture – a tradition of humanistic literature that had shown itself as politically committed, and committed, moreover, to republicanism.[5] It was the expression of civic-minded, republican cultures in Venice and Florence in which citizens and scholars had worked together to serve the *bonum commune* – a far cry from the culture evoked by Burckhardt, a world of rootless intellectuals wandering among the courts of illegitimate tyrants. This discovery of a civic humanistic tradition was for Baron the germ of his famous 'thesis'. As Baron himself believed that scholarship should serve the public good, it was important for him to understand how Italian intellectuals had made the transition from an 'otherworldly' to a 'this-worldly' outlook, from private to public commitments, and from a world in which intellectual and moral effort was aimed primarily at salvation in the next life to a world in which the civil community became the font of value. He wanted not merely to describe civic humanism, but to explain how it had come about, for to explain its genesis would be to explain the genesis of modern attitudes to the state and to what would now be called the 'public sphere'.

Baron's researches into the origins of civic humanism at length took shape in his great work, *The Crisis of the Early Italian Renaissance: Civic Humanism and Republican Liberty in an Age of Classicism and Tyranny*. In this book Baron eschewed internalist explanations for the appearance of what he called civic humanism. The civic humanism of Quattrocento Florence was not a natural outgrowth of Trecento humanism, but a new departure to be explained in terms of new political conditions around the year 1402. Before 1402 humanists had generally lacked serious political commitments; their scholarship had served limited, personal goals; their philosophy, insofar as they had one, was Stoic or otherworldly; their outward lives had been that of rootless courtiers or quietist citizens. The Florentine civic tradition, on the other hand, while it had preserved the healthy political life of the thirteenth-century commune, stood apart from the learned cultural traditions that might have given it nurture. It was only the long struggle with Giangaleazzo Visconti in the 1390s that had brought these two traditions together, creating the hybrid culture of politically committed *Bildung* that Baron called civic humanism. In the crisis of the Milanese Wars, when Florence's very existence was threatened, private scholarship of the Petrarchan variety seemed selfish and trivial. Classical learning, to retain its relevance, would have to subordinate itself to the ideological and educational needs of the state. Leonardo Bruni – for Baron the embodiment of civic humanism – quickly outgrew his youthful attraction to 'pure classicism' – symbolized by Niccolò Niccoli – and forged a new kind of classicism whose aim was to nurture and celebrate the traditions of Florentine republicanism inherited from the communal age.

Florence's victory in the Visconti wars and the new kind of humanism it engendered had, for Baron, results of world-historical importance. It meant, first of all, that Italy would not be united under a single tyranny but would become a system of city-states; as a result, the medieval communal traditions of Florence and Venice would survive to inspire a later age of republicanism.[6] Even more important, thanks to the writings of civic humanists, Florence's republican values of independent self-government, free speech, political participation and equality under law would survive, in the early modern period, to prevent a monopoly of absolutist political thought in the marketplace of ideas and to prepare the ground for the modern revolution in political ideas and practice. From an even longer perspective, the rise of civic humanism struck another blow against the Augustinian political tradition of the Middle Ages. For Augustine, the value of political activity in this world was, *sub specie saeculi*, mostly negative; *sub specie aeternitatis* it was literally nothing, since it did nothing directly to promote the health of the soul. Bruni's civic humanism challenged Augustine by reviving an Aristotelian and Ciceronian anthropology which saw self-government and other 'external goods' as necessary to the dignity and perfection of humanity. This in turn entailed a new conception of history: it was no coincidence that Bruni, the historian, was the first to detach historical events from the economy of divine providence and to make political liberty, not salvation, the theme of his history. For Baron this was a turn from 'otherworldliness' to 'reality' as the principle of history, and this view led Baron to wonder whether the new realism evident in Quattrocento visual art might not have had something to do with the atmosphere of the historical crisis he had tried to describe.

Such, in brief, were the main conclusions of Baron's *Crisis*, finished in 1952 and eventually published in two volumes in 1955 by Princeton University Press. A third volume of supplementary studies on the same themes appeared under the imprint of Harvard University Press in the same year, entitled *Humanistic and Political Literature in Florence and Venice at the Beginning of the Quattrocento*. The *Crisis* rapidly became a canonical work of Renaissance history and was republished in a condensed, one-volume edition in 1966; it has remained in print up to the present day.[7] In 1968 a collection of studies, mostly related to the 'Baron thesis', was published by the University of Chicago Press.[8] Twenty years later Princeton published the two-volume collection, containing Baron's most important articles, many of them enlarged and reworked. At the time of his death Baron was working on a biographical study of Leonardo Bruni, of which more will be said in due course.

Despite Baron's great success as a historian, his writings were never entirely free from controversy. Readers of the *Crisis* will recall that much of Baron's book is encumbered with elaborate attempts to date and re-date certain of Bruni's writings. The method employed combined traditional techniques of historical and philological criticism with what can only be called a kind of historian's connoisseurship: Baron insisted that the date of certain writings such as Bruni's *Laudatio Florentinae urbis* and *Dialogues* could be divined by correlating the 'mood' of these writings with the historical experience of the author. Many of Baron's datings have not stood up well to the test of time, and his peculiar methods have diminished rather than enhanced the plausibility of his larger conclusions.[9]

There were, of course, more serious criticisms of the Baron thesis than academic quibbling over dates. Several reviewers of the *Crisis* cast doubt on the idea that the large cultural changes Baron described could be related in any simple way to Florence's wars with the Visconti and King Ladislas – what Lucia Gualdo Rosa called Baron's 'punctilious search for mathematical correspondences between military and political events and literary texts'.[10] Other reviewers called into question Baron's insistence on the importance of Florence and the date of 1402 in the genesis of the new hybrid form of culture combining humanism and republican ideology.[11] Their scepticism was amply vindicated by subsequent research. After the work of Roberto Weiss, Giuseppe Billanovich, Nicolai

Rubinstein, Quentin Skinner, Ronald Witt and others it is clear that the roots of the humanist movement are to be found in Arezzo, Bologna and the Veneto, and that many of these *dictatores* and early humanists (a locution surely preferable to 'pre-humanists') had expressed their political commitments in classical garb, Albertino Mussato's *Eccerinis* being perhaps the best known but hardly the only example.[12] At the same time it has been amply demonstrated by Charles Davis, Emilio Panella, Quentin Skinner and others that the republican folklore of the medieval commune had been given some theoretical heft, over a century before Bruni, by scholastic and sub-scholastic writers such as Remigio de 'Girolami, Brunetto Latini and Ptolemy of Lucca.[13] The expression of these values is more mature, more secular, and more historically conscious in Salutati and Bruni, but hardly original. On the other hand, Petrarch's contemplative and politically quietist attitudes, presented by Baron as typical of humanism before 1402, have come to seem more and more exceptional, an aberration of the period between the fall of the commune of Padua in 1322 and 1400, when the humanists of Bruni's generation appeared on the scene.[14]

Other historians have taken issue with Baron's attempt to change the larger picture of Renaissance political culture. In contrast to Burckhardt's view of the Renaissance as essentially realistic and post-ideological in its politics, Baron presented the late fourteenth and early fifteenth century as a period of ideological struggle between republicanism and signory. The crisis of 1402 for Baron generated a new cultural movement emphasizing secular values and commitment to the community – a view which challenged Burckhardt's picture of a traditional society breaking apart under the pressure of egoistic individualism and illegitimate power. Several scholars, however, rejected this attempt at revisionism. Philip Jones, Peter Herde and (implicitly) Nicolai Rubinstein took Baron to task for his naive view of republican politics in medieval and Renaissance city-states.[15] They argued that these societies were in reality not as devoted to liberty as their traditions of political folklore would suggest; internally, full freedom was enjoyed only by 'property-owning burgesses of local origin and prolonged residence', while externally the freedom of subject towns was limited by the imperial claims of the metropolis. There had always been 'a strident contradiction' between the rhetoric of freedom and the reality of Renaissance government; this did not change with the humanists. In fact, Renaissance republics were oligarchies and, from a democratic point of view, had not much better claims to legitimacy than Renaissance tyrannies. For Jones and Herde, the 'titanic struggle' between monarchic and republican principles Baron saw at the dawn of the Renaissance was merely the continuation in antique dress of a century-long propaganda war between two essentially similar forms of government.

Jones' and Herde's view received further support in the mid-1960s as the work of P. O. Kristeller on Renaissance humanism began to be widely influential. Several scholars attempted to turn Kristeller's interpretation of humanism into a critique of Baron. Kristeller's view of humanism saw the phenomenon as a phase in the history of rhetoric, and drew attention to the professional employments of the humanists; for him, humanism could not be understood apart from its social and institutional context. It was not enough simply to say whether a humanist lived in a republic or a court; one should look also at the professional roles he filled. One could only make sense of humanistic literature if one saw that most professional humanists (as opposed to interested amateurs) had worked as schoolmasters, professors of literature, political secretaries and chancellors, ambassadors, court poets, and high-level civil servants. Most if not all of these professions required an expert knowledge of rhetoric. Indeed, the rise of humanism could in part be explained by changes in the nature of these professions during the early Renaissance.[16]

Kristeller's view of humanism, backed up by his comprehensive knowledge of manuscript sources, inevitably raised new questions about Baron's 'civic humanists'. Were men such as Salutati and Bruni really as rooted in the values and attitudes of the Florentine ruling classes as they had seemed to Baron? If the great Florentine chancellors were as politically committed as Baron represented them, how had Salutati managed to survive in office through the political upheavals of 1375–82? How had Bruni survived the exile and return of the Medici? Why had Bruni, immediately after the supposed crisis of 1402 and in the midst of the war with Ladislas, gone off to serve the signories of Rome and the Papal States? Why did he admire petty tyrants such as Carlo Malatesta and Braccio da Montone? Why did the Medici party take the supposed republican firebrand into the *reggimento* after 1437? Why had Bruni remained a lifelong friend of Antonio Loschi, the defender of Milanese 'tyranny', dedicating two works to him? How to explain Salutati's facile shifts, in his *missive*, back and forth between the 'new' republican ideology and the 'old' Guelf ideology? Why was there so little common ground between the coolly realistic discussions of policy found in the *Consulte e pratiche* during the 1390s and the overheated rhetoric of Salutati's public letters? How to explain Bruni's *missive* of the 1430s, which contain letters espousing policies Bruni privately disagreed with, letters both praising and damning the Medici, letters eulogizing the Emperor and the Duke of Milan? Should writings like these, and by extension Bruni's *Laudatio* and *Oration for the Funeral of Nanni Strozzi*, not be seen as pieces of political propaganda, the work of professional rhetoricians writing for specific occasions and not unspotted mirrors of sincere republican conviction?

In the last fifteen years we have begun to find answers for some of these questions, thanks to a broad revival of Bruni studies led by Lucia Gualdo Rosa and Paolo Viti. Up until about 1980 there had been, aside from Baron's own work, very little basic study of Bruni's life and works. There is even today no reliable bibliography of his works, no modern edition of his letters, and no calendar of his state papers; and the most serious biographical study of him was that of Cesare Vasoli.[17] Fewer than a dozen of the seventy-five or so works from his pen have been critically edited.[18] Scholarly work on Bruni, it seems, was long put off in deference to Baron's known interest in him. Yet few scholars in Europe were aware that Baron had spent the last twenty years of his life writing a biographical study of his hero.[19]

This unfinished study is not properly a biography, but another in the long series of *pièces justificatives* that Baron wrote in response to criticisms of his thesis; in this case the book was primarily intended as a response to the issues raised by Jerrold Seigel and Peter Herde. Baron's object throughout is to show that Bruni was not a 'professional rhetorician' but a 'civic humanist': a patriotic Florentine with a consistent political ideology shaped by his experiences in the civic world of early Renaissance Florence. So we are taken through the period of the 'crisis' once more, this time from a biographical perspective. Many of the old dating issues are raised again, together with some new ones, but there is little new research. The ruling passion is not to describe what sort of person Bruni was or to give a nuanced view of his intellectual development. Baron wants to show that Bruni's political thought and political loyalties were totally consistent from 1402 to the end of his life. Hence in Chapter 1 (much of which was published in article form in 1977)[20] we are told why Bruni's scholastic education did not give him a medieval worldview; the burden of Chapter 2 is to explain why, after the soul-shattering events of 1402, Bruni, instead of staying in Florence to serve the *bonum commune*, left Florence to serve the pope in Rome; Chapter 3 tells us why Bruni's interest in the Platonic dialogues and his hero-worship of the *condottiere* and petty tyrant Carlo Malatesta should not be seen as inconsistent with his civic humanism, and so on. While it would of course be unfair to condemn a book that was left in a very unfinished state, in this case it seems safe to say that among Baron's many scholarly talents was not that of the biographer. Baron's Bruni is a wooden puppet, an idealized projection of Baron himself, not a portrait of a man.[21] This sometimes leads to mildly comic results, as when Baron tries to explain such *jeux d'esprit* as the *Oratio Heliogabali*, an imaginary speech given by the Emperor Elagabalus to the prostitutes of Rome, in terms of a temporary fall from grace occasioned by the wicked curial milieu. Regrettably, Baron's study does little to improve our understanding of Bruni's life and thought.

A new understanding of Bruni has, however, begun to emerge in recent years. In 1980 a renaissance of Bruni studies was set off with the publication by Lucia Gualdo Rosa of F. P. Luiso's *Studi su l'Epistolario di Leonardo Bruni*.[22] This work, the foundation of modern Bruni studies, had been utilized (with Luiso's permission) by Baron half a century before in his *Leonardo Bruni Aretino: Humanistisch-philosophische Schriften* (1928); but as Baron himself observed, its curious half-existence (in proof since 1904 but not published until 1980) did much to inhibit the progress of Bruni studies.[23] Following the publication of Luiso's *Studi*, Gualdo Rosa organized an international *équipe* to survey the manuscript tradition of Bruni's *Epistulae familiares* with a view to producing a critical edition of the text. A collaborative effort was necessary because of the extraordinarily wide diffusion of Bruni's works: as the bestselling author of the fifteenth century, Bruni's works survive in about 3,200 literary manuscripts and nearly 200 incunabula.[24] Around the same time Paolo Viti organized another *équipe* to calendar Bruni's public writings as Chancellor of Florence. In 1987 his collaborators, together with a distinguished group of older scholars and some members of the Gualdo Rosa *équipe*, held a conference on Bruni's career as a public servant and Chancellor of Florence.

At this conference due honor was paid to the contribution of Hans Baron; but Hans Baron's Bruni (save in the contribution of Eugenio Garin) was nowhere in evidence.[25] Instead, a number of questions first raised by Nicolai Rubinstein and Peter Herde were quietly taken up and developed. Rubinstein himself presented a Bruni whose idealized presentation of Florentine political ideals and practice contrasted sharply with the actual functioning of politics under the pre-Medicean oligarchy.[26] He suggested that Bruni had come to identify his political outlook with that of the Medici party by the late 1430s. He pointed out, furthermore, that the context of Bruni's famous *Laudatio Florentinae urbis* was the defence of Florentine imperialism against Milanese charges of hypocrisy. Milanese propaganda argued that Florence had put down the liberties of her subject towns in Tuscany while claiming to be the defender of Italian liberties against the Milanese 'tyrant' (a charge, in Rubinstein's view, not without justice). Bruni's reply, following Salutati, reformulated the idea of liberty in a way that was to prove of great importance: he argued that liberty in the case of subject towns was not to be defined as self-government but as sharing in the liberty of the metropolis by *iure vivere* – by living in accordance with just laws free from arbitrary power. Thus in 1404 Bruni had already discovered the classic oligarchical move of redefining positive liberty as negative liberty through an appeal to law.[27]

This line of thought was taken still further in two articles by Riccardo Fubini and Anna Maria Cabrini.[28] Both articles showed how much intellectual history has benefited from the work of social historians of the last generation on the relationships between power, social class, patronage networks, marriage patterns, and political institutions such as the public debt funds of Florence. Baron had seen the Florentine republic of the late Trecento as preserving and extending the values of the popular regimes of the late Duecento. In his various articles on the sociological context of civic humanism, Baron acknowledged the existence of oligarchic tendencies in Florence after the Ciompi uprising of 1378, but he denied heatedly that the Ciompi had led to the formation of a closed and conservative ruling class.[29] In his view the Florentine political class after the commercial failures of the 1340s acquired a more open, integrated and civic-minded character, and it became 'a broad middle-class stratum of relative uniformity in property status and in political, social and economic outlook'. The social history of the last two decades has made this rosy view of the Florentine ruling class much more difficult to sustain. Recent work has argued powerfully that Florentine society in the later fourteenth and fifteenth centuries was 'not a bourgeois world, but rather one whose values were closer, more akin, to those of a feudal, aristocratic society'. It has emphasized the closed character and aristocratic ethos of Florence's tiny ruling class and largely discarded the older, romantic view of Florence as an egalitarian society in which workmen rubbed shoulders with merchant bankers as social equals.[30]

The new view of Florentine society has forced scholars to reconsider the meaning of Florence's republican discourse. Nowadays it is clear that the relationship between the political language and symbols of the commune around 1400 and the actual allocation of power is far more complex than it seemed [when the *Crisis* was first published]. If the Florentine republicanism of Salutati's and Bruni's day had preserved many of the slogans of the popular commune – 'liberty', 'participation', 'free speech' – the meaning of those slogans had changed profoundly as the regime had developed fitfully from the relatively popular regime of the 1280s and 1290s into the stable pre-Medicean oligarchy. With respect to political history, Baron was simply wrong about the significance of the Milanese wars. They had not made possible the survival of popular regimes into the high Renaissance; they had in fact solidified the grip of the oligarchy on the *reggimento* of Florence by vastly enlarging its opportunities for patronage. With respect to the history of political thought, Baron was blind to the true significance of Bruni's 'civic humanism': that it was in fact a subtle reinterpretation in oligarchic terms of Florence's traditional republican language.[31]

This new understanding of Bruni as a defender of oligarchy has been brought out with great clarity by Fubini and Cabrini. They show in detail the oligarchic prejudices informing Bruni's historical and political judgments: his preference for the central authority of the signory (the chief institutional tool of oligarchic power in Florence) to that of the popular councils, guilds and *ufficiali forestieri*; his tendency to assert the sovereignty of the commune against the empire, the papacy, and other rivals, internal and external, of the Florentine oligarchy; his praise for the emergency commissions (*Balie*) of the 1390s, which bypassed traditional popular procedures in order to permit the oligarchs to act with speed and secrecy in wartime; his preference for 'prudent and experienced men' and for expert knowledge over the judgment of the vulgar; his opposition to exiling nobles on the grounds that their experience of affairs was necessary to the commonwealth; his fulsome championship of the Parte Guelfa, that bastion of the oligarchy; his preference for the principle of merit over that of sortition in choosing public officials; his support for the Albizzi regime's attempts to assert the sovereignty of Florence against the empire; and his horror of the populist 'Ciompi' revolt of 1378.

Fubini has also emphasized an aspect of Bruni's *History* ignored by Baron: its character as a celebration, not only of Florentine liberty, but also of Florentine imperialism. This, it should be said, was one of Baron's major blind spots. If nowadays the imperial democracy and its contradictions is a familiar object of study, it was less so in Baron's day; and Baron's open partisanship of 'little Florence', the home of the brave and the free, against 'the tyrant of Milan' makes for embarrassing reading today. In fact Florence and Milan were, as opponents, pretty evenly matched; and it was Florence's imperial expansion in Tuscany, particularly the acquisition of Arezzo in 1384, which had set off the Second Milanese War; she took advantage of the chaos in Lombardy after the death of Giangaleazzo to gobble up Pisa. It was the conquest of Pisa in 1406, not the death of Giangaleazzo in 1402, that first gave Bruni the idea of writing a Florentine History.[32]

Two years after the proceedings of the 1987 conference were published, Paolo Viti published a collection of his own articles on Bruni together with a few new pieces. This collection, *Leonardo Bruni e Firenze: Studi sulle lettere pubbliche e private*,[33] constitutes the first serious study of Bruni's public correspondence, the 1,800 or so *missive* he wrote as Chancellor on behalf of the Florentine signory, only a small number of which had previously been published. These Viti places in their immediate historical context and tries to relate to the works Bruni wrote under his own name. Viti's study is particularly useful as it transcribes extensive portions from the most interesting of the *missive*, enabling readers to make their own judgment about them.

Viti's collection contains rich new archival material as well as many technical, philological and paleographical data, but it also, inevitably, repeats some old errors and creates some new ones. A more serious problem with Viti's volume is his failure to advance any convincing general interpretation of Bruni as a public servant and political thinker.

He has unearthed new data about Bruni's activities relative to the foreign and domestic politics of his day, but seems embarrassed by his own riches; he fails to use his fresh research to criticize effectively the old picture of Bruni, still less to create a new one. He declares early on in the large synthetic essay which begins the volume ('Il primato di Firenze') that he accepts with some reservations the Baronian view of Bruni:

> It thus appears evident that all the Florentine experience of Bruni, not just his work on the *Histories*, is a constant act of adhesion to the city–subject, to be sure, to certain moments of crisis in addition to his detachment as papal secretary from 1405 to 1415. (12)

He assumes throughout that Bruni has a strong ideological loyalty to republicanism as against signory, and that there is a high degree of *continuità ideale* between Bruni's private beliefs and the beliefs he was called upon to express as the spokesman for the Florentine signory. This of course creates problems of interpretation, since many letters appear to contradict those beliefs, for example, letters acknowledging the overlordship of the pope and emperor, or letters praising the Duke of Milan. Viti's solution seems to be that, whenever Bruni's *missive* agree with republican themes in (supposedly) 'private' works such as the *Laudatio* or the *Oration for Nanni Strozzi*, they can be construed as expressing Bruni's personal convictions; whenever they are at variance with the opinions 'privately' expressed by Bruni, they can be taken as 'empty', 'formulaic', 'rhetorical' or 'stereotyped'. This solution, assuming as it does a clear distinction in Bruni's writings between the public and the private, the rhetorical and the personal, is less than satisfactory.

On the other hand Viti is, to his credit, much less naive than Baron about the realities of political power in Florence, and much more willing to look at evidence which tells against Baron's roseate view of Bruni's character and beliefs. He finds new evidence not only that Bruni was tempted into the chancery of the signory of the Papal States (the pope) between 1405 and 1415, but also that he tried to prepare the ground so as to be taken into the service of the *condottieri* princes Carlo Malatesta and Giovanfrancesco Gonzaga; he was also tempted, Viti notes, to take service with Martin V even after he had received Florentine citizenship. Viti regards these acts as *trasgressioni* (369), blemishes on Bruni's record as a republican. He recognizes that Bruni could be critical of certain aspects of popular government, such as its instability (28), its cumbersome decision-making processes (39), and its anti-meritocratic bias (73). He admits that Bruni was disingenuous in the extreme about Florence's motives for its unprovoked attack on its fellow republic Lucca in 1429; if it is in fact the case, as it would seem in light of Viti's new evidence, that the Duke of

Milan secretly acquiesced in the attack on Lucca (103), then much of Bruni's justification for the war turns out to be positively mendacious. Following Fubini, Viti recognizes the jingoistic element in Bruni's writing about Florence's empire and quotes some startling passages in which Bruni talks about the natural superiority of Florentines to other peoples (5–7). He points out the ugly side of Bruni's behaviour after the Medici coup in 1434: the *missive* he composed calling for the extradition and punishment of his former friends, his willingness to act as a republican front man for the Medicean regime, his silence about the undermining of republican institutions, and his lies to the Council of Basel about the number of Florentine exiles and the seriousness of the threat they presented to public order (172–3). Following Gordon Griffiths, Viti recognizes that Bruni's description of Florentine politics in his Greek treatise *On the Polity of the Florentines* (1439) is markedly more willing to disclose the oligarchic element in Florentine government than his three previous writings on the subject.[34] Like Griffiths (and Rubinstein before him), Viti regards this shift as a sign of Bruni's changing political alignment and his acceptance of Medicean rule.

The last point reveals the anachronism in Viti's – and Baron's – approach to Bruni. Since they both regard Bruni in some degree as a republican ideologue, they can only explain inconsistencies in his thought and behaviour in terms of the chronological development of his thought or in terms of *trasgressioni*. But if we admit that Bruni's *impostazione* is primarily that of a rhetorician, the problem disappears. The *Laudatio Florentinae urbis* and the *Funeral Oration for Nanni Strozzi* are both examples of epideictic rhetoric. In epideictic rhetoric, as Bruni himself said with specific reference to the *Laudatio*, what counts is not truth but telling your audience what they want to hear.[35] A few rhetorical insincerities about Florentines not being subject to the power of a few, or having a brilliant military record, or being delighted to pay their taxes in support of a popular war effort, are excusable – just as Bruni found it excusable to praise kings for their justice, wisdom and virtue, both in his private and public correspondence. The treatise *On the Polity of the Florentines*, on the other hand, was a philosophical treatise modelled on parts of Aristotle's *Politics* (and directed to an audience that would mostly have been contemptuous of popular government). By Bruni's own theory of rhetorical genres, we must conclude that it is the philosophical treatise and not the two epideictic orations which represent Bruni's considered view of the nature of Florence's government.

If we do away with the anachronism that men such as Bruni and Salutati were ideologues (in the sense of having an exclusive commitment to one political ideology such as republicanism), we can make better sense of Viti's material. As presented by Viti, much of his new research stands in sharp contradiction to his Baronian belief that Bruni was a committed republican. If we admit that Florentine republicanism as presented by Salutati and Bruni was a rhetorical artefact not necessarily in keeping with either their private beliefs or the political realities of the time, we can at least save them from some of the more serious charges against their moral character. In fact the attitude of both Salutati and Bruni was that of permanent under-secretaries, loyal to Florence rather than to the regime, and carrying out to the best of their abilities the changing policies of successive political masters. They were also, undeniably, professional rhetoricians in the most basic sense of being paid salaries to produce propaganda for the state. They were made by their political masters to write letters and speeches that were sometimes inconsistent with or hostile to their own private convictions, but no one thought the worse of them for that. Salutati and Bruni were also human beings with wives, children and estates who made each his own accommodation with changing political realities and prudently hid whatever private views they had on party politics. As men they were useful rather than heroic; and if their consciences were not as tender as some modern historians would like, they had many other qualities we can admire. The inconsistencies among their various utterances, made under the pressure of circumstances, do not mean that they had no core convictions and values. But since they were professional rhetoricians, historians have to work much harder to detect what these were: they have to collect the evidence as fully as possible, reconstruct the context of each utterance, and, as Robert Black suggests, be sensitive to the habits of thought acquired from professional training in disciplines no longer familiar, such as grammar and rhetoric.[36] Men to whom words come easily are often able to reconcile positions that a strict logician might find incompatible, but this does not mean that their utterances are insincere or without historical interest. The writings of few if any political thinkers are perfectly consistent with each other. This is why they must be studied by historians as well as by political scientists and philosophers.

Why does it matter that Bruni, in light of recent studies, seems much more a 'professional rhetorician' than he does a 'civic humanist'? There are, in my view, two main reasons why it matters. First, it shows that the disguises of power employed by the Medici regime – their attempt to conceal the true locus of power by exercising their rule under the cloak of republican forms – were hardly original. Salutati and Bruni, as servants of the oligarchic regime of 1382–1434, had done precisely the same thing for half a century, providing a decent covering of populist rhetoric to conceal the growing concentration of power in the hands of a few *padrini*. Manipulation of republican symbols was probably more conscious and more cynical under the Mediceans, but it was not fundamentally different. From this perspective, Bruni's participation in the Medici regime should come as no surprise. The transition from the Albizzian oligarchy to the Medicean regime was neither ideologically nor politically the sharp break it is sometimes represented as being.

The second reason why the new picture of Bruni matters is because it means that the whole category of 'civic humanism' needs to be rethought – either discarded entirely or redefined so as to strip it of its exclusive links with republicanism. Bruni was always Exhibit A in Baron's definition of civic humanism: the example that became for him a kind of Weberian ideal type. If we accept that Bruni's loyalty to Florence was not primarily ideological – that the populist republicanism depicted in the *Laudatio* and the Strozzi oration does not represent his core beliefs – then Bruni begins to look much more like his fellow humanists in Rome, Ferrara, Naples and Milan, and much less like the exemplar of a separate species of humanist.[37] Like his fellow humanists, Bruni's core political convictions were about the value of virtue and eloquence, and about the value of classical antiquity as providing models of virtue and eloquence. These were universalist values, values that could be instantiated in any sort of regime or constitution; they are the values of a ruling caste, not a local political ideology. For Bruni as for Aristotle, *signori* could be good rulers, ruling in the interests of the governed, or they could be tyrants; but *populi* could also be good or bad.[38] What distinguished good governments from bad was not their constitutions but the virtues of their rulers. Bruni's belief in the value of the active life, wealth, military valour and the family – all beliefs Baron associated with his 'civic humanists' – can be documented everywhere in Italian humanist writings of the fifteenth century, not just in republican writers. The change Baron observed in the character of humanism between the generations of Petrarch and of Bruni – the move (or rather the return) of humanism to the public sphere – may be found not only in Florence and Venice, but throughout Italy, in signorial regimes as well as in republics.

Indeed, much of the scholarship on humanism during the 1980s, focusing on regional humanisms, has pointed out the universality of the themes Baron connected with the political experience of Florence.[39] If we continue to use the term 'civic humanist', it should be clearly recognized that the attempt to reform and revalorize the life of the city-state in accordance with ancient models – the great 'civic humanist' project that begins with the generation of Bruni, Poggio Bracciolini, Guarino Veronese, Gasparino Barzizza, Pier Paolo Vergerio and Niccolò Niccoli – was never a project confined to Renaissance republics. 'Civic humanism' is not Florentine, but Roman. It is a style of thought inherited from ancient Rome through Sallust, Livy, Virgil and, above all, Cicero. It aims at the reform of political communities generally by improving the moral behaviour of their ruling elites. It does this by exposing them to 'good letters', to the arts worthy of a free man, the liberal arts, the arts which make men noble, wise and good.

Taken in this more general sense, it can be said that Baron's idea of 'civic humanism' retains a core of validity, and can stand as an important supplement to the Burckhardtian understanding of the Renaissance. It is not really a contradiction, after all, to say that an age of egoism, illegitimate government, religious crisis, shallow-rooted ideologies and increasing indifference to communal values should also have been an age when educators, scholars, civil servants and men of letters everywhere urged upon their audience the need for sacrifice, patriotism and service to the common good. It is not surprising that the men of the Renaissance should have looked for cures for their own diseases of spirit. Burckhardt admired the individualism of the Renaissance, but he also recognized that, taken to an extreme, it could be destructive of civilized society. If Burckhardt drew attention to the diseases of the times, Baron was among the first to show how the age attempted its own cure, through a form of *Bildung* that aimed not only at personal distinction, but also at inculcating a sense of public duty and social conscience. Humanistic education is, like chivalry, an aristocratic form of socialization that links good behaviour with honour. That is what it has always been; that is why it is in crisis in the radically egalitarian societies of the late twentieth century. Renaissance humanists taught that true human excellence consisted in wisdom and goodness; that power unrestrained by goodness was the worst of evils. True personal distinction in the civic life had to include a sense of duty to one's community. If Baron was wrong to read his humanists as fervent partisans of republicanism, he was correct in seeing that humanism, as a cultural programme, sought more than the cultivation of the individual. It aimed also to bring scholarship and learning to bear on the task of building the virtues necessary to the preservation of civil society.[40]

Notes

1 John M. Najemy, review essay of Hans Baron, *In Search of Florentine Civic Humanism: Essays on the Transition from Medieval to Modern Thought*, 2 vols (Princeton, 1988) in *Renaissance Quarterly* 45(1992): 340–50.

2 Baron, *In Search of Florentine Civic Humanism*, II, chs 16 and 17.

3 See Felix Gilbert, *History: Politics or Culture? Reflections on Ranke and Burckhardt* (Princeton, 1990), ch. 4. Baron's own view of Burckhardt's politics was less nuanced: see his essay 'Burckhardt's *Civilization of the Renaissance* a Century after its Publication', *Renaissance News* 13(1960): 207–22, reprinted in *In Search of Florentine Civic Humanism*, II: 155–81.

4 Riccardo Fubini, 'Renaissance Historian: The Career of Hans Baron', *Journal of Modern History* 64(1992): 541–74. Sketches of Baron's career and the influences upon him had been given earlier in G. Cervani, 'Il Rinascimento italiano nell'opera di Hans Baron', *Nuova rivista storica*, 39(1955): 492–503; August Buck, 'Hans Baron's Contribution to the Literary History of the Renaissance', in *Renaissance Studies in Honor of Hans Baron*, eds Anthony Molho and John A. Tedeschi (Florence, 1971), xxxi–lviii; Eugenio Garin, 'Le prime ricerche di Hans Baron sul Quattrocento e la loro influenza fra le due guerre', in *ibid.*,

lix–lxx; and, for modern political context, Renzo Pecchioli, ' "Umanesimo civile" e interpretazione "civile" dell'umanesimo', *Studi storici* 13(1972): 3–33.

5 The term *Bürgerhumanismus*, translated as 'civic humanism', Baron first used in the introduction to his *Leonardo Bruni Aretino. Humanistisch-philosophische Schriften* (Leipzig, 1928).

6 As was pointed out by Niccolò Valeri ('An American and the Renaissance', *Newberry Library Bulletin*, 4[1956]: 88–92), this was itself a challenge to the monarchical-fascist tradition of historiography which saw Giangaleazzo Visconti's effort to unite Italy in the fourteenth century as a tragic failure to do what Vittorio Emmanuele II had succeeded in doing in the nineteenth century.

> One cannot doubt that Baron's keen opposition to the crude Machiavellism of an historical school inclined to recognize political achievement only insofar as it produces power – in isolation from every other motive, whether ideal or ethical – has sprung, like the opposition of other liberally-minded students, from a reaction against Fascist and Nazi ideologies.

Partly for this reason, Gennaro Sasso ('Florentina libertas e Rinascimento italiano nell'opera di Hans Baron', *Rivista storica italiana* 69[1957]: 250–76) argued that Baron's thesis was internationalist and ideological rather than nationalist and power-oriented.

7 For Baron's influence on American Renaissance scholarship, see *Renaissance Studies in Honor of Hans Baron*, eds Molho and Tedeschi; *The Intellectual Migration: Europe and America 1930–1960*, eds Donald Fleming and Bernard Bailyn (Cambridge MA, 1969); and Alberto Tenenti, 'Etudes anglo-saxonnes sur la renaissance florentine', *Annales* 25(1970): 1394–9. Through J. G. A. Pocock and his followers, Baron's 'civic humanism' has had a second life in the historiography of early modern Britain and America; see *The Machiavellian Moment: Florentine Political Thought and the Atlantic Republican Tradition* (Princeton, 1976), esp. chs 3 and 4. The penetration of Baron's ideas to the level of the textbook may be seen in Frederick Hartt's popular *History of Italian Renaissance Art* (New York, 1987), where Bruni is described (243) as 'a sort of Quattrocento Churchill'.

8 Hans Baron, *From Petrarch to Leonardo Bruni: Studies in Humanistic and Political Literature* (Chicago, 1968).

9 Questions about Baron's datings were first raised in a review of Baron's *Crisis* by G. Seidlmayer in *Göttingischer Gelehrnte Anzeigen* (1956): 35–63, republished in *idem*, 'Die Entwicklung der italienischen Früh-Renaissance: Politische Anlasse und geistige Elemente (Zu den Forschungen von Hans Baron)', in *Wege und Wandlungen des Humanismus*, ed. H. Baron (Göttingen, 1965), 47–74. Baron's dismissive reaction is in *From Petrarch*, 108n. For a summary of the literature criticizing Baron's datings of Bruni's early works, see my *Plato in the Italian Renaissance* (London, 1990), II, appendix 1, and the forthcoming second volume of my *Repertorium Brunianum: A Critical Bibliography of the Writings of Leonardo Bruni* (Instituto storico italiano per il Medio Evo, Nuovi studi storici; vol 1, Rome, 1997–) As Nicolai Rubenstein has remarked ('Il Bruni a Firenze: retorica e politica', in Viti, *Leonardo Bruni cancelliere della Repubblica di Firenze. Convegno di Studi*, ed. Paolo Viti [Florence, 1990], 15–28), Baron's redating of Bruni's works are mostly irrelevant to his larger conclusions.

10 Lucia Gualdo Rosa, 'La struttura dell'epistolario bruniano e il significato politico', in Viti, *Leonardo Bruni cancelliere della Repubblica di Firenze*, 372. She generally follows Baron and Garin in her interpretation of the relationship between ideology and rhetoric in Bruni's work.

11 See Sasso, 'Florentina libertas'; Seidlmayer, review of *Crisis*; Aldo Scaglione, review of *Crisis* in *Romance Philology* 10(1956): 129–37; Charles Trinkaus, review of *Crisis*, in *Journal of the History of Ideas* 17(1956): 426–43; Wallace K. Ferguson, 'The Interpretaion of Italian Humanism: The Contribution of Hans Baron', *Journal of the History of Ideas* 19(1958): 14–25. Baron replied to Ferguson in 'Moot Problems of Renaissance Interpretation: An Answer to Wallace K. Ferguson', *ibid.*, 26–34. David Quint ' in Humanism and Modernity: A Reconsideration of Bruni's Dialogues', *Renaissance Quarterly* 38(1985): 423–45, points out some internal difficulties with Baron's reading of *Dialogi ad Petrum Histrum* and their connection with the 1402 crisis.

12 Roberto Weiss, *Il primo secolo dell'umanesimo* (Rome, 1949); the work of Giuseppe Billanovich and his school on 'preumanesimo' is summarized by Guido Billanovich, Rino Avesani and Luciano Gargan in *Storia della cultura veneta*, II (Vicenza, 1976), 19–110, 111–41, and 172–270, respectively. See Rubinstein, 'Political Theories in the Renaissance', in *The Renaissance: Essays in Interpretation*, eds André Chastel, Cecil Grayson and Marie B. Hall (New York, 1982), 153–200, Quentin Skinner, 'Ambrogio Lorenzetti: The Artist as Political Philosopher', *Proceedings of the British Academy* 72(1986): 1–56, and 'Machiavelli's *Discorsi* and the Pre-humanist Origins of Republican Ideas', in *Machiavelli and Republicanism*, eds Gisela Bock, Quentin Skinner and Maurizio Viroli (Cambridge, 1992), 121–41; Skinner's critique of Baron on this point is in his *Foundations of Modern Political Thought, vol. I: The Renaissance* (Cambridge, 1978), ch. 4. See also Ronald G. Witt. 'Medieval Italian Culture and the Origins of Humanism as a Stylistic Ideal', *Renaissance Humanism: Foundations, Forms, Legacy*, ed. Albert Rabil Jr (Philadelphia, 1988), I, 29–70, and, from a different approach, Antonio Santosuosso, in 'Leonardo Bruni Revisited: A Reassessment of Hans Baron's Thesis on the Influence of the Classics in the *Laudatio Florentine urbis*', in *Aspects of Late Medieval Government and Society: Essays Presented to J. R. Lander*, ed. J. G. Rowe (Toronto, 1986), 25–51, arguing that Baron greatly overstates Bruni's independence of his classical source, Aelius Aristides, in the *Laudatio Florentinae urbis*.

13 Charles Till Davis, *Dante's Italy and Other Essays* (Philadelphia, 1984); Skinner, *Foundations*, ch. 3; Emilio Panella, 'Dal bene comune al bene del comune: I trattati politici di Remigio dei Girolami nella Firenze dei bianchi-neri', *Memorie domenicane* 16(1985): 1–198.

14 See Rubinstein, 'Political Theories'. Salutati's shifts between civic and quietist values are discussed in Witt, 'The *De tyranno* and Coluccio Salutati's View of Politics and Roman History', *Nuova rivista storica* 53(1969): 434–74, and (in a more Baronian vein) in *Hercules at the Crossroads: The Life, Work and Thought of Coluccio Salutati* (Durham NC, 1983). A convincing explanation for Salutati's inconsistencies can be found in Robert Black, 'The Political Thought of the Florentine Chancellors', *The Historical Journal* 29(1986): 991–1003.

15 Philip Jones, 'Communes and Despots: The City-state in Late-medieval Italy', *Transactions of the Royal Historical Society*, 5th ser., 15(1965): 1–96, and review of Baron's *Crisis* (2nd edn), in *History* 53(1968): 410–13; Peter Herde, 'Politik and Rhetorik in Florenz am Vorabend der Renaissance', *Archiv für Kulturgeschichte* 50(1965): 141–220; *idem*, 'Politische Verhaltensweise der Florentiner Oligarchie, 1382–1402', in Klaus Zernack (ed.) *Geschichte and Verfassungsgefüge: Frankfurter Festgabe für Walter Schlesinger* (Wiesbaden, 1973); Nicolai Rubinstein, 'Florentine Constitutionalism and the Medici Ascendency in the Fifteenth Century', in *Florentine Studies*, ed. Rubinstein (Florence, 1968). Rubinstein defends Baron against Herde with respect to Baron's interpretation of Salutati in *idem*, 'Florentina libertas', *Rinascimento*

n.s. 26(1976): 3–26, some points made earlier in Trinkaus' review of *Crisis* in *Journal of the History of Ideas* 17(1956).

16 Jerrold E. Seigel, ' "Civic Humanism" or Ciceronian Rhetoric? The Culture of Petrarch and Bruni', *Past and Present* 34(1966): 3–48; *idem, Philosophy and Rhetoric in the Italian Renaissance* (Princeton, 1968); Herde, 'Politik and Rhetorik', and 'Politische Verhaltensweise'. Baron's reply to Seigel appeared as 'Leonardo Bruni: "Professional Rhetorician" or "Civic Humanist"?', *Past and Present* 16(1968): 21–37. Kristeller has criticized Baron's view of humanism in 'Florentine Platonism and its Relations with Humanism and Scholasticism', *Church History* 8(1939): 201–11, reprinted in Paul Oskar Kristeller (ed.) *Studies in Renaissance Thought and Letters*, III (Rome, 1993), 38–48; 'Humanism and Scholasticism in the Italian Renaissance', *Byzantion*, 17(1944–5): 346–74, repr. in *Studies*, I (Rome, 1956), 553–83; 'The Active and Contemplative Life in Renaissance Humanism', in *Arbeit, Musse, Meditation, Betrachtungen zur 'Vita activa' and 'Vita contemplative'*, ed. Brian Vickers (Zurich, 1985), 141–2; 'Humanism', in *The Cambridge History of Renaissance Philosophy*, ed. Charles B. Schmitt (Cambridge, 1988), 131; *Renaissance Thought and the Arts*, ed. Paul Oskar Kristeller (Princeton, 1990), 46–7.

17 *Dizionario biografico degli italiani* (Rome, 1972), XIV, 618–33. See also my *Repertorium Brunianum* and my biography of Bruni to be published by Cambridge University Press. A biographical sketch of Bruni was also given in the introduction to Gordon Griffiths, James Hankins and David Thompson, *The Humanism of Leonardo Bruni: Selected Texts* (Binghamton, 1987), 9–46.

18 For critical editions of Bruni's writings, see the introduction to my *Repertorium Brunianum*, I.

19 For Baron's papers, see Catherine Epstein, *A Past Renewed: A Catalog of German-speaking Refugee Historians in the United States after 1933* (Cambridge, 1993), 34. Baron's papers have now been deposited at the Duke University Archives. I was able to see the papers relative to Baron's unfinished biography of Bruni thanks to the kindness of Baron's literary executor, Ronald G. Witt.

20 Hans Baron, 'The Year of Leonardo Bruni's Birth and Methods for Determining the Ages of Humanists Born in the Trecento', *Speculum* 52(1977): 582–625.

21 The degree to which Baron identified personally with Bruni will be evident to anyone who peruses Baron's papers on Bruni, with their frequent passionate outbursts against other scholars who criticized Bruni's behaviour.

22 Francesco Paolo Luiso, *Studi su l'Epistolario di Leonardo Bruni*, ed. Lucia Gualdo Rosa, Istituto storico italiano per il Medio Evo, Nuovi studi storici, fasc. 122–4 (Rome, 1980).

23 Hans Baron, 'Progress in Bruni Scholarship. A propos of F. P. Luiso's *Studi su l'Epistolario di Leonardo Bruni*', *Speculum* 56(1981): 831–9.

24 See *Per il censimento dei codici dell' Epistolario di Leonardo Bruni*, eds Lucia Gualdo Rosa and Paolo Viti (Rome, 1991). The first volume of the *Censimento dei codici dell' Epistolario di Leonardo Bruni*, ed. Lucia Gualdo Rosa, has now appeared in the Nuovi studi storici, vol. 22, published by the Istituto storico italiano per il Medio Evo (Rome, 1993).

25 Viti, *Leonardo Bruni cancelliere della Repubblica di Firenze*.

26 Rubinstein, 'Il Bruni a Firenze', extending the criticism first voiced in 'Florentine Constitutionalism' but anticipated, albeit in an extremely cursory way, in Augustin Renaudet's review of Baron's *Crisis* in *Bibliothèque d'humanisme et Renaissance* 18(1956): 322–5: 'La belle définition que, en 1428, Bruni, dans *l'Oraison funèbre pour Nanni Strozzi*, donnait des libertés florentines et

notamment de la "libertas reipublicae adeundae", restait illusoire'. Cf. Scaglione's review of the *Crisis* in *Romance Philology*: 134.

27 For an interesting parallel with classical Athens, see Martin Ostwald, *From Popular Sovereignty to the Sovereignty of Law: Law, Society and Politics in Fifth-century Athens* (Berkeley, 1986), esp. part III.

28 Riccardo Fubini, 'La rivendicazione di Firenze della sovranità statale a il contributo delle *Historiae* di Leonardo Bruni', and Anna Maria Cabrini, 'Le *Historiae* del Bruni: risultati e ipotesi di una ricerca sulle fonti', both in Viti, *Leonardo Bruni cancelliere della Repubblica di Firenze*, 29–63 and 247–319 respectively, continuing the line of Fubini, 'Osservazioni sugli *Historiarum Florentini populi Libri XII* di Leonardo Bruni', in E. Sestan, *Studi di storia medievale e moderna per Ernesto Sestan* (Florence, 1978), 1, 403–48.

29 See 'The Historical Background of the Florentine Renaissance', *History* n.s. 22(1938): 315–27 (repr. in expanded form in *In Search of Florentine Civic Humanism*, I, 3–23); 'A Sociological Interpretation of the Early Renaissance in Florence', *South Atlantic Quarterly* 38(1939): 427–8 (*Essays*, II, 40–54); 'The Social Background of Political Liberty in the Early Renaissance', *Comparative Studies in Society and History* n.s. 4(1960): 440–51.

30 Cited from Anthony Molho, *Marriage Alliance in Late Medieval Florence* (Cambridge MA, 1994); and see his 'American Historians and the Italian Renaissance: An Overview', *Bulletin of the Society for Renaissance Studies* 9(1991): 10–23. The chief dissenting voice from the recent consensus is Richard Goldthwaite, *The Building of Renaissance Florence* (Baltimore, 1980), opening chapters and conclusion; see also the striking, but ultimately inconclusive evidence amassed by David Herlihy, 'The Rulers of Florence, 1282–1530', in *City States in Classical Antiquity and Medieval Italy*, ed. Anthony Molho, Kurt Raaflaub and Julia Emlen (Stuttgart, 1991), 197–221.

31 Bruni is also treated as an oligarchic thinker in a perceptive article by Russell Dees, 'Bruni, Aristotle, and the Mixed Regime in *On the Constitution of the Florentines*', *Medievalia et humanistica* n.s. 15(1987), 1–23; and implicitly by John Najemy, 'The Dialogue of Power in Florentine Politics', in *City States in Classical Antiquity and Medieval Italy*, 269–88 and reprinted in abridged form as Chapter 4 of this volume.

32 Lorenzo Mehus (ed.) *Leonardi Bruni Arretini Epistolarum libri VIII* (Florence, 1741), I, 35–6 = Ep. II, 4 (Luiso II, 3). The Italian version of Bruni's history by Donato Acciaiuoli frequently circulates with Gino Capponi's *Conquest of Pisa*. For Baron's reading of the Florentine/Milanese rivalry in the context of modern debates about the politics of the *Kleinstaat* and the *Grossstaat*, see Pecchioli, ' "Umanesimo civile" ', 18f.

33 Paolo Viti, *Leonardo Bruni e Firenze: Studi sulle lettere pubbliche e private* (Florence, 1992).

34 *The Humanism of Leonardo Bruni*, 115.

35 See Bruni, *Epistularum libri VIII*, ed. L. Mehus (Florence, 1741), II, 111–12 (Ep. VIII.4):

> The oration was written when I was young, fresh out of Greek class. It was a boyish trifle, a rhetorical exercise. … The rhetorical genre (for a critic should consider this, too) in panegyrics of this kind calls for boastfulness and winning applause. … In civic panegyrics the speech is directed to those whom you wish to praise; the genre demands an audience, and brings together a multitude of people, not for the purpose of hearing legal cases or deciding on public policy [i.e. it is different from judicial or deliberative oratory, which according to ancient theory was

obliged to respect the truth], but in order to reap applause and pleasure from hearing its own praises sung. ... History is one thing, panegyric another. History must follow the truth, panegyric extols many things above the truth.

The insincerity of the *Laudatio* is made patent when this passage is compared with a passage from the *Laudatio* itself (Baron, *From Petrarch*, 249):

No doubt a few fools will suspect that I am trying to capture some popular favour from this panegyric of mine, and that in the process of winning your good will and disposing your minds favourably towards me as much as possible, I am trespassing on the limits of truth, mixing false things with true for the sake of rhetorical embellishment.

Bruni continues to protest in this vein for almost a page.

36 See Black, 'Florentine Chancellors'.
37 In the Preface to his translation of the *Politics* (*The Humanism of Leonardo Bruni*, 159–61), Bruni seems to have forgotten his remarks in the Strozzi oration about *popularis status* being the only legitimate form of government, for here he identifies *popularis status* with Aristotle's *democratia* and concludes, 'the popular state is therefore not a legitimate kind of government'. In the text edited by Baron as *Epistola ad magnum* [*recte* Magnae, i.e. Germany] *principem imperatorem*, dated to 1413, and attributed to Bruni (see Baron, *Humanistic and Political Literature*, 173–81), the author mistakenly identifies *democratia* as the third of Aristotle's good forms of government, and, translating it as *popularis status*, declares it to be the form of constitution in use in Florence. The attribution of this work to Bruni is suspect, for reasons I shall give in vol. II of my *Repertorium Brunianum*.
38 Bruni, as papal secretary, rather conveniently was able to condemn the Roman people in their revolt against the pope as perverse, drunken and lazy (Ep. 1.4 and 1.5, ed. Mehus, I, 6–11).
39 See John F. D'Amico, *Renaissance Humanism in Papal Rome: Humanists and Churchmen on the Eve of the Reformation* (Baltimore, 1983); Margaret L. King, *Venetian Humanism in an Age of Patrician Dominance* (Princeton, 1986); and Jerry H. Bentley, *Politics and Culture in Renaissance Naples* (Princeton, 1987), esp. 196–222.
40 Many themes in this chapter are further developed in *Renaissance Civic Humanism: Reappraisals and Reflections*, ed. James Hawkins (Ideas in Context) Cambridge: Cambridge University Press, 2000.

Figure 5.1 Political map of Italy, mid-sixteenth century.

5

GEOGRAPHIES OF POWER

The territorial state in early modern Italy

Elena Fasano Guarini

While British and American scholars have tended to privilege the history of the Florentine republic, in Italy the history of the regional or territorial state has long been the major focus. The eminent historian Federico Chabod, for example, viewed the regional state as a Renaissance creation; and he interpreted this political formation as the product of a complex process of bureaucratization and centralization through which the dominant governments of such cities as Milan, Genoa, Florence and Venice gradually brought surrounding territories under their control. Accordingly, he was able to make the claim that the territorial state was, in many respects, an anticipation of the modern nation-state – another example of the view of the Renaissance as the foundation of the modern world.

In the essay below, Elena Fasano Guarini offers a nuanced overview of recent debates among Italian scholars about the nature of the territorial state. As her work shows, there has been a shift away from, on the one hand, the centralized portrait provided by Chabod and, on the other, those models that emphasize the relation of the 'centre' (whether the prince's court or the patriciate of a dominant city) to the 'periphery' (the villages and feudal lords in the provinces). In Fasano Guarini's view, both these models are overly simplistic and fail to take into account the genuine complexity of the ways in which power circulated in the duchies, kingdoms and republics of Italy in this era. As a result, historians today are more likely to consider the state as a system of overlapping jurisdictions in which local lordships, bishoprics, towns and village communities continued to have a certain degree of independence even when they were nominally under the rule of a dominant city or prince. Thus we might not only think of Italy as a complex mosaic of states, but also of each state itself as a smaller patchwork of feudal principalities, free communes, ecclesiastical lordships, and so on. Within each territorial state, moreover, we are likely to find a mixture of contradictory forms of political organization that we can best approach not in the classical language of Renaissance political theory, but rather by attention to the most basic concerns with power as manifest in law, taxation, trade, and the use of military force.

Yet how best to grasp this political structure is, as the various models Fasano Guarini reviews, subject to considerable debate. What common

89

characteristics do they share? Did they represent, as some scholars – from Federico Chabod to Giorgio Chittolini have argued – forms of a 'Renaissance' state? Or were they, by contrast, political forms shaped by the crisis of the late Italian Renaissance and the increasing control that local aristocracies began to exercise, through a process known as re-feudalization, over their subjects? Or, finally, is it more useful, as Edoardo Grendi and Paolo Malanima have argued, to view the territorial state, at least in part, as the political expression of economic systems?

Fasano Guarini's essay, abridged, revised, and presented here with a new title, was first published in English as 'Center and Periphery', in The Origins of the State in Italy, 1300–1600, *ed. Julius Kirshner (Chicago, 1995), 74–93. Kirshner's volume provides an excellent introduction to many of the leading Italian historians whose work, still too little known in the United States and Britain, has begun to illuminate the political history of early modern Italy from new angles. For an intriguing essay that deepens the dialogue between Italian scholars on the one hand and US and British scholars on the other, see Edward Muir, 'Was There Republicanism in the Renaissance Republics? Venice after Agnadello', in* Venice Reconsidered: The History and Civilization of an Italian City-State, *eds John Jeffries Martin and Dennis Romano (Baltimore, 2000), 137–68.*

* * *

Introduction

This article addresses the history of the Italian territorial states in the early modern period, with attention to the   Duchy of Milan, the Republic of Venice, the Kingdom of Naples, Tuscany under the Medici, the Papal States, and the Republic of Genoa – undoubtedly the most powerful political systems on the Italian peninsula in this era. It is my goal to offer not so much an overview of the formation of these states as a consideration of the ways in which power was distributed within them. Was power concentrated, as many scholars have argued, in the political centres of these states? That is, did the ruling groups of such cities as Milan, Venice, Naples, Florence, Rome and Genoa dominate the territories they had conquered? Or were various institutions in the peripheral or outlying areas – towns, communes, villages, feudal lords, monasteries and castles – also sites of power, capable of contesting the authority of their sovereign? Many scholars have tackled this question by exploring the often tense contrapuntal relation between 'centre and periphery'.[1] However, as I shall suggest below, it is more helpful to approach early modern states as territorial systems in which local communities were connected not only to the centre but also to one another through a variety of economic and political networks that continued, in many cases, to guarantee them a degree of autonomy in relation to the growing power of the prince or the city which, in theory at least, was their sovereign. In fact, many historians now analyse political systems not only from the 'centre' or from 'above' but also from 'below' or from the 'periphery', with an emphasis on what we might call 'the geography of power' in the early modern period.[2]

From centre to periphery

Marino Berengo's 1967 essay on Italian postwar historiography concerning the sixteenth century is a useful starting point.[3] This work touched upon the theme of the state and its sixteenth-century developments – a theme that he linked to Federico Chabod's studies on the administration of the Duchy of Milan.[4] Chabod, despite his belief that the Italian wars unleashed by the invasion of the French king Charles VIII in 1494 had brought about the end of the Renaissance, interpreted the mid- and late sixteenth-century formation of a bureaucratic apparatus free of personal ties as a step along a path to modernity and thus placed Italian political history within the broader European context of modernization. Berengo recognized the 'extraordinary richness' of Chabod's research themes: the study of bureaucracy, for example, which was essential 'for understanding the development of a new political process' in order 'to recognize the social forces that support it' and 'to base political history upon an analysis of society'. But, according to Berengo, 'the study of the central government administration', to which Chabod had dedicated much of his work, was not 'the same as the study of power'. The latter had to take into account 'the resistance that various mediating institutions and feudal lordships, country and cities, patriciate and clergy, were able to offer to royal absolutism'. Thus 'the play of the local forces' had to be examined. Chabod's emphasis on the centre was not sufficient.[5]

Significantly Berengo, unlike Chabod, made no mention of the 'modern' or 'Renaissance' state.[6] He understood Italian politics not in terms of 'modernity' but, on the contrary, in terms of crisis and especially of the 'crisis of freedom' that, in the wake of the Italian wars, transformed the political institutions up and down the peninsula. Berengo, that is, stressed 'the decline of the true forms of Italian political life, and of one in particular that had been typical of that world: namely, the city-republic'. To Berengo, it was a decline with no redeeming features, not accompanied by the 'formation of states with solid administrative and judiciary structures', but only by a 'triumphant particularism … destined to characterize the history of the Old Regime in Italy'.[7]

Berengo was not alone in his re-evaluation of Italian political history. In an important book published in 1964, Angelo Ventura had also emphasized the long 'decadence' of the cities of the Venetian Terraferma, the mainland territories in northeastern Italy that the Venetians had conquered in the late Middle Ages.[8] His was a history of urban societies rather than states. He focused on the conflicts between 'nobility' and 'the people' and, most notably, on the process of 'aristocratization' that, in his opinion, had brought about the formation of oligarchic governments, dominated by the local nobilities, in both the larger cities and the smaller centres. Aristocratization, he argued, was closely interconnected with the erosion of freedom in the cities, first under the *signorie* (local lordships or seigneurial governments) and then under the dominion of Venice.[9] Finally, to Ventura, the Venetian Terraferma was not a 'federative' state, as a long tradition of local studies had claimed, but a dominion founded on conquest. Nor was it a unitary state, but a system characterized by a lasting schism between Venice and its territory, between 'centre' and 'periphery'.[10]

We see a similar emphasis on the interplay of the administrative centre with the feudal periphery in studies of the Kingdom of Naples and Sicily, where the role of the cities had been negligible, and where, on the contrary, the feudal–monarchic system had been fundamental. The feudal periphery, with the dynamic and violent tensions that characterized it, certainly had great importance in the works of Giuseppe Galasso and Rosario Villari. The Kingdom as a whole, itself a peripheral area (a vice-royalty) under the control of Spain and a province of the Hapsburg Empire, seemed to both scholars also to be an organic entity characterized by its own existence as a state.[11] And while they did not agree on many important matters, Galasso and Villari both maintained that the history of the Kingdom was determined by the relation between central power and feudal periphery, by the interaction of Spanish power with local institutions, by diverse and complex centripetal forces as well as by the ways in which local communities fought to protect their liberties against the pull of an increasingly powerful centre. And they concluded that it could only be understood in its totality, as the history of a single state.

The territorial state

The shift away from Chabod's model of the Renaissance state as a modern, centralized, impersonal and highly bureaucratized polity to a model that attended not only to the central sites of power in princely courts and capital cities but also to local institutions scattered throughout the periphery, was encouraged in part by a comparable shift in emphasis by historians working in other regions of Europe, especially Germany. But equally decisive was the initiative a group of Italian scholars had taken to examine in detail the territorial dimensions of the Italian states. The project – the *Atlante Storico Italiano* (Historical Atlas of Italy) – was ambitious. Not limited to the study of formal political institutions, the atlas, when completed, was intended to include maps of roads and of ecclesiastical, economic, agricultural and demographic structures. It aimed to reconstruct 'the basic features of Italian society' from different angles. The first task, the directors of the project made clear, was 'to establish the size of the states, their external boundaries and their internal jurisdictions, both public and feudal', and therefore to determine 'who, in the various territories, collected taxes and administered justice'.[12]

Significantly, the project did not imply a 'modern' and centralized vision of the state. On the contrary, it paid less attention to the powers and institutions located in the centre than to those in the periphery. It gave ample space to the analysis of particularisms, local autonomies, and fiscal and jurisdictional exemptions. For the south of Italy, the scholars naturally planned to do the research for the feudal maps first, followed only later by those of the royal jurisdictions, with the intention of eventually combining the results. But drawing maps and boundaries, thinking about their nature and quality, determining who ruled and how, and establishing who administered justice and fiscal exactions, forced the authors to think in terms of territorial or regional systems of power.[13]

Within the context of this project, my own research on Tuscany under the rule of the Medici offered a portrait of the state not as a territory that could be understood, at least not exclusively, through the relation of the centre to the periphery, but rather as an aggregation or clustering of local, particularistic and diverse centres of power.[14] Cities, towns and rural communities, each with their own councils and governing bodies, were, in effect, the basic elements in the structure of the country and in the organization of the territory. In the absence of a strong central bureaucracy, that is, local communities remained in charge of the collection and apportionment of taxes, maintaining public order, and, until Cosimo I, who ruled from 1537 to 1574, defence. While the towns and villages within the *contado* were directly subject to Florentine rule, those outside it continued to be regulated by the terms agreed upon at the time of subjugation. Accordingly they enjoyed many fiscal and jurisdictional privileges, which they were tenacious in maintaining. Moreover, from their vantage point, the state ruled by the Medici was only one of several overlapping political structures of which they were a part, for these communities were also included in a close network of leagues which were governed, in part at least, by a variety of officials (*podestà, vicari*) sent from Florence.

From the middle of the sixteenth century onward, however, those local communities outside the Florentine *contado* were increasingly subjected to the administrative and financial control of chancellors and other officials, appointed by the central government in Florence. Through these newly established bureaucratic networks, which also had a corresponding hierarchy of local governing bodies, not only was justice administered and the collection of taxes organized, but local life itself was regulated and disciplined. Furthermore, it was through these channels that the orders of the prince were transmitted and carried out; that his bans and police regulations were publicized; and that his orders to work, that is, the *opere* and the *comandate* (such as the maintenance of highways) were imposed. This was neither an 'aggregation', as Ventura claimed, nor a centralized state, but a coherent system of power, regional in scope, within which the communities continued to exist, with their functions and liberties based on an enduring set of contracts; meanwhile, the authority of the prince was strong, guaranteed by efficient instruments of control and wide-ranging government influence.[15]

In his well-known studies of the early modern Italian state, Giorgio Chittolini reached a similar conclusion.[16] While Chittolini saw, in the decline of the communes and the coming of the *signorie*, a tendency to form stable power structures and stronger centres, he did not interpret the new territorial systems as modern states, and certainly not as absolutist states. Whether focusing on the largely feudal Duchy of Milan – ruled first by the Visconti and then by the Sforza – or the small principalities in the province of Emilia, or a city-state like Florence, the fourteenth- and fifteenth-century public organization, Chittolini showed, was always based on a pact, a negotiated settlement between the central government and local authorities.[17] It was based on a division of power between the central government and a periphery that retained its vitality for a long time, resigned to the loss of its independence, to be sure, but not to that of its liberties. Chittolini adopted the term 'dualism' to describe this division of power in early modern Italian states.

In his studies of the Republic of Venice, Gaetano Cozzi also developed the concept of 'dualism'.[18] But in his work this term does not refer only to the contractual nature of the judicial relations between the Republic of Venice and its dominion, that is, the mainland territories it had conquered. It also points to the 'social, spiritual, political, economic and environmental' differences that separated Venice – which was, in any case, a strange centre placed at the borders of its state, a seafaring and mercantile city, foreign to the world of common law – from the Terraferma, which remained organized around a number of large towns and cities such as Brescia, Verona, Vicenza, Treviso, Padua and Udine, and dotted with feudal lordships and 'little princes'.[19] To Cozzi, this original 'dualism' had a deep influence on the structures and development of the Venetian state. In sharp contrast to Ventura, moreover, Cozzi maintained that this dualism did not prevent the formation of a lasting political system capable of surviving serious crises, such as the catastrophic but temporary loss of Venice's mainland territories after its defeat by the League of Cambrai in 1509, for within the course of a few years Venice had reconquered its territory.[20] Indeed, throughout its history, the authority of Venice was generally viewed as legitimate within the territories it dominated.[21] Several factors contributed to this sense of regional unity: the widespread presence of Venetian patricians who served as administrators (*podestà* and *capitani*) of the subject cities, held important ecclesiastical benefices (bishops, abbots) and owned land throughout the Terraferma; the cultural attraction exercised by Venice over the ruling classes in the provinces; and, perhaps most of all, the way in which Venice governed and administered justice. In respect to the administration of justice, what contributed most to the integration of the region was the ability of the ruling groups in Venice both to respect the autonomous statutes and the privileges of the subject cities and communities, and to assert its authority without excluding the pursuit of consensus. Venice pursued a mediation policy in local conflicts. It was willing to accept compromises and to ally itself with the oligarchies of the subject cities.[22]

For the Kingdom of Naples, scholars have insisted on the centralization processes and the erosion of the political spaces left to feudal forces in the periphery.[23] They have also discussed the disciplining of local or provincial ruling elites by the state and their degradation from political authorities to *de facto* powers. Historians, that is, have continued to see the key to the history of the Kingdom in the sixteenth and seventeenth centuries in the dialectic between these orders – a dialectic which has often been seen to coincide with that between the capital city of Naples and the feudal periphery.[24] Furthermore, starting from the peripheries, a new attention to the history of provincial towns and cities has developed in recent years. Even in the case of the Kingdom, some scholars today see the cities basically as centres of territorial aggregation, which, although they were subject to processes of rapid marginalization, were powerful enough in the late fifteenth century to act as mediators between local forces and the central government before becoming the government's agents for the repression of oppositional social groups and institutions in the sixteenth and seventeenth centuries.[25]

These changes in approach and emphasis in the study of the early modern state in Italy have had a profound influence. Not just in Italy, but elsewhere too, the traditional model of the early modern state seems less and less convincing. New models have emerged, with more nuances and a greater stress on the pluralistic and decentred nature of the territory. The notion of a 'composite' state, for example, has been applied to political systems as different as the Republic of Venice and the great European monarchies.[26] Similarly, in France scholars have begun to study the centralization and unification of the country not as a result of the methods deployed by the monarchy itself but rather by focusing on the periphery. Historians, for example, have emphasized the importance of various and disparate centres of authority in the cities and the countryside throughout France, their importance in the organization of society, and the survival of private forms of justice – whether aimed at arbitration or peace-keeping – that are hardly compatible with centralization.[27]

Microstoria and the rethinking of the territorial state

Perhaps the most fruitful and innovative development in the study of the early modern state has come from the important role that *microstoria* or 'microhistory' has assumed within Italian historiography – an approach that deliberately shifts the focus of research away from the state as a whole to single communities in peripheral or outlying areas.[28] Many scholars, working within this framework, have considered the community 'a sort of ideal unit', open to different approaches and methodologies – from the history of institutions, fiscalism and justice, to the history of *mentalités* and social anthropology.[29] In the history of communities, often identified with their most important families, historians have looked for the manifestations of social evolution as perceived from the ground up – or, if one prefers, from the periphery. Indeed, in some cases, the analysis of communities, factions and kinship groups in the outlying areas of the state has resulted in research models quite different from those used by more traditional students of institutional and administrative history. In particular, the study of the 'interdependencies between local societies and state institutions', based on categories drawn from economic and social anthropology, has challenged the familiar 'juxtapositions such as community/state and periphery/centre, which evoke the basic cultural dualism between "high" and "low" '.[30]

One of the most successful applications of this methodology is seen in the work of Edoardo Grendi and, in particular, in his study of Cervo, a small city on the Ligurain Riviera.[31] To be sure, Genoa remains an indispensable frame of reference. Genoa exercised its sovereignty over the territory around Cervo; it was the centre where high justice was administered; it imposed and collected taxes, although it had to resort to local institutions to do so and had to deal with their resistance. The *podestà* and officers who acted in the outlying communities such as Cervo were Genoese. According to Grendi, one can even identify a trend in the seventeenth century towards the consolidation of the state and the erosion of local immunities and privileges, although there was never 'a coherent state plan'.[32] Grendi believes that governing the territory required first participating in the complex interaction of 'primary associations that were radically "different", "alien" from the administrative and territorial political reality'. To understand the logic of the system he examines the reality of those associations – feuds and kinships in the communities, parishes, villages, boroughs and towns on the eastern Riviera around Cervo. Significantly, this system was not centred only around the capital city of Genoa; it was influenced also by the nature of the territory, the basic characteristics of its settlements and the distribution of resources. Its connective tissue consisted of the circuits of exchange between the villages and the towns or boroughs: the network for food provisioning; commerce in grain, oil and wine; larger operations that extended beyond the limits of the commune (such as the collection of coral); and migration. Grendi's microhistorical approach, that is, highlights 'the plurality of the protagonists in the territory' and the interaction between local powers and state functions. In this context, the state existed because it mediated conflicts between villages and towns, protecting the former; it regulated markets and supplies; it controlled the mints; and it governed the 'regional economic society', making integration possible.

Geography was clearly important. Situated between the mountains and the sea, Genoa continued to seem more like a city-state than the capital of a territory. Moreover, Genoa was engaged in financial ventures on the European stage and was, therefore, less concerned with dominating its own territories than were certain other states of the early modern period.[33] Even if Grendi's model, based on 'specific and closely focused research', cannot be extended automatically to other contexts, the 'distinctive approach' he proposes certainly can.[34] Above all, his approach enables an analysis, from the ground up, of the concrete ways in which power was exercised – a view of political realities that more traditional approaches to the history of the state, with a focus on more isolated vantage points like urban patriciates, royal courts and military fortresses, are less likely to illuminate.

Economic regions and the territorial state

Another approach that has facilitated our understanding of the decentred nature of the state has been the focus on the relation of territorial state to economic regions. Among the most familiar of these approaches has been the work of those historians who have focused on the history of single Italian cities at the time of their subjection. Whether the city in question was Vicenza, 'firstborn of Venice', or Pescia, 'in the shadow of Florence', these studies have tried to explain the early modern history of the state by examining the political, economic and cultural incorporation of the old urban centres into the new regional realities.[35] These works highlight how the responses of these cities to external stimuli and influences, their long periods of adjustment, and, at the same time, the tenacious assertion of their own local identities, were threatened by their 'relegation to the periphery'.

The theme has also been approached comparatively, as we see in the work of S. R. Epstein on Sicily, Tuscany and Lombardy. His thesis goes against the traditional view of the city as the origin of modern economic development. He maintains that the emergence of Florence as the dominant city in Tuscany during and after the fourteenth-century crisis resulted in stagnation rather than development, as demonstrated by the long decline of the other urban centres and the growing rigidity of social hierarchies. He argues that the subordination of other cities to Florence was both cause and effect of a policy of preferring dominion to integration, a policy suggested by the nature of the institutions and by the way power was used to the advantage of the dominant city. According to Epstein, conditions in Sicily proved much more favourable to economic recovery. There, not only did the crisis tip the scale in favour of the countryside, but the modification of urban hierarchies and the decline of the old metropolitan centres of Palermo and Messina allowed a more equitable distribution of resources. The Lombard system, characterized by more numerous and dynamic urban centres, was also more favourable to economic recovery than the Tuscan one. Politically, the Dukes of Milan, first the Visconti and then the Sforza, demonstrated a willingness to favour the minor centres as well as the major ones, both in the distribution of resources and the location of markets.[36]

The idea of a close link between regional state and economic region has also emerged in the work of Paolo Malanima. In his studies of the Tuscan experience, Malanima has suggested a parallel between the formation of the state and the regionalization of the economy.[37] According to Malanima, the economic region was 'a complex territorial structure consisting of interdependent realities based on forms of geographic division of labour', within which 'the different areas were like the different limbs of a body, all aiming at the same common goal'.[38] But it was not only the economy that shaped political institutions; political decisions also had far-reaching effects on the economies. This is apparent in many of the mechanisms of political power, namely: decision making on matters regarding fiscal impositions and duties; policies concerning demography, roads and hydraulics; intervention in the location of markets and manufacturing activities; and choices concerning urban planning – sometimes simply projects, at other times decisive and radical changes. The port city of Livorno (Leghorn), whose construction was a political project conceived and realized by the first Grand Dukes of Tuscany, became in a span of forty years the second most powerful city in the Duchy.[39] Around the same time, the decision by the King of Savoy to establish a new capital brought about the rapid growth of Turin in Piedmont, while the pre-existing urban network was reduced and restructured.[40] And in the Republic of Genoa in the early sixteenth century, the rise to power of Andrea Doria, who entered into a political alliance with Spain, led to the destruction of the nearby port of Savona, a city which until then had been Genoa's chief rival in the region. Indeed, both political and economic factors seem to have helped preserve or transform urban hierarchies within the system, modify the relations between city and countryside, promote or hinder the development of local centres and the proliferation of towns, redistribute resources and manpower, and shape and define economic regions. One can perhaps speak of 'centre' in the singular as a source of political decision, although certainly not of 'centralization'.[41]

In conclusion, I should like to stress two points. First, the notion of the state as a system seems to work better than the more traditional model that privileges the interplay of centre with periphery. A focus on the territory with its concrete problems, that is, proves especially useful for the analysis of political systems since, unlike a purely institutional approach, it is able to disclose the structural and dynamic aspects of such systems. As one scholar has observed, the territory is pre-eminently a historical product that reflects the history of a 'geography of power', with attention paid not so much to formal institutions as to demographic, economic and topographical factors.[42] Yet – and this is my second point – a focus on territory can also serve as the unifying framework that links institutional history to the history of extra-institutional forces, state to community, public to private.[43] From this perspective, the analysis of territory offers the possibility of connecting the study of juridical and constitutional developments, which have traditionally played such a salient role in recent research on the political history of the Italian states, with the analysis of economic and social forces – forces that have remained partly hidden by the very same institutional and legal structures that they, paradoxically, played a major role in shaping and supporting.

Notes

1 The paradigm 'centre–periphery' derives its success largely from Immanuel Wallerstein, *The Modern World-System*, 2 vols (New York, 1974 and 1980). On this work, see Alberto Tenenti, 'Centri e periferie nella vita economica dell'età moderna', *Quaderni sardi* 3(July 1981–3): 3–14. For an application of this model to artistic and cultural phenomena in Italy, see Enrico Castelnuovo and Carlo Ginzburg, 'Centro e periferia', in *Questioni e metodi*, vol. 1 of *Storia dell'Arte italiana*, ed. G. Ballati and P. Fossati (Turin, 1978), 285–352. More generally, see the monograph 'Centre and Periphery' in *Quaderni sardi* 4(July 1983–June 1984). The expression was used as the title of a volume by

Giovanni Levi, *Centro e periferia di uno stato assoluto – tre saggi su Piemonte e Liguria in età moderna* (Turin, 1985), where it applies only to the first of the three essays included, 'Come Torino soffocò il Piemonte'.

2 Claude Raffestin, *Pour une géographie du pouvoir* (Paris, 1980).

3 Marino Berengo, 'Il Cinquecento', in *La storiografia italiana negli ultimi vent'anni*, 2 vols (Milan, 1970), I: 483–518.

4 Federico Chabod, *Storia di Milano nell'epoca di Carlo V* (Turin, 1961; revised edn, 1971)

5 Berengo, 'Il Cinquecento', 488–9.

6 See Chabod, 'Was There a Renaissance State?', in *The Development of the Modern State*, ed. Heinz Lubasz (New York, 1964; original French version, 1958); and Giuseppe Galasso, 'Trends and Problems in Neapolitan History in the Age of Charles V', in *Good Government in Spanish Naples*, eds and trans. Antonio Calabria and John A. Marino (New York, 1990), 13–78 (original Italian version, 1965).

7 Berengo, 'Il Cinquecento', 495. Berengo's encouragement to study not only the centre but also the tormented life of the periphery – intermediate social institutions and local forces, feudal lordships and communities – no doubt reflected the attention to social and political conflicts that he had previously devoted to an essentially urban setting in his study on Lucca, one of the few city-states to have survived the early sixteenth-century crisis; see Berengo, *Nobili e mercanti nella Lucca del '500* (Turin, 1999; 1st edn, 1965).

8 Angelo Ventura, *Nobiltà e popolo nella società veneta del '400 e '500* (Milan, 1993; 1st edn, Bari, 1964).

9 The system that emerged was what today would be called a 'regional' state. On the definition of the regional state, see my introduction to *Potere e società negli Stati regionali italiani del '500 e '600* (Bologna, 1978), 18–20.

10 Ventura, introduction to *Dentro lo 'Stado italico': Venezia e la Terraferma fra Quattro e Seicento*, eds Giorgio Cracco and Michael Knapton (Trent, 1984), 5–15.

11 Galasso, 'Considerazioni sulla storia del Mezzogiorno d'Italia', in *Mezzogiorno medievale e moderno* (Turin, 1965), 13–59 and 'Trends and Problems in Neapolitan History'; see also Rosario Villari, *The Revolt of Naples*, trans. James Newall (Cambridge, 1993; original Italian edition: Bari, 1967).

12 Berengo, 'Premessa', in *Problemi e ricerche per l'Atlante storico italiano dell'età moderna: Atti del convegno di Gargnano, 27–29 settembre 1968* (Florence, 1971), 1–9.

13 Actually, only my map of 'La Toscana granducale al tempo di Cosimo I' and the corresponding preparatory notes were published, but the common work we carried out in preparation for the atlas represented one of the starting points for a different way of considering the Italian states of the modern period; see Elena Fasano Guarini, *Lo Stato mediceo di Cosimo I* (Florence, 1973). The map was published by the Centro Nazionale delle Ricerche (undated) and later as 'The Grand-Duchy of Tuscany at the Death of Cosimo I: A Historical Map (with enclosure)', *Journal of Italian History* 2(1979).

14 Fasano Guarini, 'Città soggette e contadi nel dominio fiorentino tra Quattro e Cinquecento: Il caso pisano', in *Ricerche di storia moderna*, I, ed. M. Mirri (Pisa, 1976), 1–94; 'Potere centrale e comunità soggette nel Granducato di Cosimo I', *Rivista storica italiana* 89(1977): 490–538; 'Considerazioni su giustizia stato società nel Ducato di Toscana del Cinquecento', in *Florence and Venice: Comparisons and Relations*, vol. 2, *Cinquecento*, eds Sergio Bertelli, Nicholai Rubinstein and C. H. Smyth (Florence, 1980), 135–68; and 'Gli statuti delle città soggette a Firenze tra '400 e '500: Riforme locali e interventi centrali', in

Statuti città territori in Italia e Germania tra medioevo ed età moderna, eds Giorgio Chittolini and D. Willoweit (Bologna, 1991), 69–124.

15 For the juridical aspects, see L. Mannori, *L'amministrazione del territorio nella Toscana granducale: Teoria e prassi di governo fra antico regime e riforme* (Florence, 1988), and *Il sovrano tutore: Pluralismo istituzionale e accentramento amministrativo nel principato dei Medici, XVI, XVIII* (Milan, 1994).

16 Giorgio Chittolini, *La formazione dello Stato regionale e le istituzioni del contado: Secoli XIV e XV* (Turin, 1979), esp. 3–35.

17 See the studies collected in Chittolini, *La formazione dello Stato regionale.*

18 Gaetano Cozzi (ed.) *Stato società e giustizia nella Repubblica veneta (XV–XVIII)* (Rome, 1980); *Repubblica di Venezia e Stati Italiani: Politica e giustizia dal secolo XVI al secola XVIII* (Turin, 1982), 217–318; and 'Ambiente veneziano, ambiente veneto, governanti e governati nel Dominio di qua dal Mincio nei secoli XV–XVIII', in *Storia della cultura veneta: Il Seicento*, eds Girolamo Arnaldi and Manlio Pastore Stocchi (Venice, 1984), 497–539. Among the studies by Cozzi's students, see, in particular, Claudio Povolo, *L'intrigo dell'onore: poteri e istituzioni nella Repubblica di Venezia tra Cinque e Seicento* (Verona, 1997); Michael Knapton, 'Tra Dominante e dominio (1517–1630)', in Gaetano Cozzi and Michael Knapton, *La Repubblica di Venezia nell'età moderna* (Turin, 1992), 465–549; and, more recently, Alfredo Viggiano, *Governanti e governati: Legittimità del potere ed esercizio dell'autorità sovrana nello Stato veneto della prima età moderna* (Treviso, 1993).

19 Sergio Zamperetti, *I piccoli principi: Signorie locali, feudi e comunità soggette nello Stato regionale veneto dall'espansione territoriale ai primi decenni del '600* (Treviso, 1991).

20 See Innocenzo Cervelli, *Machiavelli e la crisi dello stato veneziano* (Naples, 1974); Giuseppe Del Torre, *Venezia e la Terraferma dopo la guerra di Cambrai: Fiscalità e amministrazione (1515–1530)* (Milan, 1986).

21 See, for example, James Grubb, *Firstborn of Venice: Vicenza in the Early Renaissance State* (Baltimore, 1988), 99ff.; and Gian Maria Varanini, *Comuni cittadini e Stato regionale: Ricerche sulla Terraferma veneta nel Quattrocento* (Verona, 1992).

22 Michael Knapton, 'Il Territorio vicentino nello Stato veneto del '500 e primo '600: Nuovi equilibri politici e fiscali', in *Dentro lo 'Stado italico'*, 33–115; Zamperetti, 'I "Sinedri dolosi": La formazione e lo sviluppo dei corpi territoriali nello Stato regionale veneto tra '500 e '600', *Rivista storica italiana* 99(1987): 269–320, and bibliography quoted therein.

23 See, in particular, Aurelio Cernigliaro, *Sovranità e feudo nel Regno di Napoli (1505–1557)*, 2 vols (Naples, 1983).

24 Pier Luigi Rovito, *Respublica dei togati: Giuristi e società nella Napoli del Seicento* (Naples, 1981), with an introduction by R. Aiello.

25 This is particularly true for Apulia. See Angelantonio Spagnoletti, *'L'incostanza delle umane cose': Il patriziato di terra di Bari tra egemonia e crisi (XVI–XVIII secolo)* (Bari, 1981); Maria Antonietta Visceglia, *Territorio, feudo e potere locale: Terra d'Otranto tra Medioevo ed età moderna* (Naples, 1988); and, above all, Francesco Tateo (ed.) *Storia di Bari nell'antico regime*, 2 vols (Bari, 1991–2).

26 Grubb, *Firstborn of Venice* and J. H. Elliott, 'A Europe of Composite Monarchies', *Past and Present* 137(1992): 48–71.

27 Yves Durand, *Vivre au pays au XVIIIe siècle: Essai sur la notion de pays dans l'Ouest de la France* (Paris, 1984); Michel Derlange, *Les communautés d'habitants en Provence au dernier siècle de l'Ancien Régime* (Toulouse, 1987); Philippe Guignet, *Le pouvoir dans la ville au XVIIIe siècle: Pratiques politiques, notabilité et*

éthique sociale de part et d'autre de la frontière franco-belge (Paris, 1990). On the continuation of extra- and infralegal practices, see Y. Castan, *Honnêteté et relations sociales en Languedoc, 1715–1780* (Paris, 1974); and Nicole Castan, *Justice et répression en Languedoc à l'époque des Lumières* (Paris, 1980).

28 For an introduction to *microstoria* and its importance not only in political but in other aspects of early modern Italian history, see Karl Appuhn, 'Microhistory', in *The Encyclopedia of European Social History*, ed. Peter Stearns, (New York, 2001), I: 105–112, as well as Edward Muir's introduction to *Microhistory and the Lost Peoples of Europe*, eds Muir and Guido Ruggiero (Baltimore, 1991) – a selection of essays from the influential Italian journal *Quaderni storici*. Other new approaches to the history of the early modern state include the analysis of the 'patrician system', with its mechanisms of self-legitimation and co-optation as well as the study of clientage and patronage. See *Patriziati e aristocrazie nobiliari*, eds Cesare Mozzarelli and Pierangelo Schiera (Trent, 1978); Bandino Giacomo Zenobi, *Corti principesche e oligarchie formalizzate come 'luoghi del politico' nell'Italia dell'età moderna* (Urbino, 1993); Maria Antonietta Visceglia, *Signori, patrizi, cavalieri nell'età moderna* (Bari, 1992); *La corte e lo spazio: Ferrara estense*, eds Giuseppe Papagano and Amedeo Quondam; and *I ceti dirigenti nella Toscana del Quattrocento*, ed. Donatella Rugiadini (Florence, 1987).

29 Giovanni Tocci, introduction to *Le comunità negli Stati italiani d'antico regime* (Bologna, 1989), 10. I recommend this volume for its extensive bibliography up to 1989. After 1989, see e.g. D. Montanari (ed.) *Mazzano – Storia di una comunità – secoli XII–XX* (Mazzano, 1992). Other works have examined relations between communities and the central government to measure durations and transformations of regimes based on pacts. See, especially for the Papal States, Angela De Benedictis, *Patrizi e comunità: il governo del contado bolognese nel Settecento* (Bologna, 1984); Cesarina Casanova, *Comunità e governo pontificio in Romagna in età moderna* (Bologna, 1982); C. Penuti, 'Il principe e le comunità soggette: Il regime fiscale dalle "pattuizioni" al "buongoverno" ', in *Finanze e ragion di Stato in Italia e in Germania nella prima età moderna*, eds A. De Maddalena and H. Kellenbenz (Bologna, 1984), 89–100.

30 This perspective is illustrated by numerous studies published in *Quaderni storici* as well as in two recent works on Ligurian topics: Osvaldo Raggio's work on the Fontanabuona Valley in the Apennines and Edoardo Grendi's work on Cervo, a community on the Riviera. See, in particular, S. Lombardini, Osvaldo Raggio, and Angelo Torre (eds) 'Special Issue: Conflitti locali e idiomi politici', *Quaderni storici* 63(1986); Edoardo Grendi and Giovanni Levi (eds) 'Special Issue: Famiglia e comunità', *Quaderni storici* 33(1976); Giovanni Levi (ed.) 'Special Issue: Villaggi: Studi di antropologia storica', *Quaderni storici* 46(1981). But see especially, Raggio, *Faide e parentele: Lo stato genovese visto dalla Fonatanabuona* (Turin, 1990) and Grendi, *Il Cervo e la repubblica: Il modello ligure di antico regime* (Turin, 1993).

31 Grendi, *Il Cervo e la repubblica*.

32 Grendi, *Il Cervo e la repubblica*, 21.

33 Grendi, *Il Cervo e la repubblica*, 79. At the end of the eighteenth century travellers still noticed the lack of interest in the territorial government among the dominant group in the city, described as 'négociants' who 'n'ont point de pays'. See C. M. Du Paty, *Lettres sur l'Italie en 1785* (Lausanne, 1796), I: 83.

34 Grendi, *Il Cervo e la repubblica*, 20. The case of Tuscany provides a useful contrast. For a variety of reasons – including the intensely urbanized nature of the region and the pattern of its settlements – the ruling class of Florence developed a strong interest in landed property and chose, therefore, to inter-

vene directly in the territory. In addition to mediating conflicts, the Florentine government controlled local administrations and finances and organized a sytem for provisioning its subject terrorities. The system as a whole functioned through a series of offices and territorial jurisdictions, reflecting not only the supremacy of Florence but also the hierarchy of the subject cities. In some areas, like the *contado* of Pisa, the communities themselves remained vital but underwent structural transformations between the sixteenth and the seventeenth centuries. The expansion of Florentine landed property also had a profound impact on individual communities throughout the state as the development of the 'mezzadria' (the sharecropping system) brought in groups of 'foreigners' representing outside interests, whose fiscal obligations and access to markets and credit were different from those of the 'natives'.

35 Grubb, *Firstborn of Venice*; Judith C. Brown, *In the Shadow of Florence: Provincial Society in Renaissance Pescia* (New York and Oxford, 1982); Fasano Guarini (ed.) *Prato storia di una città*, vol. II, *Un microcosmo in movimento (1494–1815)* (Florence, 1986); and M. Montorzi and L. Giani, *Pontedera e le guerre del Contado: Una vicenda di ricostruzione urbana e di instaurazione istituzionale tra territorio e giurisdizione* (Pisa, 1994).

36 S. R. Epstein, 'Cities, Regions and the Late Medieval Crisis: Sicily and Tuscany Compared', *Past and Present* 130 (1991): 3–50, and 'Town and Country: Economy and Institutions in Late Medieval Italy', *Economic History Review* 46(1993): 453–77. See also S. R. Epstein, *An Island for Itself: Economic Development and Social Change in Late Medieval Sicily* (Cambridge, 1992).

37 Paolo Malanima, 'La formazione di una regione economica: La Toscana nei secoli XIII–XV', *Società e storia* 20(1983): 229–69, and 'Politica ed economia nella formazione dello Stato regionale: Il caso toscano', *Studi veneziani* n.s. 11(1986): 61–72. For an early exploration of the incorporation of a provincial city into a territorial state, in this case the Republic of Florence, see David Herlihy, *Medieval and Renaissance Pistoia: The Social History of an Italian Town* (New Haven, 1958).

38 Malanima, 'La formazione di una regione economica', 229.

39 L. Frattarelli Fischer, 'Livorno città nuova: 1574–1609', *Società e Storia* 46(1989): 872–93.

40 Levi, 'Come Torino soffocò il Piemonte'.

41 On the need for a dynamic history of the formation of states, see Fasano Guarini, 'Gli stati dell'Italia centro-settentrionale tra Quattro e Cinquecento: Continuità e transformazioni', *Società e storia* 21(1983): 617–39. On the relation between the development of the state and the formation of economic regions between the fifteenth and seventeenth centuries, see the observations by M. Mirri, 'Formazione di una regione economica: Ipotesi sulla Toscana, sul Veneto, sulla Lombardia', *Studi veneziani* n.s., 11(1986): 47–59.

42 Raffestin, *Pour une géographie du pouvoir*, 129ff.

43 Chittolini, 'Stati padani, "Stato del Rinascimento"'.

Part III

INDIVIDUALISM, IDENTITY
AND GENDER

Italy began to swarm with individuality; the ban laid upon human personality was dissolved; and a thousand figures meet us each in its own special shape and dress.

Burckhardt

The Renaissance has often been seen as a watershed in the history of individualism – indeed Burckhardt viewed this as the age in which the 'individual' first emerged as a major force in modern history. But recently scholars have rethought this claim from a number of angles, suggesting that the 'individual' is to a large degree a cultural fiction, the sources of which can be found in a vast array of social, political and sexual practices.

Samuel K. Cohn Jr. offers a fresh reading of the history of individualism from the vantage point of social history, making the case that many late medieval representations of particular persons were not, as has often been assumed, celebrations of the individual but rather memorializations of the family or lineage. Then working within a largely cultural historical perspective, Stephen J. Greenblatt attacks the idea of Renaissance individualism by arguing that for men and women of this age the belief in an internal, autonomous self was largely irrelevant. What mattered was one's social role and one's presentation of oneself in society. Renaissance social life, he suggests, was profoundly theatrical.

Another critical determinant of identity was gender. In the final two essays presented in this section, Michael Rocke and Virginia Cox offer important new interpretations of gender and sexuality in the Renaissance. Cox is attentive to social and economic forces in the construction of new notions of gender, and in particular a new theorization of women's roles, while Rocke offers a new perspective on the gender regime – and especially on the homoeroticism – of the Renaissance city. In the end, both essays make a strong case that men and women in the Renaissance lived in worlds profoundly different from our own.

Collectively, these essays raise fundamental questions about the degree to which social and political forces shaped the most basic aspects of the identity of Renaissance men and women. Readers cannot help but wonder if Burckhardt's notion of the individual has any validity at all.

6

BURCKHARDT REVISITED
FROM SOCIAL HISTORY

Samuel K. Cohn, Jr.

The Renaissance has long been associated with the rise of individualism – a theory that found its most forceful exposition in Burckhardt's The Civilization of the Renaissance in Italy *(1860). Burckhardt himself was far less celebratory of individualism than many of his critics have assumed. In fact, his view of individualism was ambivalent, and he portrayed it not only as a wellspring of artistic, literary and scientific creativity, but also as a source of many of the conflicts and acts of aggression that were woven into the history of this era. Burckhardt also explained the origins of individualism not only as a consequence of the recovery of classical texts and ideals, but also as a result of the changing political structures of Italy in the late Middle Ages. For example, despotism, according to Burckhardt, fostered a new sense of individuality not only in the despot himself but also in those who served him. 'These people', Burckhardt wrote, 'were forced to know all the inward resources of their own nature ... and their enjoyment of life was enhanced and concentrated by the desire to obtain the greatest satisfaction from a possibly very brief period of power and influence'.*

Scholars long continued to find in Burckhardt a compelling account of the origins of modern individualism; and the study of humanism, in particular, lent support to the idea that the engagement by humanists with classical antiquity – with works ranging from Plato to St Augustine – helped explain a new emphasis on selfhood and identity that many have associated with the Renaissance. But social history changed this equation. First, historians such as the French Annaliste *Emmanuel Le Roy Ladurie (discussed in the essay by William James Bouwsma in Chapter 2 above), diminished the importance of such Renaissance ideas as individualism by stressing the deep continuities in social and cultural life from the eleventh to the nineteenth centuries.*

But the relation of social history to Renaissance studies has been multifaceted. In the essay below, Samuel K. Cohn, Jr. develops a comparative analysis of the efforts by men and women in six late medieval Italian cities to assert their claims to fame and glory. Burckhardt read these claims as evidence of individuality and, in a general sense, associated individuality with the emergence of a modern civilization, in which Renaissance men and women enjoyed greater freedom than their ancestors. But Cohn is dubious of this model. Changing economic and social arrangements in both the Florentine countryside and in Florence itself tended – Cohn has argued in a variety of studies – to restrict individual choice in much of the late fourteenth and early fifteenth centuries. Moreover, here as in many of his other works, Cohn deftly shifts the analysis away from the humanist study to the social experience of the poorer classes in Italy. In particular he offers a careful analysis of some 3,400 last wills and testaments left by artisans, labourers, peasants and other groups not traditionally associated with the rise of individualism. What Cohn finds is startling: representations of particular personages in the funerary monuments of the early Renaissance were not, as so many have assumed, expressions of individualism. To the contrary, these representations, in the wake both of the Black Death of 1347–8 and of recurrence in the early 1360s, did not celebrate an individual but rather used the image of an individual to bolster the reputation of the lineage.

Cohn's essay, in short, provides a compelling example of the way in which social history can both engage traditional questions but transform the way we view them by offering a radically new and far more inclusive history of the period. Accordingly, he occupies important middle ground between Bouwsma and Le Roy Ladurie. The essay printed below originally appeared in Languages and Images of Renaissance Italy, *ed. Alison Brown (Oxford, 1995), 217–34. For a more comprehensive treatment of this theme, see Cohn,* The Cult of Remembrance and the Black Death: Six Renaissance Cities in Central Italy *(Baltimore, 1992). And for an entirely different approach to Renaissance individualism, see the important essay by Stephen Greenblatt in the chapter that follows.*

* * *

Since publication of Jacob Burckhardt's *Civilization of the Renaissance,* social historians have extended the boundaries of his 'civilization' to encompass social groups and interests that at best he subsumed with vague phrases such as 'the faith of the people'.[1] New avenues of research, perhaps most importantly the history of the family, have recently used but have qualified Burckhardt's Renaissance, some fitting new findings into the old paradigm,[2] others rejecting it altogether.[3] The social historian might, however, go beyond a simple affirmation or negation of Burckhardt (which a psychohistorian would argue is the same thing)[4] to penetrate the categories of his generalizations, showing inconsistencies in the match between, say, individualism and modernity.

Take the development of agriculture. First, a marked transformation in the countryside did correspond *grosso modo* with the Renaissance of the late trecento and early quattrocento, at least in the *contado* of Florence[5] (for Siena, it happened earlier).[6] It was a transformation that we might argue, in Whig fashion, pointed in the direction of modernity – increased urban investment, increased productivity and an intensification of market relations. From the perspective of the peasant producer, however, an organization of production spread that ran directly counter to Burckhardt's other pillar of Renaissance 'civilization' – individualism. In the place of small individual proprietors, the *mezzadria* system or sharecropping developed. Through extended family structures, the new dependent rural labourers, the *mezzadri*, while shielded from the vagaries of bad harvests, market fluctuations and taxation, lost their earlier independence as individual peasant proprietors and, in terms of Florentine fiscality, had even lost their adulthood, with both their debts and the tax laws further subjugating them to their landlords.[7]

Similarly, I have argued in *The Laboring Classes in Renaissance Florence* that the development of a more centralized and sovereign state in quattrocento Florence created new social networks for artisans and *sottoposti* in the wool industry that pointed in the very opposite direction from Burckhardt's individualism. In contrast to the social interactions of the late fourteenth century from which city-wide forces of insurrection could arise, the communities of labourers and artisans of fifteenth-century Florence turned inward around their neighbourhood parishes; relations of propinquity and kinship as opposed to free-ranging individual choice or political ideology dominated their social interactions.[8]

Burckhardt's elitist notion of civilization may now appear naive to many social historians, and the inconsistencies between state development, individualism and modernity may seem all too easy to pry apart. I would argue, however, that in one sense his approach to the Renaissance remains more sophisticated than the one taken currently by most social, economic and political historians of the Renaissance. Instead of concentrating on a single city or city-state, his investigations ranged up and down the Italian peninsula and on occasion were truly comparative, such as his first chapter on the state, where the culture of republics was compared to that of the signories.

This essay will extend its boundaries beyond the now conventional context of a single city-state and will employ a comparative framework, but will not sing Burckhardtian praises. Instead, I seek to expose a fundamental contradiction, not only within Burckhardt's classical definition but also in what has continued as one canonical view underlying art and the literary, intellectual, political and even economic history of the Renaissance.[9] This contradiction does not lie just between one development, such as the growth of the state, and another, such as individualism, but lies at the very heart of that notion so central to Renaissance historiography: individualism. My study of just under 3,400 last wills and testaments comprising over 40,000 separate, itemized bequests from six cities in central Italy – Florence, Siena, Pisa, Arezzo, Perugia and Assisi – outlines an argument about fame and glory in the Renaissance, not along the usual lines taken from humanist propagandists and the lives of their patrician or princely patrons, but for populations that included urban workers and reached into villages well off the beaten track.[10] In each of these cities testaments can be found for peasants, artisans, and even disenfranchised labourers in the wool industry. Their final choices over the distribution of property give testimony to sentiments central to Burckhardt's Renaissance.

From the supposed capital of Renaissance culture, Florence, to the market town, Assisi, which St Francis had catapulted into the history of world religions, the second strike of pestilence, in 1362 or 1363 and the years immediately following in each of these city-states, marked a critical turning point in the history of mentalities. From fragmenting their charitable bequests into small sums sprinkled over a wide range of causes, testators began to stockpile their pious gifts, focusing on less than a handful of charities and demanding later dividends that would deliver spiritual returns as well as concrete remembrance in the terrestrial sphere. As with Petrarch's experience of 1348 and his reliving of that trauma when it returned to Milan in 1361, the attitudes towards that 'scourge against mankind' changed radically with its recurrence, for patricians as well as peasants, throughout the regions of central Italy investigated by this book. More than in 'the revival of antiquity' or the acting out of antique models of behaviour,[11] the cause of the new sensibilities toward the self and 'earthly glory' can be located in matters closer to hand and more accessible to wide swaths of the population – the immediate psychological effects of the late trecento and the double experience of plague.

This history of mentality, however, can be stripped of a Whiggish teleology always pointing to the so-called modern man. Individual fame, the cult of remembrance, and earthly glory, instead of being synonymous with 'individualism', can be shown to have been deeply embedded in the development of an ideology and social structure that was antithetical to Burckhardt's 'civilization' – a throw-back to what for him, as well as for prominent social and economic historians after him,[12] was akin to the Middle Ages and feudalism.[13] Rather than concentrating on these developments over time, in this essay I wish to focus on differences over geography. While the general transition in piety marked the histories of each of these city-states, despite the wide differences in population, wealth, economy, law, government and political culture, the testamentary practices found in them were certainly not mirror images of one another, especially in the period of the most dramatic spread of the mendicant movement's preaching and culture, in the years from the 1270s to 1363.

Since Hans Baron's monumental work[14] (and for art history as far back as Vasari's *Lives*),[15] Florence has been seen as the centrepiece of a new Renaissance mentality, which from Florence – and because of Florence – emanated throughout large parts of the Italian peninsula.[16]

More recently, historians armed with anthropological studies have railed against this 'Florentine exceptionalism' and have emphasized the city's almost timeless and spaceless 'Mediterranean' characteristics.[17] My study of thousands of individual choices over property (both pious and non-pious) suggests that neither model is suitable. Instead of Florentine 'exceptionalism' or a Mediterranean world culture, the six cities divide sharply into two groups.

By the 1270s, testators in all these places began to fragment their patrimonies, and especially their pious offerings, into numerous but tiny monetary sums. In planning for the afterlife, they practised what itinerant preachers of the mendicant orders preached. Despite lives of commercial success, accumulation and usury, hard-headed artisans, shopkeepers and merchants, when making their final arrangements for their estates and souls, strove to avoid earthly hubris and 'vain' attempts to ensure earthly memory. The grip of this mendicant mentality, however, did not hold with equal tenacity from place to place. While in three of the cities (Assisi, Pisa and Siena) the mechanisms for ensuring earthly remembrance after death hardly surface in the testaments until the recurrence of plague in 1363, in the other three (Arezzo, Florence and Perugia) the ideals of earthly fame never vanished and became more pronounced through the trecento.[18]

Not only can these differences between the two groups of cities be measured by the extent to which testators fragmented and monetized their bequests; these ideals resonate through their differences in burial practices, fidecommission clauses and other restrictions on the future flow of property, as well as in testamentary commissions for art, from monumental burial chapels to ten-lire altarpieces.

Charitable legacies abound early on in the testaments from Arezzo, Florence and Perugia, that called for earthly forms of fame and remembrance. Thus an Aretine notary[19] and son of a notary, whose will dates from 1338, concentrated his last thoughts on the preservation of prized possessions and the connections between worldly things and earthly posterity. Unlike the long itemized lists of pious bequests of paltry sums to myriad ecclesiastical institutions with few strings attached, characteristic of wills in Assisi, Siena and Pisa, the biggest portion of this testament turned on only two bequests: one set aside property to finance the construction of his burial chapel and the future flow of its *ius patronatus*; the other carefully divided his private library of 156 titles bound in sixty-six volumes between the Dominican and Franciscan houses of Arezzo. He then specified in systematic detail the friars' library privileges and the rules for preserving his collection *ad infinitum* – down to the locks and cages to secure these properties' physical preservation.[20] This gift, reminiscent of Petrarch's concern with Boccaccio dispersing his library,[21] cannot find a parallel in a large sample of Sienese testaments until 1512.[22]

Letters and libraries did not, however, constitute the main avenue through which these testators sought to leave earthly imprints of their names and reputations. Aretines, Perugians and Florentines, in marked contrast to those from the other three cities, patronized works of art from their earliest surviving testaments. While only one in a hundred from Siena before 1426 left instructions to build chapels or monumental graves, nearly one in ten from Arezzo left substantial properties for the purposes of memorializing their bones and those of their future progeny.[23] In Siena, not until the latter half of the fifteenth century did testators attempt to regulate through their wills the succession of chaplains elected to skim off the *usufructus* of their landed properties, to sponsor the singing of perpetual masses in commemoration of their own and their predecessors' souls.[24] In contrast, those from the second set of towns, like the Aretine notary, early on assumed the *ius patronatus* as a familial good and passed it down through the male line. Nor did this attention to leaving lasting memorials to accompany one's bones fall simply within the purview of the well-to-do. Those who could not afford chapels in Arezzo, Perugia and Florence often individuated their earthly remains with commissions for sculpted arms, tombstones or paintings to be placed over their graves.[25] Requests for such markers are extraordinarily rare in Assisi and Pisa until the quattrocento, and do not appear in Sienese testaments until the end of that century.[26]

Testamentary patronage of other less costly works of art also present sharp differences between the two groups of cities. In a sample of 446 testaments leaving 3,088 pious bequests before 1426, the Sienese commissioned only six paintings. In Arezzo, by contrast, the desire to leave such a concrete mark for one's earthly fame in sacred places peppered the early trecento documents and increased in frequency after the recurrence of plague. These commissions, moreover, descended the social ladder to the ranks of peasants and wage-workers.[27]

On occasion, they evoked explicitly the desire for individual immortalization through their execution and maintenance. In the year of the Black Death, for instance, the son of a blacksmith living in the Casentine town of Bibbiena, located in the bishopric of Arezzo,[28] devoted a large section of his modest will to commissioning a painting, from which he desired remembrance. First, he demanded that the painter place above the sacred figures the inscription: 'this painting has been ordered by Pasquino the son of Montagne, the donor'. Then, next to the figure of Mary, the artist was to paint 'a figure in the likeness of this person Pasquino' and on the other side, his deceased father genuflecting. Above each of them a second inscription was to make it clear: 'Here is Montagne, the Blacksmith; here is Pasquino [the son]'.[29]

112

In the same year a *condottiere* employed by Florence but living in Arezzo left all of his armour to the Aretine Misericordia – all, that is, except his helmet, which he insisted be kept everlastingly above his tomb to be constructed in the Aretine church of the Servites. In his second charitable bequest, the soldier's ardour for earthly memory outstripped the self-indulgence of the blacksmith's son. In commissioning an altar-piece for the village parish of his birthplace, the soldier did not even bother with religious figures, but instead demanded that his own figure alone appear above the altar: thus casting himself as the saintly one for future parishioners to venerate. In addition to this earthly hubris over sacred matters, the image cut by the laconic terms of this testament portrays a man straight from the pages of Burckhardt's *Civilization*. He left behind a progeny of five illegitimate children to whom he bequeathed unequal sums of money.[30] Still others left small sums for church repairs, but demanded that their munificence be remembered by ordering their names to be inscribed in the beams of their parish churches.[31]

Explicit proclamations of fame and memory come as well from Perugia. In one instance, a notary's widow ordered in an annunciation that she, the testator, be painted 'in her very likeness [*ad similtudinem*]'. This, she insisted, was to preserve 'her true memory [*sue memorie in veritate*]'.[32] Another woman from a tiny Perugian village ordered her parish to have, above her grave, where her father was previously buried, a painting of St George with her father depicted quite literally tooting his horn with one hand and with the other flying a flag inscribed with the family name and arms.[33]

Furthermore, Perugians like Aretines were not content to ponder the extraterrestrial on their deathbeds, nor while negotiating their last decisions over property in good health, but they made plans that would later shape and determine the future behaviour of their heirs and other offspring. For instance, in 1393 the last demands of a Perugian nobleman reached into the future affairs of his heirs. He left his cousin as universal heir but required him to build a bridge leading to their ancestral house. The testator further ordered the bridge to be divided equally with another man and his wife and then to remain 'perpetually' the communal property of 'all those from his house [*debeat comunis dictarum domorum*]'.[34]

More than in any other town, Perugians sought ways of circumventing the passage of their properties to those they wished to exclude from the future enjoyment and possession of their patrimonies. At the same time, they pondered the plight of future heirs even beyond their immediate children and other living members of their households. The most extraordinary provision made in these documents, in any city, for the future security of offspring and descendants came from a Perugian nobleman in 1383. The 'magnificent *miles*, dominus Franciscus, son of the late dominus Ugolinus', left his sons as his universal heirs. If they should die without sons, the dowry of his daughter was to be doubled to 2,000 florins. If all his sons and their male children should die without heirs, then his granddaughter's dowry was to be also supplemented by 1,000 florins. In these cases, his residuary estate (which included landed poss-essions and houses in nine villages) should provide the funds to build a monastery on the hill called Castellare in the village of Cordig-liano. It was to be completed within one year following his death and placed under the rule of the Olivetani. All the monks were to reside perpetually in this monastery and live well with the rights and from the fruits and resources of the legacy. If the Olivetani declined his legacy, he would substitute the Sienese hospital of Santa Maria della Scala to build a hospital on this same hill within one year. In return, the knight Lord Franciscus required of the monastery or hospital that if any of the progeny of his house, male or female, legitimate or illegitimate (*spureus*), should prove 'deficient in some faculty' and 'unable to survive on his own', then the institution was obliged to accept this descendant into their community and to provide food and clothing so long as he re-mained inscribed and obedient to the superiors of this place.[35]

The Florentine testaments fit a similar pattern in both quantitative and qualitative terms; art commissions and efforts at individual and familial immortalization appear as early as the first years of the trecento.[36] Some of these would be remarkable for any period in the wills from those cities where the grip of mendicant piety held most firmly. For instance, in 1312 Ricchuccius, a parishioner of Santa Maria Novella, sought to preserve his memory by attaching it to art. At five lire a year he financed oil to be burnt continually in the Dominican church under the crucifix 'made by the distinguished painter named Giottum Bondonis' and 'in the presence of a lantern made of bones', which, he reminded the friars, he had earlier purchased for them. He further insisted that the Prior of Santa Maria Novella and the Guardian of the Franciscans at Santa Croce, when preaching, praise the earthly deeds of this testator and those of his beloved uncle, Ricchus, recalling to their assembled congregations that both had served as captains of the *laudese* confraternity of Santa Maria Novella. These churchmen were further 'to restore to memory' the time when the testator had been the executor of his former uncle's testament, and through his uncle's largesse had 'brought honour to these friaries and to the entire province through his administration'.[37]

As the example of the blacksmith's son's commission suggests, obses-sions with leaving lasting marks on earthly posterity were not confined to the testaments of the rich and prominent. In 1343 a Florentine who doubled as a tavernkeeper and gravedigger gave a field in the rural suburb of Novoli, west of Florence, to the hospital of Santa Maria della

Scala, but required the brothers of the hospital to construct a 'walled' statue of the Madonna and Child on the road in front of his field. The Madonna, constructed with bricks, mortar, and stones, was to stand at least six *brachiorum* (or fifteen feet) above the ground.[38]

Nor were these testamentary commissions always so monumental. Florentines, Aretines and Perugians often ordered the beds they bequeathed to hospitals to be painted with coats of arms and other family regalia. In one case, a blacksmith left fourteen lire for the difficult task of adorning his bed, to be given to the poor lying in the hospital of Borgo San Lorenzo, 'with an image in the likeness of the majesty of God'.[39] Other trecento testaments from these towns demanded art that could cost a pittance: wax images of the Madonna or family coats of arms to be painted on candlestick holders to stand in sacred places in perpetuity.[40]

In the face of mendicant sermons condemning the earthly hubris grounded in temporal properties and family pride, these devotional acts attest to testators' zeal to extend their earthly traces and to immortalize their names, at least in Arezzo, Florence and Perugia. In Siena, attempts to preserve the memory of lineages by plastering holy places with family coats of arms date only from the end of the quattrocento and never penetrated the testaments of artisans. In Florence, the practice, as the biting irony of one of Franco Sacchetti's stories suggests (later to be repeated gleefully by Giorgio Vasari),[41] appears early on, reaching even members of the labouring classes.[42] The 1368 testament of a wool carder, who did not even possess a family name, required the *hospitiliarius* of Santa Maria Nuova to paint his 'arms' on a torch, which he gave to the hospital and which was to be kept burning on the hospital's altar every Sunday *in perpetuum*.[43]

Attitudes towards property found in testamentary clauses governing the flow of non-pious bequests also show the same grouping and division among the six city-states. Early on, Aretines, Florentines and Perugians used their wills to govern from the grave the succession of their properties and the future behaviour of heirs. Mazes of contingency clauses to circumvent possible future demographic eventualities or an heir's failure to fulfil conditions imposed by the testator fill the final sections of these wills. These clauses often went beyond the formula preventing heirs from alienating real property. Some insisted that sons and daughters remain obedient to their mothers, brothers or uncles or else forfeit rights to the patrimony; others blocked the future flow of property, such as gifts to married daughters, with the conditions that their husbands never touch the properties. Others demanded renovations down to architectural details. Such were the demands that can be found in the testament of one Aretine merchant. In his final itemized act, instead of beseeching his heirs to have masses sung for his soul or to distribute charitable sums, he ordered them to tear down one of his stables and to construct in its place a wrap-around veranda to a house of residence in the countryside.[44] Still others drew up complex architectural plans to divide precisely the rooms among heirs, to determine not only property rights, but even their heirs' future movements – rights of passage, the use of corridors, stairways, wells and courtyards. After one such blueprint governing the future movements of heirs, an Aretine villager from Fronzola[45] sought further to ward off future squabbles between his widow and sons by demanding that they build a partition wall to divide what had formerly been a communal courtyard.[46]

Thus far, our comparative analysis may have shown little more than that the Burckhardtian notions of fame and memory cut beneath those social levels provided by his sources and that these sentiments were stronger in some places than in others. Like the Aretine *condottiere* who left behind five illegitimate children and his helmet to glorify his grave, what could be more Burckhardtian than the individual testator asserting his individuality by attempting from the grave to govern future events in the secular realm? The roots of these geographical differences, I argue, expose relationships that contradict the very terms of Burckhardt's Renaissance as well as the views of more recent historians.

Should we look for long-term, distant origins: did Roman versus Etruscan traditions or, even further back, tribal configurations of prehistoric Italy, underlie these patterns found for the late duecento and early trecento? Or, closer to our findings, did the invasions and three-centuries-long dominance of the Lombards create a social fabric for understanding these long-term structures of mentality? Instead, Marc Bloch's criticisms of 'the idol of origins' appear well advised. First, the differences among the cities do not appear to have been of such ancient origins. From the earliest testaments until 1275 the differences in the choices and patterns of bequests were minimal. Second, the geographical groupings of cities and their territories do not correspond with any of these earlier settlement patterns; they do not conveniently divide along a north/south, an east/west, a Tuscan/Umbrian, or a Lombard versus Byzantine line. It was not even a matter of propinquity; the two city-states in closest proximity – Perugia and Assisi – show as radical a difference in the pre-plague patterns of piety as any two towns in this analysis. Third, had the fifth-century invasions been the decisive force, then the area of the Duchy of Perugia, which retained Byzantine rule and Roman law, should have shown distinctive characteristics in the later Middle Ages.

Nor do these two triads of city-states divide according to population size or wealth. The political histories of these places also fail to lend much help. True, Florence and Perugia were traditional Guelf strongholds, but Arezzo and Pisa (where testamentary giving represented opposite sides of the spectrum) were the bastions of Ghibelline power in central Italy. Nor can we point to the form of government; the two city-states which placed the reins of control under the *signoria* with a single noble family were again at opposite ends – Pisa and Arezzo. Moreover, the importance of anti-magnate laws and the extent to which nobles were able to share in the political power of the mercantile elites during the trecento explains little. Two of the city-states where testators attempted more force-fully to preserve earthly memory and to manipulate future events from the grave were also ones again on opposite ends of the spectrum. While the Florentine Ordinances of Justice of 1293 became emblematic of the anti-magnate legislation sweeping through northern and central Italy in the late duecento and early trecento, the feudal lords from the rural Casentino (Pietramala) took control over Arezzo at the beginning of the trecento. In addition, these patterns over space do not correspond with religious char-acteristics, such as Domini-can popularity versus Franciscan. While sugg-estive when Dominican Florence[47] is compared with Franciscan Assisi, the correspondence ceases to hold when the other cities come into the analysis. In Arezzo, the Franciscan influence looms large in the literary and artistic evidence as well as in the statistics of pious bequests. In this early city of humanist learning, the Dominicans did not even rank second among the mendicant orders.[48]

Nor does the presence of universities help us along. Four of these cities – Perugia,[49] Siena,[50] Arezzo,[51] and to a lesser extent Pisa[52] – possessed venerable universities before the Black Death, but they do not correspond to those cities that championed a zeal for remembrance early on. The link between early centres of humanist learning and the cult of remembrance might be offered as the key for explaining the patterns of piety in Florence and Arezzo,[53] but then how is Pisa, on the other side of the spectrum in testamentary giving, to be explained – a centre of learning equal to or even more important than these cities in the late duecento?[54] Finally, despite Paul Grendler's recent and excellent overview on schooling in the Renaissance, we still know little about differences in the systems and organizations of education from city-state to city-state, especially before the quattrocento.[55] The one systematic comparative study with which I am familiar draws a distinction between the emphasis on merchant and mathematical learning in Florence as against a more literary emphasis found for Arezzo.[56] But these two cities, as we have found, were similar in their early patterns of piety and in the emphasis placed on the self and lineage.

The one structural characteristic that does correlate closely with these differences over space is the importance of the male line in property descent and its corollary, the disadvantageous property status of women.

Where concern with the souls and memory of ancestors and the devolution of property through the patrilines were strong, mendicant values proved less hegemonic. Here, at the heart of Burckhardt's classic formulation of Renaissance individualism, lies a crucial contradiction. Those societies where testators were most obsessed with earthly glory and the preservation of memory, whether achieved through clauses blocking the alienation of property or through the construction of burial complexes advertising the profane symbols of family pride, were also the ones where testators were governed most by the constraints of their ancestors. These testators' attempts to govern from the grave the future behaviour of religious beneficiaries and heirs might well be interpreted as evidence for the assertion of 'individualism' – what Stephen Greenblatt calls 'the attempt to fashion other selves'.[57] At the same time, however, these assertions of individualism acted on the societal level, creating a barrage of new restrictions on the free and individual disposition of property not only for heirs but for subsequent generations of testators. In addition, testators' efforts to memorialize their corporeal remains and to establish ancestral graves reverberated through the individual burial choices of future generations of testators. By the end of the trecento, especially women in Arezzo, Florence and Perugia rarely made independent choices any longer over their corporeal remains; they were either buried in the tombs of their husbands' lineages or, if unmarried, in those of their fathers.[58]

Furthermore, in those societies where the ideals of earthly memory were more in evidence early on, women certainly exercised less individual choice in their discretionary power over property than where mendicant values dampened any zeal for earthly self-preservation. Far from exemplifying the status of women, Florence, where the cult of remembrance was as strong as anywhere studied in this essay, was the worst place to have been born a woman, at least in terms of power over property. Fewer Florentine women determined the individual fate of their properties through the instrument of the will, and when they did, the constraints of law – the *mundualdus* – and marriage weighed more heavily on them than elsewhere. By contrast, in Pisa, where lineage was weak and the cult of remembrance less pervasive, women redacted wills early on almost as often as men. Moreover, they commonly made their choices over free property, both dotal and non-dotal, while their husbands still lived. Unlike women in Florence – where such practice was rare and when it did occur was no less than an instrument by which the husband assumed all the earlier total control over his wife's patrimony – Pisan women customarily gave their husbands only a standard fifteen lire. Finally, husbands' property settlements for their future widows were more favourable in the three cities, Assisi, Pisa and Siena, where the mendicant patterns of self-abnegation were most entrenched. To assume the *usufructus* of the husbands' property in Arezzo, Florence and Perugia, widows customarily had to relinquish their claims to their dowries, while for the other three towns the dowry remained inviolable.

More importantly, the comparative framework brings another dimension to the very character of Renaissance individualism, fame and earthly glory. The split of the towns into two groups was not random but followed at least one underlying principle: those city-states where testators tried to hold on to earthly goods past the grave, to remain alive through legalistic contingency clauses, and to proclaim their earthly fame through commissioning works of art, were places which in Burckhardt's eyes, seen from another angle, would have appeared the most medieval and feudal. They were the ones where testators invoked most often and emphatically the ideology of lineage, and which channelled property down the male line by fidecommission clauses encumbering future generations of heirs.[59] As the examples above suggest, testators in Arezzo, Florence and Perugia strove for earthly remembrance, fame and glory, but not as individuals cut from the moorings of their *domus* or clan. Rather the fame and memory these individuals expressed was that of the lineage. Their memory was inextricably bound with that of their ancestors, and family lineage provided the very channels by which this new 'this-worldly' reputation was to be perpetuated. Renaissance fame, in other words, ran down the veins of male bloodlines. In conclusion, individual choice over property for men and especially women from patrician as well as peasant families was stronger in those societies – Pisa, Siena and Assisi – where mendicant preachers had been more successful in encouraging testators to believe that family and other earthly goods were transitory matters 'held on loan', as Saint Catherine[60] railed, and 'impediments to the soul', as Francesco Petrarch proclaimed in his Augustinian-inspired last will and testament.[61]

Notes

1   J. Burckhardt, *The Civilization of the Renaissance in Italy*, trans. S. G. C. Middlemore (London, 1878; 1st edn 1860).

2   See for instance Richard Goldthwaite, *Private Wealth in Renaissance Florence: A Study of Four Families* (Princeton, 1968); *idem*, 'The Florentine Palace as Domestic Architecture', *American Historical Review* 77(1972): 977–1012; *idem*, *The Building of Renaissance Florence: An Economic and Social History* (Baltimore, 1980); *idem*, 'The Medici Bank and the World of Capitalism', *Past and Present* 114(1987): 3–31; *idem*, 'The Empire of Things: Consumer Demand in Renaissance Italy', in F. W. Kent and Patricia Simons (eds) *Patronage, Art and Society in Renaissance Italy* (Oxford, 1987), 153–75.

3   F. W. Kent, *Household and Lineage in Renaissance Florence: The Family Life of the Capponi, Ginori and Rucellai* (Princeton, 1977); and implicitly in David Herlihy, 'Family Solidarity in Medieval Italian History', in D. Herlihy, Robert Lopez and Vsevolod Slessarev (eds) *Economy, Society and Government in Medieval*

Italy (Kent OH, 1969), 173–84; and D. Herlihy and Christiane Klapisch-Zuber, *Les Toscans et leurs familles: Une étude du catasto florentin de 1427* (Paris, 1978), 525–51.

4 See e.g. Rudolph Binion, *Soundings: Psychohistorical and Psycholiterary* (New York, 1982).

5 D. Herlihy, *Medieval and Renaissance Pistoia: The Social History of an Italian Town, 1204–1430* (New Haven, 1967), 121–47; *idem*, 'Santa Maria Impruneta: A Rural Commune in the Late Middle Ages', in N. Rubinstein (ed.) *Florentine Studies* (London, 1968), 242–76; Herlihy and Klapisch-Zuber, *Les Toscans*, 268–86.

6 Philip Jones, 'From Manor to Mezzadria', in *Florentine Studies*, 193–241; I. Imberciadori, *Mezzadria classica toscana con documentazione inedita del sec. 9 al sec. 14* (Florence, 1951); Giuliano Pinto, *La Toscana nel tardo medio evo: Ambiente, economic rurale, società* (Florence, 1982); G. Pinto and Paolo Pirillo (eds) *Il contratto di mezzadria nella Toscana medievale*, 2 vols (Florence, 1987); Stephan Epstein, *Alle origini della fattoria toscana: L'ospedale della Scala di Siena a le sue terre (metà '200 – metà '400)* (Florence, 1986).

7 Herlihy and Klapisch-Zuber, *Les Toscans*, 277–8.

8 S. K. Cohn, *The Laboring Classes in Renaissance Florence* (New York, 1980).

9 See for instance Erwin Panofsky, *Tomb Sculpture: Four Lectures on Its Changing Aspects from Ancient Egypt to Bernini*, ed. H. W. Janson (New York, 1964), 67–96; Peter Burke, *Culture and Society in Renaissance Italy, 1420–1540* (New York, 1972), 29, 251, 288; Ingo Herkoltz, *'Sepulcro' e 'Monumenta' del Medioevo* (Rome, 1985); P. O. Kristeller, 'The Immortality of the Soul', in Michael Mooney (ed.) *Renaissance Thought and Its Sources* (New York, 1979), 181–96; Stephen J. Greenblatt, *Renaissance Self-fashioning from More to Shakespeare* (Chicago, 1980), 1–9; H. Baron, 'Franciscan Poverty and Civic Wealth in Humanist Thought', *Speculum* 13(1938): 1–37; Marvin Becker, 'Individualism in the Early Italian Renaissance: Burden and Blessing', *Studies in the Renaissance* 19(1972): 273–97; *idem*, 'Aspects of Lay Piety in Early Renaissance Florence', in Heiko Oberman and Charles Trinkhaus (eds) *The Pursuit of Holiness in Late Medieval and Renaissance Religion: Papers from the University of Michigan Conference* (Leiden, 1974), 177–200; and the work of Richard Goldthwaite (see note 2 above).

10 Samuel K. Cohn, *The Cult of Remembrance and the Black Death: Six Renaissance Cities in Central Italy* (Baltimore, 1992; rev. ed. 1997).

11 Federico Chabod, 'The Concept of the Renaissance', in *Machiavelli and the Renaissance* (New York, 1958), 149–200.

12 See for instance Alfred von Martin, *Sociology of the Renaissance* (New York, 1944; German edn, Stuttgart, 1932); and more recently the work thus far cited of Richard Goldthwaite, see note 2 above).

13 For a similar critique of the literature, see my *Death and Property in Siena, 1205–1808* (Baltimore, 1988), 97–158; and Diane Hughes, 'Representing the Family: Portraits and Purposes in Early Modern Italy', *Journal of Interdisciplinary History* 17(1986): 7–38.

14 H. Baron, *The Crisis of the Early Italian Renaissance: Civic Humanism and Republican Liberty in an Age of Classicism and Tyranny*, 2 vols (Princeton, 1955); other works roughly contemporaneous with Baron's heralded a similar interpretation, see e.g. E. Garin, *L'Umanesimo italiano* (Bari, 1952), translated as *Italian Humanism* (New York, 1965); *idem* (ed.) *Portraits from the Quattrocento*, trans. Victor and Elizabeth Velen (New York, 1972); Myron Gilmore, *The World of Italian Humanism, 1453–517* (New York, 1952).

15 G. Vasari, *Le vite de' più eccellenti pittori, scultori a architettori: nelle redazioni del 1550 a 1568*, eds Rosanna Bettarini and Paola Barocchi (Florence, 1966–).

16 One can certainly cite earlier examples in which Florence featured prominently as the highest expression or spearhead of a new Renaissance culture: Heinrich Leo, *Entwicklung der Verfassung der lombardischen Städte bis zu der ankunft Kaiser Friedrich I* (Hamburg, 1824); or even, 'Leonardo Bruni, *Oratio de Laudibus Florentinae Urbis*', in H. Baron (ed.) *From Petrarch to Leonardo Bruni: Studies in Humanistic and Political Literature* (Chicago, 1968), 219–63.

17 See for instance Julius Kirshner, *Pursuing Honor while Avoiding Sin: The Monte delle doti of Florence*, in *Quaderni di 'Studi Senesi'*, no. 71 (Milan, 1978); Richard Trexler, *Public Life in Renaissance Florence* (New York, 1980); Thomas Kuehn, '"Cum Consensu mundualdi": Legal Guardianship of Women in Quattrocento Florence', *Viator* 13(1982): 309–33; Anthony Molho, 'Visions of the Florentine Family in the Renaissance', *Journal of Modern History* 50/2(1978): 304–11; Elaine G. Rosenthal, 'The Position of Women in Renaissance Florence: Neither Autonomy nor Subjection', in Peter Denley and Caroline Elam (eds) *Florence and Italy: Renaissance Studies in Honour of Nicolai Rubinstein* (London, 1988), 369–81; Ronald Weissman, *Ritual Brotherhood in Renaissance Florence*; and more emphatically, *idem*, 'Taking Patronage Seriously: Mediterranean Values and Renaissance Society', in *Patronage, Art and Society in Renaissance Italy*, 25–45; P. Gavitt, *Charity and Children in Renaissance Florence* (Ann Arbor, 1990), 79, 84, 279; and most objectionably, Peter Burke, *Historical Anthropology of Early Modern Italy* (Cambridge, 1987).

18 Cohn, *The Cult of Remembrance*, ch. 3.

19 Although this testator is not identified in his testament as a notary, and in fact carries the title of 'Dominus', Ubaldo Pasqui, in 'La biblioteca di Ser Simone figlio di ser Benvenuto di Bonaventura della Tenca', *Archivio storico italiano* 54(1889): 250–5, claims that 'Ser' Simone was born around 1280, was a notary and either a judge or a lawyer and taught at the university (Studio aretino) as a Maestro.

20 *Archivio di Stato*, Florence (hereafter *ASF*), *Diplomatico* (hereafter, *Dipl.*), Domenicani di Arezzo, 1338.viii.12. According to Ubaldi, 'La biblioteca', 251, Simoneus' desires for the perpetual preservation of his library were thwarted, and his library dispersed in the campaigns of 1381 and 1384, when marauding bands of French and Italian soldiers 'barbarously' sacked churches, monasteries and private residences, 'robbing books and furnishings of every sort'. Helen Wieruszowski, 'Arezzo as a Center of Learning and Letters in the Thirteenth Century', *Traditio* 9(1953): 321–91, esp. 382–3; and in *Atti Memorie della Academia Petrarca di Lettere, Arti Scienze* n.s., 34(1968–9): 2–82, has pointed to this library as 'another important contribution to the new (humanist) movement in Arezzo', but neither she nor anyone else has commented on the testator's passion, and the measures he demanded, to preserve his library after his death, or on other aspects of the testator's zeal for earthly immortality.

21 Petrarch, *Lettere senili*, ed. Giuseppe Fracassetti (Florence, 1869), I, 5, 44–8.

22 Cohn, *Death and Property in Siena*, 90–1.

23 Cohn, *The Cult of Remembrance*, ch. 4.

24 Cohn, *Death and Property*, 102–13.

25 Cohn, *The Cult of Remembrance*, ch. 6.

26 Cohn, *Death and Property*, 61.

27 Cohn, *The Cult of Remembrance*, ch. 7.

28 In the Valdarno casentinese, 32km north of the city; see Emanuele Repetti, *Dizionario storico delta Toscana* (Florence, 1833), i, 310–13.

29 *ASF, Dipl.*, Olivetani di Arezzo, 1348:

> conventus s. Bernardi de Aretii pingi faciant fratres predicti conventus figuram s. Mariae Virginis cum filio in bracchiis in eorum maiore ecclesie et ab uno latere figuram s. Iohannis Evangeliste, et ab alio late ere figuram s. Marie Magdalene, figuram s. Antoni cum litteris ... si cum hac ipsius fieri fecit Pasquinus f[ilius] q[uondam] Montagne eius donator. Et ab una figura Virginis Marie pingatur unam ymaginem persone ipsius Pasquini et ab alia parte ymaginem Montagne olim patris sui genibus-flexis et dicatur a capite cuius eorum 'hic ist Montagne Mareschalchus, hic est Pasquinus Montagne'.

30 *Archivio di Capitolare* (Arezzo), Notarile, no. 57 (Pace Pucci), fols 143v–151v (1348.ix.21). 'Item reliquit ... ecclesie sancti Antonii de Tragetto 25 florini de auris ... in pictura et pro pictura facienda in ipse ecclesie de persona dicti testatoris ...'

31 For instance the Aretine Pierozius, son of the notary Federigi, in his 1374 will gave ten florins to repair the roof of the church of Saints Cosma and Damiano. For this charity, he demanded that his name be inscribed in one of the beams ('et ponatur inscribatur in ligno tetti nominem dicti testatoris'). *Archivio dei Laici* (hereafter *Arch. dei Laici*), reg.726, ff.60–61C (1374.vi.2).

32 *Archivio di Stato, Perugia* (hereafter, *ASPr*), Pergamene, Monte Morcino, no. 228 (1389.iii.4).

33 *ASPr*, Notarile, Protocolli, no. 22, fol. 110 r–v (1401.vi.26).

34 *Ibid.*, no. 7, fol. 84 r–v (1393.v.26).

35 *ASPr*, Pergamene, Monte Morcino, no. 202 (1383.xi.5).

36 Cohn, *The Cult of Remembrance*, ch. 7.

37 *ASF, Dipl.*, S. M. Novella (1312.vi.15).

38 *ASF, Dipl.*, S. Maria Nuova (1343.iv.25).

39 *Ibid.* (1323.ix.21).

40 Cohn, *The Cult of Remembrance*, ch. 6.

41 Vasari, *Vite*, 'Vita di Giotto', testo II, 120–1.

42 F. Sacchetti, *Il Trecentonovelle*, ed. Antonio Lanza (Florence, 1984), no. lxiii, 122–3, 'A Giotto, gran dipintore, a dato uno palvese a dipingere da un uomo di picciolo affare. Egli, facendosene scheme, to dipinge per forma the colui rimane confuso'. Sacchetti concludes with the following moral about those who do not know their place: 'osi costui, non misurandosi, fu misurato; the ogni tristo vuol fare arma a far casati; a cotali the li loro padri seranno stati trovati agli ospedali'.

43 *ASF, Dipl.*, Osp. di S. M. Nuova, 1368.viii.24.

44 *ASF*, Not. antecos., no. 9981, 38v–42v, 1416.viii.5.

45 Fronzola, Frongola, Fronzola, Fonzano: about 2km south of Poppi in the Valdarno casentinese: Repetti, *Dizionario storico*, ii, 347.

46 *Arch. dei Laici*, reg.726, 51–2, 1374.v.23; these points are elaborated on at length in Cohn, *The Cult of Remembrance*, ch. 5, 'Property'.

47 In addition to the statistics on pious giving presented here, see Frederick Antal, *Florentine Painting and Its Social Background: The Bourgeois Republic before Cosimo de' Medici's Advent to Power: XIV and early XV Centuries* (London, 1947), 74; and Daniel Lesnick, *Preaching in Medieval Florence: The Social World of Franciscan and Dominican Spirituality* (Atlanta, 1989).

48 See Cohn, *The Cult of Remembrance*, ch. 2.

49 See Giuseppe Ermini, 'Fattori di successo dello studio perugino delle origini', *Storia e arte in Umbria nell'età comunale: Atti del VI Convegno di Studi Umbri, Gubbio 26–30 maggio 1968*, part 2 (Perugia, 1971), 289–309; and *idem*, *Storia dell'Università di Perugia*, 4 vols (Florence, 1971–5).

50 Peter Denley, 'Academic Rivalry and Interchange: the Universities of Siena and Florence', in Denley and Elam (eds) *Florence and Italy*, 194:

> The thirteenth century saw the beginnings of two Tuscan *studi*, that of Arezzo, which dates almost from the beginning of the century, and that of Siena, whose origins can be traced back to documents of the 1240s, but which formally opened in 1275. (194)

51 Wieruszowski, 'Arezzo as a center for learning and letters in the thirteenth century', *Traditio* 9(1953): 321–91; and Robert Black, *Benedetto Accolti and the Florentine Renaissance* (Cambridge, 1985), 17ff.; Corrado Lazzeri and Guglielmino Ubertini, *Vescovo di Arezzo (1248–1289) e i suoi tempi* (Florence, 1920), 103–13; the 1255 statutes of the Aretine studium are the oldest of any university.

52 Angelo Fabroni, *Historia Academiae Pisanae*, 3 vols (Pisa, 1791–5).

53 See most recently, R. Black, 'Humanism and Education in Renaissance Arezzo', *I Tatti Studies* 3(1989): 171–237.

54 See Ignazio Baldelli, 'La letteratura volgare in Toscana dalle Origini ai primi decenni del secolo XIII', in *Letteratura italiana: Storia a geografia 1: L'eta Medievale* (Turin, 1987), 69–70:

> Parallelamente al fiorire del volgare scritto, rilevante la presenza della cultura latina a Pisa ... I maggiori centri di produzione dei piú antichi testi volgari sono anche fra i maggiori centri di letteratura, a tatti i livelli, in latino. ... Nell'area toscana, la coincidenza fra presenza culturale latina e attività in volgare scritto a patente a Pisa. ... La prima città in cui si coglie la novità della scrittura monumentale non isolata, ma anzi come prassi difusa, è Pisa, la prima città in Italia e in Europa.

> See also Armando Petrucci, *La scrittura: Ideologia a rappresentazione* (Turin, 1986), 3–15.

55 Paul Grendler, *Schooling in Renaissance Italy: Literacy and Learning 1300–1600* (Baltimore, 1989).

56 Black, 'Humanism and Education'.

57 Greenblatt, *Renaissance Self-fashioning*, 3.

58 Cohn,*The Cult of Remembrance*, ch. 4

59 *Ibid.*, ch. 5; also see Cohn, 'The place of the dead in Flanders and Tuscanny'

60 *I, Catherine: Selected Writings of St Catherine of Siena*, eds and trans. Kenelm Foster and Mary J. Ronayne (London, 1980), letter to monna Giovanna of Siena, 132–3.

61 *Petrarch's Testament*, ed. Theodore Mommsen (Ithaca NY, 1957). For further compactive insights and dimensions to the conclusions drawn in this essay, see my 'The place of the dead in Flanders and Tuscanny: towards a comparative history of the Black Death' in *The Place of the Dead: Death and Remembrance in Late Medieval and Early Modern Europe*, ed. B. Gordon and P. Marshall, (Cambridge, 2000) : 17–43.

7

PSYCHOANALYSIS AND
RENAISSANCE CULTURE

Stephen Greenblatt

What was self-fashioning in the Renaissance? To scholars working within the Burckhardtian tradition, Renaissance self-fashioning was the stance an individual adopted in the way he (or she) interacted with those around him (or her). Castiglione's Book of the Courtier *(1528) is explicit about the rules one must follow to fashion oneself as a gentleman (or as a court lady). Even peasants knew something about self-fashioning. In her celebrated book* The Return of Martin Guerre *(1983), Natalie Zemon Davis offers a study of the sixteenth-century French peasant Arnauld du Tilh, his theft of another man's identity, and the quite self-conscious ways he went about fashioning himself as Martin, the husband of Bertrande de Rols. In this sense, we might read self-fashioning as a wilful decision made by a particular individual to play a certain role, whether ennobling and dignified (as in the case of the courtier) or at the very least disingenuous and self-serving (as in the case of Arnauld).*

However, in his highly-influential book Renaissance Self-Fashioning: From More to Shakespeare, *first published in 1980, the brilliant English literary historian Stephen Greenblatt introduced the term 'self-fashioning' with a radically different sense in mind. To Greenblatt, self-fashioning is not the way in which people fashioned themselves, but rather the way in which certain political and religious forces in the Renaissance created the fiction of individual autonomy in the first place. His argument, in short, is about the ways in which cultural and political structures gave form to the idea of the individual – an argument deeply indebted to cultural anthropology and the work of the French philosopher Michel Foucault. Thus, rather than viewing the individual as a free-standing agent, Greenblatt sees the individual as a cultural artefact. The result of this view, at the level of elite culture, is a shift away from the romantic conception of famous artists or authors as 'geniuses' who created great works by giving expressions to their deepest beliefs, feelings or longings – a notion shared by many who take a psychoanalytic approach to Renaissance texts – to a view that stresses the way one's location in a particular society, a particular political regime, or a particular cultural ambience shaped one's artistic production. But self-fashioning can be extended to a consideration of the lives of other social strata as well, as Greenblatt does in his analysis of the case of Martin Guerre in the essay below.*

Taking explicit aim at romanticized or psychoanalytic interpretations that would valorize individual agency in such a way that 'it would appear that Arnaud du Tihl can manipulate appearances ... but he cannot seize the other man's inner life', Greenblatt responds that such an interpretative framework is 'irrelevant' to our efforts to understand the Renaissance world. As Greenblatt notes, in sixteenth-century France, even as doubts began to be cast on du Tihl's identity, 'no one bothers to invoke Martin's biological individuality or even his soul, let alone an infancy that would have seemed almost comically beside the point'. To the contrary, Greenblatt concludes that the case of Martin Guerre offers compelling evidence that early modern identity was not based on 'an authentic self beneath', but rather demonstrates that '[t]here is no layer deeper, more authentic, than theatrical self-representation'.

'Psychoanalysis and Renaissance Culture' was first published in Literary Theory/Literary Texts, *eds Patricia Parker and David Quint (Baltimore, 1986), 210–24 and again in Greenblatt's* Learning to Curse: Essays in Early Modern Culture *(London: Routledge, 1990), 131–45. It not only constitutes a provocative companion piece to Natalie Davis'* The Return of Martin Guerre, *it has also led to a fundamental unravelling of most of the traditional pieties about the nature of Renaissance individualism. Indeed, no single thinker has had a greater influence on the development of Renaissance studies in the last twenty years than Greenblatt.*

* * *

An experience recurs in the study of Renaissance literature and culture: an image or text seems to invite, even to demand, a psycho-analytic approach and yet turns out to baffle or elude that approach. The bafflement may only reflect the interpreter's limitations, the melancholy consequence of ignorance or resistance or both. But I will argue here that the mingled invitation and denial has a more historical dimension; the bafflement of psychoanalytic interpretation by Renaissance culture is evident as early as Freud's own suggestive but deeply inadequate attempts to explicate the art of Leonardo, Michelangelo and Shakespeare. The problem, I suggest, is that psycho-analysis is at once the fulfilment and effacement of specifically Renaissance insights: psychoanalysis is, in more than one sense, the end of the Renaissance.

Let me sketch what I mean by turning not to a literary text, but to a series of documents that constitute the historical record of the case of Martin Guerre. This record, part of which formed the basis of a fine historical novel by Janet Lewis, *The Wife of Martin Guerre*, has recently been amplified and analysed with great power by the historian Natalie Zemon Davis in a short book called *The Return of Martin Guerre*, and dramatized in a French film of the same title.[1]

The story is this: Martin Guerre was the only son of a prosperous French peasant who owned and farmed a property near the village of Artigat, in southwestern France. In 1538, at the tender age of fourteen, Martin was betrothed to Bertrande de Rols – a fine match for the Guerre family – but the marriage was not consummated: Martin was thought to be the victim of sorcery, and his humiliating impotence continued for eight years until the charm was finally lifted by a series of religious rituals. Bertrande became pregnant and gave birth to a son, who was given Martin's father's Basque name, Sanxi.

Martin's problems were far from over. In 1548 he seems to have had a terrible quarrel with his father, a quarrel that was almost certainly over the control and management of the family property. Accused by his father of a theft of grain, the troubled young man turned his back on parents, wife, son and patrimony, and disappeared without a trace.

Years passed. Martin's mother and father died, and in the absence of the heir the property was managed by his paternal uncle. Unable to remarry, Bertrande raised her son and waited. Then, in the summer of 1556, Martin Guerre returned. He had wandered across the Pyrenees, become a servant, then enlisted as a soldier and fought in the Spanish wars in the Netherlands. Now he seemed a changed man, kinder and less troubled. There is evidence that his resumed marriage was more loving – recorded gestures of tenderness and concern – and in the three years that followed Bertrande gave birth to two daughters. But there were also signs of strain between himself and his uncle, once again over the family property, and in 1559 this strain erupted into a series of court battles that culminated in the accusation that this was not in fact Martin Guerre but an imposter.

The extraordinary trial that followed had as its purpose the determination of the identity of the man who claimed to be Martin Guerre. Most of the inhabitants of Artigat and many from the surrounding villages were called as witnesses – from Martin's four sisters who testified that the man on trial was in fact their brother, to neighbours and friends who were divided: some upholding his claim, others swearing that he was an imposter, still others refusing to identify the prisoner one way or another. There were rumours, eagerly backed by the uncle's party, that the real Martin Guerre had lost a leg while serving as a soldier. Bertrande officially joined in the uncle's complaint, but in court she refused to swear that the defendant was not Martin Guerre, and she was seen during the period of the trial ministering to her husband, even washing his feet. It appeared either that she had been forced to become a plaintiff against her will or that she hoped that this trial would settle once and for all the question of identity, and hence authority, in her husband's favour. Her husband himself took the stand and recalled in great detail events from his childhood and adolescence that only the real Martin Guerre could have known.

The case dragged on through this trial, at the end of which the prisoner was found guilty, and then through an appeal before the Parlement of Toulouse. Finally, all the evidence had been sifted, and the court prepared its verdict, which seemed likely to be in favour of the accused and against the uncle. At this point, and without warning, a man with a wooden leg appeared in the courtroom. Bitterly upbraiding Bertrande for having dishonoured him, the man declared that he was the real Martin Guerre. The accused insisted that this was someone hired by the desperate uncle, but virtually all the witnesses now agreed that the one-legged man was in fact Martin Guerre. After the court found for the uncle, the accused man finally confessed that he was an impostor, one Arnaud du Tilh, alias Pansette. At first, it seems, he had merely intended to take advantage of his striking resemblance to Martin Guerre in order to rob the gullible household, but he had fallen in love with Bertrande and decided to assume forever the missing man's identity. Bertrande herself denied any complicity, but it is difficult to know where else Arnaud would have gone for the intimate family history, and though in Janet Lewis' novel Bertrande only senses gradually and very belatedly that her returned husband is an imposter, Natalie Davis suggests, with considerable plausibility, that the wife would have known almost at once. This certainly seems to have been Martin Guerre's own bitter conclusion.

On 16 September 1560, Arnaud du Tilh knelt barefoot in a white shirt before the church in Artigat, formally repented of his crime, and asked the forgiveness of all whom he had offended. This ritual of penitence completed, he was led to the Guerre house, in front of which a gibbet had been erected. Mounting the ladder, he asked Martin Guerre to be kind to Bertrande who had been, he declared, entirely innocent. He asked Bertrande's pardon. Arnaud du Tilh, alias Pansette, was then hanged and his corpse burned.

This case, which interested Montaigne, among others, seems to solicit psychoanalytic interpretation. Surrounded by his four sisters, his nurse and his mother, betrothed at an unusually early age, and thrust, with the familiar rowdy folk rituals, towards adult sexuality, Martin had great difficulty establishing himself in his masculine identity. He was only able to consummate the marriage after he had radically externalized the psychic threat by imagining that he had been bewitched and by undergoing a ritual cure. And when his masculinity was finally confirmed by the birth of the son to whom he gave his father's name, Martin evidently felt compelled to try to displace his father altogether – with a theft, significantly, of his father's grain, his seed. But the attempt was a disastrous failure: his father responded violently, and Martin faced an assault not merely upon his fragile masculinity, but upon his entire identity, an identity from which in effect he fled.

Not only are Martin's impotence, Oedipal transgression and flight the classic materials of Freudian speculation, but the subsequent trial seems to confirm a principle essential to the constitution of the Freudian subject: the real Martin Guerre cannot be definitively robbed of his identity, even when he has apparently abandoned it and even when its superficial signs have been successfully mimicked by a cunning impostor. To be sure, this principle of inalienable self-possession would appear far indeed from Freud's characteristic concerns: the subject of Freud is most often encountered in states of extreme alienation. Driven by compulsions over which it has little or no control, haunted by repressed desires, shaped by traumatic experiences that it can neither fully recall nor clearly articulate, the self as Freud depicts it is bound up not with secure possession but with instability and loss. Such articulation of identity as exists occurs in states of self-abandonment – in dreams and parapraxes – and the self seems lost not only to others but to the cunning representations of others within the self. No mere judicial procedure, no simple execution of the impostor, could suffice to make restitution for this theft of identity, for the criminal is already ensconced within the psyche of the victim.

Yet the intensity of Freud's vision of alienation would seem, in much of his writing, to depend upon the dream of authentic possession, even if that possession is never realized and has never been securely established. There is nothing radically new about an anthropology based upon the desire for the recovery of what was lost and yet was never actually possessed: it is already subtly articulated in Augustine, for whom fallenness is defined in terms of an innocence from which all existing humans, including infants, are by definition excluded. What needs to be posited is not an actual, historical moment of possession, but a virtual possession, a possession that constitutes a structurally determinative prehistory. The hysteric in Freud may be alienated from her own body – earlier centuries would postulate a demonic agent to account for comparable symptoms – but the alienation implies at least a theoretically prior stage of non-alienation. There are in fact moments in Freud in which he appears to glimpse such a stage actually embodied in the regal figure of His Majesty the Infant. And if the historical impact of Freud is bound up with a sustained lese majesty, that is, with an assault on the optimistic assumption of a centred, imperial self, the network of psychoanalytic scandals – the unconscious, repression, infantile sexuality, primary process – nevertheless confirms at least the romantic assumption behind that discredited optimism: the faith that the child is the father of the man and that one's days are bound each to each in biological necessity.

This necessity secures the continuity of the subject, no matter how self-divided or dispersed, so that the Rat Man, for example, is still himself when he is acting under compulsions he does not comprehend.

Identity in Freud does not depend upon existential autonomy; it is far more often realized precisely at moments in which the executive agency of the will has been relinquished. Freud's tormented subjects may lose everything, but, as Freud's narrative case studies eloquently attest, they do not and cannot lose a primal, creatural individuation. This irreducible identity is not necessarily a blessing; on the contrary, it most often figures as a burden. Along with the secret of incestuous fantasy, the Oedipus myth discloses the tragic inescapability of continuous selfhood.

We may propose then that in Freud individuation characteristically emerges at moments of risk or alienation, and hence that those moments do not so much disrupt as secure authentic identity. And with this perception we may return to Martin Guerre, for the consequence of his self-loss was to trigger a communal inquiry into the authentic Martin Guerre. This inquiry was based upon – or helped to fashion – a communal conviction that there was an authentic Martin Guerre, authentic even (or perhaps especially) in his moments of flight and eclipse. Had the one-legged man never returned, the impostor would nevertheless have remained an actor, forever at one remove from his role. Arnaud du Tilh can manipulate appearances, he can draw the surrounding world into complicity with a strategy of deception, he can improvise the mannerisms and insinuate himself into the complex social network of Martin Guerre, but he cannot seize the other man's inner life. The testimony of the community is important – in the court of law, indispensable – but the roots of Martin's identity lie deeper than society; they reach down, as psychoanalysis would assure us, through the frail, outward memories of his sisters and friends to the psychic experience of his infancy – the infancy only he can possess and that even the most skilful impostor cannot appropriate – and beneath infancy to his biological individuality.

It is here in the body's uniqueness and irreducibility, and in the psychic structures that follow from this primary individuation, that the impostor's project must come to grief. Two bodies cannot occupy the same space at the same time; my body is mine until I die, and no improvisation, however cunning, can ever overturn that elementary possession. The mind can play strange tricks, but the body will not be mocked. Martin's identity is guaranteed by the same bodily principle that guarantees the identity of Freud's patients, twisting away from themselves in a thousand tormenting ways, alienated and abused more cunningly by their own inward ruses than ever Martin was abused by Arnaud, and yet permanently anchored, even to their own horror, in the lived experience of their unique bodily being.

But these latter conclusions, though they are ones with which I myself feel quite comfortable, are not ones drawn either explicitly or implicitly by anyone in the sixteenth century. They are irrelevant to the point of being unthinkable: no one bothers to invoke Martin's biological individuality or even his soul, let alone an infancy that would have seemed almost comically beside the point.[2] This irrelevance need not in itself discourage us – the universalist claims of psychoanalysis are unruffled by the indifference of the past to its categories. It may in any case be argued that we are encountering not indifference but either a technical exclusion of certain postulates from a legal proceeding where they have no standing, or a self-evidence so deep and assured that the postulates quite literally go without saying. But I think it is worth noting that the canniest Renaissance observer of the case, Montaigne – also the canniest Renaissance observer of the self – draws conclusions that are quite the opposite to those we have drawn. Far from concluding that the trial vindicates or rests upon Martin Guerre's ultimate and inalienable possession of his own identity – a possession intensified in the experience of self-loss – Montaigne writes that the condemnation of the alleged impostor seemed to him reckless. He would have preferred a still franker version of the verdict that the Areopagites were said to have handed down in perplexing cases: 'Come back in a hundred years'. For, writes Montaigne, if you are going to execute people, you must have luminously clear evidence – 'A tuer les gens, il faut une clarté lumineuse et nette' – and there was no such clarity in the trial of Martin Guerre.[3]

I do not mean to suggest that psychoanalysis by contrast would have supported the execution of Arnaud; on the contrary, by complicating and limiting society's conception of responsibility, psychoanalysis would seem to have made it more difficult to execute convicted murderers, let alone non-violent impostors. But diminished responsibility is not diminished selfhood; indeed, for psychoanalysis the self is at its most visible, most expressive, perhaps most interesting at moments in which the moral will has ceded place to the desires that constitute the deepest stratum of psychic experience. The crucial historical point is that for Montaigne, as for the judge at the trial, Jean de Coras, what is at stake in this case is not psychic experience at all but rather a communal judgment that must, in extraordinary cases, be clarified and secured by legal authority. Martin's body figured prominently in the trial, but not as the inalienable phenomenological base of his psychic history; it figured rather as a collection of attributes – lines, curves, volumes (that is, scars, features, clothing, shoe size, and so on) – that could be held up against anyone who claimed the name and property of Martin Guerre. The move is not from distinct physical traits to the complex life experience generated within, but outward to the community's determination that this particular body possesses by right a particular identity and hence a particular set of possessions. At issue is not Martin Guerre as subject but Martin Guerre as object, the placeholder in a complex system of possessions, kinship bonds, contractual relationships, customary rights and ethical obligations. Arnaud, the court ruled, had no right to that place, and the state had the obligation to destroy him for trying to seize it. Martin's subjectivity – or, for that matter, Arnaud's or Bertrande's – does not any the less exist, but it seems peripheral, or rather, it seems to be the *product* of the relations, material objects and judgments exposed in the case rather than the *producer* of these relations, objects and judgments. If we may glimpse analysable selves – identities that invite deep psychological speculation – these selves seem brought into being by the institutional processes set in motion by Arnaud's imposture. Psychoanalysis is, from this perspective, less the privileged explanatory key than the distant and distorted consequence of this cultural nexus.

In a remarkable essay, Leo Spitzer observed years ago that medieval writers seem to have had little or no 'concept of intellectual property' and consequently no respect for the integrity or propriety of the first-person pronoun.[4] A medieval writer would incorporate without any apparent concern the experiences of another into his own first-person account; indeed he would assume the 'I' of another. In such a discursive system, psychoanalytic interpretation seems to me crippled: it is only when proprietary rights to the self have been secured – rights made most visible, we may add, in moments of self-estrangement or external threat – that the subject of psychoanalysis, both its method and the materials upon which it operates, is made possible. The case of Martin Guerre is, to be sure, a remarkable oddity, and I could scarcely claim that by itself it secured much beyond the early death of a gifted impostor. But I suggest that the accumulation of institutional decisions and communal pressures of the kind revealed there did help to fashion the historical mode of self-hood that psychoanalysis has tried to universalize into the very form of the human condition.

This attempted universalization is not the result of a mere blunder or of overweening hermeneutic ambition, for there exist, after all, complex forms of self-consciousness and highly discursive personhood in the West long before the sixteenth century. The sense of identity secured in the trial of Arnaud du Tilh has its roots in an exceedingly rich and ancient tradition, a tradition so dense and multifaceted that it provokes simultaneously an historiographical paralysis and an interpretive license. The judicial decision to terminate the life of a man who has tried to assume the identity of another is a tiny episode in a vast history, a history without convenient narrative lines, with too many precedents, with a bewildering network of contributing and limiting factors: theology, philosophy, law, social ritual, family customs. It is deeply tempting in the face of such a history to assume that it is, in effect, no history at all, that the self is at its core a stable point of reference, a given upon which to construct interpretations, psychoanalytic or other. Such interpretations, based upon a fixed value of identity, offer the intellectual gratification – consoling in the face of a frightening accumulation of traces from the past or from other societies or from the dark corners of our own lands – of a totalizing comprehension, a harmonious vision of the whole.

But this unitary vision is achieved, as Natalie Davis' book makes clear, only by repressing history, or, more accurately, by repressing *histories* – multiple, complex, refractory stories. Such stories become, in effect, decorative incidents, filigrees enchased on the surface of a solid and single truth, or (in subtler versions) interesting variants on the central and irreducible universal narrative, the timeless master-myth.

But what if we refuse the lure of a totalizing vision? The alternative frequently proposed is a relativism that refuses to privilege one narrative over another, that celebrates the uniqueness of each cultural moment. But this stance – akin to congratulating both the real and the pretended Martin Guerre for their superb performances – is not, I think, either promising or realistic. For thoroughgoing relativism has a curious resemblance to the universalizing that it proposes to displace: both are uncomfortable with histories. Histories threaten relativism, though they seem superficially allied, because the connections and ruptures with which historians are concerned sort ill with the unorganized, value-neutral equivalences that would allow each moment a perfect independence and autonomy. The power of the story of Martin Guerre, as Natalie Davis helps us understand, lies not in an absolute otherness that compels us to suspend all our values in the face of an entirely different system of consciousness, but rather in the intimations of an obscure link between those distant events and the way we are. The actual effect of relativism is not to achieve a perfectly ethical neutrality – as if we could cleanly bracket all our beliefs and lift ourselves off our moral world – but to block a disconcerting recognition: that our identity may not originate in (or be guaranteed by) the fixity, the certainty, of our own body.

But if we reject both the totalizing of a universal mythology and the radical particularizing of relativism, what are we left with? We are left with a network of lived and narrated stories, practices, strategies, representations, fantasies, negotiations and exchanges that, along with the surviving aural, tactile and visual traces, fashion our experiences of the past, of others, and of ourselves. The case of Martin Guerre offers, in this context, neither a universal myth nor a perfectly unique and autonomous event; it is a peculiarly *Renaissance* story, the kind of story that the age told itself in a thousand variations over and over again. The point of this telling is not to confirm a truth always and already known, nor – as the fate of Arnaud poignantly exemplifies – is the telling without consequences: in the judicial murder of the impostor we witness in tiny compass part of the process that secures our concept of individual existence. That existence depends upon institutions that limit and, when necessary, exterminate a threatening mobility; the secure possession of one's body is not the *origin* of identity but one of the consequences of the compulsive cultural stabilizing unusually visible in this story.

It is important to characterize the case of Martin Guerre as a *story*, not only in order to acknowledge the way that a record of these particular lives, out of so many millions lost to our view, managed to survive in the sixteenth-century narratives of Jean de Coras and Montaigne and the twentieth-century narratives of Janet Lewis, Natalie Davis, Jean-Claude Carrière and Daniel Vigne, but also in order to make the crucial connection between this relatively obscure, local series of events and the larger historical process in which they participate. For it is in stories – above all, literary fantasies – produced and consumed by those who had never heard of Martin Guerre, that the issues raised by his case escape their immediate territorial and cultural boundaries and receive their fullest rehearsal, elaboration and exploration. And conversely, the trial and execution of Arnaud du Tilh enables us to understand aspects of the social significance of these literary fantasies that would otherwise remain obscure.

Jean de Coras' account of the Guerre case was not translated into English, nor did Montaigne's brief recounting have substantial impact, but sixteenth- and seventeenth-century English writers invented, in effect, dozens of versions of this story. The drama is particularly rich in such versions, from the larcenous impersonation of the missing husband in John Marston's play, *What You Will*, to the romantic impersonations in Beaumont and Fletcher's tragicomedies, from Perkin Warbeck's regal pretentions in John Ford's play of that name to the sleazy tricks of Ben Jonson's rogues. ('But were they gulled/With a belief that I was Scoto?' asks Volpone. 'Sir', replies the parasite Mosca, 'Scoto himself could hardly have distinguished'.) Above all, there are the instances of imposture and loss of personal moorings in Shakespeare: the buffoonery of the false Vincentio in *The Taming of the Shrew*, the geometry of the paired twins in *The Comedy of Errors*, the more impassioned geometry of *Twelfth Night*. Even when there is no malicious, accidental or natural double, Shakespeare's characters are frequently haunted by the sense that their identity has been lost or stolen: 'Who is it that can tell me who I am?', cries the anguished Lear. And in the most famous of the tragedies, the ghost of Old Hamlet – 'Of life, of crown, of queen at once dispatched' – returns to his land to demand that his son take the life of the impostor who has seized his identity.

Not by accident is it in the drama that this exploration of the issue at stake in the trial of Arnaud du Tilh is most intense, for the form of the drama itself invites reflection upon the extent to which it is possible for one man to assume the identity of another. Every theatrical performance at once confirms and denies this possibility: confirms it with varying degrees of success depending upon the skill of the actor and denies it because that skill is itself perceived by virtue of the small but unbridgeable distance between the actor's real and fictive identity. All Renaissance drama is in this sense a playful enactment of the case of Martin Guerre: a convincing impersonation before a large audience that is complicit with the deception, only to bear witness at the close to the imposture's end. In some instances the impersonation seemed less playful, more dangerous than others: powerful noblemen complained that they were themselves being represented on stage, and they successfully sought a legal prohibition of the miming of living notables. But even with fictive or long-dead characters, the drama continually celebrates the mystery of Arnaud's art: the successful insertion of one individual into the identity of another. And inevitably this celebration is at the same time an anatomy, an exposing to view of the mechanisms of imposture. What is entirely unacceptable – indeed punishable by death in the everyday world – is both instructive and delightful in spaces specially marked off for the exercise of impersonation. For in these spaces, and only in these spaces, there is by a widely shared social agreement no imposture.

It is no accident too that in virtually all of these plays – and there are other instances in Shakespeare's work and the work of his contemporaries – the intrigue that arises from the willed or accidental mistaking of one person for another centres on property and proper names: purse and person are here inseparably linked as they were in the parish records that began to be kept systematically in England only in the sixteenth century. Henry VIII's insatiable craving for money to finance his military adventures abroad and his extravagances at home led him to exact the so-called Loan of 1522, which was based upon a survey undertaken at royal command earlier that year. The survey, whose financial objectives were kept secret, required authorities in the land to certify in writing the names of all the men above the age of sixteen and 'whom they belong to'. They were to record as well

> who is the lord of every town and hamlet ... who be parsons of the same towns, and what the benefices be worth by the year ... also who be the owners of every parcel of land within any town, hamlet, parish, or village ... with the year value of every man's land within the same.[5]

The secrecy built into the survey – for were its purpose known, there would have been widespread evasion and concealment – had the effect of naturalizing the relationship between name and wealth. A man's goods were to be recorded not for the specific purpose of taxation but for the general purpose of identification: to enable the kingdom to know itself and hence to know its resources and its strength.

To the momentous survey of 1522 must be added an innovation less immediately spectacular but in the long run more important: the parish records that Cromwell instituted in 1538.[6] The parish chest, which is for historical demography what the Renaissance English theatre is for literary history, signals, along with other innovative forms of Tudor record-keeping, a powerful official interest in identity and property, and identity *as* property. Precisely this interest is voiced, tested and deepened throughout Shakespeare's career. It is often said, with a sense of irony and resignation, that though we possess a surprising amount of documentary evidence about Shakespeare's life, virtually none of it is of real significance for an understanding of his plays, for most of the surviving documents are notarial records of property transactions. I think property may be closer to the well-springs of the Shakespearean conception of identity than we imagine.

Shakespeare and his contemporaries, to be sure, knew the difference between a complex individual and what the Norwegian captain in *Hamlet* calls 'a little patch of ground/That hath in it no profit but the name'. Yet I think that in all the literary instances I have cited, identity is conceived in a way that renders psychoanalytic interpretations marginal or belated. For what most matters in the literary texts, as in the documents that record the case of Martin Guerre, are communally secured proprietary rights to a name and a place in an increasingly mobile social world, and these rights seem more an historical condition that enables the development of psychoanalysis than a psychic condition that psychoanalysis itself can adequately explain.

In Renaissance drama, as in the case of Martin Guerre, the traditional links between body, property and name are called into question; looking back upon the theatrical and judicial spectacle, one can glimpse the early stages of the slow, momentous transformation of the middle term from 'property' to 'psyche'.[7] But that transformation had by no means already occurred; it was on the contrary the result (not yet perfectly realized in our own time) of a prolonged series of actions and transactions. The consequence, I think, is that psychoanalytic interpretation seems to follow upon rather than to explain Renaissance texts. If psychoanalysis was, in effect, made possible by (among other things) the legal and literary proceedings of the sixteenth and seventeenth centuries, then its interpretive practice is not irrelevant to those proceedings, nor is it exactly an anachronism. But psychoanalytic interpretation is causally belated, even as it is causally linked: hence the curious effect of a discourse that functions *as if* the psychological categories it invokes were not only simultaneous with but even prior to, and themselves causes of, the very phenomena of which in actual fact they were the results. I do not propose that we abandon the attempts at psychologically deep readings of Renaissance texts; rather, in the company of literary criticism and history, psychoanalysis can redeem its belatedness only when it historicizes its own procedures.

There are interesting signs of this historicizing – perhaps most radically in the school of Hegelian psychoanalysis associated with the work of Jacques Lacan, where identity is always revealed to be the identity of another, always registered (as in those parish registers) in language. But I want to end with a glance at a much earlier and still powerful attempt to formulate an historical conception of the self, an attempt that significantly locates the origins of this conception in language and more specifically in literary practice.

'A PERSON', writes Hobbes,

> is he whose words or actions are considered, either as his own, or as representing the words or actions of an other man, or of any other thing to whom they are attributed, whether Truly or by Fiction. When they are considered as his owne, then is he called a Naturall Person: And when they are considered as representing the words and actions of another, then is he a Feigned or Artificiall person. The word Person is latine ... as *Persona* in latine signifies the *disguise*, or *outward appearance* of a man, counterfeited on the stage; and sometimes more particularly that part of it, which disguiseth the face, as a Mask or Visard: And from the Stage, hath been translated to any Representer of speech and action, as well in Tribunalls, as Theaters. So that a *Person* is the same that an *Actor* is, both on the Stage and in common Conversation.[8]

Psychoanalysis will in effect seize upon the concept of a 'natural person' and will develop that concept into a brilliant hermeneutical system centred upon stripping away layers of strategic displacement that obscure the self's underlying drives. But in Hobbes the 'natural person' originates in the 'artificial person' – the mask, the character on a stage 'translated' from the theatre to the tribunal. There is no layer deeper, more authentic, than theatrical self-representation. This conception of the self does not deny the importance of the body – all consciousness for Hobbes derives from the body's responses to external pressure – but it does not anchor personal identity in an inalienable biological continuity. The crucial consideration is ownership: what distinguishes a 'natural' person from an 'artificial' person is that the former is considered to *own* his words and actions. Considered by whom? By authority. But is authority itself then natural or artificial? In a move that is one of the cornerstones of Hobbes' absolutist political philosophy, authority is vested in an artificial person who represents the words and actions of the entire nation. All men therefore are impersonators of themselves, but impersonators whose clear title to identity is secured by an authority irrevocably deeded to an artificial person. A great mask allows one to own as one's own face another mask.

If we conceive of a mask (as psychoanalysis has, in effect, taught us) as a defensive strategy, a veneer hiding the authentic self beneath, then Hobbes' conception must seem brittle and inadequate. But for Hobbes there is no person, no coherent, enduring identity, beneath the mask; strip away the theatrical role and you reach either a chaos of unformed desire that must be tamed to ensure survival, or a dangerous assembly of free thoughts ('because thought is free', 3.37.478) that must – again to ensure survival – remain unspoken. Identity is only possible as a mask, something constructed and assumed, but this need not imply that identity so conceived is a sorry business. In our culture masks are trivial objects for children to play with and discard, and theatrical roles have the same air of pasteboard insubstantiality. But this is not always and everywhere the case; a man who lived in the shadow of Shakespeare might have had a deeper sense of what could be counterfeited on the stage or represented before a tribunal. In his conception of a person as a theatrical mask secured by authority, Hobbes seems far closer than Freud to the world of Shakespeare and, of course, Arnaud du Tilh.

Appendix

The social fabrication of identity is, I have argued, particularly marked in the drama where, after all, identity is fashioned out of public discourse, and even soliloquies tend to take the form of rhetorical declamations. But non-dramatic literature is, in its own way, deeply involved in the pre-psychoanalytic fashioning of the proprietary rights of selfhood. Thus even in *The Faerie Queene*, where property seems to be absorbed altogether into the landscape of the mind, Spenser's concern with psychic experience is not manifested in the representation of a particular individual's inner life, but rather in the representation of the hero's externalized struggle to secure clear title to his allegorical attributes and hence to his name. If that struggle is itself a vision of the inner life, it is one which suggests that for Spenser the psyche can only be conceived as a dangerous, factionalized social world, a world of vigilance, intrigue, extreme violence, and brief, fragile moments of intense beauty – just such a world as Spenser the colonial administrator inhabited in Ireland.

What does it mean that Spenser looks deep within himself and imagines that realm as eerily like the outward realm in which he bustled? It means that for him the noblest representation of the inner life is not lyric but epic – hence the compulsion of Spenserean characters to secure their identity by force of arms. And it means too that even the most well-defended existence is extremely vulnerable to fraud – may be imitated, misused, falsely appropriated, as Arnaud du Tilh appropriated the name and property and wife of Martin Guerre.

Evil in *The Faerie Queene* has its large-boned, athletic champions, but its most dangerous agents are the impostors, those who have the power to assume with uncanny accuracy all the signs of virtue. Thus when the subtle Archimago wishes to divide the Red Cross Knight from his beloved Una, truth's allegorical embodiment, he contrives 'the person to put on/Of that good knight'. 'And when he sate upon his courser free', Spenser concludes, '*Saint George* himself ye would haue deemed him to be'. The disguise is sufficiently effective to take in Una herself – even truth cannot unmask a perfect falsehood – and the impostor's identity is only revealed after he is half-killed by the pagan Sansloy. Conversely, Red Cross' own identity – his name – is only revealed to him when he too has undergone the trials that belong to the signs he wears. And that name, first disclosed to the reader as the identity that Archimago falsely assumed, is paradoxically disclosed late in the poem to Red Cross as his true origin, an origin he can only possess at the *end* of his quest.

With the idea of an origin that is only conferred upon one at the end of a series of actions and transactions, I return to the notion that psycho-analysis is the historical outcome of certain characteristic Renaissance strategies.

Notes

1 Natalie Zemon Davis, *The Return of Martin Guerre* (Cambridge: Harvard University Press, 1983). Davis' text was originally published in French, together with a 'récit Romanesque' written by the film's screenwriter Jean-Claude Carrière and director Daniel Vigne (*Le Retour de Martin Guerre* [Paris: Robert Laffont, 1982]).
2 The only conspicuous religious element in the story is at best equivocal: Bertrande and the false Martin Guerre apparently frequented a Protestant conventicle. Natalie Davis speculates that the couple may have been seeking, in the Protestant ethos of the companionate marriage, a kind of ethical valida-tion of their deception.
3 Montaigne, 'Des boyteux' [Of cripples], in *Essais*, ed. Maurice Rat, 2 vols (Paris: Garnier, 1962), II: 478–9.
4 Leo Spitzer, 'Notes on the Empirical and Poetic "I" in Medieval Authors', *Traditio* 4(1946): 414–22.
5 Quoted in W. G. Hoskins, *The Age of Plunder: King Henry's England, 1500–1547* (London: Longman, 1976), 20–1.
6 See William E. Tate, *The Parish Chest: A Study of the Records of Parochial Administration in England* (Cambridge: Cambridge University Press, 1946).
7 It is important to grasp that this transformation is at once a revolution and a continuation; 'psyche' is neither a mere mystification for 'property' nor a radical alternative to it.
8 Thomas Hobbes, *Leviathan*, ed. C. B. Macpherson (New York: Penguin, 1968), 1.16.217.

8

GENDER AND SEXUAL CULTURE IN RENAISSANCE ITALY

Michael Rocke

Sexual and gender identities are so fundamental to our make-up that there has long been a tendency to naturalize them, to view them, that is, as an intrinsic part of our individual natures – often equating gender (masculinity/femininity) with biology (male/female). Recently, however, historians, anthropologists and other scholars have challenged this perspective. On the one hand, studies in the history of sexuality and gender have begun to cast into increasingly bold relief the fact that different societies define gender and 'appropriate' forms of sexual behaviour in various ways. This has been a major field of research in recent years. In addition to the pioneering works of John Boswell and Guido Ruggiero on the history of sexuality and gender in the Middle Ages and the Renaissance, Michael Rocke has emerged as one of the most creative scholars working on this dimension of Renaissance culture.

Rocke's approach is a vivid example of the new cultural history. He not only explores the prescriptive language of moralists and preachers such as Bernardino of Siena (1380–1444) and Girolamo Savonarola (1452–98) as well as developments in law and medicine in shaping ideas about gender in Renaissance society, he also looks to court records to examine the ways in which sexual crimes (fornication, rape, prostitution, child abuse and sodomy) were perceived and prosecuted. His essay portrays a world anxiously intent on developing clear gender definitions. The sexuality of women, especially those at the higher reaches of the social scale, was carefully patrolled through an emphasis on chastity and early marriage, while adult males were granted considerably more freedom. Indeed, for men at least, Renaissance culture was relatively tolerant of certain types of behaviour that, officially, constituted transgressions but which were, in fact, consistent with prevailing attitudes about femininity and masculinity. In the fifteenth century, for example, prostitution was not only tolerated but even legalized and regulated by governments. Brothels functioned, in part at least, as safety-valves designed to protect girls of good families from the sexual appetites of adolescent and adult males.

Rocke's most compelling illustration of the ways in which Florentines organized and understood gender, however, comes from his examination of homosexual behaviours. Renaissance culture did not categorize men or women

*as hetero- or homosexual in ways that only became normative in the nine-
teenth century. To the contrary, in the Renaissance, proper masculine
behaviour was determined not by the biological sex of one's partner but by
whether or not the adult male was the active, penetrating partner (which was
deemed acceptable whether with a man or a woman) rather than the passive,
penetrated partner (which for adult males was deemed unacceptable). Rocke,
therefore, describes a gender regime radically different from our own and
concludes his essay by underscoring 'the distance that separates the culture of
sex and gender in Renaissance Italy from that which prevails in the modern
world'.*

Rocke's essay, which is very slightly abridged here, originally appeared in
Gender and Society in Renaissance Italy, *eds Judith C. Brown and Robert
C. Davis (London, 1998), 150–70. For a further elaboration of his arguments
here, readers should turn first to his* Forbidden Friendships: Homosexuality
and Male Culture in Renaissance Florence *(New York, 1996), a book that
opens up a new window on male sociability and the role of sexuality in the
construction of Renaissance society. Students will find intriguing comparisons
and contrasts in Guido Ruggiero,* The Boundaries of Eros: Sex Crime and
Sexuality in Renaissance Venice *(Oxford, 1985) as well as in Virginia Cox's
essay 'The Single Self', which is presented in the following chapter.*

* * *

In February 1496, friar Girolamo Savonarola, campaigning to reform
the morals of Florentine society, fulminated against the sexual
debauchery that, in his view, had 'ruined the world, … corrupted men
in lust, led women into indecency, and boys into sodomy and filth, and
made them become like prostitutes'. His condemnation of erotic licence
stemmed not merely from its immorality, but also from his conviction
that the indulgence of sexual pleasures produced a dangerous confusion of gender boundaries: 'Young lads have been made into women.
But that's not all: fathers are like daughters, brothers like sisters. There
is no distinction between the sexes or anything else anymore'.[1]

Savonarola's comment reveals some central assumptions of the
culture of sex and gender in Renaissance Italy. Sexual behaviour was in
fact a basic component of the complex of cultural and social signifiers
that distinguished individuals, beyond their belonging to one biological
sex or the other, as gendered beings, as masculine or feminine. His insistence on the transformative capacity of sex to make men into women,
and presumably vice versa, indicates an awareness that gender identity
was not a natural or fixed quality but was constructed and malleable,
and as such it needed to be adequately shaped, reinforced and defended.
The friar's remarks also betrayed deep anxiety about establishing and
enforcing borders, not only between licit and illicit sexual comportment,

but also between related virile and feminine conventions and ideals, for it was in part around such confines that society was properly ordered.

Norms and ideals

In this strongly patriarchal and patrilineal society, the control of women's sexual conduct and reproductive functions was accorded especially high importance. Centuries-old philosophical, medical, legal and religious discourses on sexual difference continued to sustain the notion that women were inferior in all ways to men and subject to their dominion. Medieval understanding of female biology contributed to beliefs that women were passive and receptive in their sexual nature yet possessed a powerful yearning for semen and a more ravenous sexual appetite than that of men – a view reinforced by the Judeo-Christian myth of Eve the temptress, responsible for original sin and the fall from grace. Both religious doctrine and lay society upheld chastity as the supreme virtue of women, whether as young unwed virgins, wives or widows. The purity and modesty of the *donna onesta* was regularly contrasted with the shamelessness and incontinence of the 'indecent' woman, embodied especially in the figure of the prostitute.

The defence of female virginity before marriage and chastity thereafter also played an essential role in the pervasive culture of honour, a woman's sexual behaviour largely defining both her own standing and reputation and those of her family and of the males responsible for 'governing' her. Such concerns loomed especially large for wealthy and propertied families, for whom the guarantee of paternity determined the transmission of patrimonies and the competition for public honour carried momentous political stakes. This obsession was aptly stated by the Florentine patrician and humanist Matteo Palmieri in his *Vita Civile*:

> Wives must exercise the greatest and most extraordinary guard not only against uniting with another man, but even to avoid all suspicion of such filthy wickedness. This error is the supreme disgrace to decency, it effaces honour, destroys union, renders paternity uncertain, heaps infamy on families and within them brings dissension and hatred and dissolves every relationship; she no longer deserves to be called a married woman but rather a corrupt wench, worthy only of public humiliation.[2]

It was in part to safeguard both their daughters' virginity and the family's honour that parents rushed their girls into marriage as soon as possible after sexual maturity, usually between the ages of fifteen and eighteen. For the same reason, unmarriageable patrician girls were quickly made nuns and secluded within a convent. To preserve their chastity, women of middle- and upper-class families tended to be isolated in their homes, and their contacts with men were carefully controlled. Women at lower social levels, who generally lacked this powerful familial protection, had greater exposure to males and more freedom in their daily lives; for them, the conventions regarding virginity and chastity were probably somewhat less rigid.

Despite religious proscriptions against all extra-marital sex, standards and expectations with regard to male sexual behaviour were generally more flexible than those applied to women. No social ideal compelled men to remain virgins before marriage or demanded fidelity of them afterward. They were supposed to obey laws against rape, adultery and other illicit acts, but lax enforcement and light penalties for many offences helped dull their dissuasive force. While men were to respect the virtue of women of honourable families, they had a large pool of slaves and servants, poor or immodest women, and prostitutes with whom they could acceptably indulge their desires. This sexual liberty was reinforced by the late age at which men normally married – from their late twenties to early thirties – and by substantial rates of men who never married. Denied economic autonomy under their fathers' patriarchal rule, and forbidden significant civic roles, young men lived in a state of prolonged and powerless adolescence. These footloose bachelors were the main protagonists of the violence and sexual debauchery characteristic of Renaissance Italy. City fathers, themselves once young, viewed their profligacy with some sympathy and indulgence; it also provided an excuse for barring them from the serious business of governing, since 'they say youths should not discuss public affairs, but pursue their sexual needs'.[3]

Masculine identity did not, however, lie only in the double standard that allowed men the sexual freedoms denied to women, but also in conventions that identified manliness solely with a dominant role in sex. In this regard, males' sexual and gendered norms were as rigid as those imposing chastity on females. Potency figured among the constitutive features of masculinity, such that a man's failure to achieve erection was grounds for annulment of his marriage or for divorce.[4] The association of virility with dominance was one source of the religious ban against couples engaging in intercourse with the woman on top, an 'unnatural' position considered emblematic of woman's usurpation – or man's abdication – of males' superior status.[5] Similar notions pervaded same-sex relations, in which adult men were expected to take an exclusively 'active' role in sex with adolescents, behaviour that corresponded fully with masculine ideals, while a mature man's assumption of the receptive role was abhorred as a dangerous transgression of gender norms.

Conjugal relations and religious precepts

The church, the most authoritative source of moral teachings on sexual behaviour, established guidelines and norms which in principle were equally applicable to men and women. For all, sex was licit only within marriage, with the conscious aim of procreation, in prescribed times and conditions, and in a single position, with the couple facing and the man above. All intercourse outside marriage, as well as conjugal sex for mere pleasure, in forbidden positions, or in a manner that might impede generation, was condemned and prohibited. Although some late medieval theologians began to modify these tenets somewhat, sanctioning sensual pleasure as a reproductive aid and even permitting unconventional positions, the church's sexual orthodoxy remained restricted.[6] How closely couples observed these prescriptions is another matter and is difficult to ascertain. That moralists continued to vehemently denounce practices such as anal intercourse that could serve contraceptive aims, and the rapid decline in wives' fertility that has been observed in fifteenth-century Tuscany, would suggest that many spouses disregarded the sexual guidance of their preachers and confessors.[7]

However its teachings on sexual conduct were received, the church played an important and perhaps more effective role in forming and transmitting notions of gender. While all were supposed to bear equal liability for their carnal acts, preachers presented sexual doctrines to the faithful in ways that carried considerably different messages for men and women. The sermons of Bernardino of Siena to the Sienese and Florentines in the 1420s offer some pertinent illustrations.[8] Bernardino's preaching on conjugal life fitted well with his culture's growing emphasis on marriage as a form of companionship between spouses who were to treat each other with mutual love and respect.[9] Regarding sex, he maintained that spouses shared responsibility for preventing each other from sinning, stressed that fidelity was a duty of wives and husbands, and reproached both for sexual failings. His teachings were embedded in a framework of values, consistent with church doctrine and patrician ideals, that endorsed sexual moderation for both sexes, sustained the notion that women's frailty of reason made them more inclined than men to sin, and upheld wives' subjection to their husbands' authority. Within these traditions, however, the emphases and omissions of his remarks, or the shifts depending on the audience addressed, show some ways in which gendered assumptions framed his teachings and how ideal genders were shaped.

This can be seen most clearly in Bernardino's sermons about a basic tenet of church doctrine, that is, the equality of spouses' rights and duties with regard to the 'marriage debt': while carefully observing the proper times, position, devout spirit and procreative aim of sex, husbands and wives possessed an identical right to intercourse, which their spouse was obliged, under penalty of mortal sin, to 'render' to them. Bernardino reiterated that this injunction applied indistinctly to both partners, but in developing this egalitarian theme he employed examples and lessons that revealed and reinforced assumptions about gender difference. He normally directed his remarks on rendering the debt to wives, rather than to husbands, as if he assumed that males more commonly importuned their spouses for sex, thus implicitly fortifying notions of man's 'active' nature and pressing desire and of woman's 'passivity' and, ideally, her modesty.[10] Sexual continence and shame were considered women's crowning virtues, and when he discussed marital sex Bernardino reminded wives to remain as chaste as possible, never allowing their spouses to see them naked, to look at their 'shameful parts', or to touch them indecently. On the few occasions he acknowledged wives' prerogative to request intercourse, he in effect disempowered them by insisting on their modesty. So as to reduce a wife's temptation to commit adultery, it was better, he claimed, that the husband anticipate her request and render his carnal obligation voluntarily, rather than for her to voice her longings. While a wife was bound to respond only if asked expressly for sex and was exonerated if her husband's signals were unclear, a husband was obliged to react to the 'smallest sign' of his wife's yearning to protect her from the indelicacy of having to express her desire.[11]

Although Bernardino stressed women's virtue and modesty in carnal relations, he paradoxically also placed on them a greater burden of sexual knowledge and responsibility. He began one discussion on conjugal sex by warning that ignorance of sin exculpated neither partner, but proceeded to address only the wives, mothers and nubile girls in the congregation. Girls about to marry 'had to know how to do it', and sinned if they neglected to learn; mothers who failed to impart the facts of life to their daughters committed a serious mortal sin.[12] Rarely, if ever, did he encourage fathers to give their sons lessons in sex education.

Accordingly, Bernardino often instructed wives about the times and conditions when they could and should legitimately refuse their husbands' requests, thereby giving them some control over the frequency and character of intercourse. Although he warned both partners about the evils of unrestrained passion and specific sins, he tended to represent husbands as more inclined to 'disorderly affections' and excessive lust, which it was wives' duty to curb and correct. He insisted that, while wives were bound to obey their husbands, this never meant yielding to sinful requests. They were to refuse especially when their spouses wanted, as he implied they often did, to engage in acts *contra naturam* that impeded procreation. He also warned the wife to decline if her husband had imbibed too much wine, was crazed with lust, or desired sex so frequently that it might devitalize his seed, make him lose his senses, or cause illness or death.[13] Repeating an ancient taboo, revived vigorously in the Renaissance, he admonished women to rebuff husbands' requests for coitus during their menstrual period, which according to both popular and learned belief risked generating deformed or leprous children.[14] But in Italy, he conceded, a wife had better conceal her menstruous state and quietly render the debt, because otherwise her husband would demand anal intercourse. Bernardino also instructed wives, not husbands, to assess their mates' age and their physical and spiritual condition when considering whether or how often to consent to intercourse. He more often mentioned husbands' threats to satisfy their desires elsewhere as binding wives to render the debt, a tacit acknowledgment of men's greater opportunities to pursue extra-marital relations. It was only wives, however, whom he urged to grant consent selectively, in order to wean their husbands gradually from sex and convince them to embrace abstinence – for the church, the 'perfect state'.[15]

The law and the courts

Distinctions in the treatment of men and women also characterized the regulation of illicit sex, both in law and in court practice. Italian governments between 1400 and 1600 took a forceful role in legislating and policing sexual behaviour. Although legal norms, judiciary systems and the enforcement of sex laws varied widely, making generalization difficult, these distinctions commonly reflected male assumptions about the sexes' different natures and the need to enforce conventional gender roles and ideals. Laws and courts were influenced by beliefs that women's desires were more ravenous than men's, that women were more prone to sin, and that therefore their sexual behaviour had to be regulated more strictly. 'The laws presume that all women are usually bad', according to one commentator, 'because they are so full of mischief and vices that are difficult to describe'; a Belluno law of 1428 decreed that no woman over the age of twenty should be presumed to be a virgin, unless her virtue could be convincingly proved.[16]

Frequently, the social status, life-cycle stage or reputed virtue of the woman involved in illicit sex helped determine distinctions in guilt or penalties. This was especially true of rape and fornication, in which women were usually considered victims and absolved, but also of adultery or sodomy, in which women were often held criminally liable. Generally, the higher the woman's status was the greater the penalty levied on her seducer or lover, but finer distinctions were also drawn. The Florentine statutes of 1415 set a fine of 500 lire for men who had intercourse, whether consensual or forced, with a virgin, a respectable widow or a married woman, and allowed harsher punishment depending on the 'condition and quality of the person'. For the violation of women 'of lesser condition', the fine fell to 100 lire, while sex with a consenting servant or a prostitute carried no penalty at all.[17] Venetian authorities levied progressively milder penalties on rapists according to whether their victims were pre-pubescent girls, wives, widows or, at the bottom of the scale, sexually mature nubile women; the severest penalties were reserved for those who raped women of high status.[18]

The treatment of adultery revealed the sharpest gender discrepancies and bore the most onerous consequences for women. Despite the gender-blind injunction against extra-marital sex, in practical terms adultery was a crime of wives. Husbands' infidelity, unless with a married woman, was considered of little significance, while that of wives was deemed a most serious offence that dishonoured their spouses and undermined the conjugal bond. Courts commonly punished an adulteress more severely than her partner, and her penalty usually included the forfeiture to her husband or children of her dowry – a key commodity in the definition of a woman's honour and often her sole means of subsistence in widowhood. Sometimes adulterous husbands were also legally subject to punishment: in Venice this might mean prison or exile plus the loss of their wife's dowry. But from 1480 to 1550 not a single Venetian husband was convicted for infidelity, unlike scores of wives prosecuted from the 1360s onward.[19] This gender disparity accorded fully with religious precepts. According to Bernardino, in addition to her dowry an adulteress' husband had the right to expel her from his house, yet he forbade the wife of a philandering man to abandon him under any circumstances. He once stressed the differently gendered implications of infidelity by asserting that a husband's adultery was a greater sin, since as a man he was more rational and should therefore be more devoted, but a wife's unfaithfulness resulted in her 'perpetual shame', for she had 'no other virtue to lose' than her sexual honour.[20]

Women's shame also influenced the courts' tendency to punish them with public humiliation. Floggings and mutilations were common penalties for men too, but it appears that women convicted of sex crimes were more frequently exposed to public derision. While male adulterers were usually fined, jailed or exiled, adulteresses (besides losing their dowry) were often whipped along the streets, in various states of undress and sometimes wearing a defamatory mitre on their heads; occasionally their heads were shaved. In Pescia in 1419 an adulteress, half-naked and wearing a 'crown of shame', was placed on a donkey and whipped through the countryside.[21] In Florence between 1490 and 1515, more than half of the women convicted of sodomy with men were sentenced to a flogging or the pillory, while only a third of their partners received similar penalties; most of the men, unlike the women, were allowed to avoid the shaming by instead paying a fine. Since women's honour and reputation were more contingent than men's on community opinion, authorities tended to punish them in precisely that public fashion that would be most defamatory.

Unauthorized sexual behaviour and gendered identities

Social conventions, religious precepts and the policing of sex all played important roles in constructing and transmitting notions of gender ideals and of distinctions between the sexes, but so did sexual behaviour itself. The forms of sexual comportment that are best documented, however, are those that were illicit or occurred outside marriage, and it is consequently this realm of unauthorized sex that has proven most fruitful for historians seeking to throw new light on gender relations and identities in Renaissance Italy.

A key figure here was the prostitute, central to the sexual culture and gender system of Renaissance Italy, both for the services she provided and for the symbolic functions she performed. Christian society had long considered prostitution a distasteful but necessary evil, a 'lesser sin' that was grudgingly tolerated to prevent greater transgressions: 'Do you see that in cities prostitutes are tolerated? This is a great evil, but if it were to be removed a great good would be eliminated, because there would be more adultery, more sodomy, which would be much worse'.[22] In a sexual regime that prescribed female chastity but tacitly condoned male fornication, the prostitute played the dual role of furnishing an outlet for incontinent bachelors and philandering husbands, while also diverting their desires from adolescent males and women of 'good' families, whose virtue and honour were thus safeguarded. Prostitutes and their clients were usually exempt from laws against fornication and adultery, though authorities limited the locations and visibility of their debauchery to protect the morality of upright citizens and defend the purity of civic and sacred buildings. During the Renaissance, the notion of the public utility of prostitution underwent a significant evolution, however. From the mid-1300s, governments began to abandon earlier exclusionary policies that relegated prostitutes and brothels outside the city walls and forced such women to wear identifying signs or apparel. Instead, the state became the official sponsor of urban sexual commerce, establishing municipal brothels or designated residential areas where whores could lawfully ply their trade. Dress codes and other norms intended to distinguish prostitutes were relaxed or abandoned. Some cities created magistracies to administer the bordellos or defend whores from assault and other offences, such as the 'Officers of Decency' in Florence in 1403 and the 'Protectors of the Prostitutes' in Lucca in 1534.[23]

By around 1500, however, this attitude of tolerance was beginning to change again, in Italy as elsewhere. The complexity of the marriage market and the steady escalation in dowries made it increasingly difficult for girls to marry. Convents thrived as patrician families discarded growing numbers of unwed daughters by banishing them to nunneries, while humbler women slid into situations of solitude and poverty that made them easy recruits to the ranks of occasional and professional whores. The spread of prostitutes from brothel areas into 'honest' neighbourhoods, together with the new phenomenon of prosperous courtesans who imitated the fashions and demeanour of patrician women, heightened concerns both about the bad example these unruly females posed to chaste women and about the blurring of social and moral distinctions between the *donna onesta* and the lusty *meretrice*. The sixteenth century consequently saw a return to a more negative assessment of the ancient sexual trade. Brothels remained open, but authorities revived or tightened policies on residence or dress to stigmatize prostitutes – laws that only a few wealthy courtesans could evade by buying licences or exploiting the protection of powerful clients.[24] Influenced also by religious reform movements, there was a proliferation of institutions to convert prostitutes and to prevent poor or precarious females from slipping into the profession.[25]

Prostitutes, whether professionals in brothels, courtesans catering to upper-class clients, or women who occasionally sold themselves, undoubtedly played an important role in men's sexual education and experience, and thus in the formation of masculine identity. This was precisely one of the criticisms levelled by Catholic reformers after the Council of Trent against the evil influence prostitution had in shaping men's sexual habits and attitudes towards women.[26] In their heyday the brothels were also central institutions of male sociability, especially for young bachelors. They provided a public forum where camaraderie and erotic licence mingled with outbreaks of violence, where men tested and displayed their virility in brawls and sexual conquests. It was in the brothel, an anecdote by the Florentine humanist Poliziano suggests, that youths who were once sodomites' 'passive' boyfriends could redeem their reputations by proving their manliness with compliant whores.[27]

Unauthorized sex involving males and females encompassed far more than men's commerce with prostitutes, however. Legal records suggest that fornication, rape and adultery were typical features of the sexual culture, such activities hardly being discouraged by the light penalties usually levied on (male) offenders. But even the serious crimes of sex with nuns and (by the later 1400s) heterosexual sodomy were also commonplace occurrences on the rosters of carnal offences.[28]

Evidence on unauthorized sex tends to confirm that, for women especially, the relationship between sexual behaviour and gender was subtly but significantly shaped by their social status. This illicit realm involved men from the entire social spectrum, but the women who were implicated were – except for nuns – mainly from the class of artisans, peasants, poor labourers and shopkeepers. Women of higher status were rarely embroiled in sexual scandals or crimes, and if they were, their families had the means to conceal the disgrace, to discipline the fallen or defiant woman privately, or to ensure that their assailants or lovers were severely punished. On the whole, the protective net thrown up by patrician males around their families' females effectively minimized women's perilous liaisons with men outside their kin group. Conscious of their family's status and indoctrinated from childhood that its honour depended on their chastity, genteel women probably tended to assimilate the values and gender ideology of their class, scrupulously avoiding behaviour that could defame them as much as their fathers, husbands and kinsmen.[29] The morality of humbler women was perhaps no less principled, but their circumstances of hardship and work, or their lack of networks of male kin, exposed them to the flattery of dishonest or fickle seducers, to sexual molestation by employers and social superiors, and to assaults by individuals or gangs. Court records are littered with such stories: plebeian girls and women attacked while alone on country roads or in the fields, servants and apprentices exploited sexually by their masters, isolated widows and their daughters powerless to defend their homes and virtue against assailants. Moreover, whether forced or consensual, most sexual relations between socially dominant men and their servants, slaves and other disadvantaged women simply evaded any judiciary control. The abandoned offspring of such unions swelled the overflowing foundling homes of Renaissance Italian cities.[30]

Because the imperatives of status, property and paternity that so heavily constrained patrician women's sexual behaviour carried less force among the less wealthy, working women appear to have had their own sense of proper sexual conduct and illicit activity, implying different customs and norms from those that prevailed among the dominant classes. For both rural and urban young people of the lower classes, for instance, premarital intercourse was evidently accepted and widespread, as long as relations were initiated with an intent to marry, or at least to create a stable bond. Such romances generally came to court as fornication only when the man failed to maintain his promise of marriage and abandoned his lover, often pregnant or with a young child. The loss of virginity impaired a woman's future chances of marrying, and the tribunals to which these deflowered victims of desertion or rape turned for redress usually sought to redeem their honour and restore their marriage prospects by forcing their seducers or violators to give them a dowry or, alternatively, to marry them. Prosecution of fornication often became embroiled in ambiguities about what constituted a valid marriage, since, according to the pre-Tridentine church, this required no other formalities than the partners' mutual consent. For this same reason, long-term informal unions and clandestine marriages remained unexceptional outside the upper classes well into the sixteenth century, and even women's extra-marital relations were not uncommon.[31] Facilitated by the contacts that they forged with men through neighbourly ties, work and sociable occasions, these plebeian romances were sometimes the fruit of an intolerable marriage, the evasion from a violent or overbearing husband, and may have been aided by neighbours and relatives. Such affairs typically attracted judicial attention only when they exceeded bounds of discretion or when a wife actually fled with her lover, signalling the open rupture of her conjugal union.[32]

Studies of illicit sex have also begun to illuminate in sharp relief the problem of men's sexual abuse of children, both female and male. In Florence from 1495 to 1515, over one third of the forty-nine documented victims of convicted rapists were girls between the ages of six and twelve, and at least half were aged fourteen or under; numerous others were seduced without force or were sodomized. One man condemned in 1488 regularly picked up children begging in the market, sodomized them in his home, and then offered them to others to ravish; some of his cronies, conducted before one ten-year-old victim, were reportedly repelled by her tender age and refused to touch her, but others had no such scruples.[33] In a typical year, an average of four boys aged twelve or under would also come before the courts as victims of sodomizers, often having suffered severe anal injury. In Venice, too, pre-pubescent children were common victims of sexual abuse. A Venetian law of 1500, which prohibited pimps from prostituting girls under the age of twelve, revealed that it was regular practice to offer clients girls as young as seven to nine years of age to be sodomized. The abuse of children merits further attention, for this was evidently not merely a problem of individual aberration. The frequent subjugation of impotent juveniles probably reflects a psychosexual immaturity and aggressiveness, and an insecurity about masculine identity that had deep social, cultural and familial roots.[34]

Another prominent, if less explored, aspect of male behaviour was assaults by gangs against women or younger boys. In Florence between 1495 and 1515, nineteen out of forty-nine documented female rape victims were attacked by at least two men, and typically by three to six or more; in 1499, thirteen men abducted a married woman from her home and violated her. Many more men took part in collective ravishings (eighty-nine) than in single assaults (thirty), and among the perpetrators, patrician youths figured prominently (thirty-four of eighty-nine). Groups of men also brutally sodomized women, such as Costanza, a thirty-year-old servant sodomized and raped by fourteen youths in 1497, or Francesca, a married woman who in 1501 was anally raped by thirty assailants. Gangs attacked adolescent males as well, part of a broader context in which the sexual 'possession' of boys by groups of men, whether by force or not, was both common and deeply implicated in the fashioning of manly and social identities. The gangs that terrorized women and boys offered strength in numbers to overpower their victims and guarantee the success of their sordid ventures, but their members also gave one another psychological incentive and support, an incitement to prove their virility before their comrades as, one after the other, they humiliated their helpless prey.[35]

Besides reinforcing an impression of the aggressive and predatory character of masculine behaviour and identity, evidence about illicit sex can also provide glimpses of individuals who implicitly evaded or openly challenged not only the law but also prevailing gender conventions. A few mature men, as will be seen, defied masculine norms by taking the proscribed receptive role in same-sex relations. Women, by contrast, were not always passive victims but instead often assumed an assertive role in seeking to fulfil their sexual desires and in shaping their own affective experiences and sense of identity. Some enterprising nubile girls apparently engaged calculatingly in pre-marital sex, to circumvent parental objections over their choice of a spouse. In extra-marital affairs wives are commonly found taking the initiative, perhaps to relieve the monotony of a loveless union or escape the brutality of a cruel husband.[36] Especially striking examples of women resisting gender and social conventions to pursue erotic pleasure and male companionship come from what is, at first glance, a most unlikely source – the nunnery. Many of the women who swelled Italy's bulging convents were deposited there, willingly or not, by genteel families unable to place them in suitable marriages; not all were prepared or willing to submit to a regime of chastity or to renounce the world. Not only were nuns often implicated in sexual scandals involving laymen or priests, but some managed to conduct quite rich sexual lives, apparently shielded by a web of complicity within and perhaps outside the convent.[37] Other women confuted the submissive role assigned them in gender ideology by withstanding assailants or by denouncing abusive husbands. A distinct sense of determination and proud identity emerges from the protest that a young Florentine patrician wife, Agnoletta de' Ricci, made to her husband Ardingo, whom she publicly accused in 1497 of having repeatedly sodomized her: 'I told him that in no way did I want him to treat me like an animal, but like a woman of perfect character'.[38] Such examples serve as reminders that, though the dominant ideology of gender and sexual behaviour was powerfully constraining, it was also contestable – and contested – terrain.

Same-sex relations and masculine identity

Same-sex relations between males, classified as sodomy, provide an especially revealing perspective on the construction of masculine identity.

Ranked among the most nefarious of carnal acts in both church doctrine and legal rhetoric, sodomy – mainly but not only sex between males – was one of the most frequently prosecuted and heavily penalized crimes in Italy between 1400 and 1600. Reputedly common across the peninsula, sodomy so alarmed the governments of Venice, Florence and Lucca that they created special judiciary commissions to prosecute it (in 1418, 1432 and 1448 respectively). Penalties and patterns of control varied, but in Florence the Office of the Night, as the magistracy there was known, unearthed an exceptionally thriving sodomitical milieu. Between 1432 and 1502 as many as 17,000 males were incriminated and some 3,000 convicted for homosexual relations. Indeed, sodomy was so common and its policing in the later fifteenth century so effective that, by the time they reached the age of forty, probably two of every three Florentine men had been officially implicated.[39]

Whether this 'vice' was as pervasive elsewhere remains to be seen; nonetheless, the evidence suggests that throughout Italy same-sex relations shared similar forms, contexts and ascribed cultural meanings. Generally, homosexual behaviour had little to do with current notions of sexual orientation or identity, but was organized instead around notions of gender and life stages. For most males, same-sex sodomy was a sporadic or temporary transgression that did not preclude relations with females or imply anything about long-term inclinations.[40]

Some contemporaries saw connections between homoeroticism and the quality of relations between men and women. Bernardino of Siena singled out sodomites for their loathing and paltry esteem of women, while the Sienese *novelliere* Pietro Fortini attributed the homoerotic bent of both Florentine and Lucchese men to their universal misogyny, asserting that their 'vices are such [referring to sodomy] that they cannot bear to look at women, who they say are their enemies'. Acting in part on the belief that making public women accessible would help curtail sodomy, the governments of both Florence and Lucca promoted municipalized prostitution. This sexual equation was given a different twist by Savonarola: Florentine parents, he said, so feared the disgrace of unwed pregnant daughters that they encouraged their sons to engage instead in what they deemed the 'lesser evil' of sex with men.[41]

Notions of gender also shaped sex between males in more direct ways, while homosexual behaviour in turn had important implications for masculine identities – implications that were relevant for all males, whether they engaged in sodomy or not. Same-sex relations in Italy corresponded to a hierarchical pattern, very ancient in Mediterranean cultures and long-lasting throughout Europe, in which adult males took the so-called active, usually anally insertive role with 'passive' teenage boys or adolescents to the age of about eighteen or twenty. In Florence, the best-documented example, nine out of ten active partners were aged nineteen and above; mainly in their twenties and thirties, their mean age was twenty-seven. Of those who took the passive role, nine out of ten were between the ages of thirteen and twenty, with a mean age of sixteen. Reciprocal or age-reversed relations were rare, and limited to adolescence, while it was rarer still for mature males to have sex together. Indeed, the assumption of the receptive sexual role by adult men constituted a widely respected taboo.[42]

Sex between males thus always embodied oppositions – older and younger, active and passive, penetrator and penetrated. These were far from neutral distinctions, for contrasting values related to gender adhered to them, values such as dominance and submission, honour and shame, and, not least, masculine and feminine. These differences were neatly expressed in fourteenth-century Florentine laws, which blandly designated the active partner either as *pollutus* (morally corrupt) or as someone who committed sodomy with another, but contemptuously branded the passive as one who had dirtied or disgraced himself, or who 'willingly suffered the said crime to be inflicted upon him'.[43]

The gendered meaning of sexual roles, central to conceptions of same-sex behaviour, emerged most vividly from denunciations accusing men and boys of sodomy. Informers commonly referred to the passive partner, and only to him, with derogatory feminine expressions and metaphors. People derided sodomized boys with the epithets *bardassa*, derived from an Arabic word for slave and designating a debauched boy who offered himself to men, usually for payment; *puttana* (whore); and *cagna* or *cagna in gestra* (bitch or bitch in heat); all evoking the common-place of voracious female lust. Most often, however, informers referred to them simply as women, stating that a man kept or used a boy 'as a woman', or even 'as his wife'. What turned these boys symbolically into women was not any effeminate appearance or manner, but rather their assumption of the subordinate position in sex, which was construed in this culture as feminine. In contrast, accusers virtually never represented the 'active' partner in feminine terms, calling him at most a 'sodomite' or 'bugger'. Neither term bore overt gendered connotations other than indicating the dominant role in sex. Indeed, while passive partners were hardly ever described using these terms, both were regularly used to indicate men who sodomized women.[44] Late medieval and early modern Italians evidently found it difficult to conceive of same-sex relations – whether between males or females – outside the traditional gender dichotomy of masculine and feminine roles.[45]

These representations suggest that the sodomite, though castigated as a criminal and a sinner, was perceived as conforming to the behaviours and values defined in this culture as masculine. As long as he observed proper conventions, a man's sexual relations with boys did not compromise his status as a 'normal' and virile male. Indeed, the act of dominating another male, even if a boy, might well have reinforced it. Since sodomizing someone did not constitute deviation from 'manly' norms, and the 'womanly' role was in effect limited to very young males, this permitted all mature men to engage in same-sex activity – as very many did – without endangering their masculine identity or being relegated to a distinctive category of deviants. What was an aberration was, of course, the passive sexual role. But as this was normally restricted to the phase of physical and social immaturity, it marked only a temporary detour from a boy's progress towards manhood. In Florence, virtually all adolescent passives whose later same-sex activity is documented converted with success to a solely dominant role with teenage boys. This helps explain why passive minors usually received much lighter penalties than their companions, or, as in Florence, no punishment whatsoever, no matter how promiscuous they were. If penalties were levied, they often involved corporal punishments of the sort usually applied to women.[46]

This also accounts for the paramount significance attributed to the transition to sexual adulthood, with its expectations of adherence to virile conventions. For Florentine boys up to the age of eighteen or twenty, the passive role was considered more or less consonant with their status, but afterward most men carefully avoided the shame of being penetrated 'like a woman'. This was a crucial experiential and symbolic passage, and the border between passive and active, boyhood and maturity, feminine and masculine, was anxiously patrolled by both community and state. With a combination of embarrassment and derision, informers castigated the rare youth or older man who still 'let themselves be sodomized', emphasizing their dishonour and disgrace. The authorities often reinforced these concerns about proper masculine roles by punishing over-aged passives with exemplary penalties of public floggings, exorbitant fines or exile. So powerful was the aversion to older men's sexual receptivity, in particular, that when Salvi Panuzzi, a sixty-three-year-old citizen long notorious for sodomizing boys, publicly admitted in 1496 that he himself had been sodomized by several youths, the Night Officers condemned him to death by burning, one of only three known capital sentences they levied in their seventy-year activity. Yet while they abhorred his acts, they also feared that his execution, by rendering public his womanish 'evil ways, ... might bring shame on the entire city' and make a mockery of Florentine manhood. They therefore commuted his sentence, upon payment of a huge fine, to life imprisonment hidden away in *la pazzeria*, the prison ward for the insane.[47]

The exemplary punishments imposed on adult men for taking the 'unmanly' sexual role emphasize that individual erotic behaviour and collective gender norms and identity formed part of a seamless whole.

Informers expressed concern that the passivity of older men, a disgrace to themselves, would also implicate and malign the honour – that is, the virility – of the entire male community. By defusing the potential shame of Panuzzi's execution, and by secluding this violator of manhood among the dangerously insane, the Night Officers affirmed both the public nature of gender and the commune's role in defending the conventions that helped fashion masculine identity. Such worries were hardly limited to Florence. In 1516, Venetian lawmakers, their offended sense of masculine propriety fairly bursting from their words, resolved to stamp out 'an absurd and unheard-of thing [that] has recently become known, which can in no way be tolerated, that several most wicked men of 30, 40, 50, 60 years and more have given themselves like prostitutes and public whores to be passives in such a dreadful excess'. This revelation scandalized local commentators, in part because it evoked a deep anxiety that the hierarchy of age and gender on which masculine identity was constructed risked being subverted. One nobleman was appalled that 'Fathers and Senators', men who were 'mature, full of wisdom, with white beards' – the very symbols of patriarchy – would shamelessly allow youths to penetrate them, and he branded this 'truly a wicked and abhorrent thing, never before heard of in our times, especially among old men'. Equally menacing to their manly sense of self and civic image was the news that informed foreigners were now gleefully ridiculing the virility of all Venetians.[48] Similar concerns about defending Florentine manhood led the government of Duke Cosimo I, in a law of 1542, to single out the adult man who dared allow himself to be sodomized by ordering his public execution by burning, 'for his own punishment and as an example to others', as 'a wicked and infamous man'.[49]

Perhaps more effectively than any other contemporary erotic behaviour, the same-sex practices described here, with their age-, role- and gender-bound conventions, underline the distance that separates the culture of sex and gender in Renaissance Italy from that which prevails in the modern Western world. Little trace, if any, can be found then of the categories that today largely define sexual experience and personae; it was not, in other words, the biological sex of one's partners in erotic pleasures that significantly distinguished and classified individuals, but rather the extent to which their sexual behaviour conformed to culturally determined gender roles. In different but related ways, the norms and ideology of gender forcefully shaped and constrained the experience of sex for both women and men. And sexual activity, in turn, played important roles in fashioning gendered identities and in reinforcing – or sometimes challenging – traditional gender conventions. As historians and other scholars continue to explore the complex and still relatively uncharted universe of sexual comportments, attitudes and controls throughout the rural and urban communities of the Italian peninsula, their studies promise to further enrich our understanding of the culturally specific modes of the construction of sex and gender in late medieval and early modern Italy.

Notes

1 Girolamo Savonarola, *Prediche sopra Amos e Zaccaria*, P. Ghiglieri (ed.) 3 vols (Rome, 1971–2), vol. I, 194, 200 (23 February 1496).

2 Matteo Palmieri, *Vita Civile*, F. Battaglia (ed.) (Bologna, 1944), 133.

3 Donato Giannotti, *Opere politiche e letterarie di Donato Giannotti*, F. Polidori (ed.) 2 vols (Florence, 1850), vol. I, 230. On late male marriage and sexual behaviour, see David Herlihy, 'Vieillir à Florence au Quattrocento', *Annales, ESC* 24(1969), 1346–9; Guido Ruggiero, *The Boundaries of Eros: Sex Crime and Sexuality in Renaissance Venice* (New York, 1985), esp. 159–62; Michael Rocke, *Forbidden Friendships: Homosexuality and Male Culture in Renaissance Florence* (New York, 1996), 113–32.

4 James A. Brundage, *Law, Sex and Christian Society in Medieval Europe* (Chicago, 1987), 512; Vern Bullough, 'On being a male in the Middle Ages', in *Medieval Masculinities: Regarding Men in the Middle Ages*, C. A. Lees (ed.) (Minneapolis, 1994), 41–2.

5 Natalie Davis, 'Women on top', in her *Society and Culture in Early Modern France: Eight Essays* (Stanford, 1975), 124–51.

6 Nicholas Davidson, 'Theology, nature and the law: sexual sin and sexual crime in Italy from the fourteenth to the seventeenth century', in *Crime, Society and the Law in Renaissance Italy*, T. Dean and K. J. P. Lowe (eds) (Cambridge, 1994), 77–85.

7 David Herlihy and Christiane Klapisch-Zuber, *Les Toscans et leurs familles: une étude du catasto florentin de 1427* (Paris, 1978), 441–2; Christiane Klapisch-Zuber, 'Famille, religion et sexualité à Florence au Moyen Age', *Revue de l'histoire des religions* 209(1992), 381–92; Maria Serena Mazzi, *Prostitute e lenoni nella Firenze del Quattrocento* (Milan, 1991), 55–9, 61–86.

8 *Prediche volgari sul campo di Siena 1427*, Carlo Delcorno (ed.) 2 vols (Milan, 1989), vol. I, 538–621 (hereafter *Siena 1427*); *Le prediche volgari*, C. Cannarozzi (ed.) 2 vols (Pistoia, 1934), vol. I, 380–404 (hereafter *Florence 1424*); *Le prediche volgari*, C. Cannarozzi (ed.) 3 vols (Florence, 1940), vol. II, 173–90 (hereafter *Florence 1425*).

9 For example, *Siena 1427*, I, 556, 568–9; *Florence 1424*, I, 412; *Florence 1425*, II, 177. On increasingly positive evaluations of marriage, see Herlihy and Klapisch-Zuber, *Les Toscans*, 586–8.

10 *Florence 1424*, I, 381–404; *Siena 1427*, I, 573–603.

11 *Siena 1427*, 594, 617–18; *Florence 1425*, II, 179; *Florence 1424*, I, 393.

12 *Siena 1427*, 577–83.

13 *Florence 1424*, I, 388–9, 395–8; *Siena 1427*, I, 588–91, 593, 600, 602–3.

14 *Florence 1424*, I, 387–8; *Siena 1427*, I, 591–2. On menstruation beliefs, see Joan Cadden, *Meanings of Sex Differences in the Middle Ages: Medicine, Science, and Culture* (Cambridge, 1993), 173–6, 268; Ottavia Niccoli, '"Menstruum quasi monstruum": monstrous births and menstrual taboo in the sixteenth century', in E. Muir and G. Ruggiero (eds) *Sex and Gender in Historical Perspective* (Baltimore, 1990), 1–25.

15 *Siena 1427*, I, 592, 594–7, 600–1.

16 Brundage, *Law*, 492; quote from Giovanni Nevizzani, *Silva nuptialis* ... (Lyons, 1524), fol. 21va (cited in *ibid.*, 548–9).

17 *Statuta populi et communis florentiae publica auctoritate collecta castigata et praeposita anno salutis MCCCCVI*, 3 vols (Fribourg, 1778–83), vol. III, rubric 112, 318.

18 Ruggiero, *Boundaries of Eros*, 96–108.

19 *Ibid.*, 45–69; Giovanni Scarabello, 'Devianza sessuale ed interventi di giustizia a Venezia nella prima metà del XVI secolo', in *Tiziano e Venezia*, exhibition catalogue (Vicenza, 1980), 79; Brundage, *Law*, 517–21.

20 *Siena 1427*, I, 557; *Florence 1424*, I, 413; *Florence 1425*, II, 178.

21 Samuel K. Cohn, Jr., *Women in the Streets: Sex and Power in Renaissance Italy* (Baltimore, 1996), 114; see also Brundage, *Law*, 520; Ruggiero, *Boundaries of Eros*, 54–5.

22 Giordano da Pisa, *Quaresimale fiorentino 1305–1306*, Carlo Delcorno (ed.) (Florence, 1974), 210.

23 Richard C. Trexler, 'Florentine prostitution in the fifteenth century: patrons and clients', in *idem, The Women of Renaissance Florence* (Binghamton, 1993), 31–65; Mazzi, *Prostitute*; John Brackett, 'The Florentine Onestà and the control of prostitution, 1403–1680', *Sixteenth-century Journal* 24(1993): 273–300; Elisabeth Pavan, 'Police des moeurs, société et politique à Venise à la fin du Moyen Age', *Revue historique* 264(1980): 241–88; Romano Canosa and Isabella Colonnello, *Storia della prostituzione in Italia dal Quattrocento alla fine del Settecento* (Rome, 1989).

24 Trexler, 'Florentine prostitution', 60–5; Mazzi, *Prostitute*, 225–31, 403–7. On rising dowry values, see Anthony Molho, *Marriage Alliance in Late Medieval Florence* (Cambridge MA, 1994), 298–310. On the growth of monasteries and convent populations, see Richard C. Trexler, 'Celibacy in the Renaissance: the nuns of Florence', in *idem, The Women of Renaissance Florence*, 10–19; Judith C. Brown, 'Monache a Firenze all'inizio dell'età moderna: un'analisi demografica', *Quaderni storici* 29(1994): 117–52. On courtesans, see Brackett, 'Onestà', 293–5; *Il gioco dell'amore: le cortigiane di Venezia dal Trecento al Settecento*, exhibition catalogue (Milan, 1990).

25 Sherill Cohen, *The Evolution of Women's Asylums since 1500: From Refuges for Ex-Prostitutes to Shelters for Battered Women* (New York, 1992); Lucia Ferrante, 'Honor regained: women in the Casa del Soccorso di San Paolo in sixteenth-century Bologna', in Muir and Ruggiero, (eds) *Sex and Gender*, 46–72.

26 Brackett, 'Onestà', 293; Guido Ruggiero, 'Marriage, love, sex, and Renaissance civic morality', in J. G. Turner (ed.) *Sexuality and Gender in Early Modern Europe: Institutions, Texts, Images* (Cambridge, 1993), 25–6.

27 Angelo Poliziano, *Detti piacevoli*, T. Zanato (ed.) (Rome, 1983), 78, no. 211.

28 Rocke, *Forbidden Friendships*, 215–16; Canosa and Colonnello, *Storia*, 67–71; Ruggiero, *Boundaries of Eros*, 70–84, 118–20.

29 For unchaste women from 'good' families, see *ibid.*, 36–9, 55–64; and Mazzi, *Prostitute*, 88–96.

30 Christiane Klapisch-Zuber, 'Women servants in Florence during the fourteenth and fifteenth centuries' in B. A. Hanawalt (ed.) *Women and Work in Preindustrial Europe* (Bloomington, 1986), 69–70; Philip Gavitt, *Charity and Children in Renaissance Florence: The Ospedale degli Innocenti, 1410–1536* (Ann Arbor, 1990), 207.

31 Brundage, *Law*, 514–18; Ruggiero, *Boundaries of Eros*, 16–44, 89–108; Sandra Cavallo and Simona Cerruti, 'Female honor and the social control of reproduction in Piedmont between 1600 and 1800', in Muir and Ruggiero (eds) *Sex*

and Gender, 73–109; Gene Brucker, *Giovanni and Lusanna: Love and Marriage in Renaissance Florence* (Berkeley, 1986); Daniela Lombardi, 'Intervention by church and state in marriage disputes in sixteenth- and seventeenth-century Florence', in Dean and Lowe, (eds) *Crime, Society and the Law in Renaissance Italy*, 142–56. In Florence, unlike Venice, men condemned for fornication or rape were rarely given the option of marrying their victims, though they commonly had to provide a dowry for the unmarried ones.

32 Ruggiero, *Boundaries of Eros*, 45–69; Mazzi, *Prostitute*, 103–8.

33 ASF, OGBR 79, fols 9v–10r (8 March 1488).

34 Rocke, *Forbidden Friendships*, 162–3; Scarabello, 'Devianza', 80; Patricia Labalme, 'Sodomy and Venetian justice in the Renaissance', *Legal History Review* 52(1984): 236–7; Ruggiero, *Boundaries of Eros*, 95, 121–5, 149–54.

35 Rocke, *Forbidden Friendships*, 163, 182–9; Ruggiero, 'Marriage', 17–18; Mazzi, *Prostitute*, 110–12. Cases cited: ASF, OGBR 113, 78v (6 March 1499); ASF, UN 31, 65r–66v, 119v (21 February–5 April 1497); *ibid.* 34, 56r (26 August 1501).

36 Elizabeth S. Cohen, 'No longer virgins: self-presentation by young women in late Renaissance Rome', in M. Migiel and J. Schiesari (eds) *Refiguring Woman: Perspectives on Gender and the Italian Renaissance* (Ithaca NY, 1991), 172–4; Ruggiero, *Boundaries of Eros*, 16–69; Mazzi, *Prostitute*, 87, 103–16; Scarabello, 'Devianza', 78.

37 Ruggiero, *Boundaries of Eros*, 78–84; Scarabello, 'Devianza', 78–9.

38 ASF, UN 31, 44v (3 January 1497).

39 Rocke, *Forbidden Friendships*; Ruggiero, *Boundaries of Eros*, 109–45; Labalme, 'Sodomy'; Pavan, 'Police', 266–88; Canossa and Colonnello, *Storia*, 57–73.

40 Rocke, *Forbidden Friendships*, 87–132.

41 Bernardino of Siena, *Florence 1425*, II, 276; *Siena 1427*, I, 560; *ibid.*, II, 1158, 1160, 1166; *Novelle di Pietro Fortini*, T. Rughi (ed.) (Milan, 1923), 64; Girolamo Savonarola, *Prediche sopra i Salmi*, V. Romano (ed.) 2 vols (Rome, 1969), vol. I, 164.

42 Rocke, *Forbidden Friendships*, 94–7, 113–19. Passive partners in Venice appear somewhat younger than in Florence, though this may only reflect poorer reporting of age there; Ruggiero, *Boundaries of Eros*, 118, 121–5; Pavan, 'Police', 284.

43 R. Caggese (ed.) *Statuti della repubblica fiorentina*, 2 vols (Florence, 1910–21), vol. II, 218; ASF, PR 52, 128rv, (13 April 1365).

44 Rocke, *Forbidden Friendships*, 105–10.

45 Judith C. Brown, *Immodest Acts: The Life of a Lesbian Nun in Renaissance Italy* (New York, 1986).

46 Rocke, *Forbidden Friendships*, 51–2, 61, 99–101, 214–15; Ruggiero, *Boundaries of Eros*, 121–4.

47 Rocke, *Forbidden Friendships*, 101–5.

48 Labalme, 'Sodomy', 243 n73, 251 n160; Scarabello, 'Devianza', 82.

49 L. Cantini (ed.) *Legislazione toscana raccolta e illustrata*, 32 vols (Florence, 1800–8), vol. I, 211–13.

9

THE SINGLE SELF

Feminist thought and the marriage market in early modern Venice

Virginia Cox

Did women have a Renaissance?

This question, the title of Joan Kelly-Gadol's influential essay first published in 1977, has done more than perhaps any other single question to unveil the masculinist and patriarchal assumptions that underlay the traditional narrative of the Renaissance. For as Kelly-Gadol argued, that narrative had been one of progress in which men made decided gains. But if the emergence of a merchant culture benefited certain men, it appeared to have the opposite effect on women who, in her view, lost ground. This argument was more than an important contribution to women's history; it also constituted a major blow to the Renaissance paradigm. For if women (roughly half the population) suffered significant setbacks in the fifteenth and sixteenth centuries, why speak of a 'Renaissance' (at least a Renaissance understood as an era of progress) at all?

To a large degree, Kelly-Gadol's question has shaped much of the debate and many of the research agendas on the history of women in late medieval and early modern Europe ever since. She has had many supporters who have emphasized that the merchant families of the Renaissance cities, for example, were more constricting than their aristocratic counterparts, in which women exercised more power. As a result it has been possible to highlight the destructive patterns of patriarchal power in this period. At the same time, other scholars – especially recently – have begun to find evidence of remarkable agency and independence among women in this period. The economic historian Judith C. Brown, for example, has made an intriguing case that the labour market in Florence created new 'options' for women in the late Renaissance. To Brown, that is, this was a period of new opportunities for many Renaissance women, a view not at all inconsistent with the traditional narrative.

In the essay reprinted below, the English literary historian Virginia Cox offers a fundamentally new approach to women's history in this period. First, she does not begin with the questions of modern feminism about women's rights and liberties. Rather, she begins with the voices of Renaissance women themselves and the ways in which certain Renaissance women at least thought about their own position in society. She focuses in particular on two remarkable works: Moderata Fonte's The Worth of Women *and Lucrezia Marinella's* The

Nobility and Excellence of Women, *both first published in Venice in 1600. In these texts she discovers an arresting argument. For women, both Fonte and Marinella argue, the single state is to be preferred to marriage or to life in a convent. The argument may not sound revolutionary to us, but to women in sixteenth-century Italy it was radical, opening up the idea of an entirely new role for women, one that they themselves would choose and that would liberate them from the constraints not only of marriage and motherhood but also of the religious life.*

Like many other contributors to this volume, Cox is deeply concerned with context, but her approach is to focus on the economic factors that limited the traditional options for women. As dowry inflation increased, fathers found it increasingly difficult to contract marriages for their daughters; and many of these daughters, in turn, were increasingly reluctant to enter the monastic life. Fonte and Marinella, therefore, give value to a way of life that had earlier seemed unimaginable. They celebrate single women as women with the leisure to pursue scientific, poetic and other intellectual interests on their own, to look for a kind of completeness in their lives that traditionally had been exculsively the perquisite of men.

The original version of this essay appeared in Renaissance Quarterly *48(1995): 513–81. Given the length of the original article, it has been necessary to abridge it significantly. The author has assisted me greatly in this role, rewriting portions of the essay to accommodate the abridgements. As always, students who wish to pursue this topic in greater detail should also study the original version, along with the texts of Fonte and Marinella, both of which have recently been published in English translations: Marinella's as* The Nobility and Excellence of Women and the Defects and Vices of Men, *ed. and trans. Anne Dunhill, with an introduction by Letezia Panizza (Chicago, 1999) and Fonte's as* The Worth of Women, *ed. and trans. Virginia Cox (Chicago, 1997).*

*   *   *

The year 1600 witnessed a significant, though little noted event in Italian cultural history: the publication of the first substantial full-length works by Italian women writers arguing the case for women's moral and intellectual equality with men.[1] The writers in question were two Venetians, Lucrezia Marinella and Modesta Pozzo (Moderata Fonte); their works, respectively, a polemical treatise, *La nobiltà et l'eccellenza delle donne* and a dialogue, *Il merito delle donne.* These texts, long neglected, have recently begun to attract a certain amount of critical attention: particularly Fonte's *Merito,* far the more accessible of the two and a work, as is now being recognized, of considerable literary merit.[2]

The obvious intellectual context for these works is the long-running debate on women's equality that by the end of the sixteenth century had been consuming a steady stream of ink in Italy and Europe for over a hundred years.[3] Marinella's *Nobiltà* very self-consciously enters the lists of this debate: commissioned as a reply to Giuseppe Passi's virulently misogynistic *I difetti e mancamenti delle donne* (1599), it eruditely recapitulates a century of debate on women and pits itself explicitly against the most prestigious vernacular exponents of traditionalist positions.[4] Fonte's *Merito* has a more oblique relation to the tradition of 'defences of women', but beneath the surface *sprezzatura* of its lively and spontaneous dialogue, it too draws heavily on the stock of arguments and exempla that had accumulated over a century of debate.

To this extent, then, Marinella's *Nobiltà* and Fonte's *Merito delle donne* may be viewed as tardy interventions in a long-running *querelle* whose parameters had been set in the early decades of the sixteenth century and which had for years been running rather wearily down well-marked polemical lines. It would be mistaken, however, to regard these writers' analyses of the injustices suffered by their sex simply as a rhetorical exercise, conducted in isolation from the social realities around them. Certainly we cannot ignore the massive presence in these works of elements deriving from literary sources: it would be hopelessly naive to read them as unmediated expressions of women's discontent with their lot. But it will be my contention here that it is only by placing these works in their sociohistorical context, by tracing their links – sometimes direct, sometimes more oblique – with the realities of women's condition in Venice in the period, that we can fully understand the peculiar set of emphases they bring to bear on the subject under discussion.

Tradition and innovation in Moderata Fonte and Lucrezia Marinella

Before going on to consider the degree to which Fonte's and Marinella's writings may be seen as reflecting contemporary social realities, it will be useful first briefly to identify the respects in which these writings differ from the previous tradition of humanistic 'defences of women' alluded to above.[5] Between the fourteenth and sixteenth centuries in Italy, in their efforts to counter the essentialist conceptions of women's inferiority prevalent in contemporary scholastic culture, humanists sympathetic to women's interests – or ambitious of women's patronage – had elaborated a well-established body of arguments in favour of women's equality with men. In characteristic humanistic mode, these arguments rested largely on the evidence of classical history, which showed women to have been capable of the same achievements as men, where they had been given the opportunity to develop and exercise their natural abilities. Women's political subordination to men could not, then, it was argued, be said to have any justification in nature; nor, it was further claimed, did Christian theology offer any basis for such a discrimination between the sexes.

With its biological and theological underpinnings shot away, the myth of male superiority was revealed by Renaissance 'defenders of women' as a purely cultural and ideological construct, created to throw a veil of legitimacy over a dominance in fact rooted entirely in naked self-interest.

As will be clear from the preceding summary, the Renaissance debate on women's equality may be seen, in important respects, as foreshadowing later and more politicized variants of feminist thought. A key respect in which this earlier tradition differs from modern feminism, however, is that the powerful theoretical arguments for women's equality marshalled by Renaissance 'defenders of women' were never – or only rarely and ambiguously – pursued to the point of advocating social or political reform. This is true even of those writers who presented the relation between the sexes in the most provocatively politicized terms, describing men's dominance over women as a 'tyranny;' even here, no concrete redress appears to be envisaged in any form of emancipation for women. It is in this regard, most signally, that Fonte's and Marinella's writings may be seen as breaking new ground with respect to the previous tradition of 'defences of women'. While it would be misleading to suggest that either formulates anything approaching a coherent and fully developed programme of social reform in her writings, it is nonetheless striking that, unlike their predecessors in the *querelle des femmes*, both Fonte and Marinella do – sporadically, at least – contemplate the possibility of women rousing themselves from their 'long sleep'[6] and freeing themselves from their dependence on men. The theme of emancipation recurs in these writers' works in different contexts and with different inflections, from the fantastic to the quotidian, the deliberately utopian to the tantalizingly attainable. At one extreme – self-consciously fantastic but nonetheless expressive of real tensions – is Leonora's proposal in *Il merito delle donne* for an armed uprising by women against men.[7] More realistic aspirations centre on improved educational opportunities for women and, crucially, the opportunity to participate in public life. 'Would to God', Marinella exclaims, 'that in our times it were permitted for women to be skilled at arms and letters! What marvellous feats we should see, the like of which were never heard, in maintaining and expanding kingdoms!'[8]

Marinella is dismissive of the argument that women are unsuited to public activity: outside Italy, as she points out, women's horizons are far less circumscribed than at home. In France, Spain and England, women are permitted to succeed to fiefs and even kingdoms, while, on a humbler level in Germany, Flanders and France, they play an active role in commerce. In France, indeed, the financial reins of households and family businesses are firmly in female hands: 'men there may not spend even a *centime* unless at the request of their wives, and women not only administrate business dealings and sales but private income as well'.[9]

The capacity of women to participate in commerce cannot be contested in the face of such evidence: these foreign women, after all, 'attend to business with a diligence that is unsurpassed by the foremost merchant in all Italy'.[10]

However much wishful thinking may be involved in Marinella's description of foreign women's freedoms,[11] this passage is important in that it presents a broadening of women's opportunities as a possibility lying only just beyond her readers' grasp. The notion of women participating in public life is not being discussed in this passage as an historical curiosity or as one of the more eccentric and unworkable ideas in Plato's *Republic*.[12] What Marinella is demanding for Italian women is no more than what she claims women enjoy elsewhere in Europe at the present moment: the opportunity to exercise their native energies and talents in the public sphere.

A similar focus on aims that, if ambitious, are at least conceived of as relatively attainable, is apparent in the remarkable second book of *Il merito delle donne*. This book is largely occupied by an encyclopedic overview of the major fields of secular knowledge, from geography and meteorology to politics, law, rhetoric and medicine. It would be easy to dismiss this section of the dialogue as an empty display of erudition, an unmotivated interruption of the feminist themes of the first book. In fact, however, the place of this apparent digression in the overall economy of the work is indicated by one of the speakers, Lucrezia, when after a lengthy discussion of the medicinal properties of herbs, she replies to a companion who has suggested that discussions of healing are best left to professionals. 'On the contrary', she argues, 'it is right for us to learn about these things, so we can look after ourselves without needing help from men. In fact, it would be a good thing if there were women who knew about medicine as well as men, so men could not boast about their superiority in this field and we did not have to be dependent on them'.[13]

The hint in this passage of the possibility of women achieving effective autonomy from men is, as I have suggested, one that may help explain the intended function of this second book. If the principal means by which men exert their 'tyranny' over women is by their jealous monopoly on learning, then women's first task if they want to break free is to set about educating themselves.[14] It is perhaps exaggerated to suggest that it is concretely envisaged in Book 2 of *Il merito delle donne* that women might one day be in a position to engage in the same kind of professional activities as men. But to show a group of women conducting a reasonably informed discussion of traditional male provinces such as medicine and law was at least a strong reminder that if women were excluded from these professions, it was not because they lacked the native abilities necessary for participation in these fields.

This reading of Book 2 finds support in an extraordinary passage towards the end of the book that marks perhaps more clearly than any other the distance that separates the perspective on the question of women's equality in *Il merito delle donne* from that of the previous tradition of 'defences of women'. The 'official' theme of the second day's discussions – pursued in a semi-serious way – has been the question of whether and by what means men could be persuaded to abandon their misogynist views. At the end, one of the speakers, Cornelia, in a moment of frustration, dismisses this whole line of inquiry by pointing out that there is no use in women's attempting to win their enemies round. The only way in which women could achieve a genuine equality with men, she suggests, would be by freeing themselves from economic dependence and learning to fend for themselves.

> Would it not be possible for us just to banish these men from our lives, and escape their carping and jeering once and for all? Could we not live without them? Could we not earn our own living and manage our affairs without help from them? Come on, let us wake up, and claim back our freedom, and the honor and dignity they have usurped from us for so long. Do you think that if we really put our minds to it, we would be lacking the courage to defend ourselves, the strength to fend for ourselves, or the talents to earn our own living?[15]

While it would be rash to place too much significance on an isolated outburst in the dialogue, it is important to recognize the novelty Cornelia's proposal represents. An unstated assumption of the tradition of 'defences of women' prior to *Il merito delle donne* is that what is at stake for women is no more than a recognition on men's part of the dignity of their sex. In the words of one participant in the debate who brings this assumption into the open, women have no desire 'to escape from the unjust tyranny under which they must live'. They are content to remain in their subservient position. What is intolerable is that men fail to pay due respect to the 'dignity' and 'honour' of their sex.[16]

What is striking in the passage quoted above from *Il merito delle donne* is that Fonte's Cornelia does not stop at demanding the restitution of women's *onor* and *dignità*, but proposes instead a full-scale recuperation of their *libertà*. A world is envisaged in which women might enjoy a concrete and substantive parity, where their qualities and strengths would be not simply acknowledged but exercised. As was noted above, this utopian possibility is only occasionally glimpsed, both here and in Marinella's *Nobiltà et eccellenza*; there is nothing here approaching a coherent manifesto for social reform. This, however, is scarcely surprising given the circumstances within which these women were writing. What is more surprising – and what needs to be stressed in view of its absence from the previous tradition – is that this possibility of effective equality is envisaged at all. This aspect of their writing gives Marinella and Fonte some claim to be viewed less as exponents of the feminist thought of the century that was ending as they wrote, than as precursors of developments in the century to come.[17]

One element of novelty in the passage just quoted that deserves further attention is the emphasis it gives to the economic dimension of women's subordination. The possibility of women achieving a real and effectual equality with men is squarely perceived as dependent on their ability to 'earn their own living', to 'fend for themselves'. This attention to an aspect of women's condition almost entirely ignored in the tradition of 'defences' is a consistent feature of Fonte's *Merito*, and even in the more rarefied atmosphere of Marinella's *Nobiltà* we find traces of an awareness of the financial realities of women's lives.[18] The importance of this in assessing the originality of these texts can hardly be exaggerated: it is their firm grasp of the links between money and power, between financial self-sufficiency and freedom, that underpins much of what is most new and vital in their analyses of women's condition.

This stress on the economic realities of women's lives is an aspect of Fonte and Marinella's thought that can plausibly be related to the Venetian cultural environment. It is perhaps prudent not to exaggerate the extent to which the Venetian patriciate retained its traditional mercantile ethos in the period when Fonte and Marinella were writing: the cinquecento had seen a decisive shift away from trade towards landed investment, and the works of Venetian moralists of the period are filled with reproofs against the decadent attitudes of young patricians who neglect the mercantile traditions of their forefathers and dedicate themselves to a life of *rentier* ease.[19] Nevertheless, these complaints in themselves testify to the persistence of more traditional values, and certainly it seems safe to maintain that even at the end of the century Venice retained a more robust attitude towards money than the courts of the Terraferma in which much of the preceding discourse on women's equality had been produced.

This aspect of Venetian culture may help to account at a general level for the sensitivity Fonte and Marinella display to the economic realities of women's condition. It cannot, however, alone account for the extremely marked sense of financial grievance that pervades the treatment of women's relations with men in *Il merito delle donne*. Women are presented consistently in *Il merito* as the hapless victims of men's greed: we hear of fathers cheating their daughters of their inheritance; of brothers misappropriating their sisters' portions; of husbands mismanaging dowries; of sons reducing their widowed mothers to penury. Even the state is implicated in this conspiracy to cheat women of their dues: in a rare moment of insight into the institutional dimension of women's oppression, it is suggested that the Venetian justice system is simply a mechanism for legitimating male tyranny and greed.[20]

To understand the emphasis that is placed in the dialogue on women's financial powerlessness, it is necessary to consider the circumstances in which *Il merito delle donne* was written. The second half of the sixteenth century in Italy witnessed a series of social and economic changes which had profound and far-reaching implications for upper-class women's lives. Specifically, due to a combination of factors bearing on families' financial strategies, the prospects of marriage for women of these classes were drastically reduced. As a prolonged period of economic retrenchment coincided with a widespread adoption by the urban upper classes of aristocratic practices and aspirations, there was an increasing tendency among these classes to attempt to keep family patrimonies intact by limiting marriages to one or two in each generation, thus ensuring concentration of inheritance on a single line and preventing dispersal of resources through the payment of dowries.[21]

The consequences of this policy for women's lives, as I have suggested, were dramatic and far-reaching. Most obviously, it resulted in an influx of 'excess' daughters into convents; though not without precedent, it was during this period that the practice of *monacazione forzata* or forced claustration, most notoriously exemplified by Manzoni's *monaca di Monza*, first began to become the widespread social phenomenon it would remain for the whole of the seventeenth century.[22] At the same time, as pressure on convent places grew and the cost of placing daughters in convents increased, this period saw the appearance of the virtually unprecedented figure of the secular spinster.[23]

It is against the background of these dramatic changes in women's position and prospects that we should situate Fonte and Marinella's analyses of women's condition. At the time they were writing, vast numbers of upper-class women in Italy were finding themselves deprived of their traditional career of marriage, while a significant number – though the extent of the phenomenon is difficult to estimate – appear to have found themselves precluded as well from the alternative of the convent. This was a development whose importance can scarcely be exaggerated in a society that offered no real alternative to women of this class. The reduction in marriage opportunities cut many women adrift from the only identities their culture could offer them. At the same time, more concretely, in a society in which women's financial standing depended crucially on their possession of a dowry, the crisis in the marriage market left many women severely disadvantaged, deprived of even the limited degree of financial power and autonomy that their mothers and grandmothers had enjoyed.

Two characteristics I have noted as distinguishing Fonte and Marinella from previous 'defenders of women' are the seriousness with which they contemplate the possibility of a broadening of opportunities for women and their acute sensitivity to the economic realities of women's lives. What I want to explore now is the possibility that these novel elements in their analyses of women's condition may be linked with the set of historical circumstances I have outlined above. My suggestion will be that if it is now for the first time at the end of the sixteenth century that we find Italian women contributing to the long-running debate on the status of their sex, this may be because a whole class of women – and precisely those most likely to be readers and writers[24] – were finding their status and identity under threat.

The next section of this study will be devoted to exploring the evidence we possess, aside from Fonte's and Marinella's treatises, of the ways in which the policy of marriage limitation affected contemporary perceptions of women's role. This investigation will be limited to Venice, for although reduced nubility in the urban upper classes was a development common to the whole of Italy in this period, the extent of the phenomenon and the precise nature of its effects depended to a great deal on local social and economic circumstances. There is evidence, moreover, to suggest that the effects of marriage limitation were particularly acute and visible in Venice; this may, indeed, be one of the reasons – though the question is obviously a complex one – why it should be in Venice alone that we find women writers of this period coming forward to challenge the subordinate position allotted by society to their sex?[25]

The policy of marriage limitation in Venice and its social and psychological effects

The sixteenth century saw a decisive change in the economic life of the Venetian patriciate, a shift from the commercial activities through which the Serenissima's wealth had been accumulated to safer and less speculative investment in the farmlands of the mainland.[26] The chronology of this process, its motives and effects, are still a matter for discussion: landed investment was already becoming common in the Quattrocento, and it has been suggested that, by the early Cinquecento, Machiavelli's well known characterization of the Venetian nobility as merchants rather than genuine *gentiluomini* reflects an outsider's view of a reality which was already undergoing change.[27] In the early period of land purchases on the mainland, however, investment in property seems to have gone hand-in-hand with a continued commitment to commerce. The real change occurred in the later decades of the Cinquecento, when increased investment in land coincided with a large-scale withdrawal from trade.[28]

Moderata Fonte's *Il merito delle donne* reflects the social realities of an economy in transition. The dialogue opens with an impassioned tribute to Venice as a city of the sea, and a later passage reveals the speakers' appreciation of the 'important science' of shipbuilding and their imaginative engagement with the travails of the merchant sailor.[29] There are frequent mentions as well, however, of the pleasures and pains of life *in villa*, ranging from expressions of concern for the tribulations of tenants in the recent bad harvests to appreciations of the dancing of local shepherdesses and gleeful anticipation of the bird-hunting season.[30]

One consequence of the economic retrenchment of which the shift to landed investment was both a symptom and a cause was an increasing preoccupation with the conservation of family wealth. This concern with wealth conservation was reflected in changes in inheritance patterns during this period. It had long been customary in Venice for a father's estate to be divided equally between his sons, who then continued to live and trade together *in fraterna*.[31] This practice had been advantagous when Venice was a great trading power, as it maximized the possibilities for entrepreneurial activity. By the late sixteenth century, however, when increasingly large portions of patrician estates were in *immobili*, this practice of division threatened patrimonies with dispersion. Since custom forbade a simple transition to the practice of primogeniture practiced elsewhere in Italy, the means adopted were, first, to entail the estate; second, to limit the succession to a single line of descent by ensuring – it seems by informal agreement – that only one male member of the family married.[32]

More hung on the practice of marriage limitation than simply the fortunes of individual households: the future of the Venetian patriciate as a ruling class was perceived as being at stake. The dangers that would result for the Venetian state from a failure to keep patrician marriage rates down are clearly exposed in Ludovico Settala's *Della ragion di stato* (1627):

> And because this kind of government is made up of a determinate number of families … reason of state demands that the fathers should ensure that few of their sons marry. … for any great increase in the number of those qualified to participate in government might transform the republic into a popular regime. Moreover, the disputes over inheritance that would ensue might impoverish the nobility and bring it into disrepute, for, to live well, noblemen would be forced to engage in sordid trades. Alternatively, there is the danger that poverty among the nobility would reach intolerable levels, since it would affect so many, and that this might lead to such social upheaval that it would bring down the regime.[33]

Though the fears expressed here were not always so clearly articulated, they underlie the strategies of the Venetian patriciate from the mid-sixteenth century onwards. The imperative of marriage limitation was political as much as economic: the impoverishment of the nobility was a threat to the well-being and survival of the state.[34]

What were the consequences for women of these changes in the financial strategies of patrician households? Most crucially, they resulted in a sharp reduction in Venetian noblewomen's prospects of marriage. Dowry payments had represented an increasing strain on family resources since the early fifteenth century, as the growing exclusivity of the Venetian patriciate and the central place occupied by marriage in families' social strategies pushed up the market value of eligible matches.[35] This trend was exacerbated in the late sixteenth century with the reduction in the numbers of male patricians marrying; dowry inflation soared, and precisely at a time when the conservation of resources was imperative. The result was a tendency increasingly to concentrate what resources were available on one or two daughters, frequently the younger ones, while consigning the others to the cheaper alternative of the convent.[36]

To understand the full implications of this drastic reduction in marriage opportunities for women, it is useful to consider what it meant for women in economic terms. When marriage was an available option for the majority of patrician women, the male and female offspring of patrician families had received equal shares in their father's estate. A daughter's dowry constituted legally her share of the family patrimony and must by law be congruent with the portions of her brothers. A woman's dowry was not a privilege but her right; if a father died without providing for his daughters, their dowries were considered an outstanding debt and the obligation passed to his heirs.[37]

One result of the reduction in marriage opportunities for women in the latter decades of the sixteenth century was to undermine the principle that women were entitled to a share in the family estate.[38] Where the law continued to recognize equal inheritance rights for men and women, in actuality women's rights were dependent on their families' ability and willingness to find them a partner. The consequences of this change were more than purely formal: although it is true that a woman's dowry passed into her husband's administration during his lifetime, it remained in law her property and was returned to her on his death.[39] A series of recent studies by Stanley Chojnacki has stressed that, with the dowry inflation of the early Renaissance, patrician women came to play a far more active role in the city's economic life than is generally supposed.[40] As dowries rose, the amounts of money controlled by women became more and more significant; and Chojnacki has argued convincingly that this financial power was reflected in an enhancement of the status of married women and widows within households.

We must not be tempted to exaggerate the extent of patrician women's financial autonomy, but nor should we underestimate the very significant change it signalled for the status of women of this class when a considerable proportion of them began to find themselves excluded from the possibility of marriage. Women's power and standing in the family depended crucially on the possession of a dowry, and law and custom had encouraged them to regard a dowry as their due.[41] When at the end of the sixteenth century many patrician women found themselves dowerless and effectively disinherited, it must have been a cruel reminder of their status as pawns in the financial and social strategies of the *casa*.

How conscious were Venetian noblewomen – and men – of the late sixteenth and early seventeenth century of the extent to which women's prospects had changed since the days of their grandmothers? It is a problem to which it is difficult to provide even a conjectural answer. The changes I have been examining did not happen overnight; nor, obviously, did they affect women in a uniform way. Many women did, of course, continue to marry, and with the vast inflation in dowries those fortunate enough to find husbands were better off than before. This variety in individual destinies must to contemporary observers have obscured the broader patterns which emerge with the hindsight of history.

Nor should it be forgotten that to identify a change in the status of women, it is necessary to have a conception of women – women of a certain class at least – as a distinct social (as opposed to simply biological) group. Although this kind of feminist awareness is apparent in a highly developed form in the treatises of Fonte and Marinella, it would be rash to assume that it was an awareness shared by many of their peers. Certainly, a century of intense debate on the status of their sex had supplied literate men and women with at least the rudimentary conceptual tools for an analysis of the political and social dimension of sex difference. But it must be remembered that in their mental map of social groupings, this relatively novel and as yet faintly traced division by gender was competing with other far more clearly defined groupings of family and class.

Nevertheless, a certain amount of evidence does suggest that, at least by the early Seicento, Venetian patricians were beginning to become aware that an injustice was being done to a large section of the female members of their class. There is also some evidence of a certain discontent and resentment on the part of women, most of it, unsurprisingly, from the convents where unmarriageable noblewomen were 'stored'.[42] The majority of this evidence of women's perceptions is indirect, as is inevitable in a society that excluded women almost entirely from the means of self-expression. We are, however, fortunate enough to possess one direct testimony of the experience of a woman directly affected by the policy of marriage limitation, in the extraordinary writings of the recalcitrant nun Arcangela Tarabotti (1604–52).

Tarabotti's most memorable writings, *La semplicità ingannata* and *L'inferno monacale*, both deal with the phenomenon of forced claustration, of which she had herself been a victim.[43] The nucleus of her analysis of the phenomenon and the strongly feminist terms in which it is conducted are indicated by the original title of *La semplicità*: *La tirannia paterna*. The practice of coercing unwanted daughters to enter convents is presented as a tyrannical abuse of authority on the part of Venetian fathers intent on preserving their wealth. Any pretence at more creditable motives is mercilessly stripped away: while fathers of nuns may hypocritically pride themselves on their concern for their daughters' spiritual welfare, the least scrutiny reveals that theirs is a 'self-interested action, motivated purely by worldly pride and the desire to pile up riches'.[44]

The blame for this outrage does not, however, stop at individual fathers: their crimes are carried out with the complicity of the government itself and the church. It is this institutional involvement, in fact, that makes the practice of forced claustration so peculiarly reprehensible: 'that private citizens should commit such enormities for their own self-interest is in itself a detestable abuse, but that those in authority should allow this to happen is something that would strike horror into insensibility itself'.[45] The irony is stressed of the Venetian state's condoning a practice in flagrant contradiction of its stated principles: while ostensibly Venice is the home of liberty, in fact 'Paternal Tyranny, concealed under the majesty of senatorial robes, has set up its seat in the Ducal Palace and now rules the entire city'.[46]

Tarabotti shows herself familiar with political justifications for marriage limitation, but denies the suggestion that such considerations can justify an abuse of the magnitude she describes. She acknowledges the fear that were the patriciate to attempt to furnish all its daughters with dowries, this would reduce the nobility to bankruptcy, with dangerous results.[47] However, she suggests, if the Venetian patriciate is so concerned about the economic and political effects that would result from 'paying out so many dowries', then instead of subjecting young women to the living death of conventual life, it would do better to eliminate the excessive dowries that constitute the cause of the problem or to relax the insistence on endogamy that so limits their possibilities of marriage.[48] At the very least it could absolve women from the vows that condemn them to a lifetime of hypocrisy and allow them to live in relative peace and comfort at home. After all, as Tarabotti notes with bitter sarcasm, the dangers of an armed uprising by women overthrowing the republic is not one that should cause the Venetian government too much lost sleep:

Women cannot lay claim to your ruling status or seize it from you: they cannot even recoup those powers that you have so rashly and highhandedly usurped from them. It is true that if all nuns who lacked a vocation were on the outside, their number would be great enough to form a vast army, but they would not turn their attention to conquering kingdoms; on the contrary, they would be quite happy to remain confined within their paternal homes ... Can it be that you are afraid at the number of women in the world? What cowards! We are no longer living in the days of those valiant Amazon women, who so prudently killed their menfolk in order not to be subject to them.[49]

As this quotation illustrates, Tarabotti's denunciation of the abuse of forced claustration is embedded in a more general analysis of the subordinate condition of women. Her writings, in fact, make an illuminating point of comparison with those of Marinella and Fonte: while she goes considerably further than they, in some respects, especially in her condemnation of the institutional dimension of women's oppression, there are also interesting continuities between her work and theirs.[50] Of particular interest in the present context is the fact that like her predecessors, Tarabotti not only insists that women are naturally the equals of men, but also concretely envisages the possibility of women entering male fields of activity and competing with them directly for 'honour and gain'.[51] In Tarabotti's case these fantasies of emancipation can easily be related to the circumstances in which she was writing, circumstances calculated to provoke meditation on the limited choices society offered to women. In the case of Marinella and Fonte the links between experience and theory are less easily traced; but the similarities we find between their thought and Tarabotti's lend some support to the notion that the particular strain of feminist thought we encounter in their writings may have its genesis, in part, in the same conjunction of circumstances.

If Tarabotti's denunciation of the practice of forced claustration is unique in its radicalism, other, more complacent commentators also display a certain sensitivity to the injustice of this abuse. This is most evident in documents dealing with the problem of conventual reform. The period following the Council of Trent saw a prolonged struggle on the part of the Roman Church to tighten the notoriously lax regulations of Venetian convents.[52] However, papal projects for reform frequently met with opposition, not only from nuns themselves but also from the Venetian clergy and government, aware of the function that convents fulfilled as a safety-valve for patrician domestic finance. Comments on this issue frequently reveal a consciousness on the part of Venetian clerics and patricians of the economic roots of many novices' 'vocations', and a distinct unease about the justice of submitting unwilling noblewomen to a discipline not freely chosen.

One such comment is particularly revealing. In 1629 the Venetian Patriarch Giovanni Tiepolo, justifying to the Doge and the Senate his action in softening the regulations governing convent discipline, observed that the nuns he was concerned for were noble and brought up in the utmost luxury and refinement: their status was such that if they had been of the opposite sex, they would have been destined to government and high office. Instead, being women they had been forced to sacrifice their liberty for the good of the state and their families so that the least they could expect in return was a reasonably pleasant and unconstrained life.[53] After all, Tiepolo reflects, if the two thousand or more Venetian noblewomen stored in convents 'as though in a public warehouse' were to have insisted on remaining in the world, their action would have plunged the whole of Venetian society into a maelstrom of disorder and scandal. Set against Tarabotti's fierce outrage at the same abuse, Patriarch Tiepolo's well meaning pragmatism may seem chilling, but given the difference in their circumstances, this difference in tone is scarcely surprising. What is more interesting is the degree to which this eminent cleric's argument shares the feminist premises exhibited by Tarabotti herself or by Marinella or Fonte. Women are seen here indisputably as a social group, their position defined by custom and politics rather than nature. Their moral and intellectual equality with men is assumed, and it is accepted that only their gender precludes them from playing the same role in the life of the state. How representative Tiepolo's position on the issue is, we are not in a position to evaluate. But his arguments do suggest that some members at least of the Venetian establishment did perceive women as a group as having a justified grievance against the state.

Another striking feature of this commentary of Tiepolo's is the keen sense it displays of women as potentially a disruptive social force. The 'public warehouse' of the convents is represented as a kind of powder keg: 'if they had been able to or wished to choose some other future', the hordes of unmarried women being kept in cold storage would have had the potential to unleash a tide of 'confusion' and 'disorder' into society that we might see as an echo of the armed uprising ironically threatened by Tarabotti. Of course, as Tiepolo was well aware, women's choice in the matter was in real terms severely limited since there was little they could do to resist the decision forced upon them by family interests. But an element of choice did exist: a women's consent was required for her to enter a convent.[54] 'If they had been able to or wished to choose differently': in this fragile margin of uncertainty lay the possibility, as Tiepolo recognized, of women holding their society to ransom.

To what extent can we assume that Tiepolo's reasoning in his plea to the Senate is a reflection of the views of Venetian nuns themselves? Aside from Tarabotti, there is some evidence that this was the case. Certainly,

Venetian novices can hardly have been unaware of the financial interests which had constrained them to take the veil;[55] and it seems probable that their consent to being placed in the 'public warehouse' of the convent for the good of the family fortune was conditional on being allowed to live a reasonably untrammelled life. A nun in Udine in 1601, questioned about the authenticity of her vocation, commented artlessly that she had taken the veil 'of my own free will, because, having many sisters, it seemed to me that I had no choice', and maintained that she had not realized this decision implied any real constraints on her freedom.[56] Attempts to impose a stricter regime on convents were met with resentment; even, it seems, with revolt. A nuncio's report of 1580, following Gregory XIII's proposal for a tightening of regulations, speaks of the concern expressed in the Venetian Senate that young noblewomen, already showing signs of a reluctance to embrace conventual life, might be provoked by the proposed reforms into a position of outright defiance.[57] The fear is not merely a speculative one: even now, with the rumour of reform in the air, some young women are 'boldly refusing to take the veil'.

Even apart from direct testimonies such as this, the reluctance of Venetian nuns to accept any constraints on their freedom is amply testified by the sheer number of apparently ineffectual attempts at reform that followed each other in close succession over the period in question. Nuns, it appears, were simply not prepared to sacrifice personal comfort, freedom from dress restrictions, and access to their families and friends. It would be rash, of course, to deduce from this low-key quotidian rebellion that Tarabotti's fellow-victims shared her acute and highly politicized consciousness of the injustice of their position.[58] But such consistent infractions of conventual regulations do suggest that the *monache forzate* of this period were conscious enough of the anomalous nature of their position to consider themselves as in some sense standing outside the rules.

The practice of forced claustration, the area from which all my evidence to this point has been drawn, was only the most dramatic social consequence of the policy of marriage restriction. Another associated effect, which also aroused comment, was the appearance in society of the virtually unprecedented figure of the secular spinster.[59] As the going rate for secular dowries spiralled and the demand for places in convents increased, the monastic dowry that the convent demanded from the family of any new novice also underwent inflation. Placing a daughter as a nun remained cheaper than attempting to buy her a suitable marriage partner, but it was by no means cheap enough to be within every patrician family's means.[60] Despite the government's attempts to curb the expenses involved in placing daughters in convents, a significant number of patrician families must have found themselves with unmarried and unmarriageable daughters left on their hands.[61]

What happened to these women? Custom offered no precedent for their position and, unsurprisingly, in a society that valued women primarily as breeding stock, the lives of these patrician spinsters have vanished almost without record. A valuable clue to their fate, however, is offered by Moderata Fonte in an important passage of *Il merito delle donne* that will be discussed at greater length later in this study. The context is a rehearsal of the evils resulting to women from the improvidence and avarice of their fathers and brothers. Fathers, it is claimed, frequently fail to make provision for their daughters in their wills; and, in such cases, the poor creatures have little alternative but to turn to 'blameworthy and despicable' means. But even when a father has thought to provide for his daughter, her dowry is often usurped by her brothers, who keep her on in the house as an unpaid servant, effectively 'buried alive'.[62]

Although the blame for these women's sad fate is attributed to carelessness and cruelty rather than economic necessity, it seems reasonable to interpret the passage as a reflection of the situation outlined above. It is difficult to substantiate Fonte's claim that girls of good family were forced into prostitution for want of a dowry,[63] although the unexpected sympathy with the plight of prostitutes shown on another occasion in the dialogue might lead us to conjecture that the author knew of such cases within her own circles.[64] Where Fonte's other claim is concerned, however – that unmarried sisters were retained at home by their brothers effectively as servants – there is interesting evidence that this was indeed the case. In his introduction to a treatise in praise of virginity (Venice, 1584), the publisher Giovanni Giolito piously notes that one of God's greatest gifts to the current age has been his rekindling of the spirit of female celibacy even outside the usual context of the convent, with the creation of secular orders like that of St Ursula.[65] This new state of secular celibacy is particularly welcome because many women, though 'feeling called to observe the state of virginity', are unable to enter a convent, among other reasons, 'for the lack of a sufficient dowry'. It is patently unfair that such worldly considerations should interfere with these women's vocation; and the institution of an alternative 'second degree of celibacy' provides a valuable compromise solution to this dilemma.[66]

After this lofty beginning Giolito rapidly descends to more practical matters. Apart from the spiritual satisfaction of the individuals concerned, another advantage of this new estate is its social utility, which makes it almost a necessity. Although he insists on the voluntary nature of the commitment, and explicitly notes that secular celibacy is not merely a cheap way to dispose of one's daughters, Giolito's consideration of the 'various benefits' deriving from the presence of such 'second-grade' virgins brings us very close to the economic realities that made this 'third estate' so attractive to the Venetians of his day.

Would it not be most welcome to any father with a modest income or with many daughters, not all of whom he could afford to marry or to send to a convent (and even to those fathers who *could* afford it), that there should be a respectable third estate that would allow these young women who felt so inclined to serve God in a celibate state in their own homes, without any danger to their reputation? And, in addition, these women could help their mothers and sisters-in-law, help bring up their nephews and nieces in the fear of God and keep the house in good order.[67]

Giolito's letter and the treatise it accompanies are addressed to the congregation of St Ursula, and it is within the relatively formalized context of this order that he envisages secular celibacy. The late sixteenth century saw the appearance in Italy of a number of new or refounded tertiary orders of this kind, supplanting in some cases the older orders suppressed as a result of the Tridentine rulings on enclosure.[68] In part, these foundations can be seen as manifestations of the new forms of spirituality fostered by the Counter-reformation. Giolito's enthusiasm, however, reminds us that another factor determining their emergence was their practical usefulness as a response to the social needs of communities of declining nuptuality.

Another document of the period, slightly earlier than Giolito's *Lettera*, provides a valuable insight into the social need which orders like the Ursulines met. The *Modo di vivere proposto alle vergini che si chiaman dimesse* (Venice, 1577) by Agostino Valier or Valiero, Bishop of Verona, was published a decade before the introduction of the order of the Dimesse in Venice.[69] An advice book for unmarried women living at home with their families, Valier's treatise is valuable for our present purposes, as beneath its pious and reassuring surface it gives a good impression of the difficulties that the existence of such women presented for a society which had no recognized place for them.

Valier was well placed to speak of the problem, as he had himself after his father's death been in the position of settling his sisters. One, Laura, he married very respectably to the patrician Giorgio Gradenigo;[70] but at least one other, Donata, the dedicatee of the treatise under discussion, remained unmarried, presumably through a lack of funds for a dowry. Valier is too delicate to mention the financial considerations that might lead to the choice of an unmarried life for a woman, but in other respects his prescriptions ironically underscore Fonte's bleak description of the fate of a sister in this situation as a life sentence to unpaid service. The Dimessa can ensure her conquest of the flesh by contenting herself with eating 'the plainest of foods' and eschewing the finery of her married sisters for clothes of 'poco prezzo'.[71] Her functions in the home will include those of governess, confidante and spiritual guide, but she should not disdain, when necessary as an exercise in the virtue of humility, to 'perform any household task that may be required'.[72]

Much stress is placed in Valier's treatise on discipline and self-discipline. The Dimessa must exert great vigilance and energy in detecting and repressing her sinful urges; and she must entrust her spiritual guidance to a reliable confessor in a spirit of utter obedience.[73] Of course, this emphasis on repression and obedience is common to much of the conduct literature of the period, especially that produced in ecclesiastical circles and addressed to women.[74] In Valier's treatise, however, this advice is given a particular urgency by the fact that he is conscious of the equivocal position in which women like his sister found themselves. For all the efforts of writers like himself and Giolito to present their situation as a valid new 'estate' to be added to women's traditional estates of marriage and the convent life, spinsters such as Donata Valier must at some level have been conscious that their position was less that of pioneers than of economic refugees.[75] No cultural models existed to validate their lives, no institution existed to regulate them, and they took no formal vows of obedience to a husband or to the church. They lived in the world and could hardly be expected entirely to ignore its temptations. Valier assumes the presence in the family circle of married sisters or sisters-in-law often 'madly infatuated with worldly pleasures'.[76] The Dimessa's only protection against temptation was self-discipline and a self-imposed insulation from the world. It is not difficult to imagine the threat such women potentially presented to social stability; nor the enthusiasm with which Venetian clerics like Valier advocated the foundation of institutions like the Casa delle Dimesse of Murano (1594) to put barriers more solid than that of a voluntary deafness between these vulnerable creatures and the world.[77]

To this point in my argument, I have been considering only the negative effects on women of the policy of marriage restriction pursued by the Venetian patriciate. It should not be forgotten, however, that, at the same time that dowry inflation was condemning many women to the 'public depository' of the convent or the private one of the home, others – those fortunate enough to marry – were reaping the benefits of that same inflation. As dowries rose in a period in which the returns from trade were diminished, the importance of wives' financial contribution to the household in which they were married became ever more decisive. If we assume a continuation of the dynamic identified by Stanley Chojnacki in an earlier period of dowry inflation, the result of this may have been a further enhancement of the financial power and status of married women within families.[78] This development will, in turn, have dramatically widened the gulf in wealth and lifestyle that had always existed between married and unmarried women, even those from the same family background and social caste.[79] If, as Patricia Labalme has suggested, one of the factors we should take into account when considering the origins of the particular strain of feminist thought we find in the writings of Fonte, Marinella and Tarabotti was the 'provocative variety' of the lives led by different categories of women in Venice,[80] we should perhaps add to Labalme's contrasts between the lives of upper-class Venetian women and those of actresses, foreign women and courtesans, a further contrast within the category of upper-class women itself, between those who had been lucky enough to receive a dowry and to enjoy the social prestige and secure identity afforded by marriage, and their less fortunate sisters, condemned to an invidious future as unwilling nuns and precariously situated *dimesse*.

Such a contrast can scarcely have gone unnoticed, and it does not seem too fanciful to suggest that Venetian women's perception of this difference may have provided the first stimulus for the development of the kind of feminist sensibility we encounter in Fonte, Marinella and Tarabotti. The presence in ever-increasing numbers of unmarriageable spinsters and reluctant nuns must have sharpened women's awareness of their vulnerability and powerlessness to decide their own fate. At the same time, the inflation in dowries, by enhancing women's status within the family, must have given those women who did marry an exhilarating new sense of their worth.[81] This powerful fusion of gains and grievances, resentment and self-confidence may have given women – some women at least – the incentive to look at their condition anew.

The single self: the theme of marriage in *Il merito delle donne*

Some support for the hypothesis put forward at the end of the previous section is offered by a series of passages in Fonte's *Il merito delle donne* that deal directly with marriage, the dowry system and men's financial injustices to women. In a passage already alluded to, towards the beginning of a the first book of the dialogue a speaker denounces fathers' and brothers' unwillingness to provide as they should for their daughters and sisters. Many fathers

> do not provide for their daughters while they are alive and then finally, when they die, leave their whole estate, or the greatest part of it, to their sons, depriving their daughters of their inheritance, as though they were their neighbors' children, rather than their own.[82]

Even when a man does think to provide for his daughters, this may not guarantee their well-being:

> others, who are lucky enough to be left a dowry by their father, or to receive a share in his estate along with their brothers if he dies intestate, then find themselves imprisoned in the home like slaves by their brothers, who deprive them of their rights and seize their portions for themselves, in defiance of all justice, without ever attempting to find them a match.[83]

'In defiance of all justice' ('contra ogni giustizia'): one feature to note in this passage is the speaker's firm sense of a dowry as a woman's legal due. The obligation to marry one's daughters is a legal, not merely a sentimental, one; to fail to do so, as many men do, is a grave dereliction of duty. There are biographical reasons for Moderata Fonte's keen awareness of women's inheritance rights. She came from a legal background – her father, her two guardians and her husband were all notaries or lawyers – and there is ample evidence in *Il merito delle donne* of its author's informed interest in the profession.[84] Moreover, she herself had been personally involved in a protracted legal dispute over her share of her father's estate, which she alludes to in her verse romance *Tredici canti del Floridoro* (1581).[85] This personal experience may account for the note of bitterness in her attack in *Il merito* on fathers who die intestate without settling their daughters' futures. But more significantly, Fonte's youthful experience of battling for her own inheritance rights must have left her well placed to observe the discrepancy – a discrepancy we can assume was becoming more and more obvious – between the rights that women enjoyed under the law and the treatment they suffered in practice. The same sense of outrage at the violation of women's rights is registered by Tarabotti in her *Semplicità ingannata*, where she points out bitterly that *monache forzate* do not embrace their vow of poverty willingly, 'but spend their time with all their thoughts fixed on the world, sighing over that share of the family wealth *that is due to them under every law* but has been taken from them *in breach of all justice*' (my italics).[86]

In the passage from *Il merito* just quoted, it is only the abuses of the dowry system that are attacked. Elsewhere the dialogue goes further and attacks the assumptions on which the whole system rests. The foremost of these was, of course, that since marriage constituted a considerable financial burden for a man, it was fair for his bride or her family to offset a portion of the costs. In the passage in *Il merito* mentioned above, this conventional argument is put by one speaker, Elena, but her point is swiftly and energetically contested by another, Corinna:

> You have got it all wrong. ... On the contrary, a woman, when she marries, has to take on the expense of children and other

worries; she is more in need of acquiring money than giving it away. Because if she were alone, without a husband, she could live like a queen on her dowry (more or less so, of course, according to her social position). But when she takes a husband, especially if he is poor, as often happens, what else does she gain from it, except that instead of being her own mistress and the mistress of her own money ['comperatrice e patrona'], she becomes a slave, and loses her liberty and, along with her liberty, her control over her property, surrendering all she has to the man who has bought her, and putting everything in his hands.[87]

Several features of Corinna's speech deserve comment. One, particularly striking, is the strength of her conviction that a woman's dowry is her own, to dispose of as she wishes. In talking about women's 'control' over their dowry, their status as 'comperatrici', Corinna defiantly ignores the traditionally ambiguous status of a woman's dowry as at the same time her share of her father's estate and the purchase-price of her husband. Women's dowries in her representation belong to them as absolutely as their brothers' inheritance belongs to them, and women are – or should be – free to invest them in marriage or not as they see fit.

The passage conveys very forcefully the speaker's – or the author's – awareness of the link between financial independence and self-determination: a woman's liberty is represented as depending crucially on her maintaining control of her money. Whether this, too, was a lesson Moderata Fonte learned from her experience of fighting for control of her inheritance as a girl is something we can only speculate about. Intriguingly, though, there is some evidence in her later financial dealings of a concern with maintaining this form of autonomy: a document of 1583 reveals that, exceptionally, shortly after their marriage, her husband, Filippo Zorzi, signed over control of her dowry during her lifetime.[88]

Corinna's answer to the financial injustices of marriage is more radical than her creator's: she proposes very simply that women should renounce the married state. Marriage is not simply an unsound financial deal for women but a bad bargain altogether. 'Look what a good deal marriage is for women! They lose their property, lose themselves, and get nothing in return, except children to trouble them and the rule of a man, who orders them about at his will'.[89] Corinna's conclusion cannot be dismissed as a personal eccentricity or a gratuitous provocation: the undesirability of marriage is a constant theme of *Il merito delle donne*, and it is an argument that enjoys a large measure of consensus among the speakers. Corinna, unmarried and determined to remain so, is perhaps the most outspoken opponent of wedlock, but in case her opposition should be dismissed as owing to her inexperience, she is joined by Leonora, a young widow who vows she would prefer to drown than to marry again.[90] The only speakers in the dialogue to put in a good word for marriage are the elderly and rather sentimental Adriana and the newly married and still relatively starry-eyed Elena. But their arguments are undermined when we discover that Adriana's own two marriages have been unmitigated disasters, and that Elena's husband is already showing signs of unmotivated jealousy.[91] If marriage has any appeal, it quickly wears off: 'a wedding-cake is soon eaten'. The only woman who can describe herself as truly happy is the woman who lives without men.[92]

The polemic against marriage in *Il merito delle donne* deserves close examination as one of the most strikingly novel features of Fonte's thought, and one of the elements in her argument that seems most clearly to derive from experience rather than literary tradition.[93] Of course, it would be naive to interpret the more extreme utterances of her feminist speaker at face value as a direct incitement to Venetian women to rebel against the institution of marriage. There is undoubtedly an element of playful provocation in the dialogue, which Fonte's modern editor Adriana Chemello has rightly related to the Renaissance tradition of paradox and *serio ludere*.[94] However, there is perhaps as much of a danger in underestimating the seriousness in Fonte's attack on marriage as there is in ignoring its ludic qualities. In a society in which circumstances were daily forcing the injustices of the dowry system further into the light, it seems unlikely that readers would have interpreted an attack on this system purely and simply as an amusing paradox.

That Moderata Fonte's attack on marriage in *Il merito* is not intended as pure provocation is suggested by the fact that her speakers do not limit themselves to listing the disadvantages of the married state. They also discuss, apparently in all seriousness, an alternative to marriage: a freely chosen, entirely secular and uncloistered single life. When Corinna announces her decision to remain single at the beginning of the dialogue, her choice is commended by the unhappily married Lucrezia in enthusiastic terms:

> O happy Corinna! What other woman in the world can compare
> her lot with yours? Not one! Not a widow, for she cannot boast
> of enjoying her freedom without having suffered first; not a wife,
> for she is still in the midst of her suffering; not a young girl
> awaiting betrothal, for she is waiting for nothing but ill.[95]

Lucrezia's speech may be seen as an attempt to establish an exemplary status for Corinna by listing her chosen life as an 'estate' on a par with nubility, marriage and widowhood. Corinna's heroic singularity may be stressed, but Lucrezia expresses the hope that others will follow her example, and concludes by recommending that she write 'a volume on this subject' to dissuade innocent girls from rushing into marriage.[96]

It is difficult not to see in this proposal an allusion to *Il merito* itself. Certainly, Fonte's dialogue sets out quite systematically to tackle what would have been Corinna's first task in her 'volume': to establish a clear status and a clear identity for the secular unmarried woman, a model strong enough to compete with the model of the ideal wife and mother codified and promoted in numberless rule books of behaviour for women. This was no easy task. Not only was there no precedent for the figure of the secular unmarried woman in the previous *trattatistica* on women, but – with very few exceptions – it is difficult to think of potential models within the realm of literature. Moderata Fonte was faced in *Il merito* with a problem analogous to that of Agostino Valier in his *Modo di vivere proposto alle vergini che si chiaman dimesse*: that of creating a role and an identity for a social group not officially acknowledged to exist.

Moderata Fonte sets about this difficult task with considerable energy, ingeniously exploiting the scarce resources her culture afforded her. In her representation of Corinna, she draws on and triumphantly reverses the humanistic topos of the scholar who rejects the lure of marriage to dedicate himself to his studies.[97] By rejecting the commerce of men and giving herself over to virtue and study, Corinna is, as Lucrezia admiringly reminds her in the speech cited earlier, on the path to eternal fame.[98] What might have been presented as a purely negative decision – a rejection of the evils of marriage – becomes instead a positive, indeed a heroic, choice.

Another instance of Moderata Fonte's skill in appropriating from literary tradition is her allusion on two occasions in the dialogue to the figure of Ariosto's warrior-heroine Marfisa, almost certainly the best known literary representation available to her of a woman who had refused marriage and chosen a single life for reasons other than religion.[99] The first of these references to Marfisa occurs in the sonnet in which Corinna announces her choice not to marry, which directly quotes in its second line Marfisa's proud statement that '[non] d'altri son che mia'.[100] The second occurs in a more appropriately warlike context, when Leonora, fantasizing about organizing an Amazonian army to avenge men's wrongs against women, adopts the phoenix as her emblem in imitation of Marfisa.[101] There is a certain irony perhaps in these decorous Venetian ladies' adoption as their role-model of Ariosto's bellicose heroine. But there is an aptness in their choice as well. Apart from her independence of spirit – the quality that these references directly allude to – Marfisa is, of course, also remarkable for her prowess in the art of war. Like Corinna, she provides a positive model of spinsterhood as not simply as an escape from marriage but an opportunity for women to develop their capacities to the full.

Both Corinna's sonnet and Leonora's emblem are elements in a broader strategy in the dialogue of embroidering the bare outline of the

decision to remain single with a complex pattern of literary and icono-
graphic suggestion. The most striking example of this mythologizing
occurs in a passage at the beginning of *Il merito*, describing the *locus
amoenus* in which the dialogue takes place. This setting is a garden inherited by the hostess Leonora from an aunt who had elected not to marry
but to live alone on the income inherited from her father. At the centre of
the garden is a fountain surrounded by six laurel-wreathed statues of
women whose allegorical significance is revealed by the motto and the
emblem which each displays.[102] Three of the figures, Naivety, Deceit and
Cruelty, form a miniature narrative of the dangers of marriage: women's
innocence and naivety make them an easy prey to the deceitful words of
their suitors, who promise them love but deliver no more than a lifetime
of cruelty and suffering. The other three figures, Chastity, Solitude and
Liberty, represent the virtues and benefits of the single life wisely chosen
as an alternative by Leonora's aunt. An interesting feature of the allegory
is that this single life is not conceived of as one of cloistered retreat.
Solitude may be one of its tutelary deities, but Liberty is another; and, as
Leonora makes plain in her gloss on the statue, this liberty includes the
freedom to enjoy social intercourse untrammelled by the constraints of
marriage. The figure of Liberty, she explains, bears the emblem of a sun
to signify that her aunt was free to illuminate the whole world with her
virtue, sharing her company with 'every person of refinement', as she
would not have been able to do if married.[103]

The novelty of the ideal encoded in this allegory of an uncloistered,
sociable and creative single life for women, is perhaps best conveyed by
a comparison of Leonora's aunt's garden with another analogous but
sharply contrasted allegorical construct: the 'Temple of Chastity'
described by the humanist Antonio Loschi in his *Domus pudicicie* as an
apt setting for the early Paduan scholar Maddalena Scrovegni and brilliantly analysed by Margaret King as an emblem of male humanists'
problematic attitude to female intellectuality.[104] Loschi's description of
the *domus* reflects an obsessive and paralyzing concern with chastity: the
widowed Scrovegni is imagined enthroned on crystal in its vast white
spaces, surrounded by figures of Modesty, Virginity and Frugality. The
threat posed by a woman who insists on intruding into the masculine
sphere of intellectual activity can only be defused by denying her sexuality, deep-freezing her physical self.

The environment envisaged for the single woman in *Il merito delle
donne* could scarcely be more different. Leonora's aunt's garden is a locus
of pleasure, ripe with images of fertility and abundance and reminiscent
of the ravishing settings where the speakers of the *Decameron* or Bembo's
Asolani meet to talk of love.[105] Chastity still has its place in Leonora's
aunt's system of values, but it is a chastity transformed by its context
from a negative to a positive choice. Celibacy here does not signal a

denial but a rechannelling of sensuality, and much stress is placed throughout the dialogue on the pleasures afforded by a life without men: the company of women, the pleasures of poetry and music, good food, laughter and wine.

In proposing this ideal of a carefree, sociable and above all autonomous existence, Moderata Fonte is never in danger of forgetting that it *is* an ideal. A few scattered remarks in the dialogue make clear that Fonte was painfully aware that women who chose or were forced to remain single led a life very different from the charmed existence of Leonora's aunt.[106] Further, for a woman to choose to live alone was not only an eccentric but a potentially dangerous choice: as Lucrezia remarks at the end of the dialogue, 'with things as they are in this world', the protection of a husband, however regrettable, is virtually a necessity for women.[107] Finally, Moderata Fonte is conscious that it is illusory to talk about marriage as though it were a matter of free choice for a woman. As the lives of the speakers in the dialogue amply demonstrate, the decision to marry a woman rests with the household more than the woman herself.[108] Marfisa's phoenix is an appropriate emblem for the free and single woman for more reasons than one. At least until the longed-for day when women will be permitted to earn their own living, the option of a single life will only be available to those mythical women like Leonora's aunt, fortunate enough to enjoy an independent income and a mysterious lack of family pressure.[109]

However, the fact that a life of this kind is presented as a practical impossibility should not lead us to conclude that it is simply a literary caprice with no bearing on real women's lives. Fantasy and reality in the idiosyncratic universe of *Il merito delle donne* stand in a strangely intimate relation. The book ends with the recital by Corinna of a narrative poem on the defeat of Love at the hands of Avarice, which may be read either as a pastoral fantasy or as a shrewd commentary on the state of the Venetian dowry market.[110] Similarly, Fonte's myth of heroic spinsterhood is an excursion into the 'marvellous' that leads straight to the heart of an urgent issue of contemporary social concern.

Conclusion

Introducing my discussion of Moderata Fonte's advocacy of spinsterhood, I compared her enterprise in *Il merito delle donne* with that of Agostino Valier in his *Modo di vivere proposto alle vergini che si chiaman dimesse*. The parallel may seem a strained one: there is an enormous gulf between Moderata Fonte's shimmering fantasies and Valier's grim, prosaic rule-mongering; between the former's spirited heroines and the latter's *vergini dimesse*. However, both treatises, as I have suggested, may be seen as attempts to invent an identity for a new social group – unmarried women of the patrician and citizen classes – that the tides of economic change were beginning to wash up on the shores of the Venetian lagoon.

The collapse of the marriage market in late sixteenth- and seventeenth-century Venice was an event which had vast and far-reaching consequences for Venetian women. My contention in this study has been that one of these consequences was the emergence of the particular form of feminist thought we find in the works of Moderata Fonte, Lucrezia Marinella and Arcangela Tarabotti. An important characteristic of this strain of feminism – what perhaps best distinguishes it from the previous Renaissance tradition – is that it evinces a robust sense of women as autonomous entities, with their own economic and existential agendas.[111] Women are regarded here only secondarily as wives and mothers and muses; they are considered primarily as individuals whose worth is not measured by their usefulness to men. In Lucrezia Marinella's proud words, 'woman's proper purpose is not to gratify man, but to understand, to govern, to generate, and to adorn the world with her beauty'.[112]

It is this new sense of women as at least potentially autonomous beings that lies at the root of these writers' other novelties: their concern with the economic realities of women's condition, their fantasies of financial self-sufficiency, their criticism of the social roles traditionally allocated to women. It is here, in the sense of self that crystallizes in Moderata Fonte's myth of heroic spinsterhood, that we can identify the source of the powerful new charge of energy these writers brought to an exhausted debate. The aim of this study has been to show that this new sense of the self – the single self – cannot be accounted for without taking into consideration the peculiar set of circumstances that conspired in late sixteenth-century Venice to prise women away from their traditional notion of themselves.

Notes

1 There is some evidence of a feminist sensibility in the works of some earlier Italian women writers; see, for example, Tullia d'Aragona, *Dialogue on the Infinity of Love*, eds and trans. Bruce Merry and Rinaldina Russell, with an introduction by Rinaldina Russell (Chicago, 1997), 36–9; Veronica Franco, *Selected Poems and Letters*, eds and trans. Ann Rosalind Jones and Margaret Rosenthal (Chicago, 1999) (esp. *capitoli* 16 and 23). Defences of women's capacity for learning are also found in several earlier writers; see, for example, Laura Cereta, *Collected Letters of a Renaissance Feminist*, ed. Diana Robin (Chicago, 1997), 72–80. For a bibliography of works by Italian women published in the sixteenth and early seventeenth centuries, see *Nel cerchio della luna: Figure di donna in alcuni testi del XVI secolo*, ed. Marina Zancan (Venice, 1983), appendix III; also the bio-bibliographical section of *A History of Women's Writing in Italy*, eds Letizia Panizza and Sharon Wood (Cambridge, 2000). For an overview of women's contribution to the Renaissance *querelle des femmes*, see Joan Kelly, *Women, History and Theory: The Essays of Joan Kelly* (Chicago, 1984), 67–9, 93–4.

2 Both works are now available in English language editions: Marinella's as *The Nobility and Excellence of Women and the Defects and Vices of Men*, ed. and trans. Anne Dunhill, with an introduction by Letizia Panizza (Chicago, 1999), and Fonte's as *The Worth of Women*, ed. and trans. Virginia Cox (Chicago, 1997). A modern Italian edition of *Il merito delle donne* also exists (ed. Adriana Chemello [Venice, 1988]). All subsequent references to these texts will be to the editions cited. Where Marinella's *La nobiltà* is concerned, the Italian text used is the second Venetian edition of 1601. For biographical details of Fonte and Marinella and for secondary literature, see Panizza and Wood (eds) *A History of Women's Writing*, 301, 314.

3 There does not yet exist a comprehensive study of the debate on women in Italy. For a bibliography of primary texts, see the appendices to *Nel cerchio della luna*; for secondary literature, Letizia Panizza, 'A Guide to Recent Bibliography on Italian Renaissance Writings about and by Women', *Bulletin of Italian Studies* 22(1989): 3–24. More generally, on the debate in Europe, see Constance Jordan, *Renaissance Feminism: Literary Texts and Political Models* (Ithaca, 1990); also, on its broader intellectual context, Ian Maclean, *The Renaissance Notion of Woman: A Study in the Fortunes of Scholasticism and Medical Science in European Intellectual Life* (Cambridge, 1980).

4 On the polemics excited by Passi's *I donneschi difetti*, see *Nobility*, 15 and n37; Beatrice Collina, 'Moderata Fonte e *Il merito delle donne*', *Annali d'Italianistica* 7(1989): 142–3; Adriana Chemello, 'La donna, il modello, l'immaginario: Moderata Fonte e Lucrezia Marinella', in *Nel cerchio della luna*, 102–3; Emilia Biga, *Una polemica antifemminista del '600: 'La maschera scoperta' di Angelico Aprosio* (Ventimiglia, 1989), 35–8; Stephen Kolsky, 'An Early Seventeenth-Century Feminist Controversy', *Modern Language Notes* 96 (2001): 973–89.There were further editions of Passi's *I donneschi difetti* in 1601, 1605, 1618 and 1619 and of Marinella's *La nobiltà et l'eccellenza delle donne* in 1601 and 1621.

5 For a fuller discussion of this point, see the original version of this essay, in *Renaissance Quarterly* 48(1995): 515–20.

6 For this metaphor, see Marinella, *Nobiltà*, 120; *Nobility*, 131–2; Fonte, *Merito*, 169; *Worth*, 237.

7 Fonte, *Merito*, 163; *Worth*, 230; cf. *Merito*, 73; *Worth*, 119.

8 Marinella, *Nobiltà*, 33; *Nobility*, 80.

9 Marinella, *Nobiltà*, 29; *Nobility*, 74.

10 Marinella, *Nobiltà*, 67; *Nobility*, 118.

11 It has been suggested that Marinella's arguments on this point may derive from her observation of the practices of foreign merchant communities in Venice (see Patricia Labalme, 'Venetian Women on Women: Three Early Modern Feminists', *Archivio Veneto*, 5th series, 117[1981]: 105), and there is some evidence that the contraction in women's scope for participation in commercial activities that took place in the sixteenth century throughout Europe may have been particularly acute in Italy (see Judith C. Brown, 'A Woman's Place was in the Home: Women's Work in Renaissance Tuscany', in *Rewriting the Renaissance*, 224 and n29). It is interesting to note in this context that the English ambassador to Venice in 1612 thought the fact that Venetian women 'sell nothing abroad' worthy of comment in a draft for a report (*Venice: A Documentary History, 1450–1600*, eds David Chambers and Brian Pullan [Oxford, 1992], 27). For evidence of early modern Venetian women's participation in commerce, however, see Peter Burke, *The Historical Anthropology of Early Modern Italy: Essays on Perception and Communication* (Cambridge, 1987), 35–8; also, now, Monica Chojnacka, *Working Women of Early Modern Venice* (Baltimore, 2001).

12 For Plato's recommendation – much discussed in the Renaissance – that women participate in the civic and military life of the state on equal terms with men, see *Republic* 451c–457c; also Nicholas D. Smith, 'Plato and Aristotle on the Nature of Women', *Journal of the History of Philosophy* 21(1983): 467–78.

13 Fonte, *Merito*, 125; *Worth*, 181. See also the passage at the end of the book (*Merito*, 169–70; *Worth*, 238), where Corinna defends the group's incursion into 'male' preserves of knowledge.

14 On women's exclusion from education – a commonplace of defenders of women from Christine de Pizan onwards – see especially Marinella, *Nobiltà*, 32; *Nobility*, 83; also Fonte, *Merito*, 168, 170; *Worth*, 236, 238; and cf. also the passage from Fonte's chivalric romance, *Tredici canti del Floridoro* (Venice, 1581), cited in *Worth*, 261–3.

15 Fonte, *Merito*, 169; *Worth*, 237.

16 L'Umile Invaghito (Pompeo Baccusi), *Oratione in difesa et lode delle donne* (Mantua, 1571), cited in Francine Daenens, 'Superiore perché inferiore: il paradosso della superiorità della donna in alcuni trattati italiani del Cinquecento', in *Trasgressione tragica e norma domestica: Esemplari di tipologie femminili dalla letteratura europea*, ed. Vanna Gentili (Rome, 1983), 24.

17 I am thinking in particular here of seventeenth-century English feminists like Mary Astell; for discussions of their views, see Hilda Smith, *Reason's Disciples: Seventeenth-century English Feminists* (Urbana, 1982) and Jerome Nadelheft, 'The Englishwoman's Sexual Civil War: Feminist Attitudes Toward Men, Women and Marriage, 1650–1740', *Journal of the History of Ideas* 43(1982): 555–79. For a differing assessment of the import of the elements of social and economic criticism in Fonte, see Bodo Guthmüller, ' "Non taceremo più a lungo": sul dialogo *Il merito delle donne* di Moderata Fonte', *Filologia e critica* 17(1992): 279.

18 See, for example, Marinella, *Nobiltà*, 133; *Nobility*, 143; also the passages cited above.

19 See Pullan, 'Service to the Venetian State: Aspects of Myth and Reality in the Early Seventeenth Century', *Studi secenteschi* 5(1965): 108–17; and Ugo Tucci, 'The Psychology of the Venetian Merchant in the Sixteenth Century', in *Renaissance Venice*, ed. J. R. Hale (London, 1973), 346–78.

20 Fonte, *Merito*, 143–4; *Worth*, 204.

21 For an overview, see Gabriella Zarri, 'Monasteri femminili e città (secoli XV–XVIII)', in *Storia d'Italia. Annali 9: La Chiesa e il potere politico dal Medioevo all'età contemporanea*, eds Giorgio Chittolini and Giovanni Miccoli (Turin, 1986), 361–8 (esp. 366–7, on the social and economic factors underlying this change in families' economic strategies); also, in the same volume, Xenio Toscani, 'Il reclutamento del clero (secoli XVI–XIX)', 588–9.

22 On this phenomenon in Venice, see Zarri, 'Monasteri femminili', 400–1; Francesca Medioli, *L'inferno monacale di Suor Arcangela Tarabotti* (Turin, 1990), 111–35; also, for a revisionist view, Jutta Gisela Sperling, *Convents and the Body Politic in Late Renaissance Venice* (Chicago, 1999), 1–71. On *monacazione forzata* outside Venice, see Enrico Cattaneo, 'Le monacazioni forzate fra Cinque e Seicento', in *Vita e proceso di Suor Virginia Maria de Leyra, Monaca di Monza*, ed. Umberto Colombo (Milan, 1985), 145–95.

23 See pp. 178–85.

24 It is difficult to estimate the literacy rate among women in Italy in this period. Paul F. Grendler, *Schooling in Renaissance Italy: Literacy and Learning, 1300–1600* (Baltimore and London, 1989), 46, estimates that approximately 5–6 percent of Venetian women received some form of education in the convent or the home. See also Medioli, *L'inferno monacale*, 137–8.

25 Apart from Marinella and Fonte, feminist views are expressed by two other Venetian women writers of the late sixteenth and early seventeenth centuries: the poet and courtesan Veronica Franco (1546–91) and the *monaca forzata* Arcangela Tarabotti (1604–52). I discuss Tarabotti's work below; on Franco, see Panizza and Wood (eds) *A History of Women's Writing*, 302–3, and the bibliography cited there. To these names might perhaps be added those of two far lesser known women writers from the Venetian mainland, Maddalena Campiglia, from Vicenza (on whom see Panizza and Wood, 56–7, 289–90), and Giulia Bigolina, from Padua, whose previously unpublished writings are currently being edited, in Italian and English editions, by Valeria Finucci for Bulzoni, (Rome, 2002), and the University of Chicago Press. On factors in the social and cultural environment of Venice that may have encouraged this flourishing of feminist thought there, see Labalme, 'Venetian Women', 104–9.

26 For accounts of this process, see Pullan, 'The Occupations and Investments of the Venetian Nobility in the Middle and Late Sixteenth Century', in *Renaissance Venice*, ed. John Hale (London, 1973), 380–7; and S. J. Woolf, 'Venice and the Terraferma: Problems of the Change from Commercial to Landed Activities', in *Crisis and Change in the Venetian Economy in the Sixteenth and Seventeenth Centuries*, ed. Brian Pullan (London, 1968), 175–203.

27 See Niccolò Machiavelli, *Discorsi sopra la prima deca di Tito Livio*, in *Opere*, ed. Mario Bonfantini (Milan and Naples, 1963), 206; and Tucci, 'Psychology', 346. For estimates of the extent of investment in property prior to the War of the League of Cambrai (1509–17), see Woolf, 'Venice and the Terraferma', 188–90. On the difficulties involved in establishing when the decisive change to landed investment occurred, see also Peter Burke, *Venice and Amsterdam: A Study of Seventeenth-century Elites* (London, 1974), 101–8.

28 Woolf, 'Venice and the Terraferma', 198, identifies the half-century from 1570 to 1630 as 'the crucial period of the change to landed activities'. On the chronology of this process and the reasons for the retreat from commercial activities, see also Pullan, 'Occupations and Investments', 381–6.

29 Fonte, *Merito*, 96–7: *Worth*, 148–9.

30 Fonte, *Merito*, 89, 122–3: *Worth*, 139–40, 178–80. Fonte is doubtless speaking from experience in such passages: we learn from Fonte's biographer Giovanni Niccolò Doglioni that she spent her summers as a child on her guardian's estates on the mainland, and she herself declared ownership of a small estate near Padua in her tax return of 1582 (Doglioni, *Vita*, in Fonte, *Merito*, 6; *Life*, in *Worth*, 33).

31 See James C. Davis, *A Venetian Family and Its Fortune, 1500–1900: The Donà and the Conservation of Wealth* (Philadelphia, 1975), 85–6, 98–101; Alexander F. Cowan, *The Urban Patriciate: Lübeck and Venice* (Cologne and Vienna, 1986), 6–8.

32 On this policy of marriage restriction, see Davis, *Venetian Family*, 74–92; and Cowan, *Urban Patriciate*, 144–9; also, on the beginnings of this trend in an earlier period, Stanley Chojnacki, *Women and Men in Renaissance Venice: Twelve Essays on Patrician Society* (Baltimore, 2000), 180, 249–51.

33 Lodovico Settala, *Della ragion di stato*, in *Politici e moralisti del Seicento*, eds Santino Caramella and Benedetto Croce (Bari, 1930), 109.

34 See Brian Pullan, 'Poverty, Charity and Reason of State: Some Venetian Examples', *Bollettino dell'Istituto di storia della società e dello stato veneziano* 2(1960): 27. The problem was a real one: on the relative poverty suffered by a substantial sector of the patriciate in this period, see (besides Pullan) Cowan, 'Rich and Poor Among the Patriciate in Early Modern Venice', *Studi veneziani*, n.s. 6(1982): 147–60.

35 On dowry inflation in Venice in this period, and on government attempts to curb it, see Pullan, 'Service to the Venetian State', 138–9; Marco Ferro, *Dizionario del diritto comune e veneto*, 10 vols (Venice, 1778–81), III: 390–1. On the causes of the phenomenon, see Chojnacki, 'La posizione della donna a Venezia nel Cinquecento', in *Tiziano e Venezia: Convegno internazionale di studi, Venezia 1976* (Vicenza, 1980), 69; though cf. Donald A. Queller and Thomas F. Madden, 'Father of the Bride: Fathers, Daughters, and Dowries in Late Medieval and Early Renaissance Venice', *Renaissance Quarterly* 46(1993): 685–711; Sperling, *Convents and the Body Politic*. On dowry inflation outside Venice, see Zarri, 'Monasteri femminili', 365–6; Christiane Klapisch-Zuber, *Women, Family and Ritual in Renaissance Italy*, trans. Lydia G. Cochrane (Chicago and London, 1985), 124, 215.

36 The most detailed study of the implications of dowry inflation for women's prospects of marriage is Medioli, *L'inferno monacale*, 111–35; see also Davis, *Venetian Family*, 106–11; and Cowan, *Urban Patriciate*, 148–9; and now Sperling, *Convents and the Body Politic*. On the tendency to reserve marriage for the younger daughters in a family in order to delay the moment when dowries would have to be raised, see Medioli, 111. It should be noted that, as the example of Arcangela Tarabotti illustrates, the practice of limiting marriages was not exclusive to the patriciate, but extended down to the *cittadino* class and the richest strata of the *popolo*.

37 For a discussion of dowry law as it evolved in the medieval Italian communes, see Francesco Ercole, 'L'istituto dotale nella practica e nella legislazione statuaria dell'Italia superiore', *Rivista italiana per le scienze giuridiche* 45(1908): 191–302; 46(1910): 167–257. On women's rights under Venetian law, see Ferro, *Dizionario*, III: 380–98. On the status of the dowry as a woman's share of the patrimony, see Ercole, 211–30; Cowan, *Urban Patriciate*, 133. In practice, obviously, the allocation of dowries within a family tended to take place in a messier and more *ad hoc* way than might be suggested by looking at the law codes. On the actual workings of the dowry system in Cinquecento Venice, see Cowan, 132–42; and, on an earlier period, the various studies of Chojnacki.

38 Nuns renounced their inheritance rights on taking the veil, though a monastic dowry was paid to the convent.

39 See Ferro, *Dizionario*, III: 395; Davis, *Venetian Family*, 106–7; Pullan, 'Service to the Venetian State', 136; *idem*, 'Occupations and Investments', 390; Labalme, 'Women's Roles in Early Modern Venice: An Exceptional Case', in *Beyond Their Sex: Learned Women of the European Past*, ed. Patricia Labalme (New York and London, 1980), 132. The degree to which, even during the lifetime of both spouses, the wife's dowry continued to be considered as her own property is intriguingly illustrated by the penalties exacted for adultery and fornication in Renaissance Venice: an adulterous or absconding wife might be ordered to pay her dowry over to her husband, while a man who seduced an unmarried girl might be offered the chance to make amends by marrying her and crediting a dowry to her from his own property (Guido Ruggiero, *The Boundaries of Eros: Sex Crime and Sexuality in Renaissance Venice* [New York, 1985], 31, 33, 35, 53–5).

40 See Chojnacki, *Women and Men*, especially part II and, by the same author, 'Marriage Legislation and Patrician Society in Fifteenth-Century Venice', in *Law, Custom and the Social Fabric in Medieval Europe: Essays in Honor of Bruce Lyon*, eds Bernard S. Bachrach and David Nicholas (Kalamazoo, 1990), 163–84, 'La posizione della donna'. A factor of particular significance for Chojnacki is the freedom women had, in Venetian law and custom, to divide

their dowries as they wished, on death, among their natal and married kin: a freedom that gave them considerable leverage within both families.

41 On the central role played by dowries in Renaissance women's 'status system', see Queller and Madden, 'Father of the Bride', 698.

42 The metaphor is a contemporary one; see p. 173.

43 The term 'forced claustration' is used here for convenience, as a translation of the conventional Italian term, *monacazione forzata*. On the actual level of constraint involved, see below, note 54. On Tarabotti's life and works, see Panizza and Wood (eds) *A History of Women's Writing*, 332, and the bibliography cited there. Of Tarabotti's principal works denouncing the practice of forced claustration, her *Inferno monacale* is available in a modern edition, edited by Francesca Medioli (Turin, 1990). All subsequent references will be to this edition. References to *La semplicità ingannata* will be to the Leiden edition of 1564, published under the name of Galerana Baratotti (for the publishing history of this text, see Medioli, *L'inferno monacale*, 128, n3, 151, 158). English translations of both works, by Letizia Panizza, are forthcoming from the University of Chicago Press (*La semplicità ingannata* under its original title of *La tirannia paterna / Paternal Tyranny*).

44 *La semplicità ingannata*, 133–4. See also Book I of *L'inferno monacale*.

45 *La semplicità ingannata*, 49. For a denunciation of the church's responsibilities, see *ibid.*, 130; for an attack on reason of state, *L'inferno monacale*, 42.

46 *L'inferno monacale*, 27–8. For interesting discussions of the ways in which the cult of liberty in Venetian political thought is reflected in the writings of Fonte, Marinella and Tarabotti, see Collina, 'Moderata Fonte', 161; Labalme, 'Venetian Women', 108.

47 *La semplicità ingannata*, 137; see also *L'inferno monacale*, 93.

48 For Tarabotti's plea for men to marry 'without thinking of monetary gain', see again *La semplicità ingannata*, 137. For her suggestion that fathers might consider less ambitious matches for their daughters outside the nobility, see *ibid.*, 32–3. On the regulations governing marriages between patricians and non-patricians, see Pullan, 'Service to the Venetian State', 139–40; Cowan, *Urban Patriciate*, 168–70; and see *L'inferno monacale*, 114.

49 *La semplicità ingannata*, 137.

50 For evidence that Tarabotti was acquainted with at least some of Fonte and Marinella's work, see Labalme, 'Venetian Women', 103.

51 *La semplicità ingannata*, 100. See also *ibid.*, 102, where Tarabotti protests against women's exclusion from both politics and higher education; also 150, where, in terms reminiscent of those of Marinella in *Nobiltà*, she compares the limited opportunities allowed to women in Venice with the wider freedoms enjoyed by women elsewhere.

52 On convent reform in Venice, see L. Menetto and G. Zennaro, *Storia del malcostume a Venezia nei secoli XVI e XVII* (Abano Terme, 1987), 109–30, 145–74; Sperling, *Convents and the Body Politic*, esp. 127–69. For the broader Italian context, see Raimondo Creytens, 'La riforma dei monasteri femminili dopo i decreti Tridentini', in *Il Concilio di Trento e la riforma tridentina: Atti del Convegno Storico Internazionale, Trento, 2–6 settembre, 1963* (Rome, 1965), 45–84; Zarri, 'Monasteri femminili', 398–420; and Pio Paschini, 'I monasteri femminili in Italia nel Cinquecento', in *Problemi di vita religiosa in Italia nel Cinquecento: Atti del Convegno di Storia della Chiesa in Italia (Bologna, 2–6 settembre, 1958)* (Padua, 1960), 31–60.

53 Museo Correr, Fondo Cicogna, ms. 2570, 299–304; see also the discussions of this document in Sperling, *Convents and the Body Politic*, 3–4, 35; Labalme, 'Women's Roles', 138, n36; and Silvio Tramontin, 'Ordini e congregazioni reli-

giose', in *Storia della cultura veneta*, 4/1: *Il Seicento*, eds Giorlamo Arnaldi and Manlio Pastore Stocchi (Vicenza, 1983), 49.

54 A series of measures intended to ensure the genuineness of nuns' vocations was introduced in the post-Tridentine period; see Zarri, 'Monasteri femminili', 400–1, who concludes, however, that these measures were not enough to guarantee freedom from family pressure. On the mixture of persuasion and coercion to which prospective nuns were subjected by their families and the convents, see Medioli, *L'inferno monacale*, 31–2, 35–6, 41–2. Medioli notes that nuns had the right to renounce their vows within five years of taking them on the grounds that they had been coerced, but points out that this was near impossible in practice (*ibid.*, 125, 134, n55).

55 Medioli, *L'inferno monacale*, 170 n60, quotes an interesting letter (undated) from the libertine writer Gianfrancesco Loredan (1607–61) to his niece Laura Pasqualigo advising her to renounce her wish to marry and resign herself to the convent, presenting the choice in unequivocally pragmatic terms. On Loredan's relations with Tarabotti, see Medioli, 145, 152.

56 Cited in Zarri, 'Monasteri femminili', 386.

57 The document is discussed in Menetto and Zennaro, *Malcostume*, 178; Paschini, 'Monasteri femminili', 58–9; see also Sperling, *Convents and the Body Politic*, 30. It is interesting to note that the Senate's resistance in this case resulted in a compromise: a successive report notes that although Venetian convents will be subject to inspection, it is not planned to make the rules any tighter than they have been in the past. For evidence of resistance to the Tridentine reforms outside Venice, see Creytens, 'La riforma', 66–67; and Gaetano Greco, 'Monasteri femminili e patriziato a Pisa (1530–1630)', in *Città italiane del '500 tra Riforma e Controriforma: Atti del Convegno Internazionale di Studi, Lucca 13–15 ottobre 1983* (Lucca, 1988), 327.

58 It should, of course, be recognised that convent life could offer attractions for women, even those without powerful religious vocations. See, on this, Medioli, *L'inferno monacale*, 122; Margaret L. King, *Women of the Renaissance* (Chicago and London, 1991), 95–7.

59 On the virtual non-existence of secular spinsters at least in the upper classes before this time, see Klapisch-Zuber, *Women*, 119; also Medioli, *L'inferno monacale*, 113; Chojnacki, *Women and Men*, 179. That the phenomenon was not entirely unknown in Venice before this period is indicated by the preamble to an edict of 1420 regulating the level of patrician dowries, cited in Giulio Bistort, *Il Magistrato alle pompe nella Repubblica di Venezia: Studio storico* (Venice, 1908), 107–8, and discussed in Chojnacki, 'Marriage Legislation', which claims that the rise in dowries was leading many patricians not only to 'imprison' their daughters in convents against their will but even to resort, unprecedentedly and shamefully, to keeping them unmarried at home. The terms in which this latter expedient is described, however, indicate clearly quite how anomalous the presence of unmarried women outside the convent was felt to be.

60 On monastic dowries and the other expenses involved in placing a daughter in the convent, see Zarri, 'Monasteri femminili', 400–1; Medioli, *L'inferno monacale*, 117–18; Labalme, 'Women's Roles', 137, n30; Sperling, *Convents and the Body Politic*, 155, 176, 187–96. Medioli (118 n33) estimates the proportion between monastic and secular dowries in this period as varying between 1:3 and 1:40. On inflation in monastic dowries in Venice in this period, see Menetto and Zennaro, *Malcostume*, 184–6; on the strain they represented for family finances and on government attempts to restrict them, see Pullan, 'Service to the Venetian State', 140–3; Medioli, *L'inferno monacale*, 118; Sperling, 188–90, 222.

61 This was also the case outside Venice, see Cattaneo, 'Le monacazioni forzate', 169, and Zarri, 'Monasteri femminili', 403.

62 Fonte, *Merito*,28–9; *Worth*, 62–3.

63 I am assuming that this is primarily what is intended by Fonte's reference to 'blameworthy and despicable means', although it is possible that the phrase has a more general sense, including any kind of sexual relationship outside marriage. On prostitution in Venice in the period, see Menetto and Zennaro, *Malcostume*, 37–64; Rita Casagrande Di Villaviera, *Le cortigiane veneziane nel Cinquecento* (Milan, 1968); Antonio Barzaghi, *Donne o cortigiane? La prostituzione a Venezia: Documenti di costume dal XVI al XVIII secolo* (Verona, 1980); and Cathy Santore, 'Julia Lombardo, "Somtuosa Meretize": A Portrait by Property', *Renaissance Quarterly* 41(1988): 44–83.

64 Fonte, *Merito*, 52; *Worth*, 88–9. Little is known of the social provenance of Venetian courtesans, but for evidence that it was not unknown for women of the patrician and cittadino classes to drift into prostitution, see the letter cited in Brian Pullan, *Rich and Poor in Renaissance Venice: The Social Institutions of a Catholic State, to 1620* (Oxford, 1971), 386.

65 Agostino Valier, *La istituzione d'ogni stato lodevole delle donne cristiane*, ed. Gaetano Volpi (Padua, 1744), xxi. Giolito's letter was originally published as a foreword to a *Trattato del D. Dionisio Certosino della lodevol Vita delle Vergini* (Venice, 1584).

66 Valier, *La istituzione*, xxii.

67 *Ibid.*, xxii–xxiii. Giolito goes on to suggest other ways in which unmarried women may be of service to the community: teaching Christian doctrine in girls' schools, helping in women's hospitals and other charitable foundations and, in later life, assisting in the administration of charity.

68 For the impact of the Council of Trent's rulings on enclosure for the tertiary orders, see Zarri, 'Monasteri femminili', 402–3; and Creytens, 'La riforma', esp. 63–4 and 76. On the emergence of new orders in the later sixteenth century, see Zarri, 'Monasteri femminili', 402, 427; *idem*, 'Il "terzo stato"', in *Tempi e spazi di vita femminile tra medioevo ed età moderna*, eds Silvana Seidel Menchi, Anne Jacobson Schutte and Thomas Kuehn (Bologna, 1999), 311–34.

69 Valier's *Modo di vivere* is the first of three treatises (on, respectively, spinsterhood, widowhood and marriage) published together under the title of *La istituzione d'ogni stato lodevole delle donne cristiane* (Venice, 1577) and republished in Padua in 1744 by Gaetano Volpi (subsequent references to this text are to Volpi's edition). The Compagnia delle Dimesse was founded in Vicenza by Padre Antonio Pagani in 1579 but was introduced in Venice only in 1587, with the encouragement of Valier himself and Michele Priuli, Bishop of Verona (see Volpi in *La istituzione*, xvi; Tramontin, 'Ordini e congregazioni', 49–50; and Giovanni Mantese, *Memorie storiche della chiesa vicentina*, 5 vols [Vicenza, 1952–74], 4/1: 526–40). In the *Modo di vivere*, as Volpi notes (*ibid.*, xvi–xviii and xxi), the term 'Dimesse' is generally used to refer simply to unmarried women living at home, and it is probably in this sense that it is used in *Il merito delle donne*, where one of the speakers, Corinna, is first introduced as a 'giovene dimmessa', (Fonte 1988; *Merito*, 15; *Worth*, 45), in contrast to the other unmarried speaker, Virginia, designated 'figliola da marito' ('a girl of marriageable age'). Given Corinna's assertive character, it is unlikely that the word is being used here adjectivally in its non-technical sense of 'meek' or 'humble', while there is no indication in the rest of the dialogue that she is a member of the order of Dimesse (though cf. Guthmüller, 'Non taceremo più', 262; and Zarri, 'Il "terzo stato"', 332–3, who assume this to be the case).

70 Emmanuele Antonio Cicogna, *Delle iscrizioni veneziane*, 6 vols (Venice, 1824–53), II: 36.
71 Valier, *La istituzione*, 14, 31.
72 *Ibid.*, 17.
73 *Ibid.*, 13–16, 18–19.
74 On this literature, see Grendler, *Schooling in Renaissance Italy*, 89. Unsurprisingly, in view of the author's admiration of Carlo Borromeo, Valier's recommendations are particularly close in spirit and detail to the regulations of the Compagnia di S. Orsola, as refounded in 1567 on Borromeo's initiative: see Maria Franca Mellano, 'La donna nell'opera di San Carlo', in *San Carlo e il suo tempo: Atti del Convegno Internazionale nel IV centenario della morte (Milano, 21–26 maggio, 1984)* (Rome, 1986), 1091–3.
75 There is only one hint at a recognition of this in Valier's *Modo di vivere* (*La istituzione*, 41), when after enjoining the Dimessa to be generous in alms-giving, Valier notes that 'impecunious *dimesse*' can prove their generosity by giving freely of their time, adding that 'there are many such in Venice'.
76 *Ibid.*, 9. The author goes on to point out that not the least valuable of the social tasks the Dimessa can perform is to offer a perpetual reproach to her sinful sisters by the example of her devout and ascetic life. There are further hints the worldliness of the Dimessa's social environment at *ibid.*, 38–9, where she is warned that while visiting relatives in convents, she should avoid talk of 'theatres, parties, and trivial pastimes'; and 33, where she is enjoined to show compassion to her married sisters for the showy dressing that custom forces on them as young brides.
77 For evidence from outside Venice of the unease provoked by the phenomenon of unmarried women living outside a religious community, see Zarri, 'Monasteri femminili', 403; also Paolo Prodi, 'Vita religiosa e crisi sociale nei tempi di Angela Merici', *Humanitas* 19(1974), 307–18, and, more broadly, Sherrill Cohen, 'Asylums for Women in Counter-reformation Italy', in *Women in Reformation and Counter-reformation Europe: Public and Private Worlds*, ed. Sherrin Marshall (Bloomington and Indianapolis, 1989), 166–88, esp. 170.
78 See the various studies of Chojnacki in *Women and Men*, esp. part 2; also Labalme, 'Women's Roles', 132.
79 The difference between the extremely cloistered life led by Venetian women before their marriage and the much freer life they enjoyed afterwards is stressed in Chojnacki, 'La posizione della donna'; see also Fonte, *Merito*, 171; *Worth*, 239.
80 Labalme, 'Venetian Women', 104.
81 Evidence for this is examined in the original version of this essay in *Renaissance Quarterly*, 48(1995): 515–6.
82 Fonte, *Merito*, 28; *Worth*, 62.
83 Fonte, *Merito*, 29; *Worth*, 63.
84 See, in particular, Fonte, *Merito*, 137–8: *Worth*, 194–7.
85 Fonte, *Tredici canti del Floridoro*, ed. Valeria Finucci (Bologna, 1995), 44–5; see also *Merito*, 4; *Worth*, 33.
86 *La semplicità ingannata*, 51.
87 Fonte, *Merito*, 69; *Worth*, 114. See also, for an earlier occurrence of this argument on dowries, Labalme, 'Women's Roles', 91, n28; and, for a later one, • Tarabotti, *L'inferno monacale*, 93.
88 See Fonte, *Worth*, 37, n19.
89 Fonte, *Merito*, 69; *Worth*, 113–14.
90 Fonte, *Merito*, 21; *Worth*, 53.

91 Fonte, *Merito*, 30, 33–5; *Worth*, 64, 69–70.

92 Fonte, *Merito*, 16–17; *Worth*, 47.

93 On the absence of any serious opposition to marriage within the French Renaissance tradition of defences of women, see Lula McDowell Richardson, *The Forerunners of Feminism in French Literature of the Renaissance from Christine de Pisan to Marie de Gournay* (Baltimore, 1929), 159–60. On the evidence of my researches, the same observation could be made of the Italian tradition down to 1600. Zarri, 'Il "terzo stato" ', 334, sees Fonte as the first writer to advocate a single life for women prior to Gabrielle Suchon (1700).

94 See Chemello, 'La donna', 126–34.

95 Fonte, *Merito*, 17–18; *Worth*, 48.

96 Fonte, *Merito*, 18; *Worth*, 48–9.

97 See Daniela Frigo, 'Dal caos all'ordine: sulla questione del "prender moglie" nella trattatistica del sedicesimo secolo', in *Nel cerchio della luna*, esp. 59–66.

98 Fonte, *Merito*, 18; *Worth*, 48–9.

99 Another possible literary model is the eponymous heroine of Maddalena Campiglia's pastoral drama *Flori* (Vicenza, 1588), who rejects marriage in favour of the pursuit of literary immortality and a chaste, neo-platonic love. On Campiglia, see Panizza and Wood (eds) *A History of Women's Writing*, 56–7, 289–90.

100 Fonte, *Merito*, 18; *Worth*, 49. The opening lines of the sonnet are 'Libero cor nel mio petto soggiorna/Non servo alcun, né d'altri son che mia'. ('Free is the heart that dwells within my breast/I have no master and belong to no one but myself'); compare Marfisa's words in *Orlando Furioso*, 26: 79, 7.

101 Fonte, *Merito*, 163; *Worth*, 230. It is Elena who points out the appropriateness of Leonora's choice of device, citing the lines from *Orlando Furioso*, 36: 17–18, in which Marfisa's emblem is interpreted as denoting either her unique strength or 'her chaste resolve to live her whole life without a consort'. On Leonora's devotion to the single life, see *Merito*, 21, 23; *Worth*, 53, 56. For another use of the emblem of the phoenix in the dialogue to symbolize a freely chosen celibate life, see *Merito*, 20; *Worth*, 52.

102 On the iconography of the fountain and its sources and significance, see Chemello, 'La donna', 110–12, 146.

103 Fonte, *Merito*, 22; *Worth*, 54–5.

104 See Margaret L. King, 'Book-lined Cells: Women and Humanists in the Early Italian Renaissance', in Patricia H. Labalme (ed.) *Beyond their Sex: Learned Women of the European Past* (New York and London, 1980), esp. 78–9; *eadem*, 'Goddess and Captive: Antonio Loschi's Poetic Tribute to Maddalena Scrovegni (1389). Study and Text', *Medievalia et Humanistica*, n.s. 10(1981): 103–27.

105 For the description of the garden, see Fonte, *Merito*, 19–20; *Worth*, 50–1. Parallels with *Gli Asolani* are noted in Chemello, 'La donna', 110, n20. Particularly interesting in the context of my argument here is the detail of the fountain adorned with statues of female figures with water flowing from their breasts. On the occurrence of such figures in contemporary gardens and garden literature, and on their symbolic associations with both the fertility of nature and poetic creativity, see Claudia Lazzaro, 'The Visual Language of Gender in Sixteenth-century Garden Sculpture', in *Refiguring Women: Perspectives on Gender and the Italian Renaissance*, eds Marilyn Migiel and Juliana Schiesari (Ithaca and London, 1991), 71–113.

106 See, for example, the passage at Fonte, *Merito*, 29; *Worth*, 63 (cited above, note 83) on the fate of women whose brothers are too avaricious to marry them and who have to remain, as effectively, as unpaid servants. See also

Merito, 171; *Worth*, 239, for Adriana's warning to her daughter Virginia of the drab life which awaits her if she refuses to marry.

107 Fonte, *Merito*, 171–2; *Worth*, 240.

108 See, for example, *Merito*, 23; *Worth*, 56, where Leonora states that she was determined to follow her aunt's example and refuse to marry, until forced to by her father; also *Merito*, 17; *Worth*, 48, where we learn that Virginia would be disinclined to marry, and her mother Adriana disinclined to press the issue, if her uncles did not insist on it.

109 See Fonte, *Merito*, 22; *Worth*, 54, where Leonora notes that her aunt possessed 'a good income that she inherited from my grandfather'.

110 See Fonte, *Merito*, 173–81; *Worth*, 241–58. The poem starts with a description of a mythical age in which Love reigned the earth unchallenged, and goes on to describe the machinations of Pride and Avarice to regain their ascendancy. It concludes with an exhortation to women to scorn men's self-interested advances and dedicate themselves instead to 'worthier deeds and finer studies'. Doglioni, *Vita*, 9; *Life*, 39, records that the *stanze* were written as an independent work and only later integrated in *Il merito delle donne*, interesting evidence that the anti-marriage position sustained by Corinna in the dialogue was also maintained by the author when writing *in propria persona*.

111 See in contrast, Daenens, 'Superiore perché inferiore', 24, for the observation that in the male cinquecento tradition of defences of women, 'the image that is given of women, whether it is one of supremacy or subservience, is always an image functional to the needs and desires of men'.

112 Marinella, *Nobiltà*, 123; *Nobility*, 134. The relatively low place accorded to child-bearing on this list is worthy of note. See Chemello, 'La donna', 131, on the limited emphasis given by Fonte in *Il merito delle donne* to women's maternal role and the novelty this represents within the tradition of defences of women.

Part IV

ART, SCIENCE AND HUMANISM

．

... the Italian mind now turned to the discovery of the outward universe, and to the representation of it in speech and form.

Burckhardt

As a concept, the notion of the Renaissance is most easily applied to the artistic and intellectual history of the era, but – even here, as the essays in this section demonstrate – far more was involved in the remaking of the cultural life of Italy than the rediscovery of the ancient world.

This complexity is as evident in Anthony Grafton's quietly subversive essay on Alberti as in Katharine Park's study of Renaissance anatomies. Both these scholars expand on celebrated texts – Alberti's On Painting *and Vesalius'* On the Fabric of the Human Body *– examining the relation of these works to a broader social and cultural context. For Grafton, the context here is immediate – the social world of Florentine artists and their cultural practices – and the ways in which the humanist Alberti drew on his interactions with such artists in his thinking about the didactic and moral purposes of narrative art. For Park, by contrast, the context is far broader. She re-imagines the history of Renaissance anatomy by connecting it not only to scientific but also to religious practices involving the preservation of the bodies of saints. Both these historians, in short, ask the reader to step outside the text, to place it in the larger context of the society in which it was written, and to re-evaluate its significance by taking the context into account.*

Finally, turning to Thomas More's Utopia *and northern European humanism, David Wootton also develops a new context for understanding the most radical component of More's work: the institution of communism. While Wootton's method is largely traditional – he focuses primarily on texts – his findings are remarkable, as he discovers many anticipations of More's ideas in the works of Erasmus, a figure rarely associated with the extreme position (ostensibly) taken by More.*

All three essays offer an opportunity not only to think about how we might best understand the history of ideas; all three participate in what we might call the 'defamiliarization' of the Renaissance. Renaissance ideas – artistic, scientific and humanistic – cannot simply be read as laying the foundations of modernity; such ideas were also deeply embedded in the cultures of late medieval and early modern Europe, cultures that often had very little in common with our own.

10

HISTORIA AND *ISTORIA*

Alberti's terminology in context

Anthony Grafton

Historians of Renaissance art and culture have frequently emphasized the close association of artistic expression with rhetorical practice. The visual arts of the period, after all, were crafted not only to represent the world but also to persuade or to teach. In this sense, sculptures and paintings, which often represented scenes from the Bible or from classical mythology, resembled history itself. For Renaissance humanists viewed historical writing (here understood as a narrative of great deeds) as a moral and persuasive art, designed to instill in readers, through lessons drawn from the past, a measure of wisdom or prudence. In his treatise On Painting, *the eminent Florentine humanist and architect Leon Battista Alberti (1404–72) developed this analogy closely, arguing that grand narrative scenes in art and sculpture alike were 'histories' ('historiae', 'storie' or 'istorie') whose primary function was to stir the emotions of the viewer in a way that would move him or her to virtuous acts. It was no accident that it was precisely in this period that Leonardo Bruni, the Florentine Chancellor, was composing his* History of the Florentine People, *in which he emphasized the didactic purposes of history which teaches us, through the study of past examples, 'what we should avoid and what we should pursue'. To the Italian humanists, history was* magister vitae – *a discipline that teaches us how to live.*

In the essay below Anthony Grafton offers an analysis of the theme of 'history' in Alberti's On Painting, *a work that has traditionally been studied for its pivotal role in providing the theory of perspective (the principles Renaissance artists had begun to devise to convey the illusion of three dimensions on, for example, a two-dimensional wall painting) with mathematical and rational foundations. Grafton demonstrates how Alberti – who moved easily in the worlds of both humanist textual scholars and the workshops of painters and sculptors – drew on and transformed the language that was used by both the ancients and his own contemporaries to discuss and describe art and artistic production. Alberti's thinking about these issues was animated in part by the extraordinary clustering of great artists and architects in Florence at this time. He had arrived in the city shortly after Filippo Brunelleschi had completed his stunning octagonal dome for the cathedral – a structure that continues to define the city's skyline; while Lorenzo Giberti was working on his elaborate bronze doors to the Baptistery; and at the very time that artists and sculptors as talented as Donatello, Massaccio, della Robbia and Uccello were at work on some of their most famous projects.*

Grafton's emphasis in this essay (as in many of his writings) is on the underlying assumptions of Renaissance thinkers. He is concerned with retrieving the intellectual practices, the available analytical vocabularies, and the social contexts in which they worked. This approach enables him to cast into relief those aspects of a particular writer's works that were novel and that opened up new ways of thinking about and seeing art and the world. In the end, Grafton makes it clear that Alberti was able to create a fundamentally new language for both analysing and shaping the nature of visual representation in Renaissance culture. And, while he stresses the role that the larger cultural and intellectual context played in shaping Alberti's ideas, he does not hesitate to stress the importance of Alberti's own intellectual and cultural ambitions in the creation of a new vocabulary – a new way of seeing and representing the world.

This essay first appeared in I Tatti Studies: Essays in the Renaissance *8 (1999): 37–68, and it is this version that I reprint here, though I have excluded the passages in Latin and Italian included in the notes of the original. Grafton has reworked this essay as Chapter IV of his biography of Alberti,* Leon Battista Alberti: Master Builder of the Italian Renaissance *(New York, 2000), a text to which readers interested in a more fulsome portrait and analysis of this fascinating Renaissance figure should turn. For an introduction to Grafton's approach to the study of intellectual history, see especially his* Defenders of the Text: The Traditions of Scholarship in the Age of Science, 1400–1800 *(Cambridge MA, 1985). And, finally, for a still highly influential analysis of Alberti's* On Painting *and its significance in the development of the science of perspective, see Erwin Panofsky,* Renaissance and Renascences in Western Art *(New York, 1969), esp. 123–7; Panofsky's first studies on Alberti appeared in the 1910s and 1920s, at the dawn of Renaissance art history.*

* * *

One day in June 1446, as the Benedictine Girolamo Aliotti made his way towards Arezzo, he encountered a new 'religio' taking shape. Men dressed as penitents, women trudging on foot, boys and girls, followed cruciform banners through a cleft in the hills. Joining them, Aliotti learned that the Virgin Mary had just appeared 'in the body' to the citizens of a small town, where she had made believers out of atheists and reconciled enemies divided by ancient lawsuits and feuds. Inquiring more closely, Aliotti learned that four teenage girls had taken shelter in the local church during a heavy rain. They prayed to the Virgin to stop the downpour, which was causing serious floods, and to put an end to the civil strife which was doing even worse damage to their town. In answer to their prayers, the image of the Virgin painted on the wall of the church was 'transfigured into the true mother of the Lord our Saviour, no longer represented, but in the flesh, but breathing, but alive'.

Once transformed into its prototype, the image exhibited miraculous powers. Mockers, brought into its presence, 'began to feel the immense and terrible power of God'. Trembling, stricken, they fell helpless to the ground, like the Apostle Paul. Spectacular visions appeared to them: one saw the Virgin shooting arrows into his heart, another felt the most severe pains he had ever experienced. Contact with the image brought about conversion: immediate, irresistible, awe-inspiring. Aliotti, deeply impressed, remembered his professional responsibilities. An icon's metamorphosis into its own holy subject would constitute a miracle. Accordingly, Aliotti consulted experts on the theology of the supernatural for help in assessing what he had seen and heard. He sent a detailed account to a friend in Rome, asking for the authoritative opinions of Cardinal Turrecremata, 'the most expert theologian of our time', and Giovanni Mattiotti, the priest of Santa Maria in Trastevere who had served as confessor to Santa Francesca Romana, 'a man characterized by a special aptitude for the precise discernment of spirits'.[1]

Aliotti's social and intellectual worlds were large – large enough, in fact, to accommodate thinkers who had a very different way of looking at the power of images. He took a serious interest in the new humanistic literature of the 1430s and 1440s. Aliotti copied texts, wrote critiques, and at one point even set out to create a public library entirely composed of modern Latin texts, beginning with the complete works of Poggio Bracciolini.[2] Like many other citizens of the humanist republic of letters, he eagerly collected and read texts that dealt with the arts – for example, an anonymous work in Italian, De arte fusoria. Aliotti hoped that the painters and sculptors of Florence might be able to provide him with a more correct text of this treatise, if possible in Latin. He also made a revealing conjecture about its authorship: perhaps, he thought, 'Messer Baptista de Albertis' might have written it.[3] Aliotti's guess suggests that he already knew, or knew of, a similar work by Alberti: his treatise On Painting, the Italian and Latin versions of which both reached completion before Aliotti saw the miraculous icon.[4] This is not surprising: Aliotti, as we will see, knew and admired Alberti.

If Aliotti had decided to treat the phenomena he saw as natural rather than supernatural, he might well have consulted Alberti rather than Turrecremata, asking him to explain how a painting could so strongly affect those who encountered it. In On Painting, after all, Alberti had examined in detail the means by which a painting of the highest excellence – a 'historia', as he termed it in Latin, or a 'storia' or 'istoria' in Italian – could 'move the minds of those who see it'.[5] One can only imagine how Alberti would have gone about analysing the emotional effects wrought by the Virgin's image on the church wall. One can, however, make a more systematic effort than has yet been tried to establish exactly what Alberti had in mind when he described the 'historia' as 'the highest work of the painter'.[6]

Scholarly interest in Alberti's text and terminology goes back to the very origins of systematic art history. The Strassburg scholar Hubert Janitschek, a distinguished student of the social and cultural history of Renaissance art, translated Alberti's *Della pittura* into German more than a century ago. He also equipped the work with notes, in which he identified some of the classical and post-classical sources on which Alberti drew and the ancient and modern works of art on which he commented. Janitschek's work retains considerable value. But when he confronted Alberti's discussion of the 'historia', he read the relevant passages through a veil, one composed of the characteristic interests and assumptions of a connoisseur of painting in the 1870s. What the term 'historia' called to his mind was, naturally enough, 'history painting'. He translated 'historia', accordingly, as 'das Geschichtsbild' – a word which brings to mind heroic images of oaths and battles, represented with minute – even historicist – attention to the details of costume and setting.[7]

By contrast, John Spencer, who translated *Della pittura* into English eighty years later, contented himself with a transcription of the term: 'the *istoria*', he made Alberti write, 'is the greatest work of the painter'.[8] But in his introduction, he made clear that the term required an elaborate gloss. 'The concept of *istoria*', he explained, 'dominates the whole treatise and it is developed at length in the last half of the work'. By weaving together several of the passages in which the word occurred, moreover, Spencer produced a detailed account of what it referred to. In essence, he held, neither size nor the materials used had much to do with the meaning of a 'historia'. Rather, the term referred to a work of art that met certain formal and substantive criteria: 'It is to be built upon ancient themes with human gestures to portray and project the emotions of the actors'.[9] A 'historia', in other words, was an artistic treatment of a theme from classical history or mythology, one cast in such a way as to have a powerful effect on the emotions of anyone who saw it.

Spencer was one of the first scholars to open up what has revealed itself, in the last two generations, as a highly productive way of examining Alberti's work – one Spencer himself summed up, in the title of what has become a classic article, as 'Ut rhetorica pictura'. Alberti, he and others argued, set out to model the art of the painter on those of the humanist poet and orator. Taking the literary treatises and textbooks of Horace, Cicero and Quintilian as his chief sources, if not as his exact models, Alberti envisioned painting as a learned art. It drew its subject matter, like the orations and poems that the humanists learned to write in the schools of Vittorino da Feltre and Guarino da Verona, from the realm of ancient myth and history. And the painter hoped to produce the same sublime emotional effects as humanist oratory and poetry, by delighting and moving, as well as instructing, his audience.[10]

History, in the thought of the humanists as well as in that of the ancients, belonged to the art of rhetoric. Seen above all as a narrative designed to embody the principles of morality and prudence in the form of well-told stories about great men, history – so humanist after humanist proclaimed, echoing the sentiments of ancient historians and rhetoricians – was *magistra vitae*. Its worked examples of good and evil, effective and ineffective conduct moved readers more rapidly and more profoundly than statements of general principle could.[11]

By identifying the 'historia' as the core of the painter's enterprise – so Spencer and others after him, such as Kristine Patz, have shown – Alberti strengthened his argument that painting itself was a liberal art, comparable in function and value to rhetoric, which formed the core of the entire humanistic curriculum. Alberti himself made clear, in his later work *De re aedificatoria*, that when he applied the term 'historia' to the arts, he meant to imply that one could draw precise analogies between literature and painting:

> I look at a good painting (to paint a bad picture is to disgrace a wall) with as much pleasure as I take in reading of a good 'historia'. Both are the work of painters: one paints with words, the other tells the story with his brush. They have other things in common: both require great ability and amazing diligence.[12]

In both painting and history, as the context shows, Alberti prized above all the capacity to instruct and improve the reader or onlooker.[13]

Scholars have disagreed, however, about both the wider historical significance of Alberti's terminology and its precise interpretation. While most scholars have seen 'historia' as above all a formal term, one that denoted paintings of a particular kind, Jack Greenstein has argued that Alberti saw histories as possessing a particular kind of substance as well, a higher sense which they expressed in a figural way as traditional, even 'medieval', as their formal qualities were simultaneously classical and up-to-date.[14] But the connection between Alberti's painted histories and the ones written by humanists seems established.[15]

How then to gain a fuller and more precise sense of what Alberti had in mind when he chose 'historia' as the central term of *On Painting* – a work in which, as he himself made clear, he self-consciously set out to write something that had no clear counterpart in classical or modern literature? One way is simply by expanding the range of passages – and texts – taken into account. Scholars interested in Alberti's writing on the arts that sixteenth-century critics would associate with *disegno* have tended to assume that one can properly elucidate *On Painting* and *On Sculpture* without investigating those of Alberti's works that do not deal explicitly with these fields.

The founding figures of Albertian studies may have unintentionally encouraged later scholars to adopt this point of view. When Janitschek translated what he described as Alberti's 'shorter art-theoretical writings', and when Julius von Schlosser later compiled his classic reference work on 'the literature of art', they created a canon of works which historians of Renaissance art needed to study. In Alberti's case, this included his works on painting, on sculpture and on architecture.[16] It seems most unlikely that either of them meant to suggest that scholars could confine themselves to those works that addressed the arts explicitly: certainly neither of them did so, any more than did Janitschek's pupil Aby Warburg. But this working assumption has nonetheless governed – and limited – much of what has been written about Alberti since their time. Scholars have scrutinized *On Painting* and *On Sculpture* with imagination and care: advances have come about, usually when these works were closely compared either with their classical sources or with the work of other 'humanistic observers of painting' – to quote the subtitle of a particularly original and influential book by Michael Baxandall. Only in the realm of city planning, where Manfredo Tafuri demonstrated the vital importance of Alberti's *Momus* and *De porcariana coniuratione* to understanding his role in the Rome of Nicholas V, has this unofficial rule been broken.[17]

In fact, however, an ancient principle of philology suggests that the scholar should 'use Homer to interpret Homer' – that is, that an author's complete corpus should serve as the first port of call for those seeking parallel passages and elucidations for any given text.[18] And Alberti himself – as scholars have repeatedly argued – regularly attacked the same themes and questions in multiple works, revising his ideas as his situation changed, but remaining faithful to certain problems that preoccupied him. Other texts produced by members of his immediate circle, such as Aliotti, can also shed light on Alberti's usage. So can the ancient texts on which he drew – and to which he normally referred in an oblique, emulative way, requiring readers not simply to recognize, but to decipher his allusions.[19] In fact, passages drawn from a wide range of sources can shed light on what Alberti usually meant when he referred to 'historiae' in *On Painting*. No single definition can exhaust the word's multiple meanings and functions. Only when some future scholar has provided *On Painting* with a full commentary – rather than the haze of sources that now hangs about the text, transmitted by a series of editions with useful footnotes but nowhere analysed in full – will we know for certain from what sources Alberti drew his terminology, which terms he created himself, and how his usage in this text compares, detail by detail, with that in his other works and the writings of his contemporaries. But existing resources can be explored to some effect.

No one can exaggerate the ferocious ambition and creativity of the writer who set out to invent a terminology for discussing the arts – to claim a kind of discursive monopoly over the realm of the visual – and did so in two languages at once. But no one should forget that Alberti was only one of many highly articulate individuals in Tuscany who discussed and wrote about publicly commissioned works of art. A rudimentary terminology existed before Alberti wrote, and he drew on it, as we shall see. Sometimes, Albertian technical terms that scholars have singled out for their originality and profundity derived directly from the existing language of the artists' ateliers.[20]

At the same time, however, it would be wrong to assume that the range of meanings ascribed to 'historia' – or any other term – in Alberti's other works, in his identifiable sources, and in the language of his contemporaries includes all the senses in which Alberti himself could have used the word. Alberti was a self-consciously innovative writer. He regularly appropriated passages from ancient texts, deliberately assigning to them a meaning that their author had not had in mind, as he cited them. He wrote, moreover, in a linguistically supercharged environment – one in which small linguistic errors could cause large problems for an ambitious scholar. All humanists of the early fifteenth century wanted to write a Latin that would pass muster as classical. All of them knew, moreover, that the waters of literary life swarmed with sharks ready and eager to devour them – with critics, that is, like Lorenzo Valla, who might seek to humiliate them and destroy their literary reputations by showing that they had committed errors of grammar, syntax or semantics. When Valla decided to slay Alberti's friend and patron Poggio Bracciolini, he composed a dialogue in which the cook and stable-boy of the great teacher Guarino of Verona join their master in examining, and condemning, Poggio's Latin prose. 'Culinaria vocabula', 'Latin for the kitchen', passed into proverbial usage as a term for especially slovenly efforts at *Kunstprosa*.[21]

Alberti himself could be a sharp critic of the misuse of language. He dismissed Vitruvius, for example, in part because his prose swarmed with stylistic errors of many kinds – especially the Greek terms of which he had made wildly excessive use:

> What he handed down was in any case not refined, and his speech such that the Latins might think that he wanted to appear a Greek, while the Greeks would think that he babbled Latin. However, his very text is evidence that he wrote neither Latin nor Greek, so that as far as we are concerned he might just as well not have written at all, rather than write something that we cannot understand.[22]

And he worked in two connected intellectual environments, whose inhabitants registered the symbolic meaning of apparently small choices in wording with the precision and sensitivity to shock of earthquake meters. As a writer on painting, Alberti set out to discuss what he saw as the recent flowering of Florentine culture which he had witnessed on first visiting his ancestral city. But Florence was also the home of the savagely critical scholar Niccolò Niccoli, who notoriously despised the writings of such great moderns as Dante, Petrarch and Boccaccio, and who considered the works of his contemporaries more suited for use in the outhouse than for publication.[23] Like many others, Alberti clashed with Niccoli – and did so sharply enough that he satirized the great book collector more than once in his *Intercenales*.[24] Bitterly conscious that Tuscans tended to be hypercritical, Alberti knew to his cost that small errors in taste and usage could damage a literary reputation beyond repair.

As a papal secretary, Alberti belonged to the curia, where he and his colleagues laboured to find classical ways of asserting the majesty and power of the papal monarchy. In 1453, for example, Pope Nicholas V became the first pope since the fourth century to describe himself officially as 'Pontifex Maximus'. By reviving this title he claimed a new kind of authority over the church, the city of Rome and the Papal States, as sensitive observers did not fail to note. Nicholas did so, moreover, in highly visible contexts, no doubt chosen with great care – for example, the inscription in which he celebrated his own building of the Trevi Fountain, which offered a supply of fresh water to inhabitants of central Rome and thus revived a central function of the ancient Roman state. Alberti was very probably connected with the project; he may, indeed, have designed the inscription in question.[25] Since the curia spent much of the 1430s in Florence, Alberti had to find niches in two dangerous literary ecosystems at one and the same time.

Precision in diction requires sensitivity – especially sensitivity to the reactions that violations of norms could provoke. Alberti's sensitivity to criticism emerges clearly, not only from the texts of the *Intercenales*, which he composed in the same period as *On Painting*, but also from the numerous letters in which he asked friends to edit and correct major and minor works – ranging from *On Painting* itself to the *Intercenales* and his dialogues *On the Family*.[26] These requests, moreover, were not mere commonplaces, but genuine demands for help: like Poggio and many other humanist writers, Alberti clearly incorporated many of the corrections that friends like Leonardo Dati provided ambitious works like *Della famiglia*, which he revised and emended at their behest.[27] Like his colleagues, in other words, Alberti chose his words with painstaking care, seeking help from expert writers and critics. Like his colleagues, too, when Alberti used a Latin term in a sense which classical authority did not legitimate, he did so deliberately, in the full expectation that his readers would notice and seek to understand his choice of words. How then did he use 'historia' and 'istoria'?

'Historia', in classical Latin, can refer both to events (*res gestae*) and to narrative accounts of them (*narrationes*): both to stories in general and to formal historical narratives. Alberti regularly employed the word in these basic senses. At the age of twenty, for example, he wrote a Latin comedy about the human desire for fame – one which represented so coherent and successful an imitation of a Roman comedy, at least in the eyes of its first readers, that Alberti gave in and ascribed it to a Roman poet named Lepidus. Some years later, however, he took back the false ascription and claimed authorship of the piece, which he wanted to dedicate to Leonello d'Este, a student of Guarino and patron of letters. In the short commentary that he wrote to introduce the work, he insisted that the hero's name, 'Philodoxeus', the lover of glory, perfectly fitted a Roman hero, 'since all histories vouch for the fact that Rome was always the capital of fame'.[28] In this case, 'history' means nothing more than an account or *narratio* of *res gestae*, such as the standard account of early Roman history by Livy, a work much loved and read in Leonelline Ferrara.[29] The word figures in an even more conventional way in the *Vita anonyma*, the third-person account of Alberti's life that he himself seems to have written around 1437. This text remarks that 'he liked histories of anything so much that he considered even poor writers admirable'.[30]

Many humanists, however, used 'history' in a more precise and loaded way; to refer specifically to the sort of high, instructive account of past politics and war that retired statesmen and generals had written in ancient times. History in this elevated sense referred to narratives of the sort written by Thucydides or Polybius, which provided exemplary stories of successful and unsuccessful conduct. Readers were meant to analyse these, in order to equip themselves with the prudence needed in the active life, and then to emulate or avoid emulating the actions they depicted when faced with similar circumstances.

On 8 April 1437, for example, Alberti's friend Lapo da Castiglionchio the younger wrote to Flavio Biondo, who had sent him the first four books of his pioneering history of medieval Italy, the *Decades*, and asked for a critical assessment of the text.[31] Lapo found Biondo's text so eloquent and truthful as to need no 'emendation' – perhaps a misplaced act of editorial charity, since Pius II and other readers later criticized Biondo's prose as unpolished.[32] But he took the opportunity to explain, for his friend and no doubt for a wider readership, the value of history. He made clear that history was 'varied, multifarious and wide-ranging, and based on a great many arts and disciplines'.[33] And he identified one of its central functions as the provision of models for imitation by those involved in difficult political and military decision-making:

Precepts can be drawn from history, as from the richest imagin-able source, for every area of life: the best way to govern one's household, the method of ruling the state, the reasons for under-taking wars, how they should be waged, and how far they should be prosecuted, how friendships are to be handled, treaties are to be made, alliances to be forged, how popular disturbances are to be calmed and revolutions put down. In history we may choose some great and wise man, all of whose sayings, actions, plans, and counsel we may imitate.[34]

Alberti used 'history' in this more capacious and exacting sense of 'philosophy teaching through examples' when he conceded, in his bitter Latin work *On the Advantages and Disadvantages of Letters*, that he was too young to write a real history. Only men of full maturity and true learning could 'write histories, which would offer fitting analyses of the characters of kings and of great political events and wars'.[35]

But producing instructive narrative was not altogether simple. Like Lapo, Alberti knew that writing history presented, or could present, technical problems. Lapo noted that Biondo, writing the history of his own time, had successfully followed Cicero's 'laws for historians', avoiding falsehood and telling the whole truth:

> For you yourself were present, I think, at many events, and where you were not, you learned about them by going into the matter and interrogating those who were there. And you accepted as true those accounts that rested on the most reliable witnesses, and rejected as falsehoods and fictions those that derived from popular gossip and rumor.[36]

Critical problems arose with special frequency when the historian had to write an account of events that had taken place before his own time, and had to decide which of the older reports he considered credible before composing his own work. Lapo's praise of Biondo – like the classical sources on which he drew – insisted that a history must be truthful as well as instructive, and tacitly admitted that the historian might not always find it easy, or possible, to pursue these two goals at once.

An episode that took place early in Alberti's career in the papal curia ensured his awareness of this point. Biagio Molin engaged him to write the biography of an early Christian martyr, one Potitus, who had been put to death in the time of the pagan emperor Julian. Adopting a method often followed by humanist historians, Alberti set out to impose a proper rhetorical form on a narrative provided by Molin, presumably in the form of short medieval texts in Latin or Italian.[37] These told him that Potitus, a Christian soldier in the best spirit of Monty Python, suffered beatings and worse at the hands of the Romans: they tore out his eyes and tongue as well. Yet he continued, even without his tongue, to confess the true god, and by doing so impressed the animals in the arena so deeply that they refused to eat him. The task that confronted Alberti was to retell these stories in a suitably modern – that is, classical – way.

Alberti – unlike Aliotti – had little love for miracles. In a letter to his friend Leonardo Dati, on whose literary judgment he regularly relied, Alberti confessed that he found the historical status of Potitus' martyrdon problematic:

> I was a bit worried, since, like you, I feared that scholars might entertain the doubt that this history ['historiam'] of Potitus of ours is a childish, invented tale ['fabulam']. For I knew what men of learning usually seek in a history ['in historia']: they expect a full account of the event in question, the places, the times, and the quality of the actors. And I saw that the ancients had given clear and full accounts of the acts of the apostles and the lives of the popes and the other martyrs. But I saw that this history ['istoriam'] of Potitus was transmitted so carelessly that I could easily infer that ignorant men, rather than those scholars of great learning, produced it.[38]

Simply using the traditional, crude narratives first placed at his disposal, Alberti felt that he could not fix the chronology or geography of Potitus' heroic end precisely. Bad historians and worse scribes had scrambled the entire account beyond recognition. Accordingly, Alberti collected all the works by early Christian writers he could find in the curia that might shed light on Potitus' life, and used these primary documents to establish what he considered a plausible identity and date for his protagonist. He also amused himself by putting into the mouth of the emperor Julian a phosphorescent denunciation of the anti-social habits and idleness of the Christians.

In this case, Alberti treated history as something more than a well turned narrative about events already known to the author: it was, or should be, a reflexive, scholarly genre that required its practitioners to be deft at research, honest with themselves and others and able to assemble and compare multiple sources for a single event. Not even the precision of the critical procedures he applied allayed all his doubts about Potitus. But by stating them he could at least make clear his own sense of what the genre demanded, wrapping his argument up with an apposite quotation from *De oratore*: 'But as to what scholars think about the carelessness of the scribes or some historians, we can speak elsewhere'.[39] Alberti's situation here was delicate. He seems to have cared sincerely about historical accuracy. Later in life, writing on the supremely delicate subject of Stefano Porcari's conspiracy against Nicholas V, he seems to have given a highly accurate version of the speech in which Porcari denounced the pope for having deprived the Romans of their ancient rights of citizenship.[40] In the case of Potitus, however, he could only indicate – by including the letter in which he described his critical techniques with the life itself – what he saw as a contradiction between the historian's two obligations, to be truthful and to be instructive.

Alberti's unusual work apparently found some admiring readers. It must have been his success with Potitus that made Aliotti see him as the ideal biographer of Ambrogio Traversari – a man not only erudite, but also one so holy that lilies miraculously sprouted on his grave. For as soon as Traversari died, Aliotti began to agitate for Alberti to be appointed his official biographer: once again, he would have worked with a set of documents provided him by the sponsors of the life in question.[41] Yet Alberti declined or evaded the commission – perhaps because he would have found it difficult to discharge in a way both principled and effective. Even within the classical senses of history, in other words, difficulties lurked.

Alberti, moreover, sometimes employed the term in one of its classical senses, but to an unclassical – or at least unconventional – end. When he dedicated the Italian form of *On Painting* to Brunelleschi, he remarked that he regretted that 'so many excellent and divine arts and sciences, which we know from their works and from historical accounts ['per le istorie'] were possessed in great abundance by the talented man of antiquity, have now disappeared and are almost entirely lost'.[42] Here – as elsewhere – 'storia' meant only an authoritative narrative about the past (perhaps, quite precisely, Livy's history of Rome). In other passages, however, Alberti manipulated the well worn terms in ways that showed his characteristic independence of received views. Book 35 of Pliny's *Natural History* treated painting not only as the object of aesthetic analysis but also as a historical subject, the development of which could be reconstructed Olympiad by Olympiad and artist by artist. This erudite work, based on elaborate researches described in a well known letter by the younger Pliny, clearly represented a scholarly effort to tell the truth about the past – and by doing so to offer serious lessons about the way in which human efforts had perfected the arts. Pliny, moreover, built his critical 'history' from little 'histories', using a series of stories about the most proficient ancient artists – Zeuxis, Apelles, and the rest – to embody the central morals of his tale. In doing so, he followed well established precedent. Ancient chroniclers and historians regularly included in their works information about the history of culture, usually in the form of heurematological remarks – identifications of the individuals or communities responsible for the invention or first use of a weapon or other device. Lapo wrote appreciatively of the usefulness and pleasure of history, which taught not only moral lessons, but also:

who founded the great cities, who devised the arts, who first began to educate the human race, which was rough and unculti-vated, who assembled men in cities, who gave them laws, who introduced the worship of the gods, who first instructed them in sailing, agriculture, and letters, and who began to deal with mili-tary affairs.[43]

Alberti, though he occasionally made one of Pliny's stories fit his own, quite different ends, made it clear that he did not mean to emulate the Roman scholar's way of talking about the arts.[44] He maintained, in the Italian text, that he did not want 'to tell stories like Pliny, but to write an original, systematic treatment of the art of painting'.[45] In the Latin version, he stated that unlike Pliny, 'he did not want to review the history of painting'.[46] In each version of his remark Alberti criticized the standard ancient text on painting. Though Alberti used the terms 'storia' and 'historia' here in classical senses, in other words, he did so only in order to declare himself free to depart from classical precedent whenever he liked. Accordingly, there is no reason to assume that he always had the classical model of rhetorical history in mind when he discussed painted and sculpted histories. Moreover, the rhetorical tradition as Alberti understood it included not only the Greek and Roman classics, but also Byzantine texts in which the term 'historia' meant simply 'a painting' or 'a representation' – as it also did in the Latin and Italian of Alberti's day, as we will see. Even when Alberti conformed to what he saw as the canons of the pure classical style, in other words, he could use the term 'historia' in a sense not attested in ancient literature.[47]

At times, Alberti deliberately departed even further from classical norms. Cicero had made clear, in his *Brutus*, that orators normally applied the term 'historia' to true events, not to myths. A 'historia' could be many kinds of tale – but not the false one properly known as a 'fabula'.[48] Alberti certainly knew this newly discovered work by Cicero, which he cited at the conclusion of *On Painting*, and he referred to it directly when he noted the fabulous nature of the story of Potitus.[49] But he deliberately flouted Cicero's distinction when he referred to the story of the Calumny of Apelles as an ideal 'historia' or 'istoria', and even more directly when he described the story of Narcissus' metamorphosis into a flower in Latin as a 'fabula', and in Italian as a 'storia'.[50] A history, in other words, might be the sort of high rendering of individuals in action which humanists liked to deliver in perfect Latin; but it might also be, paradoxically, a myth. Alberti's reader had to think twice each time the word occurred before knowing for certain to what it referred.

What then was a history, for Alberti, most of the time? In the first place, it seems to have been not only a painting, but in most cases a large-scale painting executed in a public place. At times, to be sure,

Alberti writes as if absolute size and placement played no role in identifying a painting as a 'historia'. Early in *On Painting*, for example, he describes the picture plane in general terms, which would fit anything from a panel painting to a panorama:

> First of all, on the surface on which I am going to paint, I draw a rectangle of whatever size I want, which I regard as an open window through which the *historia* is to be seen: and I decide how large I want the human figures in the painting to be.[51]

But in Book 3, where Alberti gives his most detailed account of the process of composing a 'historia', he recommends that the painter work out his entire 'invention' in advance, before he sets brush to surface. Otherwise, he cannot be sure 'that nothing at all will crop up in the work, the nature and position of which we did not precisely know'.[52] Alberti here provides the painter with precise instructions on how to carry out this task. He must lay out his entire work in detailed sketches, and then he must transfer his designs directly from these to the surface he intended to adorn: 'In order that we may know this with greater certainty, it will help to divide our models into parallels, so that everything can then be transferred, as it were, from our private papers and put in its correct position in the work for public exhibition'.[53] Alberti's terminology is suggestive: a 'publicum opus' or 'publico lavoro' must normally be a large-scale work meant to be displayed in a public building – exactly the sort of work which required the procedures Alberti described. That helps to explain why Alberti so strongly emphasized that the painter 'should not adopt the common habit of painting on very small panels. For I want you to become used to working on large-scale images, which indeed come as close as possible in size to the objects you wish to represent' – clear evidence that he saw paintings with life-size or near life-size figures as the chief work of the painter.[54]

The nature of the public work in question, or one form of it at least, is easy enough to establish. Paolo Uccello used exactly the technique Alberti recommended, squaring off a sketch of the monument to Sir John Hawkwood, now preserved in the Uffizi, before he transferred his design to the wall of the Florentine cathedral, to serve as the basis for his fresco. He did so, moreover, in the summer of 1436 – exactly at the time that Alberti seems to have finished *Della pittura*.[55] Elsewhere Alberti advised painters that if they included the face of a well known individual in their 'historia' or 'storia', it would 'attract the eyes of all onlookers'.[56] And he asked the artists who read *On Painting*, if they valued his advice, to include his portrait 'in suis historiis' – 'in their histories'.[57] Florentine fresco painters – notably Masaccio – regularly included portraits of famous men, including scholars like Alberti, in their frescoes.[58] Finally, when Alberti wanted to give an example of a good modern history, he cited the *Navicella* of Giotto – a mosaic in the Vatican which no longer survives, and which represented Jesus and the Apostles on the Sea of Galilee.[59] There seems every reason to infer, then, that Alberti, for all his interest in and knowledge of written histories, used the term in the first instance in a deliberately up-to-date sense, to refer to large-scale works of art that included a number of figures engaged in a complex action and that were meant for public display. Alberti claimed, in his later work on architecture, to prefer removeable panel paintings to frescoes, and clearly considered that the term 'historia' could apply to both.[60] For the most part, however, Alberti must have envisioned painted 'historiae' as frescoes, the context of which could be – as the example of the *Navicella* shows – biblical as well as mythological or historical.

The qualities that Alberti ascribed to the ideal 'historia' are too well known to require detailed discussion. It should contain no more than eight or nine characters, varied in age, gender, dress and attitude. Most of them should be playing parts in a single story, but one chosen individual could be looking out at and gesturing towards the onlooker, inviting him or her to examine the action more closely. All of them should have bodies, clothing and attitudes that fit their sexes, stations and ages. Copiousness without chaos, variety without indiscipline, decorum above all – these characteristics clearly fit a painting designed on the grand scale and intended for public display, like the frescoes of Masaccio, whom Alberti explicitly praised in his dedicatory letter to Brunelleschi.[61]

Yet by Alberti's own account, not all 'historiae' were painted. He made clear in his critique of older 'historiae' that the term embraced the work of 'the ancient *sculptors and painters*'. For he complained, in *De pictura*, that 'You will hardly find any "historia" by one of the ancients that is properly composed, in painting or modelling or sculpture'.[62] It is not clear whether Alberti had in mind here the work of ancient artists, as Greenstein holds, or that of medieval Italian painters, as seems more likely (in *On the Family*, after all, Alberti described earlier members of the Alberti family as 'the ancients'). But it is clear that a 'historia', in Alberti's sense, could be a work of sculpture as well as painting. A 'historia' in this sense – a sculpted work that included, like a painted 'historia', multiple figures carrying out a single action – would have to be a relief. And indeed, Alberti singled out for praise, along with Giotto's *Navicella*, what he called a 'historia [or 'storia'] at Rome which represents the dead Meleager' – a stone sarcophagus relief.[63] In *De re aedificatoria* Alberti regularly used the term to refer to the sort of reliefs which encrusted the Arch of Constantine and the columns of Hadrian and Trajan.[64] Alberti did not mean, by his choice of title, to restrict his theories to the single artistic genre of painting.[65]

Moreover, Alberti did not create a critical language out of whole cloth. The vocabulary of art in Florence was already well developed and widely diffused long before he wrote his treatise. The thirty-four members of the jury empanelled to decide who should fashion the first Baptistery doors presumably discussed the relative merits of Brunelleschi and Ghiberti, not to mention the other contestants, in some detail. If Alberti hoped to find an audience ready to accept and use his own terminology, he was more or less bound to adapt terms that already existed to his purposes. The art language that existed when Alberti set to work, in other words, provided the resisting medium that he chiselled and polished until it took on a coherent new form.

'Historia' and 'storia' belonged to this language. Established terms for works of art in late fourteenth- and fifteenth-century Italy, both words could and often did refer to narrative paintings. But they also very often denoted sculpted reliefs – more particularly, reliefs that represented a fairly large number of individuals at once.[66] Dante had used 'storia', in a celebrated passage in Canto 10 of *Purgatorio*, to refer to panels cut from the living rock.[67] And many Florentines, both writers and artists, employed the term regularly in this specific, technical sense. Leonardo Bruni, when he proposed his plan for the second new set of doors for the Baptistery in 1424, insisted that the twenty 'storie' to appear on the new doors must be both meaningful and brilliantly executed. To that end, he argued, an adviser should be hired, who was in a position to advise Ghiberti on the various 'storie' he would represent (Ghiberti made the same play on the meaning of 'storia' in his *Commentaries*).[68] Matteo degli Organi, who built and rebuilt organs for the Florentine cathedral, wrote to the Operai of the Cathedral of Prato in 1434 to urge that they should cease complaining because Donatello was taking so long to execute his reliefs for the outdoor pulpit of the Chapel of the Girdle of the Blessed Virgin. The sculptor, he explained, had just finished 'quella storia di marmo', and all connoisseurs agreed that he had created something uniquely beautiful.[69] The official documents in which the Operai of the Florentine cathedral discussed the monies paid to Luca della Robbia for his reliefs for the Cantoria referred to the panels consistently as 'storiae marmoris' – histories in marble.[70]

Ancient reliefs, also called 'historiae' and 'storie', fascinated the artists of the early fifteenth century. The first systematic sketches from the antique, now usually attributed to the workshop of Pisanello, include a good many figures drawn from Roman reliefs. True, these were usually pulled from context and redrawn in a way more decorative than precise by Pisanello's pupils, who showed little interest in the qualities of depth and composition that most interested Alberti.[71] But ancient reliefs also powerfully attracted Ghiberti and Donatello, and these artists – the ones whom Alberti explicitly praised – recovered and improved on the principles of composition, anatomy and perspective that their ancient counter-parts had employed.[72] Bacchic sarcophagi struck the most original artists of Alberti's time as an aesthetic revelation. In the Florentine 'horizon of expectation' of the 1430s, 'relief sculpture' was prominent among the senses that would have come to the mind of a reader of *De pictura* or of *Della pittura*.

Why, then, when Alberti set out to characterize the ideal form of painting, did he use as his central term one charged with non-classical senses strongly established in normal practice? Why suggest that ancient and modern reliefs embodied the ideal qualities which painters, as well as sculptors, should strive to attain? The answer seems clear. Alberti set out, in *On Painting*, to create an aesthetic language that was not only descriptive, but prescriptive. He wanted to convey a particular set of aesthetic ideals about the characteristics that a truly excellent work of art should possess. The artists whom Alberti admired most – to judge from his letter to Brunelleschi – were sculptors. Three of the five individuals he mentioned in that famous text, Ghiberti, Donatello and Luca Della Robbia, were at work in the 1430s on relief panels which embodied, to a greater extent than any paintings then being created, some of Alberti's aesthetic preferences. They employed sophisticated systems of perspec-tive, represented anatomically plausible bodies in solid, well balanced poses, and attained considerable variety of expression and gesture. In Ghiberti's case, and sometimes in Donatello's, they used these formal devices to tell a single coherent story.

The sculptors achieved all of these effects not by the deployment of rich decorative materials, which generally displeased Alberti, but by the application of their skilled hands.[73] Aby Warburg, in his doctoral disser-tation, notoriously connected Alberti's evocation of the expressive power of 'bewegtes Beiwerk', 'moving accessories', like hair and clothing, with Botticelli's mythologies, as well as with the somewhat earlier reliefs of Matteo de' Pasti and Agostino di Duccio in the Tempio Malatestiano at Rimini and elsewhere: 'The concern … with capturing the transitory movements of hair and garments, corresponds to a tendency prevalent among Northern Italian artists, which finds its most telling expression in Alberti's *Libro della pittura*'.[74] In fact, however, Alberti's description also corresponds closely to Della Robbia's reliefs for the Cantoria and Donatello's for Prato, both of which were at least in part being carved in Florence as he wrote his book. Many scholars have observed that the relief sculpture of the 1430s was far more 'Albertian' than the paintings carried out in Florence in the same period.[75] Alberti presumably chose the term 'historia' at least in part because he wanted to make that point clear, both to the patrons who would read his book in order to find out which artists they should choose to support and to the artists themselves.[76] By using a term at once classical and non-classical, and by giving enough clues that an alert contemporary could grasp what he was doing, Alberti created something that had both the authority of antiquity and the lustre of modernity – exactly as he did when he transformed medieval churches in Rimini and Florence by wrapping them in facades that adapted classical forms to new functions.

At the same time, however, Alberti did something more: he made clear, to the *literati* who would read the Latin text of his work, that the term 'history' was not just polysemous, but unstable. The humanists, as we have seen, followed ancient precedent in defining history as a set of genuine facts, attested by the best sources or witnesses available. But they also insisted that the study of history should serve an affective and moral purpose. Historical accounts taught their readers the principles of morality and prudence, correct behaviour decorously carried out – and they did so in the most effective possible way, presenting them not as arid, abstract statements but as concrete, moving embodiments of the truth. But these two views of history could exist only in a tight state of tension. Faced with evil or indecorous conduct, the historian had to violate either the commandment to tell the complete truth or the commandment to provide reliable moral guidance couched in the most attractive form – a point Alberti himself felt keenly, as we have seen, when forced to play the hagiographer.[77]

A generation after Alberti, Lorenzo Valla would return to this point. Stimulated by a reading of Aristotle's *Poetics*, a text which proclaimed poetry superior to history because it did not strive for completeness and accuracy, Valla insisted that historians too were artful writers, who deliberately omitted and shaped their materials and crafted their characters' speeches as lessons in good rhetoric and good morality. He thus admitted that the historian had to serve not one but two Clios, whose demands sometimes contradicted one another; and he cast his lot with the Clio who demanded truth to the established principles of morality and decorum.[78] In effect, Alberti had already made the same point in *On Painting*. When he insisted that the painter's *historia* could have the same beneficial effects on its audience as a written history – whether its contents came from the realm of myth, that of fact about the ancients, or sacred history – he implied that only style and execution, not the correspondence of the content to truth, determined the emotional effectiveness of a 'history'.

Here too Alberti opposed ancient authority. Sallust noted, in his widely read history of the war against Jugurtha, that

> I have often heard Quintus [Fabius] Maximus, Publius Scipio, and other outstanding Roman citizens say that when they contemplated the images of their ancestors, they were inflamed with desire for virtue. And it was not the wax used in those

images, nor their appearance, but the memory of the events, that made this flame grow so strongly in the hearts of virtuous men that they could not rest until their virtue equalled their reputation and their glory.[79]

Alberti agreed with Sallust about the relative insignificance of the artist's materials, but disagreed about the formal qualities of his work. These – not the verbal tradition that was passed on with it – made a visual history work.

Alberti's friend Lapo seems to have been very struck by the novelty of this argument.[80] In fact his letter of spring 1437 to Biondo – a friend of both men – seems to have represented in part his response to *De pictura*. Lapo insisted, forcefully, that true histories would have even more effect on their readers than the finest images – just because they were truthful:

> When we hear or read of some great effort or risk, undertaken not for gain or profit but for the freedom of the country, for the safety of its citizens, for security, we all praise it to the skies, we are struck with admiration for it, and if possible we want to imitate it. This is clear from fables and pictures. Even if the affairs shown in them are invented, they still affect us by different senses so that we feel the warmest affection for those of whose outstanding deeds we have heard, or seen depicted in a painting. If these things are so powerful, imagine how effectively virtue will be instilled by a history which presents real, not imaginary, characters, and real, not invented, events, and speeches not brought forth to show off the author's skill but set out as they were held.[81]

Lapo's insistence on the affective and educative value of truth was most unusual, as Mariangela Regoliosi has pointed out, in humanist writing about history.[82] And he made his argument in the context of an extended analogy between the effects of written histories and those of myths and paintings. It seems highly likely that he advanced this view so forcefully because he had read Alberti's text and became concerned at what he saw as an injudicious exaggeration of one side – the expressive and inspiring one – of history. It is also possible that Lapo's praise of cultural history, quoted above, represents a response to Alberti's slighting remark about Pliny. Alberti's work on painting was – as many scholars have pointed out – aimed chiefly at an audience of *literati*. It seems all the more appropriate that one response to it came in a text on written 'historiae'.

It remains unclear why Alberti compared the 'historia' to the 'colossus', insisting that the former, rather than the latter, constituted the painter's chief and highest work. And it is equally uncertain exactly how

Alberti's earliest readers understood his arguments – though at least one of them, Angelo Decembrio, who incorporated parts of *On Painting* directly into his own *De politia literaria*, seems to have had Alberti's classical, Mantegnaesque notion of the consistent, relief-like 'historia' in mind when he made his hero, Leonello d'Este, condemn the anachronisms seen on Flemish tapestries that represented stories from ancient history.[83]

It does seem certain, however, that Alberti hoped to persuade both artists and patrons that they should collaborate in the creation of a new kind of large-scale art – one brought into being by the painter's brush, but ruled by the disciplined, austere aesthetic code of relief sculpture, ancient and modern. Alberti never meant to strip the artist's *historia* of its association with the high, dramatic narratives of the Old and New Testaments, nor to alter its goal – one of the traditional ones for religious art – of inspiring the proper emotions. He saw the *historia* as rhetoric in paint, and rhetoric as the art of expressing and inspiring emotions. But he wanted the *historia* to be rhetoric of a particular, humanistic kind. Like the miraculous image conjured into being by the pious girls admired by Aliotti, Alberti's *historia* would inspire emotions. But unlike the irresistible, transfixing sorrows and pains injected into onlookers by wonder-working icons, these would be disciplined by the ancient aesthetic and ethic of decorum. The term itself would apply to allegorical paintings, later created by Botticelli to represent Alberti's ideal 'historia', the *Calumny of Apelles*, as well as to frescoes of the traditional religious kind. All motions, all attitudes, all gestures represented by the artist would follow the code of appropriateness to person and place. And the experience of looking at the completed work *in situ* would take place, as its creation had, on a high aesthetic plane, as the onlooker painstakingly identified and examined the means the painter had used to obtain his effects.[84] Like a stone relief rather than a wonder-working icon, the *historia* would remain at a distance from its viewer. The emotions it inspired would be not only recollected, but experienced, in tranquillity. And the semantic range of the term itself, as Alberti used and reused it, would have suggested as much to a contemporary reader. Perhaps it is not so surprising after all that Aliotti turned for advice not to his iconoclastic friend, the Florentine critic, but to the Roman experts in the discernment of spirits.

Notes

1 G. Aliotti, *Epistolae et opuscula*, ed. G. M. Scaramalli (Arezzo, 1769), I: 180–7. On the larger context of these women's visions and the way the image of the Virgin figured in them, see C. Frugoni, 'Female Mystics, Visions, and Iconography', in *Women and Religion in Medieval and Renaissance Italy*, eds D. Bornstein and R. Rusconi, trans. M. J. Schneider (Chicago and London, 1996),

130–64, and P. Dinzelbacher, *Heilige oder Hexen?* (Zurich, 1995; repr. Reinbek bei Hamburg, 1997). For Francesca Romana and Giovanni Mattiotti, see A. Esposito, 'S. Francesca and the Female Religious Communities of Fifteenth-century Rome', also in *Women and Religion*, 197–218 at 199–200.

2 Aliotti, *Epistolae*, I: 274–6.

3 *Ibid.*, I: 406.

4 Most scholars accept the view that Alberti completed *De pictura*, the Latin form of his work in Florence by 1435 and *Della pittura*, the Italian form, before July 1436, when he dedicated it to Filippo Brunelleschi. See C. Grayson, 'Studi su Leon Battista Alberti', *Rinascimento* 4(1953): 45–62 at 54–62; and 'The Text of Alberti's *De pictura*', *Italian Studies* 23(1968): 71–92, both reprinted in his *Studi su Leon Battista Alberti*, ed. P. Clut (Florence, 1998), 57–66, 245–69. See, however, L. Bertolini's pointed summary of later discussions, emphasizing that some internal evidence supports the priority of the Italian text, in *Leon Battista Alberti*, eds J. Rykwert and A. Engel (Milan, 1994), 423–4.

5 L. B. Alberti, '*De pictura*', in *On Painting and On Sculpture*, ed. and trans. C. Grayson (London, 1972); and in Alberti, *Opere volgari*, ed. C. Grayson, (Bari, 1960–73), III, 41.

6 *Ibid.*, 60; cf. 33, 35.

7 L. B. Alberti, *Kleinere Kunsttheoretische Schriften*, ed. and trans. H. Janitschek (Vienna, 1877).

8 L. B. Alberti, *On Painting*, trans. J. R. Spencer (London, 1956; repr. with corrections, New Haven, 1966), 70, translating *Della pittura*, 33.

9 *Ibid.*, 23–8, at 24.

10 This approach to Renaissance art theory was first pursued by R. W. Lee, who emphasized the role of poetics in his classic article 'Ut pictura poesis', *Art Bulletin* 22(1940): 197ff., later reprinted in book form (New York, 1967); for Alberti and rhetoric, see esp. appendix 2, 'Inventio, Dispositio, Elocutio'. The role of ancient literary theory in Alberti's work was clarified by C. Gilbert, 'Antique Frameworks for Renaissance Art Theory: Alberti and Pino', *Marsyas* 3(1943–5): 87–106. More recent studies, while dwelling on the structure and models for *On Painting*, have tended to stress rhetoric more than poetics; see esp. J. R. Spencer, '*Ut rhetorica pictura*: A Study in Quattrocento Theory of Painting', *Journal of the Warburg and Courtauld Institutes* 20(1957): 26–44; E. H. Gombrich, 'A Classical Topos in the Introduction to Alberti's *Della pittura*', *ibid.*, 173; A. Chastel, 'Die humanistischen Formeln als Rahmenbegriffe der Kunstgeschichte und Kunsttheorie des Quattrocento', *Kunstchronik* 5(1954): 119–122 and *Art et humanisme à Florence au temps de Laurent le Magnifique* (Paris, 1959); S. L. Alpers, '*Ekphrasis* and Aesthetic Attitudes in Vasari's *Lives*', *Journal of the Warburg and Courtauld Institutes* 23(1960): 190–215; A. Ellenius, *De arte pingendi* (Uppsala and Stockholm, 1960); C. W. Westfall, 'Painting and the Liberal Arts: Alberti's View', *Journal of the History of Ideas* 30(1969): 487–506; L. Bek, 'Voti frateschi, virtù di umanista e regole di pittore. Cennino Cennini sub specie Albertiana', *Analecta Romana Instituti Danici* 6(1971): 63–105 at 100; M. Baxandall, *Giotto and the Orators* (Oxford, 1971) and *Painting and Experience in Fifteenth-Century Italy* (Oxford, 1972); N. Maraschio, 'Aspetti del bilinguismo albertiano nel "De pictura"', *Rinascimento* ser. II, 12(1972): 183–228, esp. 187–99; D. R. Edward Wright, 'Alberti's *De pictura*: Its Literary Structure and Purpose', *Journal of the Warburg and Courtauld Institutes* 47(1984): 52–71; D. Rosand, '*Ekphrasis* and the Renaissance of Painting: Observations on Alberti's Third Book', *Florilegium Columbianum*, eds K.-L. Selig and R. Somerville (New York, 1987), 147–63; R. Kuhn, 'Albertis Lehre über die Komposition als die *Kunst* in der Malerei', *Archiv für Begriffsgeschichte* 28(1984): 123–78; N. Michels,

Bewegung zwischen Ethos und Pathos (Münster, 1988), esp. 1–65; P. Panza, *Leon Battista Alberti: Filosofia e teorie dell'arte* (Milan, 1994), 115–26; G. Wolf, '"Arte superficiem illam fontis amplecti": Alberti, Narziss, und die Erfindung der Malerei', in *Diletto e Maraviglia*, eds C. Göttler, U. M. Hofstede, K. Patz and K. Zollikofer (Emsdetten, 1998), 10–39. M. Gosebruch, '"Varietas" bei L. B. Alberti and der wissenschaftliche Renaissancebegriff', *Zeitschrift für Kunstgeschichte* 20(1957): 229–38 (cf. also *Kunstchronik* 9[1956]: 301–2), H. Mühlmann, *Aesthetische Theorie der Renaissance: L. B. Alberti* (Bonn, 1981); and C. Smith, *Architecture in the Culture of Early Humanism* (New York and Oxford, 1992) concentrate on connections between rhetoric and architecture in Alberti's thought, but have much to offer students of *On Painting* as well. K. Patz, 'Zum Begriff der "Historia", in L. B. Albertis "De pictura"', *Zeitschrift für Kunstgeschichte* 49(1986): 269–87; and J. Greenstein, *Mantegna and Painting as Historical Narrative* (Chicago and London, 1992), both rightly stress Alberti's originality and eclecticism in the use of classical sources.

11 See in general G. Nadel, 'Philosophy of History before Historicism', *History and Theory* 3(1964): 291–315; R. Landfester, *Historia magistra vitae* (Geneva, 1972); M. Miglio, *Storiografia pontificia del Quattrocento* (Bologna, 1975); R. Koselleck, 'Historia magistra vitae: Ueber die Auflösung des Topos im Horizont neuzeitlich bewegter Geschichte', *Vergangene Zukunft* (Frankfurt, 1984), 38–66; E. Kessler, 'Das rhetorische Modell der Historiographie', in *Formen der Geschichtsschreibung*, eds Reinhart Koselleck, Heinrich Lutz and Jörn Rüsen (Munich, 1982), 37–85; and, for the larger context, E. Cochrane, *Historians and Historiography in the Italian Renaissance* (Chicago and London, 1981).

12 Alberti, *On the Art of Building in Ten Books*, trans. J. Rykwert, N. Leach and R. Tavenor (Cambridge MA and London, 1988), 7.10, 220 (slightly altered); for the original see *De re aedificatoria*, ed. G. Orlandi, trans. P. Portoghesi (Milan, 1966), II, 609–61. This passage has been quoted in a similar connection by M. B. Katz, *Leon Battista Alberti and the Humanist Theory of the Arts* (Washington DC, 1978), 20.

13 Alberti, *De re aedificatoria*, II, 610 n2.

14 Greenstein, *Mantegna and Painting*, ch. 2.

15 Two exceptions should be noted: Grayson dismissed the question as insignificant in his introduction to *On Painting and On Sculpture*, 13, as do C. Hope and E. McGrath in 'Artists and Humanists', *The Cambridge Companion to Renaissance Humanism*, ed. J. Kraye (Cambridge, 1996), 161–88 at 166. The authors in question rightly point out that Alberti did not coin the term 'historia' – a point on which others have repeatedly gone wrong. But the fact that the term was not new does not imply that Alberti's usage was conventional or simple.

16 See J. Schlosser Magnino, *Die Kunstliteratur* (Vienna, 1924) translated as *La letteratura artistica* by F. Rossi, 3rd edn, ed. O. Kurz (Florence, 1977, repr. 1979), 121–9.

17 See M. Tafuri, '*Cives esse non licere*'. Niccolò V e Leon Battista Alberti, Ricerca del Rinascimento. Principi, Città, Architetti (Turin, 1992), 33–88.

18 For the earliest formulation and application of this rule, see L. D. Reynolds and N. G. Wilson, *Scribes and Scholars*, 3rd edn (Oxford, 1991), 13–14.

19 See e.g. A. Grafton, *Commerce with the Classics* (Ann Arbor, 1997), ch. 2.

20 C. Hope, 'Aspects of Criticism in Art and Literature in Sixteenth-century Italy', *Word and Image* 4(1988): 1–10 at 1–2.

21 See R. Pfeiffer, 'Küchenlatein', *Philologus* (1931): 455–9, reprinted in *Ausgewählte Schriften*, ed. W. Bühler (Munich, 1960), 183–7.

22 Alberti, *On the Art of Building in Ten Books*, trans. Rykwert *et al.*, 6.1, 154; for the original, see Alberti, *De re aedificatoria*, II, 441.
23 See esp. H. Harth, 'Niccolò Niccoli als literarischer Zensor: Untersuchungen zur Textgeschichte von Poggios "De avaritia"', *Rinascimento* n.s. 7(1967): 29–53.
24 G. Ponte, 'Lepidus e Libripeta', *Rinascimento* 12(1972): 237–65.
25 M. Miglio, 'Il ritorno a Roma. Varianti di una costante nella tradizione dell'antico: le scelte pontificie', *Scritture, scrittori, e storia*, II (Rome, 1993), 144.
26 See L. Goggi Carotti's note on this point in her edition of L. B. Alberti, *De commodis litterarum atque incommodis* (Florence, 1976), 42–3.
27 See e.g. the famous letter of Leonardo Dati and Tommaso Ceffi to Alberti, offering a critique of *I libri della famiglia*, in Dati, *Epistolae xxxiii*, ed. L. Mehus (Florence, 1743), 13, 18–20; and C. Grayson's note in Alberti, *Opere volgari*, I, 380. Such exchanges, often resulting in substantial revisions, formed a normal part of the humanist system of publication before printing, on which see the classic study of P. O. Kristeller, 'De traditione operum Marsilli Ficini', *Supplementum Ficinianum*, ed. Kristeller, 2 vols (Florence, 1937); Harth, 'Niccolò Niccoli', and, more recently, A. Grafton, 'Correctores corruptores? Notes on the Social History of Editing', in 'Editing Texts/Texte Edieren', ed. G. W. Most, *Aporemata: Kritische Studien zur Philologiegeschichte*, II (Göttingen, 1998), 54–75.
28 'Leon Battista Alberti, *Philodoxeos fabula*: Edizione critica a cura di Lucia Cesarini Martinelli', *Rinascimento* 2nd series, 17(1977): 111–234, at 144–5.
29 See Grafton, *Commerce with the Classics*, ch. 1.
30 R Fubini and A. Menci Gallorini, 'L'autobiografia di Leon Battista Alberti. Studio e edizione', *Rinascimento* 2nd series, 12(1972): 21–78, 77.
31 For a critical text and suggestive analysis of Lapo's letter, see M. Regoliosi, '"Res gestae patriae" e "res gestae ex universa Italia": la lettera di Lapo da Castiglionchio a Biondo Flavio', in *La memoria e la città*, eds C. Bastia and M. Bolognani (Bologna, 1995), 273–305.
32 Pius II, *Memoirs of a Renaissance Pope*, ed. L. C. Gabel, trans. F. A. Gragg (New York, 1959), 323.
33 Regoliosi, 'Res gestae patriae', 294.
34 *Ibid.*, 295–6.
35 L. Alberti, *De commodis litterarum atque incommodis*, 41; cf. Cicero, *De oratore*, 2.36. On the date and circumstances of Alberti's work see now L. Boschetto, 'Nuovi documents su Carlo di Lorenzo degli Alberti e una proposta per la datazione del *De commodis litterarum atque incommodis*', *Albertiana* 1(1998): 43–60.
36 Regoliosi, 'Res gestae patriae', 303.
37 See G. Ianziti, *Humanistic Historiography under the Sforzas* (Oxford, 1988).
38 L. B. Alberti, *Opuscoli inediti di Leon Battista Alberti. 'Musca', 'Vita S. Potiti'*, ed. C. Grayson (Florence, 1954), 86–7.
39 *Ibid.*, 87.
40 See A. Modigliani, *I Porcari* (Rome, 1994), 495.
41 Aliotti, *Epistolae*, I, 32–4, 44–6, 67–8.
42 Alberti, *Della pittura*, 'Prologus'.
43 Regoliosi, 'Res gestae patriae', 301.
44 See L. Barkan, *Unearthing the Past* (New Haven and London, 1999), ch. 2.
45 Alberti, *Della pittura*, 26.
46 *Ibid.*

47 See C. Dempsey's important note in *The Portrayal of Love* (Princeton, 1992), 29–30, n24. On the debt of the humanists to Byzantine rhetoric, see esp. Baxandall, *Giotto and the Orators* and Smith, *Architecture in the Culture of Early Humanism*.

48 Cicero, *Brutus*, 42; in fact, Cicero did not observe this distinction at all times (see e.g. *Ad Atticum*, 1.16.18), and in poetry 'historia' could have a sense very close to 'fabula' (e.g. Ovid, *Amores*, 2.4.44).

49 Alberti, *On Painting*, 63; see Grayson's note *ad loc.* (see note 5 above), and Goggi Carotti's edition of Alberti, *De commodis litterarum*.

50 L. B. Alberti, *De pictura*, 26 (on Narcissus), 53 (on the Calumny).

51 *Ibid.*, 19.

52 *Ibid.*, 61.

53 *Ibid.*, 61.

54 *Ibid.*, 57. The whole passage reveals Alberti's preference for the large image.

55 Alberti, *On Painting*, 135, n18. Cf. also F. Ames-Lewis, *Drawing in Early Renaissance Italy*, (New Haven and London, 1981) and Rosand, '*Ekphrasis* and the Renaissance of Painting'.

56 Alberti, *De pictura*, 56.

57 *Ibid.*, 63.

58 J. Pope-Hennessy, *The Portrait in the Renaissance* (London and New York, 1963).

59 Alberti, *De pictura*, 42; cf. Baxandall, *Giotto and the Orators*, 129–30 and plates 3 and 5(a).

60 Alberti, *De re aedificatoria*, 7.10; *L'architettura*, ed. Orlandi (see note 12 above), II, 609.

61 See esp. the *locus classicus*, *De pictura*, 40.

62 Alberti, *De pictura*, 21. Cf. F. Balters, *Der grammatische Bildhauer. Kunsttheorie and Bildhauerkunst der Frührenaissance: Alberti, Ghiberti, Leonardo, Gauricus* (Aachen, 1991).

63 Alberti, *De pictura*, 37.

64 Alberti, *De re aedificatoria*, 8.6, 9.4, 8.4, 8.3.

65 A. Niehaus, *Florentiner Reliefkunst von Brunelleschi bis Michelangelo* (Munich, 1998), 22–8.

66 See K. Patz and P. Toynbee, 'A Note on *Storia, Storiato*, and the Corresponding Terms in French and English, in Illustrations of *Purgatorio*, X, 52, 71, 73', *Mélanges offertes à M. Emile Picot par ses amis et élèves*, 2 vols (Paris, 1913), I, 195–208.

67 Dante, *Purgatorio*, 10.52, 71, 73.

68 Leonardo Bruni to Niccolò da Uzzano, spring 1424, in R. Krautheimer and T. Krautheimer-Hess, *Lorenzo Ghiberti* (repr. of 2nd edn, Princeton, 1982), 372.

69 Matteo di Paolo to the Operai of the Cathedral in Prato, 19 June 1434, in C. Guasti, *Il pergamo del Donatello pel Duomo di Prato* (Florence, 1887), 19.

70 G. Poggi, *Il duomo di Firenze* (Florence, 1909; repr. 1988), e.g. Doc. 325.

71 See most recently A. Cavallaro, 'I primi studi dall'antico nel cantiere del Laterano', in *Alle origini della nuova Roma: Martino V (1417–1431)*, Atti del Convegno, Roma, 2–5 Marzo 1992, eds M. Chiabò, G. D'Alessandro, P. Piacentini and C. Ranieri (Rome, 1992), 401–12.

72 See Niehaus, *Florentiner Reliefkunst*.

73 Cf. J. Bialostocki, 'Ars auro potior', *Mélanges de littérature et philologie offertes à Mieczyslaw Brahmer* (Warsaw, 1966), 55–63.

74 A. Warburg, 'Sandro Botticelli's *Birth of Venus and Spring*', in *The Renewal of Pagan Antiquity: Contributions to the Cultural History of the European Renaissance*, ed. K. W. Forster, trans. D. Britt (Los Angeles, 1999), 95; for the original see

Warburg, *Gesammelte Schriften: Studienausgabe*, eds H. Bredekamp, M. Diers, K. W. Forster, N. Mann, S. Settis and M. Warnke (Berlin, 1998), I, part 1, 10–11.

75 See e.g. Krautheimer and Krautheimer-Hess, *Lorenzo Ghiberti*, but the argument is an old one: note e.g. H. Kaufmann, *Donatello* (Berlin, 1935) 63–6; and cf. Niehaus, *Florentiner Reliefkunst*.

76 Aliotti's testimony, cited above, confirms the view that Alberti expected to be read not only by his fellow humanists and by erudite princes of the state and church, but also by artists – as he certainly was, by Filarete, Leonardo and a number of others.

77 On the long-term consequences of this aporia in the humanistic theory of history see U. Muhlack, *Geschichtswissenschaft im Humanismus und in der Aufklärung* (Munich, 1991).

78 L. Valla, *Gesta Ferdinandi regis Aragonum*, ed. O. Besomi (Padua, 1973), 3–5; admittedly Valla insists that the historian is also truthful.

79 Sallust, *Bellum contra Iugurtham*, 4.5–6.

80 See C. Celenza, *Renaissance Humanism and the Papal Curia* (Ann Arbor, 1999), 156, for Lapo's praise of Alberti.

81 Regoliosi, 'Res gestae patriae', 298–300.

82 See the important notes *ibid.*, and Miglio, *Storiografia pontifica*, 47–50.

83 M. Baxandall, 'A Dialogue on Art from the Court of Leonello d'Este. Angelo Decembrio's *De Politia Litteraria* Pars LXVIII', *Journal of the Warburg and Courtauld Institutes* 26(1963): 304–26. In this case, Decembrio clearly ascribed his own (and Alberti's) tastes to Leonello, who in fact eagerly collected the tapestries in question. See N. Forti Grazzini, 'Leonello d'Este nell'autunno del Medioevo. Gli arazzi delle "Storie di Ercole"', *Le muse e il principe: Arte di corte nel Rinascimento padano. Saggi* (Modena, 1991), 53–62 at 61–2.

84 Alberti, *On Painting*, 40.

223

11

THE CRIMINAL AND THE SAINTLY BODY

Autopsy and dissection in Renaissance Italy

Katharine Park

The publication of Andreas Vesalius' On the Fabric of the Human Body *in 1543 has long marked a watershed in the history of Renaissance science. Vesalius was by no means the first anatomist of Renaissance Italy, but when he published this exquisitely illustrated book, he went to great lengths to underscore the importance of his own innovative methods. The frontispiece, the most compelling representation of the Vesalian revolution, depicts this famed Paduan professor performing a dissection. He stands at the centre of an amphitheatre crowded with onlookers, for the most part medical students but curious townspeople as well. His science is both public and revolutionary. From this point on, the opening of the human body will serve as the basis of new knowledge. In this respect, Vesalius' book – along with Copernicus' book* On the Revolution of the Heavenly Orbs, *published in the same year – is part of a familiar narrative of the emergence of modern science. Whether gazing into the microcosm of the human body or outwards into the heavenly macrocosm, Renaissance 'scientists' opened up new vistas and began to lay the foundations of the modern world.*

Yet Vesalius was not the first Renaissance anatomist to dissect a body. In early fourteenth-century Bologna, the anatomist Mondino de' Luzzi used the opened human body to illustrate Galenic teachings to his students. But Vesalius was the first to have 'read' the human body not as an illustration of ancient theories but rather as a text that itself could transform medical knowledge. But why did it take nearly 250 years for Renaissance anatomy to move from using the dissected body as an illustration of what was known to an object of research?

One theory – still current today – is that a deeply entrenched cultural taboo against opening cadavers in both classical antiquity and medieval Europe held medical research in check. The dead body was seen as filthy, even polluting – and it required rapid burial. Thus, when anatomical dissection first began, the bodies were uniquely those of executed criminals; and dissections were rare, with governments carefully controlling the conditions under which professors of anatomy could perform their work. Only with the Reformation and a new view of the body as God's handiwork would Europeans begin to overcome this taboo and explore it as an object of fascination and beauty.

In the essay below, Katharine Park demolishes the myth of the medieval antipathy towards the opening of the dead body. Her evidence makes it clear that, at least from the early fourteenth century on, medieval men and women opened the bodies not only of criminals but also of 'saints', those men and women whose lives they judged to be holy. Moreover, they opened the body to read internal organs such as the heart and the gall bladder for signs of sanctity (which could also be made manifest, as in cases of the stigmata, on the exterior of the body). Medieval doctors also performed autopsies, looking not for a pattern (or a proof that Galen was right) but rather for an abnormality that could explain a death. In her research Park finds no evidence that any of these practices provoked feelings of Religions horror or disgust.

Not only does the medieval taboo against the opening of the body turn out, in Park's analysis, to be a myth, but feelings of anxiety about dissection appear to have increased in the wake of the development of Vesalian anatomy. Yet the anxiety was not based on the fear of pollution so much as on the fear that the body of a loved one might be dishonoured. The story Park tells, therefore, reverses the traditional narrative. Paradoxically, it was in the sixteenth century as new anatomical practices began to develop that popular resistance to the opening of the human body first began to appear.

Park's essay originally appeared in Renaissance Quarterly 47(1994): *1–33, and I have reproduced it here with only minor changes to the notes. The history of Renaissance science is a burgeoning field, in which a number of scholars – most notably Mario Biagioli and Paula Findlen – have begun to transform our understanding of scientific practices and communities in this period. For a counterpoint to Park's interpretation, see Andrea Carlino,* The Books of the Body: Anatomical Ritual and Renaissance Learning *(Chicago, 1999).*

* * *

On 17 August 1308, Chiara of Montefalco died in the small Umbrian monastery of which she had been the abbess. Her fellow nuns did not take any steps to preserve her body. Nonetheless, for five days it remained uncorrupted and redolent of the odour of sanctity, despite the blazing summer heat. At that point – not wanting to tempt fate further – the community decided to embalm the precious relic. In the words of Sister Francesca of Montefalco, testifying some years later at Chiara's unsuccessful canonization procedure, 'They agreed that [her] body should be preserved on account of her holiness and because God took such pleasure in her body and her heart'.[1] They sent to the town apothecary for 'balsam and myrrh and other preservatives', as the apothecary himself testified,[2] and they proceeded to the next step in contemporary embalming practice, which was evisceration.

Sister Francesca's narrative continues:

And after the other nuns had left, Sister Francesca of Foligno, who is now dead, and Illuminata and Marina and Elena, who is now dead, went to cut open the body, and the said Francesca cut it open from the back with her own hand, as they had decided. And they took out the entrails and put the heart away in a box, and they buried the entrails in the oratory that evening. On the following evening, after vespers or thereabouts, the said Francesca, Margarita and Lucia and Caterina went to get the heart, which was in the box, as they later told the other nuns. And the said Francesca of Foligno cut open the heart with her own hand, and opening it they found in the heart a cross, or the image of the crucified Christ.

Over the course of the next two days, Francesca of Foligno and her fellow nuns cut into the heart yet again, finding even more miraculous marks of Chiara's sanctity, all formed of flesh: the crown of thorns, the whip and column, the rod and sponge, and tiny nails. Encouraged by these signs, they examined the other organs, which they had disinterred from the oratory, and discovered – again in the words of Francesca of Montefalco – that

inside Chiara's gall bladder ... there were three things that seemed to be round, so that they could not relax or rest until they knew what they could be. So they consulted with Maestro Simone of Spello [the communal doctor of Montefalco and physician to the monastery] in order to ask him if these objects could have been caused by some illness. And they placed the gall bladder in his hand so that he could open it up. He did not want to do this because, as he said, he did not feel himself worthy. So Francesca cut open the gall bladder and found in it three small stones.[3]

At this point – and here we take up the testimony of Chiara's brother, a Franciscan friar also in Montefalco – the nuns then came to the Franciscan convent to show him his sister's remarkable heart. From there they all proceeded to the church of Santa Croce where they displayed it to a host of townspeople, several of whom were healed by its miraculous power.[4]

I want to make two points about Sister Francesca's striking narrative. The first is that although we may find her account disquieting, there is no sign that her contemporaries reacted in the same way. Her narrative was corroborated by dozens of witnesses, including the cautious Maestro Simone himself, and neither they nor the ecclesiastical authorities charged with investigating Chiara's claim to sainthood indicated any reservations – or even any surprise – about the events of that hot week in August. Some questioned the nuns' credulity, but none impugned their piety. Indeed, Chiara's post-mortem was not an isolated instance. We can find a close analogue in the case of Margarita of Città di Castello (d. 1320), a Dominican tertiary whose heart was also extracted during embalming and was found to contain three stones engraved with images of the Holy Family, a procedure performed before the high altar in the presence of what her anonymous biographer called a 'multitude of friars'.[5]

My second point is that the events described by Sister Francesca coincide with the emergence of autopsy and dissection as a regular and integral part of both legal practice and medical training in the cities of northern and central Italy. I aim here to explore the implications of these events and this conjunction – it is, I will argue, no coincidence – for the period between the first recorded Italian autopsy in the 1280s and the work of Andreas Vesalius and his contemporaries in the mid-sixteenth century. In the process, I hope to lay to rest the persistent misconception that there was in medieval and Renaissance Europe a deep-seated 'taboo' connected with corpses and the closure of the body. According to the most recent versions of this myth, opening the body was seen not only as dangerous, contaminating and polluting, but also as a violation of the divine prohibition on forbidden knowledge – perhaps even 'the model for all such prohibitions', in the words of Marie-Christine Pouchelle.[6] From this point of view, the practice of dissection was essentially punitive. Restricted to the cadavers of condemned criminals, it functioned to prolong their sufferings during execution into death. The medieval and Renaissance anatomist, despite elaborate social, verbal and pictorial strategies designed to distance himself from these associations, nevertheless acted as an arm of the coercive state. First cousin to the executioner and torturer, he inscribed its penalties on the helpless bodies of those who transgressed its norms.[7]

The myth of medieval resistance to dissection is an old one, and like the flat-earth myth with which it is often associated, it has proved protean and apparently impossible to kill. Its late twentieth-century incarnation is especially vivid and attractive, invoking the traditional schism between medieval religiosity and the scientific rationalism of the Renaissance (here given a novel negative twist) while also mobilizing our liberal sympathies concerning capital and corporal punishment. It is also, like its more triumphalist predecessors, partial and distorted, imposing a false unity on the long millennium between Augustine and Vesalius and ascribing to the people of that period modern anxieties and a modern sensibility essentially alien to their own. The true situation, as it turns out, was considerably more complicated. From at least the early twelfth century, opening the body was a common funerary practice, as the examples of Chiara of Montefalco and Margarita of Città di Castello indicate. Over the course of the fourteenth century, it also established itself in Italian medicine as not only tolerated but frequently requested on the part of individuals and their families. Not until the mid-sixteenth century do we begin to see persistent hints of a new popular suspicion concerning dissection. I will argue that this suspicion was not rooted in age-old taboos; rather, it grew out of dramatic new anatomical practices widely perceived as violating not the sanctity of the body, in the first instance, but the personal and familial honour expressed in contemporary funerary ritual. And it was reinforced by new, and not unwarranted, fears that anatomists themselves occasionally acted as executioners.

Opening the body: autopsy and dissection before 1500

The first recorded case in Italy of a human body being opened for inspection dates from 1286. In that year, according to the chronicler Salimbene,

> there was in Cremona, Piacenza, Parma, Reggio, and many other Italian cities and bishoprics, a great mortality among both humans and hens. And in Cremona, one woman lost forty-eight hens in a very short time. A certain physician had some of the [hens] opened and found [that] … there was a vesicular aposteme on the tip of each hen's heart. He also had a dead man opened and found the same thing

– a coincidence so suggestive that it moved a Venetian physician to issue a bulletin warning against the dangers of eating chicken and eggs.[8]

The practice of autopsy to determine the cause of death was quickly transferred from a public health to a forensic context in Bologna, which boasted the most advanced medical and legal faculties of the day. From the mid-thirteenth century the commune of Bologna, like several other north Italian cities, had appointed a pool of well respected local doctors who could be called on to testify in trials involving assault and suspected murder. Initially they worked from external inspection, but by shortly after 1300 we find them performing autopsies on victims in order to look for hidden and internal causes of death, most commonly when poison was suspected. In 1302 – the first recorded case of this sort – Azzolino degli Onesti was opened up at the judge's request by a commission of two physicians and two surgeons, who concluded from their examination that 'the said Azzolino had not died of poison, but rather and more certainly from a large quantity of blood that had gathered around the great vein, called the chilic vein, and the nearby veins of the liver'.[9] Similarly in 1307, one year before the opening of Chiara of Montefalco, a woman named Ghisetta was submitted to an autopsy and found to have

228

died as a result of internal bleeding from a wound that appeared superficially as healed.[10] We can find another roughly contemporary example in Pietro d'Abano's *On Poisons*, which mentions the autopsy of a Paduan apothecary who had accidentally swallowed a lethal quantity of mercury.[11]

It seems clear, therefore, that the first cases in which bodies were opened and their contents inspected all involved autopsies and post-mortems – procedures carried out on a corpse to gain information about the physical state of a particular individual. In the cases of Chiara and Margarita the concern was simply extended to their spiritual state. By the middle of the thirteenth century, in fact, it was widely assumed that the saint's body differed from that of other people, in the way that the victim of plague or poisoning was recognizable by certain unmistakable signs. These differences were not confined to incorruptibility and the odour of sanctity but also included external and internal marks, such as stigmata and the alien structures found in Chiara's and Margarita's hearts.[12]

Post-mortems of this sort did not destroy the contours of the body. Thus they were fully compatible with contemporary Italian funerary practices, whether these involved embalming the corpse or immediately transporting it to church for burial, wrapped in the traditional pall. They appear in fact to have grown out of the increasingly common practice of embalming, which, as we saw in the cases of Chiara and Margarita, normally involved evisceration and was used to preserve the bodies of saints, of people who had died some distance from their chosen place of burial, and of notables whose funerals might take some time to organize and prepare. The task of preparing the body – one early chronicler even called it an 'anatomy'[13] – was often left up to the attending doctor, though cooks and confessors might also serve, and we know of several instances prior to the late thirteenth century in which this provided (apparently incidentally) the occasion for judgments regarding pathology and cause of death.[14]

In order to judge the nature and significance of individual anatomical and physiological differences, doctors had to have some idea of human norms. Thus it makes sense that contemporary with the appearance of formal autopsies in the years around 1300 we find the first evidence of a different but related practice – dissections aiming to illustrate and explicate those norms. These were designed to accompany the teaching of medicine and associated with the reformed medical curriculum put into place at the university of Bologna by the circle around Taddeo Alderotti. It is unclear whether the first dissections preceded or followed the first forensic post-mortems. Although Taddeo was probably dissecting cadavers a decade before the post-mortem of Azzolino in 1302, the first unambiguous account of such a dissection refers to 1316 and appears in the influential anatomy textbook of his student Mondino de' Liuzzi.[15] Certainly, the two developments were closely related; thus one of physicians who performed the autopsy on Azzolino's cadaver, Bartolomeo da Varignana, also taught medicine with Taddeo at Bologna.[16]

The earliest dissections seem to have taken place in private houses (as did other forms of teaching) and were probably relatively informal, involving only the master and a small group of disciples. They are for that reason relatively difficult to document. To my knowledge, only one such case (presumably quite atypical) made its way into the public record. In 1319 four students of Master Alberto of Bologna were prosecuted for robbing a grave and bringing the corpse to the house where he lectured 'so that the said Master Albert could teach them to see what is to be seen in the human body'.[17] The practice of dissection seems to have been codified quite quickly, however – partly doubtless to avoid such episodes – in the form of the regular, university-sponsored anatomy. As described by Mondino, these four-day exhibitions took place once or twice a year and were performed on the bodies of condemned criminals, both male and female, supplied to the medical faculty by the *podestà*.

The anatomy differed in purpose and completeness from the civil or forensic post-mortem. Rather than explaining the spiritual or physical state of a single individual, it aimed to illustrate to medical students general anatomical and physiological principles. And unlike the more limited autopsies, it involved the complete or near complete disaggregation of the body, including the face, as Mondino's description of the anatomy of the eyes and jaws makes clear. The remnants of these dissected bodies may well have been given some sort of funeral by local authorities or by the students and teachers involved, but the ceremonies must have been altered to suit the circumstances, since Italian funerary ritual centered on the physical object of the corpse, normally covered only by a cloth and usually exhibited with its face exposed.[18]

Over the course of the fourteenth century both autopsy and dissection became increasingly common, spreading rapidly to other northern Italian cities. During the summer of 1348, for example, the communes of both Florence and Perugia paid doctors to open the bodies of several people who had succumbed to the mysterious new epidemic devastating their inhabitants, and the same thing happened in Padua during the plague of 1363.[19] Similarly, over the course of the mid-fourteenth century the universities of Perugia, Padua and Florence moved to require attendance at one or more dissections for candidates for the degree of doctor of medicine, a requirement also quickly adopted by the new colleges of doctors springing up within the Italian guilds.[20]

Dissections of this sort, like autopsies of plague victims, were relatively infrequent: guilds, colleges and universities typically mandated only one or two a year. Far more common by the time we reach the fifteenth century were the post-mortems performed by doctors on their private patients. Consider, for example, the death in 1486 of the Florentine patrician Bartolomea Rinieri, as described by her husband in his *ricordanza*:

> Early in the morning my wife Bartolomea died at the age of forty-two or thereabouts. She died of a diseased womb; this caused a flux which had lasted about eighteen months and which no doctors could cure. She asked me to perform an autopsy on her so that our daughter or others could be treated. I had this done, and it was found that her womb was so calcified that it could not be cut with a razor.[21]

Bartolomea's story was typical; a patrician who could afford the best in medical care, she requested her own post-mortem. In many such cases, in fact, the initiative came from the patient or his or her family, and the reason most commonly invoked was the fear of hereditary disease. When people, particularly mothers, died of mysterious and incurable illness, they or their families frequently worried that the same disease might strike their children or siblings, and they hoped that autopsies would provide their family doctors with all possible information concerning prevention and cure.

A similar case was recorded by Bernardo Torni, Professor of Medicine at Pisa at about the same time. A Florentine judge had asked Torni to perform an autopsy on his young son, 'for to lose one's offspring is hard', Torni wrote,

> harder to lose a son, and hardest [to lose him] to a disease not yet fully understood by doctors. But, for the sake of the other children, I think that to have seen his internal organs will be of the greatest utility.

Torni diagnosed the problem as an obstruction in the vein leading to the liver, and he closed his opinion with a referral to a trustworthy local doctor, prescriptions for several different preventive medicines for the other children, and a promise to keep himself informed regarding their health.[22]

Not all clients were motivated by parental love, however. The fifteenth-century Florentine physician Antonio Benivieni recalled one case in which relatives had a man examined post-mortem 'rather to expose the ignorance of his doctors than to know the nature of his illness'.[23] Benivieni also records the only instance I have found so far of familial resistance to the practice. His treatise *On Some Hidden and Wondrous Causes of Disease and Healing*, compiled in the years before his death in 1502, includes almost twenty examples of autopsies he performed or witnessed in the context of his own medical practice. On one occasion, however, when he wanted to open a patient who had died of vomiting and diarrhoea, 'the relatives refused permission', as he put it, 'through I don't know what superstition'.[24]

As this example shows, not all the inhabitants of Renaissance Italy were comfortable with the practice of opening the body. Nonetheless, there is no sign of a general (or even common) prohibition concerning the opened corpse *per se*. Historians searching for evidence of such a prohibition often invoke the famous bull of Boniface VIII, *Detestande feritatis*, promulgated in 1299 and reissued in 1300. But an informed reading of this bull and its reception reveals a different story. Boniface's decree condemned not dissection or autopsy but a much more extreme funerary practice that involved dismembering the body and boiling the flesh off the bones in order to allow them to be more easily transported for distant burial.[25] Although common among the aristocracy and royalty of northern Europe, this practice was not current among Italians, who seem to have had considerably ˙less investment in their place of burial and who, if they wished temporarily to preserve a cadaver, relied on embalming, as we saw in the case of Chiara of Montefalco.[26] Nowhere in the bull did Boniface prohibit evisceration, which seems to have been accepted as a practical necessity even by canonists and theologians with a strong investment in bodily integrity. Several years later, in 1303, he did refuse a French bishop's request to prepare his brother's corpse for transportation home from Italy, forbidding him to 'cremate, boil, or even cut into it'.[27] But neither the bull nor the letter had any discernible impact on either funerary or dissecting practices in Italy (unlike France), except that it prevented Mondino from demonstrating several small bones in the head; these 'cannot be well seen unless they are removed and boiled', he noted, 'but owing to the sin involved in this I am accustomed to pass them by'.[28] From all available evidence, Boniface's bull and letter were taken as irrelevant by generations of Italian medical professors, private doctors, judges, city councils, and even by later popes, several of whom were themselves embalmed.[29]

This is not to say that thirteenth- and fourteenth-century Italians had no interest or investment in the fate of the physical body after death – merely that this seems on the whole to have been a less charged issue in Italy than in northern Europe, both in theory and in practice.[30] Unlike their northern counterparts, Italian nobles and princes did not typically make elaborate provisions for their corpses; they neither stipulated that they be dismembered for interment in several separate sites, nor did they request heroic measures of preservation – evisceration, sealing in animal hides, boiling – to allow their bodies to be transported long distances for burial.[31] Italian embalming techniques usually aimed only to preserve the corpse for a few days to allow for the organization of the funeral, and only candidates for sainthood such as Chiara or Thomas Aquinas had their bodies divided, in order to diffuse their magical powers over as wide a territory as possible. Similarly, the debates over bodily integrity that so exercised northern canonists and theologians seem to have found few echoes among Italian writers.[32] Boniface VIII was of course the principal exception, and he may have taken the position he did for personal or political reasons. Certainly he was aware of its novelty.[33]

If there were no obvious taboos surrounding opening the body, then, how can we explain the often cited fact that formal university anatomies were typically performed on the corpses of condemned criminals? Does the practice indicate a punitive intent? Here I think the answer is complicated and hinges on the universal stipulation that the criminal be of foreign birth and preferably of low degree. In the words of the anatomist Alessandro Benedetti, writing in 1497, 'By law only unknown and ignoble bodies can be sought for dissection, from distant regions without injury to neighbours and relatives'.[34] I would argue that these people were dissected in the first instance *qua* poor foreigners rather than *qua* criminals, as is clear from the mid-fifteenth-century statutes of the University of Bologna, which required only that the cadaver belong to a person who came from at least thirty miles away.[35] This hypothesis gains further support from the fact that hospital patients were the next major group to come under the dissector's knife, as we will shortly see. Like hospital patients, foreign criminals had no relatives nearby with an investment in a conventional and honourable funeral, and usually no money to guarantee one for themselves.

In other words, these people risked dissection because they were marginal members of society, but they were marginal on account of their poverty and geographical origin as much or more than their judicial status. The latter merely provided a jurisdictionally tidy solution to the problem of supplying medical faculties with cadavers, since the rector of the university, who oversaw dissections, and the *podestà*, who oversaw executions, were both municipal officials. There was indeed a stigma associated with public dissection – 'may God preserve us from such a fate', wrote one early fifteenth-century doctor[36] – but this did not arise from the opening of the body *per se*, as is clear from the widespread private practice of autopsy and embalming. It lay rather in the dramatic violation of personal and family honour involved in public dissection, as Benedetti's reference to relatives and neighbours implies. Not only was public dismemberment the dramatic penalty for particularly loathsome crimes, but dissection required lengthy public exposure of the naked body (also used as a humiliating punishment). This gave the anatomization of female subjects a particular charge in a society that associated female honour with chastity and avoidance of the public eye.[37]

Furthermore, dissection compromised the identifiability and hence also the personal identity of the corpse, symbolized by its exposed face, and forced alterations in the ritual of the funeral, which played such an important part in family honour and prestige.[38]

The importance of funerary ritual appears clearly in the university and municipal statutes and records concerning dissection. In Florence, for example, students attending a dissection were required to pay five lire for 'having the cadaver brought to the church after the anatomy, and having it buried, and celebrating an office for its soul',[39] while the books of the *Otto di Guardia*, the police magistracy that supplied criminal bodies to the university, scrupulously noted that these were to receive a proper funeral.[40] Faced in the middle of the fifteenth century with a shortage of foreign criminal cadavers for their public dissections, the Venetian college of doctors and surgeons required students attending the dissection not only to pay for but also to attend the subsequent funeral in hopes of encouraging local families to offer their dead for dissection.[41] It would be interesting to know if anyone agreed.

The anatomical renaissance

As this last provision suggests, the supply of cadavers for public dissection was sharply limited. Executions were rarer in fifteenth-century Italian cities than we often imagine – Florence averaged between six and seven a year, for example – and only a very small proportion of executed criminals fitted the criteria established by the university and guild: foreigners of low birth hanged during the winter months (in the days before refrigeration summer dissections were unusual, for obvious reasons).[42] Nonetheless, the problem of supply did not appear critical, thanks largely to the limited demand for cadavers. Anatomy in this period was a static discipline, and dissections had a pedagogical end. It was widely acknowledged that 'no one can be a good or fully trained doctor unless he is familiar with the anatomy of the human body', in the words of the 1388 statute of the University of Florence,[43] but there was little sense of anatomy as an arena for research. In this sense, dissections functioned rather like an extension of anatomical illustration. Their goal was not to add to the existing body of knowledge concerning human anatomy and physiology but to help students and doctors understand and remember the texts in which that knowledge was enclosed.[44]

The situation changed dramatically in the years around 1490, with a remarkable flowering of interest in anatomy as a problem not just of teaching but also of research. This enthusiasm for anatomy was not confined to doctors, but swept up contemporary artists and other laymen, as is well known. Some artists began to perform their own dissections,[45] while prominent citizens became a fixture at university anatomies, which later in the sixteenth century developed into theatrical events attracting an enthusiastic and often raucous crowd. The reasons for this change are complicated. They include the revival of antique art, with its interest in naturalism; the new enthusiasm of humanist doctors and scholars for the works of the Greek medical writer Galen of Pergamon, whose lost treatise on anatomy was recovered at exactly this time; and as we move into the sixteenth century the increasing availability of printed and illustrated works of anatomy designed as 'coffee-table' books for a general audience interested in medicine and the secrets of the natural world.[46]

Here, however, I want to focus not on the causes of this renewed interest in anatomy but on its effects. The size of the audience increased dramatically in formal university dissections, which now began to assume a truly public character. The 1405 statutes of the University of Bologna allowed no more than twenty students at the anatomy of a male cadaver, and thirty at that of a female. In his *Commentaries on Mondino* (1521), in contrast, Jacopo Berengario da Carpi claimed to have demonstrated the placenta of a hanged woman to 'almost five hundred students at the university of Bologna, together with many citizens'.[47] These larger audiences could no longer be accommodated in private houses but required more spacious quarters: temporary structures of seats and risers set up in the interiors of churches, for example, and later in the sixteenth century, permanent anatomy theatres.[48] As part of the same process, the demand for dissectable bodies quickly escalated beyond the meagre but regular trickle supplied by the local gallows, and families (if any) swayed by the prospect of a free funeral. We can get some sense of the numbers involved when we consider that the fifteenth-century medical professor Bartolomeo da Montagnana wrote with considerable authority, having opened at least fourteen bodies. By 1522 Berengario claimed to have anatomized several hundred.[49]

Berengario's *Commentaries* give a clear sense of the new hunger for cadavers that drove early sixteenth-century anatomists.[50] He dismissed public dissections as useless displays, of interest only to tyros and curious townspeople. The true anatomist, he emphasized, worked in private, slowly and methodically, surrounded only by a handful of students. Rather than choosing his bodies for their size and typicality (the case with public dissections), he sought out bodies of all descriptions: male and female, virgin and sexually experienced, young and old, healthy and sick, starved and well fed. This allowed him both to explore normal anatomy and to develop a sense of the range of natural variation. Berengario in particular advocated dissecting foetuses at different stages of development, and he called for repeated dissections, since exploring one organ often involved destroying others.[51] ('May the reader note how much I have laboured to understand the *rete* [*mirabilis*] and its location', he wrote, 'and I have dissected more than a hundred human heads almost solely on account of this *rete*.)[52] Only by dint of such varied and repeated observations could the anatomist truly come to understand the divine craftsmanship with which the human body had been created.

But how were all of these bodies to be obtained? The most obvious source for doctors was of course post-mortems, and there is considerable evidence that they began increasingly to recommend these to their patients' families, even when the family was itself satisfied as to the cause of death, as we already saw in the case of Antonio Benivieni.[53] But few doctors had practices large enough to generate vast numbers of corpses, and this was obviously not an option for artists at all. Thus they looked more and more to the other traditional source of cadavers: poor foreigners and others without families nearby to worry about their funerary rites. Only a very few of these ended up on the gallows; far more died in local hospitals, many of which were founded as charitable institutions to serve precisely this group of people. Beginning in the 1480s there is increasing evidence of this new source of supply. Thus we find Leonardo da Vinci working with cadavers obtained from hospitals in Florence, Rome, and apparently Milan.[54] In Venice, similarly, the anatomist Niccolò Massa had an ongoing relationship in the 1520s and 1530s with the Hospital of Saints Peter and Paul, which had also become the site of the annual dissection sponsored by the Venetian College of Surgeons, and he managed on one occasion to convince the surgeon employed by a local monastery to convey to him the body of one of his patients there, 'a stranger passing through town on a pilgrimage'.[55]

In time, however, even the hospitals proved inadequate to the task. They could not meet Berengario's need for foetuses, for example, and he was reduced to buying them clandestinely from local midwives.[56] But it is only in the next generation that anatomists began to rely heavily on unofficial or extralegal sources of supply. This shift is already evident in Massa's *Introductory Book of Anatomy* (1536) where he discussed cranial sutures on the basis of 'the heads of dead people in cemeteries'.[57] Massa's skulls probably came not from private graves but from ossuaries where the bones of those long dead were stored after being exhumed to provide more space in the crowded urban burial grounds. Some of his colleagues, however, were less discreet. Grave-robbing was not a new phenomenon; we have already come across the early fourteenth-century case of the students of Master Alberto of Bologna, while the university statutes from 1405 refer vaguely to 'quarrels and rumours ... in finding or searching for bodies'.[58] But the lack of surviving documentation suggests that such cases were rare. Furthermore, the grave violated by Master Alberto's students had not been chosen at random: hanged the previous day, its occupant belonged to the class of condemned criminals earmarked as appropriate anatomical subjects. In the early days of dissection, respectable citizens, however scandalized by the sacrilege involved, could still count themselves safe from a similar fate.

With the increasing currency of dissection, this was no longer the case. In Bologna, according to Lodovico Frati, students attempted to remove corpses awaiting burial from private houses, while Alfonso Corradi says that in Padua they also assaulted funeral processions.[59] But Vesalius marks the real turning point. One of the most surprising aspects of his great treatise *On the Fabric of the Human Body* (1543), compared to the works of his predecessors, is his lack of respect for persons and his candid pride in the acts of daring and deception required to obtain what he considered an adequate supply of cadavers. He and his students forged keys, rifled tombs and gibbets, and stole in and out of ossuaries in a series of night-time escapades that he recounts with evident relish and amusement, particularly when female bodies were involved (this was often the case, given the small number of women executed for capital crimes).[60] The following passage is typical:

> The handsome mistress of a certain monk of Sant'Antonio ... died suddenly, as though from strangulation of the uterus or some quickly devastating ailment, and was snatched from her tomb by the Paduan students and carried off for public dissection. By their remarkable industry they flayed the whole skin from the cadaver lest it be recognized by the monk who, with the relatives of his mistress, had complained to the municipal judge that the body had been stolen from its tomb.[61]

It was this sort of practice that inspired a Venetian law from 1550 that punished grave-robbing, which it associated with the growth of private dissection, by heavy fines.[62]

It is not until the middle of the sixteenth century, in other words, that we begin to find clear signs of persistent public concern regarding anatomical practice in Italy, and even then this concern coexisted with well documented popular enthusiasm for the spectacle of dissection.[63] The reservations of Italian city dwellers, unlike their English counterparts, concerned not dissection in general but the specific prospect that they or their loved ones might come under the anatomist's knife. Initially these reservations focused on traditional issues: funerary ritual and family honour – hence Vesalius' own decision to delete from the revised edition of the *Fabrica* (1555) some of the more lurid passages concerning his quest for cadavers.[64] Increasingly, however, popular anxieties began to find another focus – the fear of vivisection. Beginning in the 1530s, a haze of unsavoury stories on this topic gradually collected around the names of famous anatomists. Berengario became an early target, and Falloppia noted the rumour that he lost his position at the University of

Bologna for having vivisected Spanish twin brothers with syphilis.[65] Similar rumours also attached themselves to Vesalius, supposed to have undertaken his fatal pilgrimage in penance for carrying out an autopsy on a still-living Spanish noble.[66]

There is no evidence to support these particular allegations. Nonetheless, the accusations are not completely preposterous. It was not unknown for the hanged to revive (in which case they went free, presumably on the principle of double jeopardy); Antonio Benivieni recorded an incident of this sort.[67] More to the point, Berengario emphasized the importance of vivisection while noting that this was only incidentally practised by doctors suturing wounds, lancing boils, trepanning skulls and performing other surgical operations.[68] Vesalius included an even more striking and suggestive observation in his discussion of moisture in the cardiac membranes, which, inconveniently for the anatomist, dissipates shortly after death. 'Eager to see this water', as he put it, he opened the body of a man who had just died in an accident and took out what he described as 'the still pulsing heart'.[69]

Thus the rumours concerning human vivisection are themselves telling, even as rumours, reflecting what was seen as (and may well have been) the dangerous and unseemly haste with which sixteenth-century anatomists appropriated fresh cadavers for dissection. These anxieties were not confined to the uninitiated, and they merged with the increasing fear of being buried alive. One of the growing number of Italian testators to specify an unaccustomed waiting period between death and interment was the anatomist Niccolò Massa, who – drawing perhaps on personal experience – asked to be left unburied for two days 'to avoid any mistake'.[70]

Whether or not the sixteenth-century anatomical hunger for cadavers actually put the living at risk, it certainly forged unprecedented links between anatomists and the administrators of criminal justice. Sometimes anatomists' enthusiasm for corpses, no matter what their provenance, served the interests of criminals. In 1518, for example, Caterina di Lorenzo was hanged in Rome after killing a man and handing his body over for dissection, in an apparently novel attempt to dispose of the corpse.[71] More often anatomists collaborated with the judges in concrete and sometimes disturbing ways. In his *Letter on the China Root* (1546) Vesalius lamented the burden of negotiating with judges concerning time and mode of execution,[72] and there are clear indications that anatomists sometimes eliminated the middle man by carrying out capital sentences themselves. Alessandro Benedetti noted in his *History of the Human Body* (1497) that 'those who live in prison have sometimes asked to be handed over to the colleges of physicians rather than to be killed by the hand of the public executioner', adding that 'cadavers of this kind cannot be obtained except by papal consent'.[73] Fifty years later, Falloppia offered an even more explicit recollection:

> The Grand Duke of Tuscany ordered a man to be given over to us, for us to kill as we wished and then dissect. I gave him two drams of opium, but he suffered from quartan fever, and its crisis halted the effect of the drug. The man, exulting, asked that we give him a second dose, so that if he did not die, we would intercede for a pardon with the duke. I gave him another two drams of opium, and he died.[74]

There is no evidence here that dissection itself, at least in this period, was considered part of the criminal's penalty – a way, as it became in England, of intensifying the ultimate sentence.[75] Nor does it seem to have been seen by either judges or criminals as specifically punitive in intent. There is no particular reason to doubt Benedetti's claim that criminals might prefer the anatomist's opium to the public humiliation of the executioner's rope. Nonetheless, the new enthusiasm for dissection brought anatomist and executioner into ever closer association. Anatomists had no cause to regret the dramatic increase in executions that accompanied the rise of absolutist government in Italy from the middle of the sixteenth century, while their own methods echoed their rulers' increasing recourse to unusual and extreme forms of execution – what Samuel Edgerton has called 'an officially sanctioned policy of desecration and mutilation of the criminal's body'.[76]

The later sixteenth-century fascination with flaying and dismemberment was not confined to the arenas of medicine and justice; as William Heckscher has pointed out, it also marked the arts of the period, with their graphic images of torture, punishment, martyrdom and rape. It is too simple to argue, as Heckscher does, that public anatomies directly inspired artists to produce work of this sort.[77] But the dissections, the images and the grisly executions may all reflect in one way or another a culture of coercion and exemplary violence that characterized the theory and practice of absolutist rule.[78]

The criminal and the saintly body

As Caroline Bynum has argued, the body has a history, and

> there is something profoundly alien to modern sensibilities about [its] role in medieval piety. ... Medieval images of the body have less to do with sexuality than with fertility and decay. Control, discipline, even torture of the flesh is, in medieval devotion, not

so much the rejection of physicality as the elevation of it – a horrible yet delicious elevation – into a means of access to the divine.[79]

Few of us can identify with the relish with which pious men and (especially) women of the thirteenth, fourteenth and fifteenth centuries embraced – at least as a vicarious ideal – not only penitential practices such as drinking pus or saliva, but also the experiences of mutilation and dismemberment. By the same token we should not read our own anxieties back into the earlier period. The people of the Middle Ages and early Renaissance had a heavy investment in the integrity of their funerary rituals, but this did not necessarily extend to the integrity of the corpse. At the centre of popular Christianity, as Chiara of Montefalco's story reminds us, lay the magical charisma of relics: the dead and dismembered bodies of the saints. The association of dismemberment and sanctity continued to permeate popular attitudes well into the sixteenth century, and may help to explain the general Italian tolerance of anatomy and dissection.

We can gain some insight into the nature and logic of that association through the story of the martyrdom of the first Saint Ignatius, as recorded in the *Golden Legend* (c.1260) of Jacopo da Varagine. Condemned by the emperor Trajan to a daunting series of tortures, including being eaten by wild animals, Ignatius welcomed these with equanimity: ' "O salutary beasts", he cried,

> "when will they come, when will they be granted to me, when will they be allowed to use my flesh? I will invite them to devour me, and I will pray them not to hold back in any way, nor to fear touching my body. ... I know well the things that are useful to me: fire and the cross, animals, the division of the bones, those who will rend all my members and my entire body."[80]

When his executioners asked why he continually called on Christ, he told them, "I have his name written on my heart, and for that reason I can't help remembering it", so that after his death those who had heard him, wanting to test this, extracted his heart from his body and split the whole heart down the middle [and] found written on it the name of Jesus Christ in letters of gold. Whence many believed in God'.[81]

Jacopo's version of this story reflects the intensely somatic nature of Christian spirituality in the late Middle Ages, and the central role it assigned to the opened and dismembered body. Ignatius' body, like that of Chiara of Montefalco, acted not only as his avenue to sanctity, but also as the site of the signs that attested to that sanctity and (through his relics) as the instrument of his holy power.[82] At the same time Ignatius' story reaffirmed the importance of proper funerary ritual: Jacopo emphasized that the lions at the end refused to eat the saint's mutilated body so that his fellow Christians could give it an 'honourable burial'.[83]

These same themes resonate through the history of Renaissance anatomy, linking the saint and the criminal with the martyr in the middle. Not only did many of the more creative Italian methods of execution – grilling, rolling in a spiked barrel, pulling the flesh off with red-hot pincers – echo the torments of famous martyrs, but the confraternities that took as their mission the comfort of condemned criminals regaled them on the way to their deaths with the stories of those martyrs whose modes of execution most closely echoed their own.[84] As recent historians of those confraternities have shown, the Renaissance ideology of execution exploited these associations, portraying the criminal's death as exemplary; in addition to being an act of vengeance and a warning to others, it was also the culmination of a process that aimed to reconcile the criminal with those who condemned him through a final act of atonement explicitly identified with Christ and the saints.[85] This served to legitimize those executions by associating the justice of the state with the will of God.

From this point of view the criminal's subsequent dissection, which in the days before the permanent anatomy theatre sometimes took place in church, itself resembled a sacrament – the penultimate act in a potential drama of redemption. (The last act, as the story of Ignatius indicates, still consisted of the reunion of the criminal's dismembered parts in a Christian grave.)[86] Similar associations permeated the écorchés in the anatomical treatises of Berengario da Carpi, the most elaborately illustrated works of their kind before Vesalius' Fabric. These included two male figures in the stance of saints holding their instruments of martyrdom, the executioner's rope and axe (Figures 11.1 and 11.2), as well as a series of heroic nudes – one complete with aura – willingly participating in their own dissection by holding up the layers of skin hiding their abdominal muscles (Figure 11.3). Most striking of all, however, was the image chosen by Berengario to illustrate the muscular anatomy of the arms: a flayed figure of the crucified Christ (Figure 11.4).[87]

There is in fact considerable evidence for the continuing association of the criminal and the saintly body in Renaissance Italy. Both saint and criminal were exemplary figures, models of all that was to be emulated or shunned. The deeds of both were assumed to be supernaturally inspired, whether by God or the devil, and their bodies were sites of special power. As anatomists themselves demonstrated, the criminal's body, like the saint's, could differ physically from that of other people. Benivieni dissected a notorious thief and found his heart covered with hair, while Realdo Colombo described the extra rib and swollen uterine

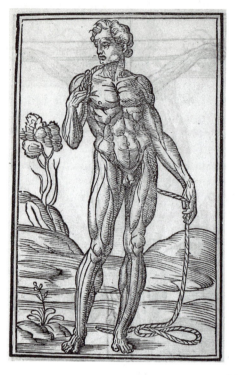

Figure 11.1 Ecorché showing the exterior muscles of the front.

Source: Jacopo Berengario da Carpi, *Commentaria cum amplissimis additionibus super anatomica Mundini*, fol. 519 (Bologna, 1521). Photo: National Library of Medicine.

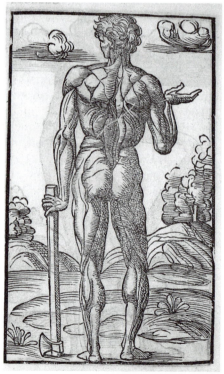

Figure 11.2 Ecorché showing the exterior muscles of the back.

Source: Berengario, *Commentaria*, fol. 520v. Photo: National Library of Medicine.

Figure 11.3 Ecorché showing the abdominal muscles.

Source: Berengario, *Isagogae breves perlucidae ac uberrimae in anatomiam humani corporis*, fol. 6v (Bologna, 1523). Photo: National Library of Medicine.

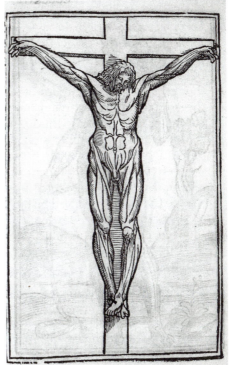

Figure 11.4 Ecorché showing the muscles of the arm.

Source: Berengario, *Commentaria*, fol. 519v. Photo: National Library of Medicine).

veins of a notorious 'demoniac' and infanticide.[88] Some of these devia-
tions could be explained by medical principles – Benivieni attributed the
thief's hairy heart to an unusually hot complexion – but others smacked
clearly of the supernatural, especially in the cases of repentant
criminals.[89] In one of her most famous letters, Catherine of Siena
described the blood of the decapitated Niccolò di Toldo as so fragrant
that she could not bear to wash it off, while others attributed incorruptibility to the bodies of great sinners and healing virtues to the body parts
of the executed.[90] Thus, according to Vasari, the sixteenth-century
sculptor Silvio Cosini of Fiesole made a vest out of the skin of a criminal
corpse he had stolen for dissection and wore it over his shirt for its
magical and protective powers.[91]

We can see other remnants of this saintly aura in an anecdote in
Benedetti's otherwise quite sober anatomy textbook. 'It happened once
when a dissection had been completed at the university of Padua', he
wrote,

> that a certain student kept the bones for his own use. Halfway on
> his journey to Venice at night, he left his boat to dine and went to
> an inn with his companions. Along came a most impudent squad
> of tax collectors looking for contraband merchandise and found
> the box of bones the student had left behind in the boat. When
> they asked to whom these belonged and received no reply, the
> tax collectors carried off the bones and opened the box next
> morning in the presence of their overseers. When they found the
> bones, picked clean of flesh and shining white, lying among
> odorous herbs, they began to worship them with bared heads as
> though they were the relics of some saints. Then they brought
> the box to the highest magistrate. In the crowd that assembled
> before him Francesco Sanudo, a man of high reputation and
> standing in the legal profession, revealed that the bones were the
> remains of an anatomical dissection and ordered them to be
> restored to the student of medicine, who had by this time lodged
> a complaint about the stolen box. Everyone laughed loudly to
> see the frustrated greed of the tax collectors. And now,

Benedetti concluded, 'let us return to the vertebrae of the neck'.[92]

Notes

1 Sr Francesca's testimony transcribed in *Il processo di canonizzazione di Chiara da
   Montefalco*, ed. Enrico Menestò with Silvestro Nessi (Scandicci [Florence], 1984),
   339. See also Piero Camporesi, *The Incorruptible Flesh: Bodily Mutation and
   Mortification in Religion and Folklore*, trans. Tania Croft-Murray and Helen Elsom
   (Cambridge, 1988), 3–7 (based on a seventeenth-century account of the same

events) and in general ch. 1; and the various articles in *S. Chiara da Montefalco e il suo tempo*, eds Claudio Leonardi and Enrico Menestò (Perugia, 1985).

2 *Il processo di canonizzazione*, 428.

3 *Ibid.*, 341.

4 *ibid.*, 296, 453.

5 *Vita beatae Margaritae virginis de Civitate Castelli* in *Analecta bollandiana* 19(1900): 27. The embalming was done by two surgeons at the request of the municipal government.

6 Marie-Christine Pouchelle, *The Body and Surgery in the Middle Ages*, trans. Rosemary Morris (New Brunswick NJ, 1990), 82; see also 70 and in general ch. 5. Pouchelle cites as evidence the poor reputation of Nero, who was supposed to have had his mother killed and opened in order to see the womb that bore him – although it is hardly necessary to invoke a taboo against dissection in order to understand medieval reservations concerning his behaviour.

7 Pouchelle, *The Body and Surgery*, ch. 1; see also Glenn Harcourt, 'Andreas Vesalius and the Anatomy of Antique Sculpture', *Representations* 17(1986): 28–61; and esp. Jonathan Sawday, 'The Fate of Marsyas: Dissecting the Renaissance Body', in *Renaissance Bodies: The Human Figure in Renaissance Culture, c.1540–1660*, eds Lucy Gent and Nigel Llewellyn (London, 1990), 112–35, both evidently influenced by Michel Foucault, *Discipline and Punish: The Birth of the Prison*, trans. Alan Sheridan (New York, 1977), part 1; and Francis Barker, 'Into the Vault', in his *The Tremulous Private Body: Essays on Subjectivity* (London, 1984), 72–112. Similar ideas appear in an English context, to which they appear considerably more appropriate, in Ruth Richardson, *Death, Dissection and the Destitute* (London, 1988), ch. 1.

8 Salimbene de Adam, *Cronica*, ed. Giuseppe Scalia, 2 vols (Bari, 1966), II: 894. The practice of autopsy to determine cause of death may have been current considerably earlier in the Byzantine Empire. For a case reported by William of Malmesbury in the twelfth century, see Ynez Violé O'Neill, 'Innocent III and the Evolution of Anatomy', *Medical History* 20(1976): 429–30, n5. The most comprehensively documented account of the early history of autopsy and dissection is still Walter Artelt, 'Die ältesten Nachrichten über die Sektion menschlicher Leichen im mittelalterlichen Abendland', *Abhandlungen zur Geschichte der Medizin und der Naturwissenschaften*, H. 34(1940).

9 Cited in Artelt, 'Die ältesten Nachrichten', 17. On the use of expert medical testimony in Bolognese legal practice, see in general Edgardo Ortalli, 'La perizia medica a Bologna nei secoli XIII e XIV: normativa e practica di un istituto giudiziario', *Atti e memorie della Deputazione di storia patria per le province di Romagna*, n.s. 17–19(1965/6–1967/8): 223–59; and Eugenio Dall'Osso, *L'organizzazione medico-legale a Bologna e a Venezia nei secoli XII–XIV* (Cesena, 1956). On early autopsies in particular, see Loris Premuda and Giuseppe Ongaro, 'I primordi della dissezione anatomica in Padova', *Acta medicae historiae patavina* 12(1965–6): esp. 124–7.

10 Nancy G. Siraisi, *Taddeo Alderotti and his Pupils: Two Generations of Italian Medical Learning* (Princeton, 1981), 113. For another example from 1335 involving a woman poisoned by her husband, see Artelt, 'Die ältesten Nachrichten', 18.

11 Pietro d'Abano, *De venenis* (Mantua, 1473), ch. 3, fol. [5].

12 See in general André Vauchez, *La sainteté en Occident au derniers siècles du Moyen Age d'après les procès de canonisation et les documents hagiographiques* (Rome, 1981), 499–518; and Caroline Walker Bynum, 'The Female Body and Religious Practice in the Later Middle Ages', in *Fragments for a History of the*

Human Body, eds Michael Feher with Ramona Naddaff and Nadia Tazi (New York, 1989), I: 163–9, who points out that corporeal marks of sainthood were particularly characteristic of holy women.

13 Cited in Dietrich Schäfer, 'Mittelalterlicher Brauch bei der Überführung von Leichen', *Sitzungsberichte der preussischen Akademie der Wissenschaften* (Berlin, 1920), 496. For a survey of late medieval funerary practice, see R. C. Finucane, 'Sacred Corpse, Profane Carrion: Social Ideals and Death Rituals in the Later Middle Ages', in *Mirrors of Mortality: Studies in the Social History of Death*, ed. Joachim Whaley (New York, 1982), ch. 2; and (for Italy) Sharon T. Strocchia, *Death and Ritual in Renaissance Florence* (Baltimore, 1992), part I. On embalming in the Middle Ages, see in general Paul Diepgen, 'Über Leicheneinbalsamierung im Mittelalter', *Janus* 26(1922): 91–4; Schäfer, 'Mittelalterlicher Brauch'; Pierre Duparc, '*Dilaceratio corporis*', *Bulletin de la société nationale des antiquaires de France* (1981): 360–72; and especially Ernst von Rudloff, *Über das Konservieren von Leichen im Mittelalter: Ein Beitrag zur Geschichte der Anatomie und des Bestattungswesens* (Freiburg, 1921), 22–39. The techniques of embalming and autopsy are so similar that it is almost impossible to distinguish them in contemporary images; see, for example, the conflicting interpretations of one of the earliest European representations of an open body, in the Bodleian, MS. Ashmole 399 (*c*.1300), in Loren MacKinney, *Medical Illustrations in Medieval Manuscripts* (London, 1965), 100–1 and fig. 96; and Artelt, 'Die ältesten Nachrichten', 12, n13. On the other hand, it is clear that the image does not refer, as is often claimed, to a dissection.

14 E.g. Schäfer, 'Mittelalterlicher Brauch', 492; and Gerhard Wolff, 'Leichen-Besichtigung und -Untersuchung bis zur Carolina als Vorstufe gerichtlicher Sektion', *Janus* 42(1938): 265–6.

15 Mondino de' Liuzzi, *Anothomia* (Pavia, 1478), [26]. English trans. in Edward Grant (ed.) *A Source Book in Medieval Science* (Cambridge MA, 1974), 733; and facsimile edition in *Anatomies de Mondino dei Luzzi et de Guido de Vigevano*, ed. Ernest Wickersheimer (Paris, 1926), [7]–[50]. On the early history of anatomy and dissection at Bologna, see Siraisi, *Taddeo Alderotti*, 110–13; and in general Siraisi, *Medieval and Early Renaissance Medicine: An Introduction to Knowledge and Practice* (Chicago, 1990), ch. 4; G. Martinotti, 'L'insegnamento dell'anatomia in Bologna prima del secolo XIX', *Studi e memorie per la storia dell'università di Bologna* 2(1911): 3–32; Artelt, 'Die ältesten Nachrichten', 18–20.

16 See Artelt, 'Die ältesten Nachrichten', 17; and Siraisi, *Taddeo Alderotti*, 45–9.

17 Trial record transcribed in Piero Giacosa, *Magistri salernitani nondum editi: Catalogo ragionato della esposizione di storia della medicina aperta in Torino nel 1898* (Turin, 1901), 603–8 (quotation at 607). The authorities showed no particular interest in the dissection itself but concerned themselves exclusively with the sacrilege involved in disturbing a recent grave.

18 Strocchia, *Death and Ritual*, 21–2, 39–40; and B. Cecchetti, 'Funerali e sepulture dei veneziani antichi', *Archivio Veneto* series I, 34(1887): 265–84. See also Jacques Chiffoleau, *La comptabilité de l'audelà: Les hommes, la mort et la religion dans la région d'Avignon à la fin du Moyen Age (vers 1320–vers 1480)* (Rome, 1980), 121, 132; and Philippe Ariès, *The Hour of our Death*, trans. Helen Weaver (New York, 1981), 168–70. For a graphic illustration of the relatively exposed condition of the corpse during the funeral, see the illumination in the *Liber regulae* of the Roman hospital of Santo Spirito in Sassia from *c*.1300, reproduced in Vincenzo Monachino, Mariano da Alatri, and Isidoro da Villapadierna, *La carità cristiana in Roma* (Bologna, 1968), fig. 52.

19 Florence: Katharine Park, *Doctors and Medicine in Early Renaissance Florence* (Princeton, 1985), 97; Perugia: Vincenzo Busacchi, 'Necroscopie trecentesche a scopo anatomo-patologico in Perugia', *Rivista di storia della medicina* 9(1965): 160–3 (including transcriptions of two chronicle entries); Padua: Premuda and Ongaro, 'I primordi', 127.

20 Raffaele Ciasca, *L'arte dei medici e speziali nella storia e nel commercio fiorentino dal secolo XII al XV* (Florence, 1927), 279; Park, *Doctors and Medicine*, 38–9; Giuseppe Ongaro, 'La medicina nello studio di Padova e nel Veneto', in *Storia della cultura veneta*, eds Girolamo Arnaldi and Manlio Pastore (Vicenza, 1981), III/3: 94; Premuda and Ongaro, 'I primordi', 128.

21 Archivio di stato di Firenze: Conventi soppressi-95, 212, fol. 171; transcribed in Park, *Doctors and Medicine*, 53–4. For a similar case from 1478, see the *ricordanza* of Filippo di Matteo Strozzi in Archivio di stato di Firenze: Carte strozziane, series 5, 22, fol. 97.

22 Bernardo Torni, *Relatio anatomica*, in Lynn Thorndike, *Science and Thought in the Fifteenth Century* (New York, 1929), 126, 131; Latin text 290–4.

23 Antonio Benivieni, *De abditis nonnullis ac mirandis morborum et sanitationum causis*, in *L'inizio dell'anatomia patologica nel Quattrocento fiorentino, sui testi di Antonio Benivieni, Bernardo Torni, Leonardo da Vinci*, eds A. Costa and G. Weber (Florence, 1952), 636. This edition of Benivieni contains sixty-five cases omitted from the version edited and translated by Charles Singer and Edmond R. Long (Springfield IL, 1954).

24 Benivieni, *De abditis nonnullis* (Springfield IL, 1954), 80.

25 See Elizabeth A. R. Brown, 'Death and the Human Body in the Later Middle Ages: The Legislation of Boniface VIII on the Division of the Corpse', *Viator* 12(1981): 221–70, for a detailed discussion of the circumstances surrounding the bull and the issues raised by it. Text in *Les registres de Boniface VIII*, eds Georges Digard, Maurice Fauçon, Antoine Thomas and Robert Fawtier, 3 vols (Paris, 1907–21), II: 576–7 (no. 3409).

26 Details on the history and geography of these practices in Brown, 'Death and the Human Body', 226–34; and the sources in note 13 above.

27 Brown, 'Death and the Human Body', 239. Text in *Les registres de Boniface VIII*, III: 754 (no. 5218). In the same year, the French cardinal Jean Lemoine glossed *Detestande feritatis* as applying also to evisceration (Brown, 250).

28 Mondino, *Anothomia*, [47]; translated in *A Source Book*, 739. On the bull's much greater effect in France, see Artelt, 'Die ältesten Nachrichten', 23–4; Mary Niven Alston, 'The Attitude of the Church toward Dissection before 1500', *Bulletin of the History of Medicine* 16(1944): 229–32; Brown, 'Death and the Human Body', 250–1.

29 Ernst von Rudloff, *Über das Konservieren von Leichen*, 19–22; and Wolff, 'Leichen-Besichtigung', 265. It is not clear how many of the fourteenth-century cases involved opening the body. See Alston, 'Attitude of the Church', 235–6, for a transcription of the physician Pietro dell'Argelata's description of eviscerating and embalming Alexander V in 1410.

30 See Katharine Park, 'The Life of the Corpse: Division and Dissection in Late Medieval Europe', *Journal of the History of Medicine and Allied Sciences* 50(1994): 111–32.

31 See Agostino Paravicini Bagliani, 'Storia della scienza e storia della mentalità: Ruggero Bacone, Bonifacio VIII e la teoria della "prolongatio vitae"', in *Aspetti della letteratura latina nel secolo XII: Atti del primo convegno internazionale di studi dell'Associazione per il Medioevo e l'Umanesimo Latini*, eds Claudio Leonardi and Giovanni Orlandi (Perugia and Florence, 1986), 244–50, on the differing funerary instructions given by Italian and northern European cardinals in the

later thirteenth and early fourteenth centuries, and in general Cecchetti, 'Funerali e sepulture' (fourteenth-century examples); and Samuel K. Cohn Jr, *Death and Property in Siena, 1205–1800: Strategies for the Afterlife* (Baltimore, 1988), 114.

32 On these debates and the philosophical and theological issues they raised, see Bynum, 'Material Continuity, Personal Survival and the Resurrection of the Body: A Scholastic Discourse in its Medieval and Modern Contexts', in her *Fragmentation and Redemption: Essays on Gender and the Human Body in Medieval Religion* (New York, 1991), 260–9; Brown, 'Death and the Human Body', 235–45; Francesco Santi, 'Il cadavere e Bonifacio VIII, tra Stefano Tempier e Avicenna: Intorno a un saggio di Elizabeth Brown', *Studi medievali* 28/2(1987): 861–78.

33 For Boniface's personal concern with fame, immortality, and the fate of the corpse, see Paravicini Bagliani, 'Storia della scienza', 274–9; for his possible political motivations, Brown, 'Death and the Human Body', 247–9.

34 Alessandro Benedetti, *Anatomice, sive historia corporis humani* (Paris, 1514), fol. 10v; trans. in *Studies in Pre-Vesalian Anatomy: Biography, Translations, Documents*, ed. and trans. Levi Robert Lind (Philadelphia, 1975), 83. See in general Martinotti, 'L'insegnamento dell'anatomia', 50; Ciasca, *L'arte dei medici*, 280; M. G. Nardi, 'Statuti e documenti riflettenti la dissezione anatomica umana e la nomina di alcuni lettori di medicina nell'antico "studium generale" fiorentino', *Rivista di storia delle scienze mediche e naturali* 47(1956): 242. Thus the 1388 statute of the University of Florence required the dissectee to be 'captiva progenie, paucorum amicorum, et propinquorum' (*Statuti della università e studio fiorentino dal anno 1387 [Florentine style], seguiti da un'appendice di documenti dal 1320 al 1472*, ed. Alessandro Gherardi [Florence, 1881], 74).

35 *Statuti delle università e dei collegi dello Studio bolognese*, ed. Carlo Malagola (Bologna, 1888), 319 (amendment of 1442); note that no such restrictions were mentioned in the statute of 1405 where the dissection had only to be licensed by the rectors to avoid 'rixe et rumores in reperiendis seu querendis corporibus' (*Statuti*, 289).

36 Leonardo Bertapaglia, *Recollectae habitae super quarto Avicennae*, in Guy de Chauliac, *Ars chirurgica* (Venice, 1546), fol. 299v. This account is certainly not by Bertapaglia but by one of his contemporaries at Padua; see Thorndike, *Science and Thought*, 68–9.

37 On dismemberment, Antonio Pertile, *Storia del diritto italiano dalla caduta dell'impero romano alla codificazione*, 2nd edn, 6 vols in 8 (Turin, 1892–1902), V: 269; Camporesi, *The Incorruptible Flesh*, 19–22. On public exposure, Samuel Y. Edgerton Jr, *Pictures and Punishment: Art and Criminal Prosecution during the Florentine Renaissance* (Ithaca NY, 1985), 65.

38 Strocchia, 'Death Rites and the Ritual Family in Renaissance Florence', in *Life and Death in Fifteenth-Century Florence*, eds Marcel Tetel, Ronald G. Witt, and Rona Goffen (Durham NC and London, 1989), 120–45. Boniface VIII, who objected to any mutilation of the corpse, laid particular stress on its face; see Paravicini Bagliani, 'Storia della scienza', 255.

39 *Statuti della università*, ed. Gherardi, 75 (statute of 1388). According to the books of the confraternity of Santa Maria della Croce al Tempio in Florence, the remains of dissected criminals were buried in the confraternity's chapel of Santa Maria in Campo; see Biblioteca Nazionale di Firenze: MSS. II, I, 138, e.g. *ad annos* 1421 (no. 25), 1436 (no. 169), 1444 (no. 206). The Bolognese statute of 1405 set maximum expenses at sixteen lire for the dissection of a man and twenty for that of a woman, but does not further specify where the

money is to go, or why female cadavers were more expensive. See *Statuti*, ed. Malagola, 289–90.

40 See, for example, Luca Landucci, *Diario fiorentino dal 1450 al 1516*, ed. Iodoco del Badia (Florence, 1883), 273, n1.

41 Ciasca, *L'arte dei medici*, 280. Adriano Prosperi, 'Il sangue e l'anima: Ricerche sulle compagnie di giustizia in Italia', *Quaderni storici* 17(1982): 962, points out that it was often hard to find people to attend the funerals of the executed and that this was one of the principal motivations behind the founding of the confraternities for the comfort of condemned criminals.

42 Figures based on the first fifty years (1420–69) of records kept by the confraternity of Santa Maria della Croce al Tempio. Of the 331 people executed during that period, fewer than a fifth were foreigners and only ten were women. See Biblioteca Nazionale di Firenze: MS. II, I, 138, *ad annos* 1420–1469, tabulated according to form of execution in Edgerton, *Pictures and Punishment*, app. B.

43 *Statuti della università*, ed. Gherardi, 74.

44 Siraisi, *Medieval and Early Renaissance Medicine*, ch. 4. Roger K. French, 'A Note on the Anatomical *Accessus* of the Middle Ages', *Medical History* 23(1979): 465–8, explores the way in which medieval anatomists applied the rhetorical techniques of textual commentary to the explication of physical structures in the body.

45 See Bernard Schultz, *Art and Anatomy in Renaissance Italy* (Ann Arbor, 1985), chs 2–4.

46 See in general Giovanna Ferrari, 'Public Anatomy Lessons and the Carnival: The Anatomy Theater of Bologna', *Past and Present* 117(1987): 55–61; Roger K. French, 'Berengario da Carpi and the Use of Commentary in Anatomical Teaching', in *The Medical Renaissance of the Sixteenth Century*, eds Andrew Wear, Roger K. French, and Iain M. Lonie (Cambridge, 1985), 42–74; *Studies in Pre-Vesalian Anatomy*, 3–19; Schultz, *Art and Anatomy*, ch. 2.

47 *Statuti*, ed. Malagola, 289 (statute of 1405), translated in *University Records and Life in the Middle Ages*, ed. and trans. Lynn Thorndike (New York, 1944), 283; Jacopo Berengario da Carpi, *Commentaria cum amplissimis additionibus super anatomia Mundini* (Bologna, 1521), fol. 222v.

48 See Ferrari, 'Public Anatomy Lessons', 61–6, 72–87; Martinotti, 'L'insegnamento dell'anatomia', 76–8.

49 Bartolomeo da Montagnana, *Consilia Montagnane* (Lyon, 1525), fol. 202v (consilium 134); Berengario, *Isagogae breves perlucidae ac uberrimae in anatomiam humani corporis* (Bologna, 1523), fol. 2 (preface); translated in *A Short Introduction to Anatomy*, trans. L. R. Lind (Chicago, 1959).

50 References in French, 'Berengario da Carpi', 54–61.

51 See also Niccolò Massa, *Liber introductorius anatomiae, sive dissectionis corporis humani* (Venice, 1536): fol. 26, translated in *Studies in Pre-Vesalian Anatomy*, 193.

52 Berengario, *Commentaria*, fol. 459.

53 See note 24 above.

54 On Leonardo's anatomical work, see in general Schultz, *Art and Anatomy*, 67–100; Martin Kemp, *Leonardo da Vinci: The Marvellous Works of Nature and Man* (Cambridge MA, 1981), 257–61, 285–94. On his work at the hospital of Santa Maria Nuova in Florence, Kemp, *Leonardo*, 257; on his dissections in Milan (probably at the Ospedale Maggiore), C. Biaggi, 'Gli studi anatomici all'Ospedale Maggiore nel secolo XV: Leonardo a Milano', *Ospedale Maggiore* 44(1956): 405–10; on those in Rome (probably at the hospital of Santa Spirito), Adalberto Pazzini, 'Leonardo da Vinci e l'esercizio dell'anatomia in Roma',

Sudhoffs Archiv 37(1953): 329–37. For a survey of the functions of Italian hospitals in this period, see Katharine Park, 'Healing the Poor: Hospitals and Medical Assistance in Renaissance Florence', in *Medicine and Charity before the Welfare State*, eds Jonathan Barry and Colin Jones (London, 1991), 26–45.

55 Massa, *Liber introductorius*, fol. 56v; see also fols 10 and 26 (translated in *Studies in Pre-Vesalian Anatomy*, 216 and 181–2). On the Venetian College of Surgeons, *Studies*, 82, n7.

56 French, 'Berengario da Carpi', 53.

57 Massa, *Liber introductorius*, fol. 78; translated in *Studies in Pre-Vesalian Anatomy*, 233.

58 *Statuti*, ed. Malagola, 289; translated in *University Records*, 283. For the 1319 case, see note 17 above.

59 Lodovico Frati, *La vita privata di Bologna dal secolo XIII al XVII* (Bologna, 1900), 118, recounting (without sources) a case in which the body of a young girl was successfully stolen, and another in which the friends of a spinner who had recently been killed drove off the students with rocks and the help of the police. Corradi, as cited in Martinotti, 'L'insegnamento dell'anatomia', 37, n1.

60 On Vesalius' female cadavers, see C. D. O'Malley, *Andreas Vesalius of Brussels, 1514–1565* (Berkeley, 1964), 436, n7.

61 Andreas Vesalius, *De humani corporis fabrica* (Basel, 1543; facsimile edn Brussels, 1964), 538; translation based on O'Malley, *Andreas Vesalius*, 113–14.

62 Jacopo Facciolati, *Fasti gymnasii Patavini*, 2 vols (Padua, 1757), II: 208–9.

63 Ferrari, 'Public Anatomy Lessons', 98–9.

64 O'Malley, *Andreas Vesalius*, 278.

65 Gabriele Falloppia, *De morbo gallico* (1563), in Falloppia, *Opera omnia*, 2 vols and appendix (Frankfurt, 1600–6), I: 728. This statement does not appear in all editions, and its authenticity is dubious; see Martinotti, 'L'insegnamento dell'anatomia', 103, n1; and Vittorio Putti, *Berengario da Carpi: Saggio biografico e bibliografico, seguito dalla traduzione del 'De fractura calvae sue cranei'* (Bologna, 1937), 91–5. An English translation of the latter: *On Fracture of the Skull or Cranium*, trans. L. R. Lind (Philadelphia, 1990).

66 On this rumour and its sources, see O'Malley, *Andreas Vesalius*, 304–5, with accompanying notes. In a variation on this theme, Michelangelo, who also engaged in dissection, was rumoured to have murdered a porter in order to depict more accurately the sufferings of the dying Christ. References in Martinotti, 'L'insegnamento dell'anatomia', 102, n1.

67 Benivieni, *De abditis nonnullis* (Springfield IL, 1954), 162–3; see also Peter Linebaugh, 'The Tyburn Riot against the Surgeons', in *Albion's Fatal Tree: Crime and Society in Eighteenth-century England*, eds Douglas Hay, Peter Lindebaugh, John G. Rule, E. P. Thompson and Cal Winslow (London, 1975), 102–5.

68 Berengario, *Commentaria*, fols 4v–5.

69 Vesalius, *De humani corporis fabrica*, 584.

70 Text of will in *Studies in Pre-Vesalian Anatomy*, 325–7; quotation from 326. See also Cecchetti, 'Funerali e sepulture', 265–6, and – for two near misses in the late fifteenth century – Benivieni, *De abditis nonnullis* (Florence, 1952), 650, 651.

71 Vincenzo Paglia, *La morte confortata: riti della paura e mentalità religiosa a Roma nell'età moderna* (Rome, 1982), 125.

72 Vesalius, *Epistola … radicis chynae*, in his *Opera omnia anatomica et chirurgica*, eds Hermann Boerhaave and Bernhard Siegfried Albini, 2 vols (Leiden, 1725), II: 680.

73 Benedetti, *Anatomice*, fol. 10v; translated in *Studies in Pre-Vesalian Anatomy*, 83.
74 Falloppia, *De tumoribus praeter naturam*, ch. 14, in his *Opera omnia*, I: 632.
75 Linebaugh, 'The Tyburn Riot', 76.
76 Edgerton, *Pictures and Punishment*, 145; see also 232–3; and Paglia, *La morte confortata*, 111. Graphs and statistics for Rome in Paglia, apps I and II, and for Florence in Edgerton, app. B.
77 William S. Heckscher, *Rembrandt's Anatomy of Dr Nicolaas Tulp: An Iconological Study* (New York, 1958), 87.
78 *Ibid.*, 46. See also Carroll's interpretation of contemporary rape imagery in Margaret Carroll, 'The Erotics of Absolutism and the Mystification of Sexual Violence', *Representations* 25(1989): 3–30; and Foucault, *Discipline and Punish*, part I, on corporal punishment as a paradigm of absolutism.
79 Bynum, 'The Female Body', 161–2.
80 Jacopo da Varagine, *Leggenda aurea*, ed. Arrigo Levasti, 3 vols (Florence, 1924), I: 308.
81 *Ibid.*, I: 311.
82 Chiara's own martyrdom was self-imposed in the form of strenuous ascetic practices. Testimony in *Il processo di canonizzazione*, 98–9, 167–8, 330. On the role of the saint's body in late medieval Christianity, see in general Bynum, 'The Female Body'; Bynum, 'Bodily Miracles and the Resurrection of the Body in the High Middle Ages', in *Belief in History: Approaches to European and American Religion*, ed. Thomas Kselman (Notre Dame, 1991); Vauchez, *La sainteté*, 499–518; Pouchelle, 'La prise en charge de la mort: Médecine, médecins et chirugiens devant les problèmes liés à la mort à la fin du Moyen Age (XIIIe–XVe siècles)', *Archives européennes de sociologie* 17(1976): 249–78.
83 Jacopo da Varagine, I: 310.
84 Pertile, *Storia del diritto italiano*, V: 265; Paglia, *La morte confortata*, 84.
85 See in general Edgerton, *Pictures and Punishment*, ch. 5; Paglia, *La morte confortata*; and esp. Prosperi, who argues ('Il sangue e l'anima', 983–6) that this identification of criminal and martyr was rooted in the need of the authorities to be forgiven by their victim and to assimilate their legal judgments to the law of God.
86 See Bynum, 'Material Continuity, Personal Survival', for a compelling statement of the significance of this ultimate emphasis on the unity of the body. There are strong eucharistic resonances in Jacopo da Varagine's version of Ignatius' final speech: 'Io sono grano di Cristo, sarò macinato co' denti de le bestie, acciò ch nasca uno pane bianchissimo' (I: 310).
87 On Berengario's illustrations, see Lind, 'Introduction', in Berengario, *Short Introduction*, 23–7; and esp. Putti, *Berengario da Carpi*, 165–99. Figures 1 and 2 appeared in the *Commentaries on Mondino* (1521) as well as in *Short Introduction* (1st edn 1522). Figure 3 and the other self-demonstrating *écorchés* appeared first in the *Short Introduction*. Figure 4 appeared in both the *Commentaries* and the first edition of the *Short Introduction*, but was omitted – probably because of questions concerning its appropriateness – from later editions of the latter.
88 Benivieni, *De abditis nonnullis* (Springfield IL, 1954), 163–6; Realdo Colombo, *De re anatomica libri XV* (Venice, 1559), 60, 173–4.
89 The boundary between natural and supernatural disease and healing was extraordinarily permeable and fluid in this period; see Park, *Doctors and Medicine*, 50–2.
90 Catherine of Siena, *Lettere di Santa Caterina*, ed. Niccolò Tommaseo (Rome, 1973), letter to Raimondo da Capua (1375), 63. On incorruptibility, Philippe

Ariès, *Hour of our Death*, 360; Louis-Vincent Thomas, *Le cadavre: de la biologie à l'anthropologie* (Brussels, 1980), 42–3. On healing powers, Camporesi, *The Incorruptible Flesh*, 19; Linebaugh, 'The Tybourn Riot', 109–10; Pieter Spierenburg, *The Spectacle of Suffering: Executions and the Evolution of Repression, from a Preindustrial Metropolis to the European Experience* (Cambridge, 1984), 30; Elfriede Grabner, 'Der Mensch als Arznei: Alpenländische Belege aus einem Kärtner Schauermärlein', in *Festgabe für Oskar Moser: Beiträge zur Volkskunde Kärntens* (Klagenfurt, 1974), 81–95. Heckscher, *Rembrandt's Anatomy*, 164–6, n180. The confraternities for the comfort of the condemned sometimes gathered up their body parts and instruments of execution, in the manner of relics. Prosperi, 'Il sangue e l'anima', 994, n8.

91 Giorgio Vasari, *Le vite de' più eccellenti pittori, scultori ed architettori*, ed. Gaetano Milanesi, 9 vols (Florence, 1878–85), IV: 483. Vasari is most disapproving of this episode and notes that Cosini interred the vest after being reprimanded by a priest.

92 Benedetti, *Anatomice*, fols 121–121v; translated in *Studies in Pre-Vesalian Anatomy*, 132–3.

12

FRIENDSHIP PORTRAYED

A new account of *Utopia*

David Wootton

If the study of the ancient world – its ruins and its texts – did much to animate the intellectual and cultural life of the Renaissance, the overseas discoveries of Columbus and later explorers were equally if not more revolutionary. On one level, as is well known, these discoveries – the news of which reached many Europeans through the letters of the Florentine explorer Amerigo Vespucci – led to conquests, the destruction of many of the indigenous peoples in the Americas, and the emergence of new societies. On another level, they enabled the creation of a new imaginative literature, in which Thomas More's Utopia, *first published in 1516, holds an important place. As one of the two major interlocutors in the dialogue, Raphael Hythloday – whom More portrays as having 'signed up with Amerigo Vespucci' – observes at the conclusion to Book 1, travel to distant places makes it possible to see ways of life different from one's own and perhaps to admit that political and social arrangements can be better elsewhere than they are at home.*

Utopia, *therefore, becomes an imagined place that enables readers to rethink the world in which they live. Hythloday tells of a land ('Utopia', a pun, means both no-place ['ou-topos'] and a good place ['eu-topos']) with fundamentally different institutions and values from those of sixteenth-century England. He describes a world with universal education, gender equality and religious freedom; but the most radical difference lies in Hythloday's report that in Utopia everything is owned collectively; there is, in short, no private property. How serious More was about this proposal has long been a contested issue among scholars, but there is no question that this work constitutes, along with Machiavelli's* The Prince, *one of the most influential reflections on politics and society written in the early sixteenth century.*

How one should read More's Utopia *– whether as a satire or as a serious work or, indeed, whether as a work in which More praises or condemns communism – remains a matter of debate among historians. Without doubt much of the text was ironic and paradoxical. It is well known, for example, that More and Erasmus were close friends and that Erasmus had written his* Praise of Folly *(again a pun, this time on More's name ['morus', from the Greek, means fool]), while a guest at More's home in England. Like Erasmus, More believed it* *possible to address the most difficult issues of his day through irony. He was able to be serious and not so serious at the same time. In the essay below, Wootton extends our understanding of the relationship of More to Erasmus by demonstrating the way in which More's* Utopia *was indebted to Erasmus' writings, in which the Dutch humanist, drawing both on Plato and the New Testament, argued for the common ownership of goods and equality as the basis of friendship.*

Paradox was also woven into More's life. A wealthy lawyer and a brilliant humanist, he became an advisor to Henry VIII and rose to become Lord Chancellor of England. He was a devout Catholic who believed profoundly in Erasmus' call for reform but sharply rejected the proposed reforms of Martin Luther. More helped his king compose a defence of the seven sacraments, and he himself eventually composed some of the most vehement anti-Lutheran diatribes of the day. But More is best known for his own struggles of conscience. Though loyal to Henry, he ultimately could not bring himself to support the king's divorce from Catharine of Aragon or to sign the Act of Succession of 1534 that established the Anglican Church. More died a martyr, convicted of treason. One of his last works was his Dialogue of Comfort against Tribulation, *written while he was imprisoned in the Tower of London. Given the way in which More's life unfolded, one of* Utopia's *central questions – whether virtue can survive in the messy world of politics and wealth – is especially haunting.*

Wootton's essay originally appeared in History Workshop Journal *45(1998): 30–47. For the text of* Utopia *itself, there are two attractive alternatives: Thomas More,* Utopia, *with Erasmus'* The Sileni of Alcibiades, *ed. David Wootton (Indianapolis, 1999); and Thomas More,* Utopia *ed. David Harris Sacks (Boston, 1999), both with excellent introductions. Finally, among the many indispensable scholarly essays on More, see J. H. Hexter, 'Intentions, Words, and Meanings: The Case of Thomas More',* New Literary History *6(1975): 529–41; and Stephen Greenblatt, 'At the Table of the Great: More's Self-Fashioning and Self-Cancellation', in Greenblatt's* Renaissance Self-Fashioning *(Chicago, 1980), 11–73.*

* * *

In the summer of 1515 Thomas More (1478–1535) was a successful young lawyer employed in trade negotiations with the Netherlands and soon to enter the King's Council. An astute onlooker might have been able to predict his future promotion to Lord Chancellor, but his death as a Counter-reformation saint was unimaginable, for the Reformation had yet to begin. At this point More's closest allegiance was to Erasmus (1469–1536) and his network of reformers, who sought to emphasize not theology or the sacraments but rather Christ's moral teaching. That summer More invented the Utopia, a literary form dear to radicals ever since; he had a model, of course, in Plato's *Republic*, but More, drawing on the conventions of travel literature, described his ideal society as if he had walked its streets and sat in its gardens.[1] Moreover, Plato had been far from clear whether his conception was practical or merely ideal; while the reality-effect More constructed in *Utopia* was designed to convince the reader that he was offering a blueprint for reform.

Utopia portrayed an island which had had no contact with the world known to us for more than a thousand years, an island 'discovered' by Raphael Hythloday. Because of the success with which he portrayed a land so unlike his own, More's vision has been hard to situate in the context of Renaissance intellectual life. Indeed, in a number of important respects More's text appears to be extraordinarily in advance of its time. *Utopia* is often heralded as the founding text of modern communism: the concept of communism was already well known from the *Republic* and the New Testament, but one has to wait for the Diggers to find its practice recommended again. *Utopia* portrays a remarkably egalitarian society with an elaborate structure of representative government; More lived in an intensely hierarchical society, and no-one spoke up for equality again until the Levellers.[2] In *Utopia* all citizens (a few scholars excepted) work with their hands, and work is organized so as to maximize leisure. In early modern England only gentlemen and the clergy had soft hands; everyone else laboured through the hours of daylight. The Enlightenment was well under way before Locke, in the privacy of his notebooks, returned to the idea of universal labour and its concomitants, universal education and a shorter working day.[3] In sixteenth-century England, printing press, compass and gunpowder heralded a world of technological revolution, but most trades still employed tools familiar to the Romans. The Utopians, by contrast, hunger for technological progress: they have learnt, for example, to incubate eggs, despite being without thermometers or thermostats, steam or electricity. It is hard to find evidence of a comparable conviction that technology can transform the world before Francis Bacon (1561–1626).[4] And, of course, sixteenth-century England was backward looking: its philosophy and science came from Ancient Greece, its literature and religion from Ancient Rome and its empire, while its law and constitution claimed to be descended from time immemorial. The author of *Utopia* is prepared to abandon tradition and reshape society from scratch; he is also prepared to recognize and seek to explain change within his own society, providing a devastating account of the advance of pasture at the expense of arable, and the consequent increase of unemployment and of crime as sheep devour men. Even the death penalty – the core institution of every previous system of criminal law – seems to him pointless, for exterminating criminals has no effect if one does nothing to eliminate the causes of crime.

Utopia is thus a conundrum. It is often mentioned along with Machiavelli's *The Prince* (1513–16) as a text which marks the transition from medieval to modern; but it is easy to show how *The Prince* is grounded in Machiavelli's daily life, while *Utopia* seems to float free of More's own experience, as lost in time as it is in space.[5] Faced with this puzzle, the modern scholarly literature offers readers of *Utopia* a simple choice: if, on the one hand, you accept that More admires the institutions of *Utopia*, then you must turn to Erasmus and his network if you want to identify the intellectual antecedents of *Utopia*. This line of argument was pioneered by J. H. Hexter.[6] The Erasmians, for example, argued that true nobility is virtue: the egalitarianism of *Utopia* has its origins in this implicit attack on the feudal aristocracy of the day.[7] Alternatively, Richard Sylvester and his followers seek to persuade you that the first half of *Utopia* is a dialogue between a character called More and a character called Hythloday; far from sharing Hythloday's enthusiasm for Utopian society, the author More, we are told, shares his namesake's scepticism of Utopian communism. More has conjured up modern radicalism only in order to expose its weaknesses.[8]

This essay places itself firmly in the 'Erasmian' camp, despite the fact that its opponents have in recent years seemed to be steadily gaining ground. *Utopia*, I will suggest, pays homage to Erasmian principles, and I will show that if its close relationship to one Erasmian text in particular is recognized, its communism and radicalism become much easier to understand. I will not be so foolish as to suggest that *Utopia* ceases to be ambiguous and puzzling, for many of the ambiguities are intentional and the author quite deliberately conceals himself behind his characters, but the real puzzle of *Utopia* lies, I will maintain, in More's decision to conceal its original subject, which is friendship. By this act of concealment he did indeed go some way towards inventing modernity, implying for the first time that the political is impersonal.

In 1500 Erasmus published a brief collection of 818 Greek adages; in 1508 this grew to a large folio volume, the *Adagiorum Chiliades*. Early in 1515 an expanded edition included a number of political discussions which, it has recently been argued, are relevant to the interpretation of *Utopia*.[9] Seven further editions appeared during Erasmus' lifetime, the last containing 4,151 adages. The *Adages* is a peculiar volume, and its peculiarity explains its limited interest for modern scholars. Suppose that, a thousand years from now, scholars come across references to 'Essex girls', or find themselves puzzling over the statement that 'You don't need a weatherman to know which way the wind blows'. Then they will feel the need for a volume comparable to Erasmus' *Adages*. There Erasmus takes Ancient Greek phrases which either appear to be fragments of proverbs ('To drive out one nail by another' [I.ii.4], 'Thieves fear a noise' [I.ii.66]) or references to mysterious stereotypes ('To play Cretan with a Cretan' [I.ii.29], 'Luckier than the Strobili of Carcinus' [I.ii.68]) and explains (in Latin, the language of scholarship) where they originate, what they mean, and how they are taken up and echoed in later literature.[10] The result is an idiosyncratic and unwieldy encyclopedia of classical learning. The *Adages* is as large as a telephone book (the modern translation will occupy six volumes when it is complete), but lacks any discernible order: fortunately a helpful index was published in 1549.[11] In the sixteenth century it was presumably used as a source of wisdom ('If you are wasteful at holiday time, you may be in want at ordinary times, unless you live sparingly' [I.ii.69]) and of amusing sayings ('A party-frock for the cat: This is often said when an honour is bestowed on those who are unworthy of it' [I.ii.72]). The insights to be gained from such a work are unpredictable. 'Man is but a bubble' (II.iii.48) not only recalls the transience of life, but also reminds one how different bubbles were in an age without detergent, for Erasmus feels bound to pause to tell us what a bubble is: 'a bubble is that round swollen empty thing which we watch in water as it grows and vanishes in a moment of time'. In 1965 Margaret Mann Phillips published a valuable selection from the *Adages* which focused particularly on the 'political' adages added in the edition of 1515 ('To tax the dead' [I.ix.12]; 'War is sweet to those who do not know it' [IV.i.1]).[12] However, it is scarcely surprising that it is Erasmus' *Praise of Folly*, not the *Adages*, which appears in the Penguin Classics; that it is *The Education of a Christian Prince*, not the *Adages*, which has recently been translated for the Cambridge Texts in the History of Political Thought.[13] In the Toronto *Complete Works*, which began to appear in 1974, the first volume of the *Adages* was published in 1982; two volumes are still awaited, and the scholarly world can hardly be said to be holding its breath.[14] Still, pick up the *Adages* and start at the beginning (an odd recommendation, like starting at the beginning of a dictionary), and you will find yourself suddenly, entirely unexpectedly, on a voyage to Utopia.

First of all the *Adages* is 'Between friends all is common' (I.i.1) which stands 'as a favourable omen at the head of this collection'.[15] Erasmus gives some fifteen classical instances of the use of this adage, and remarks, 'If only it were so fixed in men's minds as it is frequent on everybody's lips, most of the evils of our lives would promptly be removed'. Plato of course is amongst those who made use of it:

Plato is trying to show that the happiest condition of a society [*felicissimum reipublicae statum*] consists in the community of all possessions: 'So the best kind of city and polity and the finest laws [*Prima quidem igitur civitas est et reipublicae status ac leges optimae*] are found where the old saying is maintained as much as possible throughout the whole city; and the saying is that friends really have all things in common'.

In 1515 Erasmus added a further sentence: 'Plato also says that a state would be happy and blessed in which these words "mine" and "not mine" were never to be heard'. Erasmus traces his favourite saying back to Pythagoras, and in the 1515 edition he adds the claim that Pythagoras actually established a community in which all things were shared in common, realizing Christian principles long before Christ. 'This is called in Latin, in a word which expresses the facts, *coenobium* [i.e. cloister – a word with monastic overtones], clearly from community of life and fortunes'.

In the preface to the *Adages* Erasmus had defended the study of adages:

> Aristotle, according to Synesius, thinks that proverbs were simply the vestiges of that earliest philosophy which was destroyed by the calamities of human history. They were preserved, he thinks, partly because of their brevity and concise-ness, partly owing to their good humour and gaiety; and for that reason are to be looked into, not in sluggish or careless fashion, but closely and deeply: for underlying them there are what one might call sparks of that ancient philosophy, which was much clearer sighted in its investigation of truth than were the philoso-phers who came after.

He then pointed to this same opening proverb as an example of 'the many uses of a knowledge of proverbs:

> anyone who deeply and diligently considers that remark of Pythagoras, 'Between friends all is common' will certainly find the whole of human happiness included in that brief saying. What other purpose has Plato in so many volumes except to urge a community of living, and the factor which creates it, namely friendship? If only he could persuade mortals of these things, war, envy and fraud would at once vanish from our midst; in short a whole regiment of woes would depart from life once and for all. What other purpose had Christ, the prince of our reli-gion? One precept and one alone He gave to the world, and that was love; on that alone, He taught, hang all the law and the prophets. Or what else does love teach us, except that all things should be common to all? In fact that united in friendship with Christ … as members of one Head and like one and the same

body we may be filled with the same spirit, and weep and rejoice at the same things together. This is signified to us by the mystic bread, brought together out of many grains into one flour, and the draught of wine fused into one liquid from many clusters of grapes. Finally, love teaches how, as the sum of all created things is in God and God is in all things, the universal all is in fact one. You see what an ocean of philosophy, or rather of theology, is opened up to us by this tiny proverb.[16]

The second adage is equally pertinent: 'Friendship is equality. A friend is another self' (I.i.2).

Plato in Book 6 of the *Laws* quotes it as an old saying and accepted as a proverb: 'There is a saying old and true and finely phrased, that equality is the maker of friendship'. ... The law of the Hebrews does not differ from this, when it commands us to love our neighbour as ourselves.[17]

Erasmus does not single out this proverb to discuss in his preface; instead, alongside 'Between friends all is common', he discusses 'The half is more than the whole' (I.ix.95): 'What doctrine was ever produced by the philosophers more salutary as a principle of life or closer to the Christian religion?'[18] Turn to this proverb, and it too turns out to be about equality, 'which is according to Pythagoras both parent and nurse of friendship'.[19] Erasmus (drawing on Hesiod) attacks 'the unbridled luxury of kings and rich men, showing how inferior their splendours are to the moderate life of ordinary folk' and quotes Euripides:

Better far, my child
Embrace equality, which binds friend to friend,
City to city and ally to ally.
Equality's the natural source of law;
The less is ever hostile to the greater –
Hence endless discord. But equality
Prescribes for men limits and balances,
And numbers all things.[20]

It would not be an exaggeration to say that Erasmus has advertised these two adages, 'Between friends all is common' and 'Friendship is equality', as encapsulating the whole of moral philosophy and as epitomizing Christian teaching. Out of respect for their author, Pythagoras, he then proceeds to collect together all the other proverbs associated with him. 'Although at first blush, as they say, some of these injunctions may seem superstitious and laughable, yet if one pulls out the allegory one will see that they are nothing else but precepts for the good life'.[21] Of the thirty-six additional proverbs he presents, some are easy to interpret as moral precepts: 'Exceed not the balance', for example, 'that is, You shall not do anything which is not just and right'. Or 'Do not eat your heart out, that is, Do not torture your own soul with cares'. 'Walk not in the public highway. ... This piece of advice agrees with the teaching of the Gospel, which recommends us to avoid the broad way where most people walk, and take the narrow way, trodden by few but leading to immortality'. Other Pythagorean adages are more resistant to Erasmus' moralizing interpretation: 'Stir not the fire with a sword'; 'Abstain from beans'; 'Do not make water on clippings from nails or hair'; 'Always have the bedclothes folded up'.[22]

But one other reminds us immediately of *Utopia*:

> Do not sit on the grain measure ... For my part at least, since when one is dealing with this kind of precept it is not only allow-able but necessary to make a guess, I should say that this Pythagorean riddle ... means that we should not idly seek leisure and sustenance from others, but acquire through our own industry the means to sustain life decently. For it is parasitical and dishonourable 'to live on the crumbs from another man's table', and have no skills whereby one can pay for the food in one's own home. ... The remark of the Apostle Paul concurs with this, and it too is in common circulation: 'If any will not work, neither shall he eat'.[23]

In Utopia, not only is labour nearly universal, but there are rules to ensure that those who do not work may not eat.[24]

Erasmus concludes his discussion of the Pythagorean maxims by invoking the man he most admired (Christ alone excepted):

> St Jerome also records this Pythagorean principle, in which that great man seems to have comprised the whole of moral philos-ophy: 'These things we must chase from us, and cut away by all means in our power – sickness from the body, ignorance from the mind, gluttony from the belly, sedition from the state, discord from the family, intemperance in short from every activity of life'.[25]

In Utopia we find, not only universal education and free health care, but also a proto-Puritanical distaste for gluttony and intemperance: 'there are no wine-bars, or ale-houses, or brothels; no chances for corruption; no hiding places; no spots for secret meetings'.[26]

I started by explaining that *Utopia* is a puzzling text because it seems to have no Renaissance antecedents: who else aside from More admired communism, praised equality, advocated labour? The answer should now be obvious: Erasmus did. And in the few sentences he added to the 1515 edition he almost invited a description of the best form of common-wealth, which would be the happiest: *De optimo reipublicae statu* is *Utopia*'s subtitle, and 'Utopia', we are told (supposedly by Hythloday's nephew), can mean either Nowhere (from Outopia), or Happy Place (from Eutopia).[27]

The correspondence between the preoccupations of the opening pages of the *Adages*, particularly as revised for the 1515 edition, and those of More in *Utopia*, begun a few months after the new edition appeared, is too great to be a coincidence simply because these preoccupations are so exceptional in their time and place. Of the idiosyncratic characteristics of the value system of *Utopia*, only the preoccupations with technology and social change are missing from the Pythagorean adages, and perhaps they should both be regarded as a necessary consequence of taking labour seriously. Even something of the dialogic structure of *Utopia* might be said to be implicit in the *Adages*, where contrasting proverbs are often pitted against each other: 'Walk not in the public highway' versus 'Do not walk outside the public highway' (I.i.2); 'Even a fool oft speaks to the point' (I.vi.1) versus 'Fools in their folly speak' (I.i.98); 'A friend is another self' (I.i.2) versus 'Each one loves himself more than his friend' (I.iii.91). In 1511 Erasmus had published *The Praise of Folly*, entitled in Latin *Encomium Moriae*: a pun on 'Praise of More'. It was natural that when More set out to produce his first substantial literary work it should take the form of an homage to Erasmus, and that where Erasmus had praised folly (by which Erasmus meant Christian values, which seem foolish to the world), More in his turn should praise what Erasmus had identified as being the epitome of true wisdom, the Pythagorean princi-ples of communism, equality and hard labour.

This is a simple hypothesis which fits the facts. Can we find supporting evidence in its favour? We would hope to discover, I would suggest, evidence of three types: first, evidence that other readers, familiar with Erasmus' work, recognized that *Utopia* was taking up a theme from the *Adages*. Second, evidence that the *Adages* invited the sort of reading which More must have given them in order to find in them the inspiration for *Utopia*. And third, and most problematic, evidence that More was conscious that there was some sense in which *Utopia* could be said to be a book about friendship.

Late in 1516 *Utopia* was seen through the press of Dirk Martens of Louvain by Erasmus and Peter Giles.[28] Giles was a friend of both Erasmus and More; *Utopia* is in effect dedicated to him, and he appears in it as responsible for introducing Hythloday, the discoverer of new-found lands, to More, the ambassador of the King of England. Giles and Erasmus added to More's text various accompanying documents: a map of Utopia (see Figure 21.1), a poem written in the Utopian language, and prefatory letters by distinguished people such as Busleyden and Desmarez. One of them added marginal glosses – Erasmus in all likelihood, for amongst the early ones are a series of synonyms for 'adage' (*proverbium, paroemia, apophthegma*): clearly, reading *Utopia* brought the theme of adages to mind.[29]

There was a further edition in 1517 (Paris, supervised by Lupset), and two in 1518 (Basel, supervised by Erasmus). In each of the first three editions the number, order and placing of the texts accompanying *Utopia* was changed. The second edition, for example, included a second letter from More to Giles, commenting on the reception of *Utopia*; somewhat surprisingly, this was dropped from later editions. But from the second edition onwards, one letter held pride of place, a letter from Guillaume Budé to Thomas Lupset thanking him for presenting him with a copy of *Utopia*. This letter, though neither Lupset nor Budé was directly involved in the original production of *Utopia*, was of such importance that Erasmus held up printing of the third edition until a copy of it could be obtained, though he was, by contrast, happy to overlook More's own addition to the text.[30] In translation, Budé's letter occupies six pages, but at its heart lies an extended attack on the inequality of property in contemporary society. By contrast,

> the founder and controller of all property, Christ, left his followers a Pythagorean rule of mutual charity and community property; not only so, but he confirmed it unmistakably when Ananias was sentenced to death for violating the rule of community property ... The island of Utopia ... is said (if the story is to be believed) to have imbibed, by marvellous good fortune, both in its public and its private life, truly Christian customs and authentic wisdom, and to have kept them inviolate even to this day. It has done so by holding tenaciously to three divine institutions: equality of all good and evil things among the citizens (or, if you prefer, full and complete citizenship for all); a fixed and unwavering dedication to peace and tranquillity; and utter contempt for gold and silver.[31]

The claim that Pythagoras had practised communism was far from being a commonplace: Erasmus had made it on the basis of a mistaken emendation which had introduced *coenobium* into early printed texts of Aulus Gellius.[32] It would seem, then, that Budé has the first of Erasmus' *Adages* in mind. He is offering the interpretation of *Utopia* that one

Figure 12.1 A map of the island of Utopia. From the first edition of *Utopia*, Louvain, 1516.

Source: British Library.

familiar with Erasmus' own writing (later in the letter he describes Erasmus as a close friend) would offer: that Utopian communism is both Pythagorean and Christian. Erasmus then validated that interpretation by placing Budé's letter in a place of honour as an introduction to More's text. In order to do so, he displaced to the end of the book a letter in praise of Utopian communism by Busleyden – 'Its great strength lies in the fact that all squabbles over private property are removed, and no one has anything of his own. Instead, everyone has everything in common for the sake of the common good' – a letter in which there is prominent reference to Plato, but none to Christ or Pythagoras.[33]

Budé's letter stands in direct opposition to what has been termed the new orthodoxy in the interpretation of *Utopia*, and naturally lay at the heart of Hexter's interpretation, which the new orthodoxy attacks. Budé insists that Utopia embodies a truly Christian way of life; Hexter echoes him; Skinner, a careful scholar who has defended this view in the past, now says 'This interpretation cannot survive'.[34] It is certainly true that the Utopian religion, which (for example) approves suicide, is at odds with Christian doctrine at certain points; but we have not only Budé's assurance that a communist way of life is a Christian one, but Erasmus', and once one recognizes that *Utopia* echoes themes from the *Adages* it becomes far harder to conclude that More intended to portray the fundamental institutions of Utopia as being at odds with Christianity. To have done so would have been to attack Erasmus, who was *Utopia*'s chief sponsor. More may, however, be inviting the reader to wonder what Christianity offers above and beyond what Pythagoras taught: the significance of the sacraments (treated by Erasmus as mere symbols in the preface to the *Adages*) is presented as being particularly problematic for the Utopians, many of whom convert to Christianity but who have no priest.[35]

Budé's letter not only insists that Utopia is to be understood as a Christian society; it also insists that *Utopia* provides practical proposals for reform:

> Our own age and ages to come will discover in [More's] narrative a seedbed, so to speak, of elegant and useful concepts from which they will be able to borrow practices to be introduced into their own several nations and adapted for use there.[36]

By contrast, the new orthodoxy insists that the careful reader is supposed to recognize that Hythloday is an impractical theorist, and that Utopia should not be imitated. Reading *Utopia* against the *Adages* does not provide new evidence that More wanted to see Utopia's institutions copied (as not only Hythloday but even the fictional 'More' implied they should be) as the Utopians copied the technology of printing press and compass, but it does remind us that Erasmus thought that the values of Utopia are eminently practical, for they are embodied wherever friends love one another.[37]

It would be a mistake to argue that Erasmus' *Adages* presents a coherent moral or political view. Because of their encyclopedic character, all opinions are to be found within, and readers are therefore free to find in them what they want. In the Bodleian Library in Oxford there is a copy of the 1515 edition of the *Adages* which has been heavily underlined by two early hands.[38] First came a reader who used red ink. He or she had a consistent interest in the theme of poverty, underlining 'Slaves have no leisure' (II.iii.46) and 'Poverty is the mother of wisdom' (II.vi.55), and a corresponding interest in the competitive nature of man, annotating 'Everyone wants things to go better for himself than for others' (I.iii.91), 'Self-love' (I.iii.92), and 'Man is a wolf to man' (I.i.71). This reader took the view that it is more than human for one man to help another (I.i.69), and, naturally, Erasmus' angry discussion of how 'Everything bows to money' (I.iii.87) is heavily underlined. When he or she reads the key Pythagorean adages that stand at the beginning of the volume it is with an eye for injustice. This reader approves the sentiment that 'Human affairs have never gone so well that the best pleases the majority'.[39] 'Red Pen' predictably approves the view, in Erasmus' discussion of labour, that 'it is parasitical and dishonourable to live on the crumbs from another man's table'.[40]

Later, a second reader, writing in an italic hand in black ink (which in at least one place lies on top of the red), heavily annotated the lengthy political adages of 1515, 'To tax the dead' (I.ix.12), 'You have obtained Sparta, adorn it' (II.v.1), and 'The Sileni of Alcibiades' (III.iii.1). This reader might have enjoyed reading Machiavelli, for in 'Adopt the outlook of the polyp' (I.i.93), an adage recommending that one adapt oneself to the circumstances in which one finds oneself, he or she underlined a passage from Plautus: 'Not a soul can be worth anything, unless he knows how to be good and bad both. He must be a rascal among rascals, rob robbers, steal what he can'.[41] In the Pythagorean adages, this second reader's eye is caught by another key phrase. 'Plato also says that a state would be happy and blessed in which these words "mine" and "not mine" were never to be heard'.[42] The passage is underlined and annotated in the margin.

I have argued that Budé recognized themes from the *Adages* in *Utopia*. Now I believe I can reasonably claim that the *Adages* invited the sort of reading that More must have given it to find within the text the inspiration for *Utopia*, for communism, equality and the dignity of labour catch these two readers' attention, just as they must have caught More's. Indeed we might say that, after Budé, these two readers were the sort of audience at which *Utopia* was directed, for they were in a good position to recognize at once the family resemblance between the Pythagorean adages and the teachings of Hythloday.

Hexter's little book on *Utopia* was subtitled 'the biography of an idea'. His starting point was the realization that More had written Book 2, the description of the island of Utopia, first, and Book 1, the debate about how to reform contemporary England, second. We can now offer a fuller account of the biography of More's idea. *Utopia* began as the description of the ideal Pythagorean community whose existence Erasmus had announced in 1515. Its form as travel literature followed from this original conception. Its peculiar characteristics – communism, equality, universal labour – were not invented by More but presented to him by Erasmus. More's task was to prove that these were indeed the characteristics of an ideal society. Of necessity, one of his concerns was to explore the question of what it meant to lead a Christian way of life without being a Christian: he therefore attributed to the Utopians a rational religion but deprived them of the sacraments. As he worked he identified a crucial theoretical problem: even if the Pythagorean conception of an ideal society could be realized in practice, such a society would inevitably find itself embroiled in conflicts with its neighbours. And in order to be sure of triumphing in such conflicts it would have to behave in a brutal and cynical fashion. Part of More's solution to this problem was to invent the Zapoletans, an evil race of bloodthirsty mercenaries who ensure Utopian victory in war, but whose deaths on the battlefield cause the Utopians to rejoice. But the Utopians cannot escape moral responsibility so easily: Utopia cannot apply the same standards to the treatment of the people outside its boundaries as it does to those within.[43]

Within Utopia there are no boundaries of class, and gender distinctions are reduced to what More may have imagined was their irreducible minimum. Every citizen is properly treated. But this presents a quite different problem. If you love your neighbour as yourself, if you treat every citizen as your friend, then love and friendship themselves become invisible because, instead of being exceptional and exclusive, they are normal and universal. Just as 'free love' is incompatible with romance, universal friendship is incompatible with the special status attributed to a friend. The absence of boundaries makes friend and citizen one and the same. *Utopia* may have begun as an account of true friendship, but it took shape as a discussion of communism, equality and labour, not friendship.

Perhaps More originally intended to preface *Utopia* with a discussion of the relationship between friendship and citizenship, as Plato prefaced the *Republic* with a discussion of whether justice was the same in the soul and the city. Perhaps he preferred to leave the book as a riddle (Erasmus had called 'Do not sit on the grain measure' a Pythagorean riddle), expecting the reader to grasp that it is friends not citizens who have everything in common. In any event, well informed readers would have recognized that there was some sense in which *Utopia*, even though it contained no explicit representation of friendship, was a book about friendship. They would have found the modern literature, which never mentions friendship in the context of *Utopia*, peculiarly blinkered. All I need to complete my argument is evidence indicating More regarded friendship to be the underlying, if concealed, subject-matter of *Utopia*. Fortunately, such evidence exists.

In the first line of the 1518 editions of *Utopia* Erasmus refers to 'my [friend] More'. The first line of More's text is addressed to 'my dearest Peter Giles'. The last sentence of More's 'preface', his letter to Giles, reads 'Farewell sweetest Peter, and farewell to your excellent wife; love me as you always have, and I for my part love you [*ego te amo*] more than ever'. Giles, we are later told, is the epitome of the perfect friend: 'with his friends so open-hearted, affectionate, loyal and sincere that you would be hard-pressed to find another man anywhere whom you would think comparable to him in all the marks of friendship'.[44] Sent as a manuscript to Erasmus and Giles, adorned and published by them, *Utopia* is itself a gift exchanged between friends.

By May of 1517, a few months after the publication of *Utopia*, Erasmus and Giles had commissioned another gift. A diptych painted by Quentin Metsys (see Figs 12.2 and 12.3) shows Erasmus and Giles sitting at opposite ends of a desk, surrounded by books. In his hand Giles holds a letter in More's handwriting, while Erasmus wears a ring given to him by More. Erasmus is working on his paraphrase of *Romans*, but his eyes are on a book which Metsys holds forward over the table edge, as if presenting it to the painting's owner. Lisa Jardine has argued, I think convincingly, that the book is the first edition of *Utopia*, a quarto volume like the one shown, which Giles and Erasmus had jointly seen through to press.[45]

When More received this painting, precious gift from his friends, he responded with two Latin poems. The first describes the painting itself, seeking to immortalize it, for More protests that wood is perishable, while this image of Erasmus and Giles deserves to live for ever. The second is entitled 'The Picture Speaks':

> Such friends as once were Castor and Pollux,
> Such I present Erasmus and Giles to you.
> More grieves to be separated from them,
> Joined as he is to them by so great a love

Figure 12.2 Erasmus, by Quentin Metsys (1517).

Source: Her Majesty Queen Elizabeth II.

As anyone could have for his own self.
They arranged to satisfy their absent friend's longing for them:
A loving letter [*amans littera*] represents their spiritual identity; I
represent their physical identity.[46]

What is the *amans littera*? There would be no problem if the word was
either *epistola* (a letter such as one sends in the post) or *libellus* (a book).[47]
A *littera* (the word is rare in the singular, more common in the plural) can
be a carved letter (as on a tombstone), handwriting (as in a signature), a
letter (for posting), a text, or a book. The general assumption has been

Figure 12.3 Peter Giles, by Quentin Metsys (1517).
Source: Private collection.

that More is referring to some letter that has not survived.[48] This seems to me to miss the convention of the poem, which is explaining how we should read the picture. The *amans littera*, I suggest, is *Utopia* itself, the volume which Giles is portrayed presenting to More. For *Utopia* portrays the true spirit of friendship: 'Between friends all is common', 'Friendship is equality'. 'All citizens after all are one another's friends', wrote Erasmus in 1531.[49] Had this been the epigraph to *Utopia*, More's book would long ago have ceased to be a riddle, and, far from seeming to be without precedent, would have easily been identified as a contribution (if a somewhat unusual one) to the Renaissance literature on friendship.[50]

For the Renaissance the theme of friendship was inextricably intertwined with that of politics, for rulers governed through their friends. The political *was* personal. In 1512, for example, Erasmus had dedicated a new translation of Plutarch's *How to Tell a Flatterer from a Friend* to Henry VIII: this was a practical guide to statesmanship.[51] The theme of friendship led naturally to the question of what sort of advice councillors should give to kings, the subject of the first book of *Utopia*. More, in 1516 as he finished *Utopia*, was torn between the true friendship he had with Erasmus (who visited him as he was finishing off his work on the book) and the friendship he might hope to form with his monarch. The two parts of *Utopia* reflect this division of loyalties.

Twenty years ago Stephen Greenblatt published a brilliant account of More as a man addicted to role-playing, a stranger even in his own home.

> There is always, it seems, a 'real' self – humanistic scholar or monk – buried or neglected, and More's nature is such that one suspects that, had he pursued wholeheartedly one of these other identities, he would have continued to feel the same way. For there is behind these shadowy selves still another, darker shadow: the dream of a cancellation of identity itself, an end to all improvisation, an escape from narrative. The dream, as I shall argue, is played out in *Utopia*, and its consequence is that More's life, and not simply his public life in the law court or the royal administration but his private life in his household or among his friends, seems composed, made up. If we may believe Roper, this quality extended even to his choice of a wife.[52]

Greenblatt goes on to tell the famous story of how More married, not the woman he loved, but her older sister. But he offers nothing to support the suggestion that More was a stranger to his friends. Greenblatt assumes that the choice of a wife is the ultimate test of a capacity for authenticity. But did it seem like that to More? He lived in a world where there was a cult of friendship, not of companionate marriage.[53] Giles appears in Greenblatt's account only as (quoting *Utopia*) 'a native of Antwerp, an honourable man of high position in his home town' and as (in Greenblatt's own words) one of 'a distinguished community of Northern European humanists, men who knew More personally or by reputation and who discuss his work among themselves in that special personal spirit one reserves for the books of friends'.[54] Here friendship is elided with acquaintance, and the friend of a friend is equated with a friend. But Giles was someone to whom More was 'joined by as great a love as anyone could have for his own self'; he was 'his sweetest friend', someone to whom he could write *ego te amo*. For More, and for the men of his day, it was a friend, not a wife, who was 'another self'.

If there were moments of authenticity in More's life they were in his relationships with his friends, and for him friendship involved a cancellation of identity, the recognition of another as one's true self.[55] Castor and Pollux are the ideal expression of true friendship because they are indistinguishable one from another. If Utopia appears as a land where men and women share a common identity (More does not even bother to record the name of a single Utopian, with the exception of Utopus, their founder), one would expect nothing more of a Pythagorean or a Christian community. It is because *Utopia* is about friendship as realized in such a community that in it More dramatizes the merging of identities, the loss of self-consciousness, the abandonment of role-playing. *Utopia* portrays the spiritual identity of friendship in general, not of a particular group of friends, because friendship, since it involves the relinquishing of individuality, the willingness to weep and rejoice at the same things together, is always the same wherever you find it. Metsys had portrayed two friends and, indirectly, the absent More. More's loving text portrayed one soul capable of inhabiting innumerable bodies, as many grains form one bread, many grapes one wine.

There is one last type of evidence for which we should look: a reflection in the *Adages* of the impact of Erasmus' reading of *Utopia*. In April 1518 Erasmus wrote to More to tell him a new edition of the *Adages* was on its way to him. He especially recommended to him two adages which appeared transformed in this edition: 'Esernius versus Pacidianus' (II.v.98) and 'As warts grow on the eye' (II.viii.65).[56] Both are attacks on clerical corruption, and particularly on the mendicant orders; Erasmus may well have thought they would remind More of the debate between the fool (*morio*: perhaps an alter ego for More himself) and the friar in *Utopia*.[57] But 'As warts grow on the eye' begins with a lengthy, new attack on the evil advice given to rulers by their counsellors, which is directly reminiscent of the 'Dialogue of Counsel' in *Utopia*, in which Hythloday insists that it would be impossible for anyone who gave honest advice to be taken seriously at court. Erasmus is horrified that

> villages are burnt down, fields laid waste, churches despoiled, innocent citizens butchered, things sacred and profane utterly confused, while all the time the prince sits idly playing games of chance, dancing, amusing himself with court fools, hunting, womanizing, drinking. O for the line of Brutus and his like, now long extinct! Where is Jove's thunderbolt, now blind or blunted?

For there is no doubt that these corrupters of princes will pay God their due penalty, though we may not live to see it. And meanwhile we must bear with them, lest tyranny give place to anarchy, an almost more pernicious evil.[58]

Even the fear of anarchy is reminiscent of *Utopia*, where More had protested to Hythloday that communism must lead to 'continual bloodshed and turmoil'.[59]

More would have read these new passages with pleasure, and seen in them evidence that he and Erasmus were engaged in a common enterprise. Perhaps he cast his eye too over the Pythagorean maxims that had inspired *Utopia*. If he did, he may have noticed a small but significant innovation in 'Feed not things that have sharp claws' (I.i.2). The entire commentary now reads as follows:

Shun rapacity, explains Tryphon. For my part I think it agrees with the saying of Aeschylus, which I shall give in its due place, 'The lion's cub must not be fostered in the state', that is, no admittance for 'people-devouring kings', as Homer has it, *or for those who create factions and powerful individuals who concentrate the wealth of the citizens in few hands, which is now the usual practice.*[60]

But the passage I have placed in italics was added in the edition of 1517/18, after the publication of *Utopia*.

In *Utopia* More had invented the word 'oligopoly' to describe the concentration of wealth in few hands. Erasmus had written 'Reader note well' in the margin of *Utopia*'s attack on 'the various commonwealths flourishing today' as 'nothing but a conspiracy of the rich, who are advancing their own interests under the name and title of the commonwealth'.[61] More had described with care the economic and social change that was reinforcing oligopoly, dramatizing his argument by referring to people-devouring sheep.[62] Having portrayed friendship, which shares all things, in Book 2, he had turned in Book 1 to portray greed, the natural product of self-love, which inevitably causes poverty and distress. He had shown that greed is not necessarily a private vice, for it is built into the operations of the market system, making even the sheep rapacious. *Utopia* may be a work portraying a form of love now lost; to read it may require an archaeology of the affections; but More's social analysis still seems up-to-date. In his brief addition to 'Feed not things that have sharp claws' we see Erasmus wrestling with More's double recognition, that oligopoly is wrong, and yet it is the result of everyday practices. The text which inspired *Utopia* gives way momentarily, imperceptibly, fleetingly to a text inspired by *Utopia*, as if to demonstrate that these friends indeed have everything in common.

Notes

1 See the poem praising *Utopia* as superior to the *Republic* which accompanied all the early editions of More's work: Thomas More, *Utopia: Latin Text and English Translation*, ed. G. M. Logan, R. M. Adams and C. H. Miller (Cambridge: Cambridge University Press, 1995), 19. For a modern English edition, see *Thomas More, Utopia, with Erasmus' The Sileni of Alcibiades*, ed. and trans. David Wootton (Indianapolis and Cambridge: Hackett, 1999).

2 On the 'modernity' of the Levellers, see David Wootton, 'The Levellers', in *Democracy: the Unfinished Journey*, ed. John Dunn (Oxford: Oxford University Press, 1992), 71–89.

3 John Locke, 'Labour', in *Political Writings*, ed. D. Wootton (Harmondsworth: Penguin, 1993), 440–2. For the connection with *Utopia* see 116.

4 But not impossible: on the Dover harbour project of 1584, see David Wootton, 'The Study of Society, 1450–1750', in *History of Humanity: Scientific and Cultural Development*, eds P. Burke and I. Habib (London: Routledge, 1999).

5 For example, J. H. Hexter, 'Thomas More: On the Margins of Modernity', *Journal of British Studies* (1961): 20–37.

6 J. H. Hexter, *More's Utopia: The Biography of an Idea* (Princeton: Princeton University Press, 1952).

7 Quentin Skinner, 'Sir Thomas More's *Utopia* and the Language of Renaissance Humanism', in *The Languages of Political Theory in Early Modern Europe*, ed. Anthony Pagden (Cambridge: Cambridge University Press, 1987), 123–57.

8 R. S. Sylvester, ' "Si Hythlodaeo Credimus": Vision and Revision in More's *Utopia*' (1968), in *Essential Articles for the Study of Thomas More*, eds R. S. Sylvester and G. Marc'hadour (Hamden CT: Archon Books, 1977), 290–301.

9 Richard J. Schoeck, *Erasmus of Europe* (Edinburgh: Edinburgh University Press, 1993), 157. On the adages of 1515 and *Utopia*, Dominic Baker-Smith, *More's Utopia* (London: Harper Collins, 1991), 62–4, 66–7, 141–3.

10 The numbering is that of the last edition to appear in Erasmus' lifetime, taken up in all later editions.

11 Joannes Vasaeus, *Index rerum et verborum copisissimus ex Des. Erasmi Rotterodami Chiliadibus* (Coimbra, 1549), which must suffice until an index to the Toronto edition is published.

12 Margaret Mann Phillips, *The Adages of Erasmus: A Study with Translations* (Cambridge: Cambridge University Press, 1965); an abbreviated paperback appeared as *Erasmus on His Times: A Shortened Version of The Adages of Erasmus* (Cambridge: Cambridge University Press, 1967).

13 Desiderius Erasmus, *Praise of Folly and Letter to Maarten van Dorp, 1515*, trans. Betty Radice, ed. A. H. T. Levi, revised edn (Harmondsworth: Penguin Books, 1993); *The Education of a Christian Prince*, trans. N. M. Cheshire and M. J. Heath, ed. Lisa Jardine (Cambridge: Cambridge University Press, 1997).

14 Desiderius Erasmus, *Collected Works*, vol. 31, trans. Margaret Mann Phillips, ed. R. A. B. Mynors (Toronto: University of Toronto Press, 1982); vols 32, 33, 34, trans. and ed. R. A. B. Mynors (Toronto: University of Toronto Press, 1989; 1991; 1992). I follow this translation, reproducing the Latin where I vary from it significantly.

15 Erasmus, *Collected Works*, vol. 31, 29–30. On this adage, see Kathy Eden, ' "Between friends all is common": the Erasmian Adage and Tradition', *Journal of the History of Ideas* 59(1998): 405–19; also John C. Olin, 'Erasmus' *Adagia* and More's *Utopia*', in *Miscellanea Moreana: Essays for Germain Marc'hardour*, ed. Clare M. Murphy, Henri Gibaud and Marto A. Di Cesare (Medieval and Renaissance Texts and Studies, Binghamton: 1989), 127–36.

16 Vol. 31, 14–15. Erasmus returned to the praise of Pythagoras in III.x.1, added in 1536.

17 Vol. 31, 31. Erasmus stressed that 'Plato did not think everything should be offered equally to old and young, learned and unlearned, stupid and wise, strong and weak, but that distribution should be made to each according to his worth'. The Utopians would have agreed: More, *Utopia*, 143.

18 Vol. 31, 30.

19 Erasmus, *Collected Works*, vol. 32, 230.

20 Vol. 32, 229, 230.

21 Erasmus, *Collected Works*, vol. 31, 32.

22 Vol. 31, 32–50.

23 Vol. 31, 34.

24 More, *Utopia*, 145.

25 Erasmus, *Collected Works*, vol. 31, 50.

26 More, *Utopia*, 145.

27 *Utopia*, 2, 19, 31n.

28 *Utopia*, 270–1.

29 *Utopia*, 27n, 36, 40, 44; also 76, 90, 94.

30 *Utopia*, 272. Erasmus' letter to Froben, which appears in front of Budé's letter in the two Froben editions of 1518 (5–7) is an introduction as much to More's *Progymnasmata* as his *Utopia*.

31 *Utopia*, 13.

32 Erasmus, *Complete Works*, vol. 31, 30n.

33 More, *Utopia*, 253.

34 Hexter, *More's Utopia*, revised edn (New York: Harper Torchbooks, 1965), 43–8; Skinner, 'Sir Thomas More's *Utopia*', 148.

35 More, *Utopia*, 221.

36 *Utopia*, 19.

37 *Utopia*, 49 (More) and 107 (Hythloday).

38 The call mark is Allen c 36.

39 Erasmus, *Collected Works*, vol. 31, 41.

40 Vol. 31, 34.

41 Vol. 31, 135.

42 Vol. 31, 30.

43 George M. Logan, *The Meaning of More's Utopia* (Princeton: Princeton University Press, 1983), 244–5.

44 More, *Utopia*, 4, 30, 38, 43.

45 Lisa Jardine, *Erasmus, Man of Letters* (Princeton: Princeton University Press, 1993), 27–41. See also Lorne Campbell, Margaret Mann Phillips, Hubertus Schulte Herbrüggen and J. B. Trapp, 'Quentin Matsys, Desiderius Erasmus, Pieter Gillis and Thomas More', *Burlington Magazine* 120(Nov. 1978): 716–25, and St Thomas More, *Complete Works*, vol. 3, part 2, eds C. H. Miller, L. Bradner, C. A. Lynch and R. Oliver (New Haven: Yale University Press, 1984), 422. The book needs to be one which jointly involved Erasmus and Giles, which rules out the second (octavo) and third (quarto) editions of *Utopia*. Alan Cromartie suggested to me that it might be Erasmus' New Testament, the best of all gifts, and unquestionably a book about true friendship. But this had appeared relatively long ago (March 1516), and was in any case a folio volume of approximately a thousand pages (Schoeck, *Erasmus of Europe*, 185), quite unlike the handsome quarto volume portrayed by Metsys. That volume is too thick to consist only of *Utopia*, but such a short work would normally have been bound with other pamphlets.

46

Tabella Loquitur: Quanti olim fuerant Pollux et Castor amici./ Erasmum tantos Aegidiumque fero./ Morus ab hi dolet esse loco, coniunctus amore/ Tam prope quam quisquam vix queat esse sibi./ Sic desyderio est consultum absentis, ut horum/ Reddat amans animum littera, corpus ego.

(More, *Complete Works*, vol. 3, part 2, 298)

On the translation of *absentis* see the note on 423.

47 I owe this point to David Womersley.

48 Allen translates *littera* as 'letter [?]': Desiderium Erasmus, *Opus epistolarum*, eds S. Allen, H. M. Allen and others, 12 vols (Oxford: Clarendon Press, 1906–58), vol. 3, 106. Campbell and others (see note 45 above) and the Yale edition both have 'letter'. Jardine has 'letters', which must be wrong (31 and note). For a poetic usage of the plural meaning 'in words' or 'on paper', see More, *Utopia*, 18. It is theoretically possible that the *amans littera* was an inscription on the picture frame, now lost. But none of the texts associated with the painting mention any such inscription.

49 Edward J. Surtz, *The Praise of Pleasure: Philosophy, Education, and Communism in More's Utopia* (Cambridge MA: Harvard University Press, 1957), 173, quoting from Erasmus' *Apophthegmata* (1531) on Lycurgus and the Spartans.

50 On this, see David Wootton, 'Francis Bacon: Your Flexible Friend', in *The World of the Favourite*, eds J. H. Elliott and Laurence Brockliss (New Haven: Yale University Press, 1999); and the fine essay by Alan Bray and Michel Rey, 'The Body of the Friend', in *English Masculinities, 1660–1800*, eds T. Hitchcock and M. Cohen (London: Addison Wesley Longman, 1999).

51 L. J. Mills, *One Soul in Bodies Twain: Friendship in Tudor and Stuart Drama* (Bloomington: Principia Press, 1937), 80.

52 Stephen Greenblatt, *Renaissance Self-fashioning from More to Shakespeare* (Chicago, University of Chicago Press, 1980), 32.

53 Lawrence Stone, *The Family, Sex and Marriage in England, 1500–1800*, 2nd edn (Harmondsworth: Penguin Books, 1979), 217–53.

54 Greenblatt, *Renaissance Self-fashioning*, 34.

55 The classic text is Michel de Montaigne's essay 'Of Friendship': see Jean Starobinski, *Montaigne in Motion* (Chicago: University of Chicago Press, 1985), 36–53.

56 *The Correspondence of Erasmus*, vol. 5, trans. R. A. B. Mynors and D. F. S. Thomson, ed. G. Bietenholz, *Collected Works* (Toronto: University of Toronto Press, 1979), 402.

57 More, *Utopia*, 77–81.

58 Erasmus, *Collected Works*, vol. 34, 75.

59 More, *Utopia*, 105.

60 Erasmus, *Collected Works*, vol. 31, 43.

61 More, *Utopia*, 244. For a discussion of More's political economy see my introduction to Thomas More, *Utopia*.

62 More, *Utopia*, 63.

Part V

RELIGION
Tradition and innovation

… their belief in God began to waver.
Burckhardt

The Renaissance is often thought of as an age of secularization, a period when religion began to play a less pronounced role than it had – or is assumed to have done – in the medieval world. But historians no longer approach the Renaissance with this assumption. The late medieval and early modern world remained profoundly religious, and it would be difficult to make sense out of the experience of communities and individuals without taking this into account.

The essays in this section provide a glimpse into two very different approaches to the history of Christianity in the Renaissance. Edward Muir's essay 'The Virgin on the Street Corner: The Place of the Sacred in Italian Cities' is representative of what might called the 'anthropological turn' in historical studies. He is curious not so much about what Renaissance Christians believed as what they practiced, and he focuses in particular on the pragmatic and social function of saints and the cult of the Virgin Mary in four Italian cities. By contrast, Euan Cameron's work ' "Civilized Religion": from Renaissance to Reformation and Counter-reformation' attends more directly to the intellectual history and, in particular, the play of humanist ideas about civilty on developments in both Protestantism and Catholicism in the early modern world. Between these two branches of Christianity, Cameron notes profound differences in the ways in which each appropriated the humanist heritage and the ways in which each approached popular religious beliefs and practices. Finally, as readers will observe, Muir and Cameron have profoundly different views of the nature of popular Catholic practices. To what degree are their differences a result of the types of sources and approaches they use?

13

THE VIRGIN ON THE STREET CORNER

The place of the sacred in Italian cities

Edward Muir

Devotion to the saints and to the Virgin contributed significantly not only to the religious but also to the social and political landscape of late medieval Europe. Indeed, Italians not only venerated saints; they also viewed the relics of the holy martyrs as powerful loci of the sacred that were diffused throughout their communities, in churches, shrines and even niches along the exterior walls of urban buildings; and they called upon the holy dead for assistance in times of crisis. Women appealed to Santa Margarita at the time of childbirth; the faithful invoked San Rocco and San Sebastiano at times of plague; while the blind and those with failing eyesight called upon Santa Lucia. As a result their shrines were often surrounded by ex votos in various forms: miniature replicas of the body part that had been healed (an arm, a hand, a leg, the heart, and so on); small painted panels that narrated the cure; or brief writings that gave thanks to the saint for the miracle received.

In the essay below, Edward Muir explores the ways in which cults – especially the, devotion to the Virgin Mary – played an active, constitutive role in forging a sense of communal identity. Precisely because the images and relics associated either with the Virgin or with a particular saint were often the focus of intense religious feeling, they not only presented the image of an ideal world but also served as the focal point for social tensions. Political rulers, religious leaders and the people themselves were acutely aware of the different roles that a cult could assume. The cult of St Mark in Venice is a perfect example. Venetian devotions were highly particularistic, with various guilds, confraternities and parishes often defining themselves in relation to a particular saint such as St Martin or St Thomas. But St Mark was the patron of the city as a whole, and Venetians turned to St Mark as a unifying devotion in a highly diverse urban environment.

To be sure, studies of the cult of saints have long served to open up a window onto salient aspects of late medieval and Renaissance popular religious beliefs and practices. But Muir's essay – largely informed by social and cultural anthropology – makes it possible to analyse religious behaviour not from the perspectives of either the official teachings of the Roman Catholic Church or of those Protestant reformers who condemned these practices, but rather as constituent dimensions of the social order, simultaneously underscoring the diverse ways in which extra-religious factors conditioned the nature of these traditional devotions. To accomplish this, Muir builds here on earlier studies of ritual behaviour in Italian cities – an area of research in which he, along with such scholars as Richard Trexler, has played a pioneering role, beginning with his book Civic Ritual in Renaissance Venice *(Princeton, 1982). But Muir's analysis here picks up on a new theme: the power of images and the small social dramas that those who encounter them re-enact. In such a world, the meaning of a sacred image or other holy object varied according to the social context in which it was placed – a feature of Renaissance social and religious life that Muir's comparative analysis (he explores religious behaviour in four Italian cities) brings out nicely. Finally, Muir's essay is an important reminder of the vitality of traditional religious beliefs and practices in the Renaissance – practices that would, in fact, persist well into the early modern and modern periods.*

This essay first appeared in Religion and Culture in the Renaissance and Reformation, *ed. Stephen Ozment (Sixteenth-Century Studies and Essays, vol. 11) (Kirksville MO, 1988), 25–40. See, by way of comparison and contrast, Peter Burke, 'How to be a Counter-reformation Saint', in* The Historical Anthropology of Early Modern Italy: Essays on Perception and Communication, *ed. Burke (Cambridge, 1987), 48–62; as well as Rudolph Bell and Donald Weinstein,* Saints and Society: The Two Worlds of Western Christendom, 1000–1700 *(Chicago, 1982). Above all, it is useful to contrast Muir's essay with the following chapter in which the historian Euan Cameron offers an intriguing overview of some of the more subtle ways in which humanist ideas led to significant changes in both Protestant and Catholic culture.*

* * *

On nearly every street corner in the back alleys of Venice, one can still find the Virgin Mary.[1] She usually presents herself as a modest statue or crude painting, or sometimes only a faded picture postcard set up within a *capitello* (niche or frame) on the outside wall of a house or church. Thousands of images of Mary, the saints and Christ proliferated throughout the city, encouraged by religious orders and parish priests, but most often produced by neighbourhood or private devotions. Beginning in 1450, the republic charged a local patrician with responsibility for watching over these images, and in the residential neighbourhoods they still flourish. Historians can never recapture all their functions and meanings in the little and great dramas of urban activity, but these Madonnas and saints had many lives. Some depicted the patron of the parish church, extending the sacrality of the church outward through a neighbourhood cult; others worked miracles, cured the afflicted and guarded against plague; some succoured the poor, protected against street crime, or discouraged blasphemy; and most reminded the living of their obligations to pray for the dead.[2] Saintly images created a setting where reverential behaviour was appropriate, and the ubiquity of images may point to a social style characterized by formality and the pervasiveness of ritual and theatricality in daily life. Intercessors with the divine permeated urban spaces in many Italian cities to such a degree that rigid distinctions between sacred and profane, so typical of the Reformation, must have seemed alien, even irreligious, to many who lived in towns magically tied together by little shrines. Italian towns, moreover, were themselves mystical bodies, a corporation both in the legal sense and the literal one of a number of persons united in one body, nourished and protected by a civic patron saint.[3] Citizenship was not just a legal distinction but one of the principal social influences in identity formation.

But situating little holy places about the city like fountains hardly guaranteed appropriate behaviour. In an attempt to reduce street violence, Udine followed such a strategy by erecting images at the entrances of each quarter and on certain houses and by encouraging neighbourhood cults, but the city fathers largely failed to pacify their community.[4] Local context determined the social significance of holy places, and the multiple touch-stones of the sacred in Italian cities – street-corner Madonnas, parish churches, monasteries, confraternity chapels, even government buildings – created tangled, overlapping, and conflicted religious commitments among believers which resembled the agonistic character of their social lives.[5] In the relationship between place and the sacred, one finds contradictory tendencies – some that promoted tensions and urban conflicts, others that fostered spiritual community. By focusing on the relationship between social behaviour and the character of the holy, one can see both how humans create sacred objects and places and how these influence behaviour.

In her essay, 'The Sacred and the Body Social in Sixteenth-century Lyon', Natalie Zemon Davis analyses the symbolic configurations of urban religion and treats Protestantism and Catholicism as 'two languages which, among many uses, could describe, mark and interpret urban life, and in particular urban space, urban time and the urban community'.[6] Whether or not the sacred could be localized in space became, after all, a major issue in the theological conflict between Catholics and Protestants, the former insisting on the divine presence in the Eucharist and treating relics as special objects of devotion, the latter refusing to acknowledge such an impious mixing of spirit and matter. But the dispute was never purely theological. Relations with the sacred provide an idealized pattern of earthly social relations, and changes in attitudes towards the sacred altered the means by which Renaissance townspeople might form their social identity.[7] Even before the

Reformation many Italian cities exhibited religious heteroglossia, to adopt Bakhtin's term: multiple languages through which various social groups approached and understood the location of the sacred.[8] Structured in part by dogma and in part by the relations between clergy and laity, a language of religious symbolism is also the product of the 'distinctive experience of the people who use it'.[9] It is this peculiarly lay language of the sacred that wants recapturing, an argot discovered in what Angelo Torre calls the 'consumption of devotions'.[10] Despite many dialectal variants, two forms, I would suggest, dominated in Italian cities.

One might be called the prophetic language, unstable in time and space, appearing, disappearing and reappearing according to the vicissitudes of events. Prophecies played a major role in lay culture, as Ottavia Niccoli has shown in her analysis of the pamphlets sold by itinerant ballad singers and preachers after piazza performances. During the political disintegration of Italy after 1494, editions of prophecies multiplied, but after the Peace of Bologna in 1530, they virtually disappeared, except perhaps in Venice.[11] The notorious plasticity of prophecies, subject to highly imaginative reinterpretations, made them alluring in unstable times but apt to evanesce after a short time.

The second kind of sacred language, and for our purposes the more important, might be called the iconic, in which holiness tended to adhere to an object or a place, sometimes in direct defiance of theological doctrine. The sacred presented itself in temporal cycles rather than with apocalyptic finality and had a more fixed relationship to space than the prophetic language, although all venerated objects were potentially mobile and some actually so, regularly moving about the city in processions. The iconic language offered citizens immediate and personal intimacy with the saints rather than the future collective salvation promised by the prophets, and images and relics had intensely meaningful relationships with urban spaces, not only because the devout wished to see and touch such objects, but also because the moving of images and relics through city streets in processions celebrated *communitas*. The perpetuation of the procession's salubrious effects was one of the objectives in erecting images of the Virgin in public places. Virgins in many locations created a different kind of procession, one actively experienced by citizens as they walked about following their daily affairs.[12]

The meanings conveyed and behaviours evoked by these images, however, could hardly be controlled or predicted. In particular, women may have reacted very differently from men to the Virgin, and since Jews could not be expected to respond as Christians, authorities had to face the reality that their cities were never fully united. In Venice and other cities where ghettos were established, residential segregation created zones free from Catholic notions of sacred spaces, and the movement of non-Christian residents about the rest of the city was carefully restricted, since they would not be influenced toward righteousness by the Virgin Mary or St Francis. In a few cases Jews were even allowed to destroy Christian images painted on the walls of their houses, although the reaction of the Christian populace to such perceived defilements might be quite violent.[13] Despite the variety of behaviour stimulated by such images, established norms defined appropriate responses.

Most Italian urban laymen and women were likely to seek communion with the saints through a proper self-presentation rather than through an agonized Augustinian self-examination on the issue of sincerity. In his recent historical anthropology of Italy, the 'land of façades', Peter Burke proposes what he calls the 'sincerity threshold'. Higher in the north of Europe than in the south, the sincerity threshold operates on a

> kind of sliding scale ... so that a stress on sincerity in a given culture tends to be associated with a lack of emphasis on other qualities, such as courtesy. ... Paradoxical as it may seem on the surface, sincerity cultures need a greater measure of self-deception than the rest – since we are all actors – while 'theatre cultures', as we may call them, are able to cultivate the self-awareness they value less.[14]

Burke seems to mean that it is more important in the north than the south to make statements of intention correspond to overt actions. In the southern theatre cultures, norms are more often established in behavioural rather than verbal terms; thus, the issue of intention and sincerity is less likely to arise. The goal of social relations in a theatre culture is similar to that of dramatic acting: to create the appearance of effortless, natural behaviour even though all may be calculated. Such an emphasis on appearances correlates with the belief, which anthropologists find characteristic of Mediterranean societies, that 'seeing' is the only reliable source of knowledge.[15] The Virgin hovering in every street required a performance, and even for the pious the most important thing was to bring this off.

Thus, when approaching the various sacred images and objects, the devout conveyed reverence through a demonstration that one had been properly socialized.[16] To calm a riotous crowd, priests would proceed through the city with a miracle-working image or relic. But there also remained a deep ambiguity about the range of behaviours acceptable in the presence of the sacred. Its separation from the corruption of business activity (seemingly required of Christians by the example of Christ's casting out the money-changers from the temple) was often transgressed in Renaissance Italy, where the market needed holy objects to facilitate business and where, for many, religious behaviour was merely another form of negotiation. Requiring an atmosphere of trust for the extension of credit and the firming of business deals, traders and artisans sought to sanctify their commercial dealings by notarizing, signing and witnessing their contracts in a church, where the parties might be invested with a fear of divine punishment for breaking their word.[17] One of the oldest standing churches in Venice, for example, is in the centre of the Rialto market, and elsewhere saints' shrines became the site for market fairs. Such profane uses provoked protests from reforming preachers such as Bernardino of Siena, but they enjoyed little success in isolating churches from the mundane, at least until the Counter-reformation.

Ambiguity about the proper use of churches, of course, reached back to the concept of sacred space peculiar to Christianity. Peter Brown has argued that one of the distinguishing characteristics of early Christianity was its belief in the mobility of the sacred.[18] Christians replaced sacred wells, caves, and trees with Christ's eucharistic body and the corpses of martyrs to the faith, objects which could be moved from place to place. Churches and monasteries were holy because of the ceremony of consecration but also because of the activities they permitted and the objects they contained: 'The place does not sanctify the man but the man the place', and the church is not essential to the relic but the relic to the church. In devotional practice holiness was revealed in gradations of intensity: some things were more holy than others. Even St Bernardino argued that a sacrilege against a holy object was far worse than one simply perpetrated within a holy place.[19]

Such distinctions manifested themselves in numerous ways. Ex votos clustered around a reliquary or a miracle-working image reflected a sensitivity to the location and intensity of the holy, and pilgrimages encouraged belief in the efficacy of gaining access to sacred objects.[20] Lay devouts often seem to have considered images as signs that indicated the presence of the saint rather than as symbols that brought the saint's spiritual qualities to mind. The impulse to decorate and embellish churches (especially altars) may have come in part from an underlying anxiety about the mobility of the sacred. A saint who was ill treated or forced to dwell in shabby surroundings might just allow his or her body to be 'translated' elsewhere. And the theft of relics was always a danger. Many of Venice's most important relics, including the body of St Mark and the head of St George, had in fact been stolen in North Africa or the Near East and brought to Venice by travelling merchants and crusaders.[21] Anxious about such possibilities, Italian citizens and clerics sought to fix sacred objects in particular places by arguing – often through hagiography, pious legends, and apparitions – that a saint favored a certain place or church. The emanations of ecclesiastical buildings confused spirit and matter in a manner that would become especially offensive to reformers. Although Catholic theology placed strict limits on sanctified objects and rejected as pagan the notion that places could be sacred by themselves, popular practice tended nonetheless to create sacred places. Leon Battista Alberti, who saw all spaces in the mathematics of proportionality and geometry, was puzzled by the mystic hierarchy of places created, he thought, by popular beliefs. But in recognizing how widespread such attitudes were, he conceded that the architect must prescribe fixed places for religious statues.

> I wonder how most people can so credit the opinions transmitted by our ancestors that it is believed that a certain picture of a god [or saint] situated in one place hears prayers while a statue of the same god a short distance away is unwilling to heed appeals? Not only that but when these same, most venerated images are moved to a different place, the people lose faith in them and quit praying to them. Such statues, therefore, must have permanent, dignified locations set aside for them alone.[22]

Complex social patterns and traditions enmeshed sacred places in a profusion of ambiguities that forced concessions to popular beliefs, which were themselves often highly creative. At the present state of research perhaps all that can be achieved is a very tentative suggestion of the varieties of these relationships. To do so, one might compare Venice, Florence, Naples and Udine. As often happens in Italian history, systematic comparisons are difficult, especially because research in these cities has concentrated on different periods. Given the diversity of Italian regions, moreover, it would be absurd to argue that these cities are representative or typical, but they do encompass a calculated variety by including two major city-republics and two cities linked by formal feudal ties to the countryside and dominated by a 'foreign' power. By the end of the sixteenth century Naples was the largest of these cities, indeed the largest of Christendom. With a population of 280,000, it was twice the size of Venice, three times that of Rome, four times that of Florence, and nearly twenty times the population of Udine.[23] Within each of these cities diverse social groups expressed their devotion in various ways. Diversity seems to have been most dramatic in Naples, least evident in Venice. Particularly before 1530, Florence displayed a range of competing forms, and the laity of Udine lacked a deeply rooted Christian language of the sacred, at least in comparison to that of other Italian towns.

As a 'theatre state' Venice, like Counter-reformation Rome, most effectively interpreted an iconic language for the purposes of maintaining public order.[24] The doges succeeded in permanently capturing St Mark for themselves, and although Mark was the patron of all Venetians, after the fourteenth century he was so surrounded by institutional barriers that he was limited to silent service at the placid centre of the state cult. In Venice processional routes included the whole city and tied the neighbourhoods to a ceremonial centre where a vast architectural frame set apart ritual performances. In Piazza San Marco, as in Rome's Piazza San Pietro, a large public square retained a special character derived from the sacred activities that took place there, and through an escalation of magnificences during the late sixteenth century, these two cities defiantly reasserted the incorporation of the sacred into worldly spaces.[25]

The salient feature of Venice's distinctive cityscape was its centre, where the most prestigious and powerful institutions clustered around the Doge's Palace and adjacent Basilica of St Mark. Exhibiting weaker forms of neighbourhood organization than in other cities and a high level of residential mobility evident as early as the thirteenth century, Venetian parishes played a small role in forming citizens' social identity.[26] Males from patrician families pursued rewards and influence by competing for civic offices and seeking government favours; thus in Venice patronage was more city-wide and less neighbourhood-bound than in Florence, Genoa, or probably most other Italian cities.

Venetian patronage, however, may have been peculiarly sex- and class-specific. Dennis Romano has suggested that Venetian patrician women, in contrast to their husbands, developed well articulated local patronage networks largely because women were secluded in their palaces and seldom appeared in public beyond the parish confines. Romano has found evidence that lower-class women in the fourteenth century frequently chose a patrician woman from their own parish to act as executor of their wills, whereas lower-class men almost never designated a male patrician to serve in this delicate capacity. Neighbourhood patronage among males in Venice fell to the better-off commoners, especially to the secondary legal elite of *cittadini*, who dominated, for example, the parish-level priesthood. A Venetian priest's influence came less perhaps from his role as confessor, spiritual advisor and preacher than from his involvement in the secular world. Parish priests served as executors of wills, held the power of attorney, acted as notaries, invested in commercial ventures, and were particularly valued as sources for small loans.[27] Apparently indifferent to parish affairs, the upper-class male Venetian experienced the sacred by joining a city-wide confraternity or by acting as a lay patron for a monastery or mendicant church, as did Italians of other cities. In fact, a significant minority of wealthy Venetians sought burial sites outside of their parish and paid for tombs in convents, monasteries or mendicant churches often located at some distance from the family house or palace.[28]

For the various annual feasts the Venetian doge and signoria attended special masses throughout the city, and in comparison to other cities, especially Florence, Venice more often commemorated historical events important for the entire city in its civic liturgy and less often recognized local patrons or important ecclesiastics.[29] Lay officials exemplified their control by dominating sacred places. Unlike Florence, neither parishes, *sestieri* (quarters), nor any other neighbourhood division was ever represented after the fourteenth century in a Venetian ritual. The constituent elements of the Corpus Christi rite in Venice, for example, were corporate groups, especially the confraternities, which were carefully regulated by the Council of Ten, and the greatest annual festival, the marriage of the doge to the sea, engaged secular and ecclesiastical hierarchies, arranged according to a rigid protocol of precedence, in a mystical union with the watery environment.[30] In comparison to other Italian cities except perhaps Rome, Venice displayed the most precise hierarchy of sacred and profane spaces, a time-bound, sometimes inverted, occasionally subverted hierarchy, but nevertheless a symbolic scheme which organized much of the urban plan. In most other cities the relative strength of private power ensured that private groups would successfully compete with public authority by elevating their private spaces to a high symbolic position.

The goal of the public control of space, to be perhaps too crudely simple, was to influence the loyalties and obligations of individuals. To accomplish this, the sacred was employed iconically to work a miraculous restructuring of social obligations in a way impossible merely through the legal expansion of public domination over urban spaces. In Venice, the necessity of controlling a difficult habitat, that ever recalcitrant space that would disappear into the sea without consistent intervention, led to the subordination of neighbourhood-based loyalties in the interest of collective ecologic survival. Only the highly personalized street Virgins and saints had strong neighbourhood ties, but the central government encouraged devotion to these images and they never seem to have threatened the hegemony of St Mark, who had a greater, more unifying, and more lasting hold on Venetian loyalties than anyone or anything else. The civic triumphed in Venice, not completely, perhaps, but completely enough to allow centrally located institutions to dominate the Venetian social and spatial order.

Multicentred Florence, in contrast, had various sources of social power and a physical geography with several distinct and dominant visual foci.[31] Major institutions were dispersed throughout the city, creating a physical geography that was visually and conceptually chaotic. Up to the end of the fifteenth century Florence was the home of prophetic publications in Italy, a sign of instability furthered by the absence of a single source of the sacred that triumphed over all others.[32] In Florence, neighbourhood clients were still the base for a political career, and in contrast to Venice there was a greater tendency for patricians to identify with their neighbourhood by sponsoring works for the local church, as the Medici did so famously with San Lorenzo.[33]

Outside of the political class, Florentines found their most vital daily contacts in their face-to-face relationships in the neighbourhood piazza. These neighbourhoods, like those in Venice, did not conform to the stereotype of the medieval city in which members of the same craft lived close together in the same district. Most neighbourhoods were socially heterogeneous, containing both the palaces of the rich and the tenements of the poor, and members of many different trades. With a few exceptions, industry was organized on such a small scale that artisans in the same trade had no special incentive to live in close proximity to one another. Apart from ethnic ghettos of foreign workers, residential segregation was normal only for the artisans in a few specialized crafts, so that the majority lived among and married the daughters of craftsmen in other professions, although during the fifteenth century, as Samuel Cohn has argued, members of the Florentine working class may have begun to experience higher rates of parish, if not occupational, endogamy than before.[34] The extended family, although it had lost its thirteenth-century corporate status, remained a vital social unit, serving as the organizing force behind Florentine commerce, qualifying one for membership in guilds and other corporate groups, continuing as a component of prestige, and influencing one's honour, status, and ability to participate in urban politics.[35]

Neighbourhood could also generate strong animosities and jealousies, for the piazza served as a common stage, bringing together a citizen's many, sometimes incompatible, roles of kinsman, friend, political ally, tax assessor, business partner, client, parishioner. Managing them and maintaining numerous potentially conflicting loyalties was an arduous task through which the most valuable social commodity of honour could be won or lost.[36] The specific role of neighbourhood in social life varied by class, by status, by age, and almost certainly by sex. For the Florentine citizens who were politically eligible and wealthy enough to pay taxes, the *gonfaloni* and quarters of the town had significant meaning. It was, after all, around the banner of the *gonfalon* that each male citizen assembled under threat of fines during the city's chief civic pageant, the feast day of St John the Baptist. For the socially marginal – the poor and the working classes, adolescents and women – neighbourhood boundaries were more fluid and amorphous, and could include piazza, street corner or alley, but generally coalesced around the parish. In the fourteenth century and again in the late fifteenth century, the *popolo minuto* organized neighbourhood festive bands which staged mock and occasionally real turf battles during feast days. By the middle of the sixteenth century, the parish, newly energized by the forces of Catholic reform, was the only remaining source of corporate solidarity, in the wake of the collapse of *gonfaloni* and guilds.[37]

As a counterweight to neighbourhood loyalties, Florentine city fathers promoted civism with the cult of St John the Baptist, whose popularity spread from the Romanesque Baptistery where all of Florence went to be baptized. The Baptistery and the adjacent cathedral became the spiritual centre of Florence, and the beginning and end for most processions. In addition, government buildings, especially the city hall, represented political salvation through the display of sacred signs and symbols. A raised platform in front of Florence's hall, for example, became an altar during civic ceremonies, thereby directly imputing divine sanction to public authority.[38]

The mobility of the sacred and the annual liturgical cycle conspired to give every major neighbourhood and its chief lay patrons a chance to demonstrate their charisma to the entire city, a chance to link the collective honour of its inhabitants to devotion to the city's chief saints. During the Florentine feast of the Magi, the link between space, sacred charisma and earthly honour was especially obvious. In this Medici-sponsored celebration of the fifteenth century, representatives of each of the three quarters of Florence, dressed as Magi kings, paid homage to the fourth quarter, passing the Medici palace and walking on to 'Bethlehem', the Medici-dominated convent of San Marco, to adore the Christ child.[39] In contrast to Venice, private groups in Florence enhanced their charisma and their claims by manipulating sacred spaces. There the sacred was subject to the same particularist forces as was the secular. Among the constants of Florentine history are that every regime laid claim to legitimacy by employing the city's vocabulary of sacred space and that social ties to local places constrained the thoroughgoing expansion of public over private space.

Naples shows even more dramatically the strangely contradictory forces playing upon sacred objects and place names, which were ritually invoked by authorities for social control and adopted by intermittent rebels to legitimate themselves and to cleanse the body politic of evil rulers. One of the distinguishing features of Naples may have been that its central sacred object, the relic of St Janarius, recurrently stimulated prophetic enthusiasms through the prognostic capabilities of the triennial liquification of the saint's blood.[40] Since the liquifications only began after St Janarius' translation to Naples in 1497, the cult evolved during Naples' domination by foreign powers, principally Spain; and since social strife was manifest through struggles over the control of the cult, its socio-political role was ambiguous.[41]

Almost every year the archbishop, civic deputies and the viceroy argued over rights of precedence in the ceremonies. For example, in 1646, the year before the revolution of Masaniello, the archbishop provocatively announced that the relics were his alone and denied the laity any rights to them. During the revolution the following year, the cathedral diarist assigned to· describe the liquifications laconically recorded, 'there is nothing to note because there was the revolution'.[42] But the people saw visions of St Janarius and employed his image on rebel coins, stealing his favour, in effect, from the archbishop, who was constrained from presiding over the regular liquification miracle. Additionally, a dark, miracle-working image of the Virgin offered special assistance to the poor of the fruit market; and on several occasions, while the authorities squabbled over the blood of St Janarius, her feast days supplied the occasions for piazza uprisings. In 1647, in fact, the market-place church of Santa Maria del Carmine served as the stage for Masaniello's raptured but short-lived revolutionary performance.[43] The great Neapolitan revolution consisted, in large part, of a competition among saints. After Masaniello's death, the archbishop interpreted a dramatically complete liquification as a sign of the saint's pleasure with the suppression of the rebellion: 'In particular', reads the cathedral diary,

> His Eminence commented more than once about never having seen [the blood] so beautifully [liquified], since after calamitous times [in the past] it had always appeared thus as a happy augury for our city ... which has in the end been liberated from the tyranny of the mob.[44]

Even more than those of Florence, the sacred and political centres of Naples were widely dispersed; its cathedral housing the miraculous relics of Janarius lay far from the Castel Nuovo, where thick stone walls protected the viceroys. Large sections of the city were divided among the noble barons, and the packed popular quarters clustered around the market-place, where the Carmelites and other orders provided the spiritual services the parish clergy neglected. Unlike Venetian doges or the Medici of Florence, no Neapolitan authority succeeded in capturing for itself the charisma of St Janarius through the sacralization of urban spaces and institutions: a failure that helped keep Naples permanently decentered and politically heterogenous.

An even more extreme example of such a failure might be Udine, a city where social divisions had clear cultural and linguistic correlates. In the early sixteenth century, Udine and the surrounding Friulan countryside witnessed some of the most widespread and violent revolts by artisans and peasants in Renaissance Italy. In 1511 more than twenty palaces in Udine were looted and burned, and perhaps two dozen castles besieged and damaged in the nearby countryside. What is most remarkable about these disturbances, especially when compared to the nearly contemporaneous revolts in the South Tyrol and Upper Swabia, is the absence of any religious content. Even the urban riots of Udine lacked the sensitivity to symbolic places so evident in similar disturbances in Florence and Naples.

This relative poverty of Christian imagery was widespread, even though for nearly four centuries the region had been an ecclesiastical principality under the patriarchs of Aquileia, and still had an exceptionally large religious establishment, constituting nearly 4 per cent of the population of Udine alone. But this establishment was notoriously neglectful of its pastoral duties. Even after Trent, suburban parish churches were still being used as barns, and the functioning of Udine's cathedral was jeopardized by a lack of liturgical vessels and ill repair. One report noted that the roof leaked so badly that divine offices might as well be said in the open. A visiting cardinal lamented that cathedral canons were infamous street fighters, most parish priests were illiterate and incapable of reciting the mass, and the monasteries were dangerous places where the monks divided into armed camps. The cathedral chapter and the civil government were forever bickering over the administration of the divine cult, but artisans and suburban peasants were apparently indifferent to the expressive possibilities of religious ritual and sacred places, neither invoking the saints nor following a ritual geography during disturbances.[45] Their models of representation derived from other sources: the vendetta, factional loyalty, magic, and carnival practices; while the populace was far more open to Protestant doctrines than the Venetians, Florentines or Neapolitans. The Cardinal of San Severina complained in 1535 that monasteries in Udine could barely survive from what charity trickled in from the laity because 'this land is close to German places infested with Lutheran lies'.[46] Lacking a charismatic centre, the extremely agonistic society of Friuli was symbolically atomistic, failing to accept any social bodies larger than family and faction.

The gap between ecclesiastical institutions and popular spiritual life was so vast that the town remained in a semi-feudal, almost clannish environment in which animal totems and heraldic blazons carried greater emotive power than relics and images. Neighbourhoods in Udine demarcated factional turfs, and even the images of the Virgin erected about the city (probably in imitation of Venetian practice) seem to have been largely ignored by the laity. Much as the Spanish viceroy of Naples – the Venetian *luogotenente* in Udine, who after 1420 was officially in charge – who lived as the outsider he was, separated from the citizens on a strongly fortified hill within the city, the cathedral and monasteries, extensions of factional patronage systems, were thoroughly incapable of providing refuge from the recurrent strife.[47] Udine might not represent so much a failure of cognition or of faith as a failure of Christianity and of political institutions to create a civic culture by encouraging the veneration of images in public places.

In all these cities, conflicting forces exerted pressure on the sacred. On the one hand, relations with the sacred presented an idealized pattern for human social relations that emphasized the virtues of hierarchy, deference and obedience and that encouraged civic concord by investing urban places with a hallowed character. Ecclesiastic and secular authorities cooperated by representing the sacred in ways that would serve desirable social ends, but their effectiveness largely depended on the ability of the civil government to marshal support and suppress opposition. Although all governments appeared to legitimate themselves through divine sanction, only those regimes that built or forced some degree of social consensus succeeded in achieving legitimacy.

On the other hand, agonistic relations among individuals and urban groups – families, neighbourhoods, guilds, classes – were projected onto the sacred, creating counter-pressures that gave spiritual sanction to civil conflicts. In Venice the Virgin encouraged passivity; in Naples she sponsored rebellion. In all of these cities, sacred places and objects were approached and understood through public performances and rituals, but the meaning of gestures of reverence came not from the form of the performance itself but from what one might call the social script. In the theatre states, the authorities made certain that they wrote the script and dominated the stage. The sincerity threshold was quite low because performing well brought rewards even if it masked crude self-interest and significant social conflict. In other cities, sacred performances were competitive – they constituted street fighting by another means – and the sincerity threshold was higher precisely because there was little agreement over the social script or even the most appropriate stage.

Where the sacred was most completely interwoven into the urban fabric, where the spiritual was most readily manifest in objects, where the incandescence of the holy could be found in the most mundane places, such as in Venice and Florence, one also finds the most effectively institutionalized, most politically sophisticated, the most economically advanced cities. Communities that failed to infuse urban spaces with a spiritual presence or to control their sacred objects were more awkwardly organized, more conflict-ridden, more economically backward, and perhaps more often open to religious reformist ideas. Such a pattern is, of course, the exact inverse of what traditional Durkheimian sociology might lead one to expect, and differs also from the more recent revisionist view that all societies are equally ritualized.[48] It is not the amount of ritual that counts, but its character and its relationship to social behaviour and verbal protestations.

The proper balance between ritual and the word, performance and intention, spirit and objects in representing the sacred was certainly one of the more vexing issues of the sixteenth century. Debated by theologians and humanists, these issues met the hard realities of daily social life in the cities. When one recalls Luther's reaction to his Roman sojourn, or Erasmus' complaints about the moral laxity among celebrants of the liturgy and lay believers alike, one wonders how much of the Reformation may have come from misunderstandings of the various dialects of popular devotion, misunderstandings that were stumblings, in effect, upon the threshold of sincerity.

Notes

1 Portions of this article have been adapted from an article co-authored with Ronald F. E. Weissman, 'Social and Symbolic Places in Renaissance Venice and Florence', in *The Power of Place*, ed. John Agnew and James Duncan (London and Boston MA: Allen & Unwin, 1989). I am grateful to Professor Weissman for his many insights which have contributed to this article and also wish to thank Patricia Fortini Brown, Linda L. Carroll, Natalie Zemon Davis and Lionel Rothkrug for their criticisms and suggestions. Professor Rothkrug emphasizes the significance of the difference between the adjectives 'holy' and 'sacred', a distinction which the Germans lacked. See his 'German Holiness and Western Sanctity in Medieval and Modern History', *Historical Reflections* 15(1988): 169, an article Professor Rothkrug kindly sent me before its publication. In Italian the distinction would be between *santo* and *sacro*, but Italian usage does not always correspond exactly to the English differences between holy and sacred, and in both languages the terms are commonly used interchangeably. Since this article is about the social and spatial context of religious images, relics and objects, exact semantic distinctions create the appearance of a greater theological precision than is possible, given the character of the evidence. I will follow, therefore, contemporary Catholic usage of the terms 'holy' and 'sacred' and do not intend to imply a precise distinction between them.

2 Antonio Niero, 'Per la storia della pietà popolare veneziana: Capitelli e immagini di santi a Venezia', *Ateneo Veneto* n.s. 8(1970): 262–7 and *idem*, 'Il culto dei santi nell'arte popolare', in A. Niero, G. Musolino and S. Tramontin, *Sanctità a Venezia* (Venice: Edizioni dello Studium Cattolico Veneziano, 1972), 229–89. Cf. M. Nani Mocenigo, 'I capitelli veneziani', *Le Tre Venezie* 17(1942): 224–7; and Paolo Toschi, 'Mostra di arte religiosa popolare', *Lares* 13(1942): 195–7.

3 Hans Conrad Peyer, *Stadt und Stadtpatron im Mittelalterlichen Italien* (Zurich: Europa Verlag, 1955). Ernst H. Kantorowicz, *The King's Two Bodies: A Study in Medieval Political Theology* (Princeton: Princeton University Press, 1957).

4 Antonio Battistella, 'Udine nel secolo XVI: La religione e i provvedimenti economico-sociale', *Memorie storiche forogiuliesi* 20(1924): 5.

5 Ronald F. E. Weissman, 'Reconstructing Renaissance Sociology: The "Chicago School" and the Study of Renaissance Society', in *Persons in Groups: Social Behavior as Identity Formation in Medieval and Renaissance Europe*, ed. Richard C. Trexler (Binghamton: Center for Medieval and Early Renaissance Studies, 1985), 44–5.

6 Natalie Zemon Davis, 'The Sacred and the Body Social in Sixteenth-century Lyon', *Past and Present* 90(1981): 42.

7 William A. Christian Jr, *Apparitions in Late Medieval and Renaissance Spain* (Princeton: Princeton University Press, 1981).

8 Mikhail Bakhtin, *Rabelais and His World* (Cambridge MA: MIT Press, 1968). Katarina Clark and Michael Holquist, *Mikhail Bakhtin* (Cambridge MA:

Harvard University Press, 1984). Tzvetan Todorov, *Mikhail Bakhtin: The Dialogical Principle* (Minneapolis: University of Minnesota Press, 1984), 56, 72–3, 77.

9 Davis, 'The Sacred and the Body Social', 67.

10 'Il consumo di devozioni: rituali e potere nelle campagne Piemontesi nella prima metà del Settecento', *Quaderni storici* n.s. 58(1985): 181–2.

11 Ottavia Niccoli, 'Profezie in piazza: Note sul profetismo popolare nell'Italia del primo Cinquecento', *Quaderni storici* 41(1979): 514–15. Cf. *idem*, 'Il re dei morti sul campo di Agnadello', *Quaderni storici* 51(1982): 929–58. I have not yet been able to consult Niccoli's new book on prophecies [though now see her *Prophecy and the People in Renaissance Italy*, trans. Lydia G. Cochrane (Princeton: Princeton University Press, 1990)]. On the survival of a prophetic tradition in Venice after the period Niccoli discusses, see Marion Leathers Kuntz, *Guglielmo Postello e la 'Vergine Veneziana': Appunti storici sulla vita spirituale dell'Ospedaletto nel Cinquecento* (Venice: Centro Tedesco di Studi Veneziani, Quaderni no. 21, 1981). John Jeffries Martin discussed a late sixteenth-century millennialist group of Venetian artisans in 'The Sect of Benedetto Corazzaro', a paper presented at the Sixteenth-century Studies Conference, Tempe, Arizona, 30 October 1987 [now published as Chapter 8 in his *Venice's Hidden Enemies: Italian Heretics in a Renaissance City* (Berkeley: University of California Press, 1993)].

12 Niero counted 406 images of the Virgin in the streets of Venice. 'Il culto dei santi', 264–85.

13 Michele Luzzatti, 'Ebrei, chiesa locale, "Principe" e popolo: Due episodi di distruzione di immagini sacre alla fine del Quattrocento', *Quaderni storici* 54(1983): 847–77.

14 Peter Burke, *The Historical Anthropology of Early Modern Italy: Essays on Perception and Communication* (Cambridge: Cambridge University Press, 1987), 12–13. Cf. David I. Kertzer, *Ritual, Politics, and Power* (New Haven: Yale University Press, 1988).

15 David D. Gilmore, 'Anthropology of the Mediterranean Area', *Annual Reviews in Anthropology* 11(1982): 197–8.

16 Richard C. Trexler, *Public Life in Renaissance Florence* (New York: Academic Press, 1980), 45–128. Cf. Moshe Barasch, *Gestures of Despair in Medieval and Early Renaissance Art* (New York: New York University Press, 1976). Michael Baxandall, *Painting and Experience in Fifteenth-century Italy: A Primer in the Social History of Pictorial Style* (Oxford: Clarendon Press, 1976), 56–71.

17 Trexler, *Public Life*, 111–12, 263–70.

18 Peter Brown, *The Cult of the Saints: Its Rise and Function in Latin Christianity* (Chicago: University of Chicago Press, 1981), 86–105.

19 Quotation from Francesco da Barberino as translated in Trexler, *Public Life*, 52–4.

20 Cf. Burke, *Historical Anthropology*, 209–10.

21 Edward Muir, *Civic Ritual in Renaissance Venice* (Princeton: Princeton University Press, 1981), 78–102. Patrick J. Geary, *Furta Sacra: Thefts of Relics in the Central Middle Ages* (Princeton: Princeton University Press, 1978).

22 Leon Battista Alberti, *L'Architettura [De Re Aedificatoria]*, ed. Giovanni Orlandi (Milan: Edizioni il Polifilo, 1966), 2: 661–3 (book 7, ch. 17). The translation is mine. The passage is analysed in Joan Gadol, *Leon Battista Alberti: Universal Man of the Early Renaissance* (Chicago: University of Chicago Press, 1969), 150–1. Also see Lionel Rothkrug, 'Holy Shrines, Religious Dissonance and Satan in the Origins of the German Reformation', *Historical Reflections* 14(1987): 146; and *idem*, 'German Holiness', 161–4.

23 Fernand Braudel, *The Mediterranean and the Mediterranean World in the Age of Philip II*, 2 vols (New York: Harper & Row, 1972), I: 345.

24 Cf. Clifford Geertz, *Negara: The Theatre State in Nineteenth-century Bali* (Princeton: Princeton University Press, 1980), and Burke, *Historical Anthropology*, 10, 174.

25 Muir, *Civic Ritual*; Charles Stinger, *The Renaissance in Rome* (Bloomington: Indiana University Press, 1985); Burke, *Historical Anthropology*, 168–82.

26 Stanley Chojnacki, 'In Search of the Venetian Patriciate: Families and Factions in the Fourteenth Century', in *Renaissance Venice*, ed. J. R. Hale (London: Faber and Faber, 1973), 59–60. Rona Goffen, *Piety and Patronage in Renaissance Venice: Bellini, Titian, and the Franciscans* (New Haven: Yale University Press, 1986), 27–8.

27 Dennis Romano, *Patricians and Popolani: The Social Foundations of the Venetian Renaissance State* (Baltimore: Johns Hopkins University Press, 1987), 91–102, 131–40. Romano has further discussed the decline of Venetian parishes after 1297 in a superb paper, 'Politics and Parishes in Early Renaissance Venice', presented at the annual conference of the Renaissance Society of America, New York, 18 March 1988. Also see Richard Mackenney, *Tradesmen and Traders: The World of the Guilds in Venice and Europe, c.1250–c.1650* (Totowa NJ: Barnes & Noble, 1987), 47.

28 Romano, *Patricians and Popolani*, 102–18; Mackenney, *Tradesmen and Traders*, 56–61; Brian Pullan, *Rich and Poor in Renaissance Venice: The Social Institutions of a Catholic State, to 1620* (Oxford: Blackwell, 1971), 33–196.

29 Muir, *Civic Ritual*, 212–23.

30 *Ibid.*, 119–34.

31 My analysis of Florence closely follows Muir and Weissman, 'Social and Symbolic Places', and is particularly indebted to Ronald F. E. Weissman, *Ritual Brotherhood in Renaissance Florence* (New York: Academic Press, 1982), and Trexler, *Public Life*. Also see Giorgio Simoncini, *Città e società nel Rinascimento*, 2 vols (Turin: Einaudi, 1974); and Richard Goldthwaite, *The Building of Renaissance Florence* (Baltimore: Johns Hopkins University Press, 1980).

32 Donald Weinstein, *Savonarola and Florence: Prophecy and Patriotism in the Renaissance* (Princeton: Princeton University Press, 1970); Niccoli, 'Profezie in piazza', 505.

33 Dale Kent and F. W. Kent, *Neighbours and Neighbourhood in Renaissance Florence: The District of the Red Lion in the Fifteenth Century* (New York: J. Augustin, 1982). Cf. Goldthwaite, *Building of Renaissance Florence*, 12–13.

34 Samuel Kline Cohn, *The Laboring Classes in Renaissance Florence* (New York: Academic Press, 1980).

35 Francis William Kent, *Household and Lineage in Renaissance Florence: The Family Life of the Capponi, Ginori, and Rucellai* (Princeton: Princeton University Press, 1977). Alfred Doren, *Le arti fiorentine*, 2 vols (Florence: Le Monnier, 1940). John M. Najemy, *Corporatism and Consensus in Florentine Electoral Politics, 1280–1400* (Chapel Hill: University of North Carolina Press, 1982). Dale Kent, *The Rise of the Medici: Faction in Florence* (Oxford: Oxford University Press, 1978).

36 Weissman, *Ritual Brotherhood*; Kent and Kent, *Neighbours and Neighbourhood*.

37 Weissman, *Ritual Brotherhood*; Trexler, *Public Life*.

38 Trexler, *Public Life*, 49.

39 *Ibid.*, 424–45.

40 Tommaso Costo, *Giunta di tre libri al compendio dell'Istoria del Regno di Napoli. Ne' quali si contiene quanto di notabile, e ad esso Regno appartenente e accaduto, dal*

principio dall'anno MDLXIII insino al fine dell'Ottantasei. Con la tavola delle cose memorabili, che in essa si contengono (Venice: Gio. Battista Cappelli e Gioseffo Peluso, 1588), 120.

41 G. B. Alfano and A. Amitrano, *Il miracolo di S. Gennaro in Napoli* (Naples: Scarpati, 1950), 145. Cf. Giuseppe Galasso, 'Ideologia e sociologia del patronato di San Tommaso d'Aquino su Napoli (1605)', in *Per la storia sociale e religiosa del Mezzogiorno d'Italia*, eds G. Galasso and Carla Russo, 2 vols (Naples: Guida Editoti, 1982). I wish to thank John Marino for bringing Galasso's article to my attention.

42 Archivio dell'Arcivescovado, Naples (hereafter AAN), MS titled *I diari dei ceremonieri della cattedrale di Napoli*, 3: 165. Franco Strazzullo, *I diari dei cerimonieri della cattedrale di Napoli: Una fonte per la storia napoletana* (Naples: Agar, 1961), xxi.

43 Burke, *Historical Anthropology*, 191–206. Rosario Villari, 'Masaniello: Contemporary and Recent Interpretations', *Past and Present* 108(1985): 117–32. Cf. Rothkrug, 'Holy Shrines', 175–6.

44 AAN, 'I diari dei cerimonieri della cattedrale di Napoli', 2: 173.

45 Battistella, 'Udine nel secolo XVI', 1–17. The situation in Friuli paralleled the prince-bishoprics in Germany. Rothktug, 'German Holiness', 162.

46 Battistella, 'Udine nel secolo XVI', 7.

47 These comments come from a book I am currently preparing on vendetta and factional strife in Friuli during the fifteenth and sixteenth centuries [see now Muir, *Mad Blood Stirring: Vendetta and Factions in Friuli during the Renaissance* (Baltimore: Johns Hopkins University Press, 1993)].

48 Cf. the comments on this issue in Burke, *Historical Anthropology*, 223–4.

14

'CIVILIZED RELIGION'

From Renaissance to Reformation and Counter-Reformation

Euan Cameron

The religious reforms of early modern Europe – both the development of Protestantism and the equally far-reaching changes that took place in the Catholic world – were a consequence, in part at least, of the new intellectual energies and passions of Renaissance humanists. Scholars have long been familiar with the role humanist scholarship played in the shaping of the Reformation. Valla's demonstration that the Donation of Constantine was a 'forgery' and Erasmus' annotated edition of the New Testament served as springboards for the work of many of the religious reforms of the sixteenth century. In the essay below, Euan Cameron explores the connection between humanism and religious reform from a new angle: namely, the humanist concern with 'civility' and the ways in which this concern played out in both Protestant and Catholic cultures in the early modern period. The theme of civility first emerged as a major issue in the historical sociology of Norbert Elias (1897–1990); Cameron's essay constitutes an early effort to explore this theme in relation to religious reform.

In his examination of Protestant culture, Cameron identifies a paradox. While Luther was dogmatic, Protestantism in general was not. Rather – and here the influence of Renaissance humanism seems to have been quite strong – Protestants tended to acknowledge the provisional nature of creeds and confessions. Moreover, like the humanists, Protestant educators and ministers took aim at what they saw as 'vulgar religion' – the mechanistic assumptions behind much popular spirituality that placed more emphasis on, say, a transaction with a particular saint than on an individual's ethics. As a result, the call for 'civilized religion' in the Protestant world meant, first, an attack on traditional Catholic practices and, second, attacks on folk beliefs, witchcraft and demonology. In the Protestant sphere, therefore, the civilizing process had a far-reaching impact on popular religious culture and, ultimately, on society in general. Changes in religion played an important role in the shift from a largely feudal culture based on patronage systems to a more individualistic social order based on merit.

Cameron also identifies a paradox within early modern Catholicism. While many of the Catholic reformers adopted humanist rhetoric, they did not accept humanist pluralism but insisted instead on the unity of the truth (and, therefore, the unity of creeds and catechisms). Consistent with this was a deep concern with heresy and error – a concern that led to an emphasis on preaching, confession and the Inquisition. Finally, unlike Protestantism, Catholicism continued to make use of traditional religious practices and rituals in order to bolster popular support for the church. In Asia and the Americas, moreover, Catholic priests and friars continued to make appeals to saints and the miraculous as part of their strategies for conversion – strategies which, in turn, continued to influence modes of preaching in Europe itself. As a result, according to Cameron, Catholicism tended to be less flexible and to adapt rather less easily to change in the early modern period than did Protestantism.

Nonetheless, Cameron's essay makes it clear that the afterlife of Renaissance humanism was, in general, important in the shaping of early modern European culture. In fact, an argument can be made that it was in the religious sphere that humanism had its greatest popular impact, especially in the Protestant world. At the same time, it is useful to compare and contrast Cameron's methodology with Muir's essay in the preceding chapter. Cameron's approach is equally historical, but he tends to give more weight to intellectual developments in the shaping of popular religious practices; in contrast Muir tends to give more weight to social and cultural factors.

This essay first appeared in Civil Histories: Essays Presented to Sir Keith Thomas, *eds Peter Burke, Brian Harrison and Paul Slack (Oxford, 2000), 49–66. For a different approach to many of the themes raised here, see James D. Tracy, 'Erasmus among the Postmodernists:* Dissimulatio, Bonae Letturae, *and* Docta Pietas *Revisited', in* Erasmus' Vision of the Church, *ed. Hilmar M. Pabel (Kirksville MO, 1995). For other assessments of the nature of early modern Catholicism, see John W. O'Malley,* Trent and All That: Renaming Catholicism in the Early Modern Era *(Cambridge MA, 2000) and the rich bibliography O'Malley includes.*

*   *   *

Many writers who advocated 'civilized' behaviour in the early modern period wrote in an overtly religious spirit. Erasmus, whose *On the Civility of the Manners of Children* inaugurated the early modern conduct book, treated refinement of manners as one of the minor branches of his broader project to create a sincere, rational Christian ethic.[1] In Giovanni della Casa's *Galateo*, written *c*.1551–5, it is a bishop who corrects the manners of a duke through his servant (the eponymous Galateo).[2] The followers and imitators of Friedrich Dedekind's *Grobianus* were largely written by German Protestant clerics.[3] The *Oráculo manual y arte de prudencia*, written by the Jesuit Baltasar Gracián in 1647, and Jean-Baptiste de La Salle's *Règles de la bienséance et de la civilité chrétienne à l'usage des écoles chrétiennes*, first published in 1703, became key texts for 'civil' conduct.[4] The clerics who wrote conduct manuals undoubtedly believed that religion, and religious instruction in particular, could make people more 'civilized': that it could restrain their passions and moderate the excesses of their natures.[5] An important revision of Norbert Elias' thesis has proposed that the early modern conduct book derived ultimately from the rules of disciplined behaviour cultivated in medieval monasteries, rather than manuals of courtly etiquette.[6]

Yet 'civility' is not associated just with Christianity as such. Rather, it has been linked with a particular shift in the cultural styles and tastes of western Europe between the late Middle Ages and the Renaissance. It saw 'civil' and 'civility' displace 'courteous' and 'courtesy' as the fashionable terms to denote approved conduct.[7] It is associated with behavioural changes, crudely definable as a move from chivalric and feudal honour to courtly refinement or bourgeois respectability. Practically, this entailed a preference for privacy versus life in the public view; for restraint versus the exhibition of emotion; and for selective and discreet generosity rather than extravagant displays of munificence. It also intersected with a more rational, individualistic attitude to the place of man in society: merit was to be preferred over hierarchy or lineage, ethical standards over the liens of patron and client, and positive law over the force of tradition and convention.[8] How far did the influences run in the other direction? Was there such a thing as 'civilized religion' – that is, religion reshaped under the influence of the Renaissance cultural developments just described? Even to ask this question entails a particular attitude to religious belief and practice. It requires that religion be treated, not just as the expression of timeless absolute principles in daily life and thought, but as a cultural phenomenon, reflecting the values of the society that cultivates it.

I

The obvious point at which to start is the change in religious priorities associated with the Renaissance. Renaissance 'humanist' religion was overwhelmingly concerned with the ethical life of the individual (hence, *inter alia*, the conduct books). Erasmus laid himself open to the charge of turning Christ into nothing more than an ethical example.[9] Religious writers who shared this preoccupation tended to identify and oppose two particular evils in religion: dogma and 'superstition'.

Erasmus mercilessly traduced those intellectual clerics who elaborated a bewilderingly complex, linguistically barbarous dogmatic theology. He argued that they wasted their energies and failed to instil real (that is, ethical) piety.[10] The key to theology, for Erasmus, was, first, to keep it short and simple; and, second, not to insist on absolute uniformity in details of belief. In a letter written to a Bohemian nobleman in 1519,

Erasmus condensed the 'sum of Christian philosophy' into less than a dozen lines, then encapsulated the principle of doctrinal pluralism in words both astonishing and ironic in view of the date of the letter: 'If any man wishes to pursue more abstruse questions ... he is welcome to do so with this restriction, that to believe what commends itself to this or that man should not at once become compulsory for everybody'.[11] In the adage *quot homines, tot sententiae* ('there are as many opinions as there are people'), Erasmus warned that

> the apostle Paul also seems to have alluded to this [proverb], when he advises that to prevent rivalry we ought to allow everyone to abound in his own opinion. If the mob of theologians were to listen to this advice, there would not nowadays be so much strife over trivial little issues.[12]

Erasmus' indifference to uniformity of dogma had its parallels in the Renaissance papal curia, where (according to Pier Antonio Bandini) no one was considered a courtier or a gentleman unless he held, in addition to the approved doctrines, his own private heresy;[13] or in the eclectic, Neoplatonic theology of German humanists such as Mutian, Celtis or Reuchlin.[14] Most undogmatic humanists (unlike Erasmus) kept their religious speculations private, the preserve of an inner circle of initiate friends.[15] Many were moderate and cautious, distrusting enthusiasm and fervour. They tended to express themselves ambivalently or ironically, and favoured discussion of alternatives over the rhetoric of absolutes.[16]

Second, the early Renaissance humanists reacted against a medieval practical theology where ritual observances and abstinences earned specific rewards, and where the church formed a great collective forum for the exchange of grace between God, the priesthood, and the souls of the living and the dead. Fasting and penance, for example, came to be regarded as 'uncivilized' or 'barbarous' to the extent that they claimed to exchange fleshly mortifications for spiritual benefits.[17] Lives and legends of saints that promised rewards for the mechanical observance of their cults, or that celebrated holy men for reconciling people through mutual restitution and social reintegration, came likewise to be condemned as 'uncivilized'.[18] Saints were no longer expected to behave like the unscrupulous and partial patrons of unruly feudatories: ethics, and the individual's moral standards, became all-important.

Erasmus continued the critique of the fifteenth-century Italians in his own way. He ridiculed as 'superstition' at best, and cynical exploitation at worst, the popular piety that traded in special vows, bogus relics, or abstinences unfounded in scripture.[19] To criticize 'superstition' was not, of course, distinctive to humanists: scholastics, led by Thomas Aquinas, had done the same for generations.[20] However, humanists tended to ridicule as human folly what medieval clerics had denounced as the deception of demons.[21] Moreover, Renaissance humanists extended their critique beyond the obviously forbidden areas of the folk magic that lived parasitically on the official cult, into more areas of sanctioned and approved religiosity than anyone before them.

If the writers of the Renaissance represent 'civility' in the religious sphere, then it is reasonable to regard their *bêtes noires*, elaborate dogma and vulgar superstition, as the epitome of 'uncivilized', or, as they said themselves, 'barbarous' religion. Without the value judgements, one might still claim that both scholastic theology and traditional Catholic piety, with its quantifiable grace and performative rituals, were the religious embodiments of medieval culture, of 'archaic' society with its organic structure and feudal, reciprocal values. The humanists' opposition to dogma and superstition may not exhaust the attributes of 'civilized religion', but it offers a starting point.

What became of this attitude after the Reformation? Before c.1520, there appeared no serious risk that the great edifice of sacerdotal authority and sacramental ministry could be shaken. It had been safe for a few choice intellectuals to raise learned doubts about doctrine, or quietly to mock the credulity of the piously uneducated. After the schism, that relaxed attitude could no longer be sustained. Humanists chose a side to take, and defended it vigorously.[22] To argue, as Erasmus did, that issues such as predestination simply did not need to be discussed, would no longer do. When Luther commented, criticizing Erasmus' religion, that 'the Holy Spirit is no sceptic', he was not accusing Erasmus unfairly of sheer unbelief. He was identifying a cultural gulf, a difference of principle over the legitimate scope of certainty in religion, which divided the early Renaissance from the early Reformation.[23]

The humanist aversion to dogma appears largely dormant until the mid-seventeenth century. A handful of freethinkers and spiritualists, such as Sebastian Franck or Caspar Schwenckfeld, or critical individualists such as Sebastian Castellio, refused to submit to any rigid form of Protestantism.[24] Hendrik Niclaes and the Familists practised an urbane, secretive dissent apparently attractive to some of Elizabeth I of England's courtiers.[25] Spiritual *libertins* and religious sceptics of seventeenth-century France like Gabriel Naudé would, from different standpoints, oppose both superstition (especially that of vulgar Catholicism) and fanatical dogmatism (especially that of militant Protestantism), in the name of a rational, non-credal faith.[26] However, these individualist freethinkers were an infinitesimal minority among the religiously minded of early modern Europe.

The task here is to analyse what became of 'civilized religion' in the confessional age: specifically, what became of the Renaissance humanists' aversion to rigid doctrinal definitions, and their mockery of a traditional religion that 'bargained' with the deity and with the dead for protection and favour. In the mainstream churches, one finds a highly complex and paradoxical state of affairs. The cultural and religious legacy of the Renaissance could not be ignored, but it was certainly transformed.

II

The humanists opposed any attempt to pin down the faith to detailed dogmas. In contrast, as Wilhelm Dilthey put it in the nineteenth century, Luther's faith 'is not the exit of dogma ... on the contrary, it has this dogma in all respects as its necessary presupposition. It stands and falls with the dogma'.[27] Paradoxically, the Renaissance humanists' *skills* of persuasive rhetoric, a fluent and attractive written style, and progressive and systematic schooling were used in the era of confessional orthodoxy to inculcate precisely the sort of dogma that Erasmus so decried.[28] More bewilderingly still, one can see a plausible connection between the credalism of the post-Reformation era and the humanists' desire for a *personal* commitment to faith. This shift towards the individual's religious commitment marked a distinct change from the 'archaic' modes of social organization identified by historians like Marvin Becker.[29] Whereas medieval popular religion, with its priestly and saintly intercessions, embodied the contemporary social principles of reciprocity, patron–client relationships and vicarious atonement,[30] none of the early modern churches officially encouraged the idea that one person could be godly on behalf of another, or that one godly action was interchangeable with another.[31] This ideal of conscious, educated commitment required a trained clergy and a trained laity. Both Protestant and Catholic churches set about this task with similar aims and similar techniques. However, the frameworks within which they worked led, ultimately, to very different outcomes.

In Protestant countries, clergy education was reformed either by recasting the existing universities to provide for the new style of clergy training; or by setting up new colleges and academies specifically to train pastors. Generally speaking, the first route was followed in kingdoms and principalities where old universities were already available to be adapted, as in most Lutheran states, and also in England and Scotland. The second route was chosen either where the existing universities were beyond the control of the reformed church (as in France) or where the state was too small to have supported a full university (as in Strasbourg, Geneva, Herborn or Neustadt).

Where possible, Protestant clergy were trained within the mainstream of academic life. The medieval philosophies that had supported traditional theology were stripped from the curriculum – for instance, by

Philipp Melanchthon for Lutheran Germany. One might have expected Melanchthon to have imposed theological standards on everything. In fact, the reverse seems to be true. Melanchthon resisted becoming a member of a theological faculty, and regarded his true home as in the arts.[32] His humanistic natural philosophy was certainly made *consistent* with his Protestantism; but the attempt recently made to tie his philosophy in with rigid Lutheranism does not seem fully persuasive.[33]

On the whole, Protestant centres of education were not like seminaries. Most did not just teach clergy; seldom were they hermetically sealed from the ideas current in the world outside. Even rare exceptions, such as the 'cloister schools' of Württemberg, fed their products into the (quite cosmopolitan) University of Tübingen for final training.[34] The Genevan academy's primary *raison d'être* was to train ministers: yet soon after Calvin's death the Genevan bourgeoisie gave it the substance, if not the name, of a university by introducing other disciplines besides theology.[35] Cultural and intellectual diversity was guaranteed by the refugee or transient communities of foreign students and pastors-to-be.[36] Zurich sent its students abroad to both Calvinist and Lutheran (especially Philippist) universities to complete their education.[37] The theoretically 'Calvinist' university of Heidelberg continued to use Melanchthon's textbook of theology.[38] Scotland, with four universities by 1600, still sent students not only to Calvinist centres, but also to Baltic Lutheran universities such as Rostock or Helmstedt.[39] Exposure to a diversity of opinions was not sought for its own sake. In some countries, especially strict Lutheran states, foreign education was seen as positively dangerous and to be discouraged.[40] It took place, first because there was often no alternative; and second, because many Protestants, especially Calvinists, were inclusive rather than exclusive in their attitudes to the orthodoxy of brother churches.

The same plurality of voices was heard in the instruction of the Protestant laity. Laypeople were introduced to dogma through catechesis. While the ideal of Protestant education may have been to inculcate absolute verbal uniformity on teaching, among the young especially,[41] no reformed catechism actually achieved total ascendancy even within the major denominations. When Luther's two catechisms appeared in 1529, many rivals were in print in Germany, often with Luther's encouragement.[42] In the reformed tradition, Calvin's catechism came too late on the scene to influence Zurich or Strasbourg, for example. The widely used Heidelberg catechism of 1563 followed a slightly different line of development from Genevan thought.[43] Moreover, as the Protestant confessions suffered internal fissures and schisms, rival factions produced competing credal documents; attempts to mediate and reconcile often simply increased the number of documents in circulation, like the Zurich consensus of 1549, the Second Helvetic

Confession of 1566, or the Lutheran Formula of Concord.[44] The catechism in the English Book of Common Prayer was so short and summary (as John Knox complained very early on) that it encouraged the formation of new, unofficial catechisms for the ready market in religious instruction.[45]

Of course, many of these catechisms and confessions expressed the same essential ideas, but at different levels of sophistication and with different emphases. Credal diversity was not embraced deliberately. Nevertheless, because the reformed doctrine of the church did not require any supranational unity of churches, it was inevitable that the church in each region or nation would acquire its own style and formulas. Minor differences in creeds or worship did not prevent churches from regarding each other as fellow members in the invisible Christian communion.[46] As confessions of faith and catechisms multiplied, it would become harder to believe that one form of words, and only one, was eternally correct. This semantic diversity must, in the fullness of time, have made easier the acceptance that all verbal expressions of the faith were provisional and relative.

The process reached a peak in mid-seventeenth-century England. The claims of so many rival religious leaders to exclusive truth – quite contrary to their intentions, one need hardly add – cancelled each other out. As Thomas Hobbes put it,

> it is unreasonable in them, who teach there is such danger in every little errour, to require of a man endued with reason of his own, to follow the reason of any other man, or of the most voices of many other men; which is little better, than to venture his salvation at crosse and pile.[47]

The wave of humanist-inspired education that followed in the wake of the Counter-reformation presents some interesting contrasts to its Protestant equivalent. It became axiomatic that priests should receive a formal academic training, even if the seminaries envisaged by the Council of Trent in many instances took a long time to appear. The Society of Jesus, which led the first wave of educational reforms,[48] adopted Renaissance educational techniques enthusiastically. Like the French secular colleges and Johann Sturm's Strasbourg *Gymnasium*, Jesuit colleges structured their teaching around graded classes, where examinations had to be passed before students could move from one grade to another.[49] Antique texts, carefully expurgated and selected, formed the core of the arts curriculum. Jesuits like Nadal tried to retrieve some works of Erasmus from their blanket condemnation in the *Index*, and continued to use his grammatical writings.[50] The florid 'copious' rhetoric of the early Renaissance came back into vogue, after it had fallen from favour elsewhere in Europe, as a means to an emotive, alluring pulpit style.[51] Ciceronian Latin survived longer than nearly anywhere else, save perhaps some English public schools.[52]

Catholic educators, Jesuits above all, gathered the harvest of the literary Renaissance. However, Jesuits then and later pointed out that scholarship was cultivated not for itself, but as a means to godliness.[53] Educators presumed that religious truth was unique and indivisible, and reflected that unity through strict uniformity. The Jesuit *Ratio studiorum*, approved in 1599, was one of the most prescriptive documents ever produced, on the content, form and method of what was taught. Sympathetic commentators, as well as its critics, speak of its 'pedagogic totalitarianism' and its 'authoritarian humanism'.[54] Even Catholics engaged in internal controversy over the content of orthodox tradition insisted that truth was indivisible.[55]

Counter-reformation educators took steps to protect their students from any exposure to heterodox ideas. To discuss opinions from sources not officially approved was forbidden in the *Ratio studiorum*. In-house textbooks were written by such Jesuits as Orazio Torsellini, author of manuals on grammar and history.[56] In the universities of Spain and Portugal, the *cursus philosophicus* detached Aristotelianism from many of the contentious debates that had troubled early Renaissance Italy.[57] Pupils could be secluded from the wider intellectual world, principally future clergy but also members of the lay elite. Such seclusion could be achieved by the seminary system (often run by Jesuits) but also became current in seventeenth-century France.[58] This conviction of the absolute unity and permanence of their teaching materials could not fail to have a paralysing effect. In Jesuit hands, humanist literary techniques went hand-in-hand with an entirely unhumanistic dependence on Aristotle and Thomas Aquinas, prescribed by Loyola at the start. Late scholasticism itself had been anything but static, and the adoption of Thomas' *Summa*, rather than Peter Lombard's *Sentences*, as a set text carried on the most forward-looking trends in fifteenth-century theology.[59] Jesuit Aristotelianism in the sixteenth century exploited the new scholarly work on the text of the philosopher.[60] However, and despite the claim that neo-Aristotelianism offered some autonomy for the natural sciences, the doctrine of substances and accidents was held sacrosanct when challenged by Descartes, precisely because to deny it would cast into doubt the official dogma of transubstantiation .[61] Nothing could be less humanist than to enthral natural philosophy to a religious dogma, expressed in scholastic categories.

The same conviction about the absolute unity of truth is seen in the production of an official catechism for the church, the *Roman Catechism*, authorized after Trent and published in 1566. After its appearance other individuals' catechisms, very numerous in the period *c.*1530–60, became much rarer, in complete contrast to the position in Protestant countries.[62] Even the three scrupulously orthodox catechisms of the Jesuit Peter Canisius were controversial in some quarters.[63] There were obvious dangers inherent in adopting a particular written formula of over 500 pages as 'a book in which to find catholic truth in all certainty'.[64] One of the lessons of the early Renaissance was, allegedly, that the relationship between words and the things that they describe is not fixed, but can entail ambiguities and uncertainties.[65] If that is so of language in general, it must be infinitely more so of religious language. Yet a recent analyst of the Roman catechism describes it as a 'timeless exposition of a timeless faith'.[66] The new redaction of the *Catechism of the Catholic Church* in 1994[67] provoked criticism from some Roman Catholic theologians over whether a single catechism could be produced and imposed by authority to be appropriate to all peoples across the world.[68] If a single catechism is not appropriate to all countries, *a fortiori*, it is not appropriate to all times. Yet this insight, a cliché in Protestantism since late-nineteenth-century liberalism, presents Catholicism with some difficulty, such is the influence of its Counter-reformation heritage.

The different outcomes of the Protestant and Catholic handling of dogma reflect, to a large measure, their different doctrines of the church, and, behind that, different ideas about the relationship of the divine to the human. An admirer of the Catholic system might argue that Protestantism succumbed to credal pluralism – and thereby equipped itself to face the modern era – through failure, while Catholicism became petrified because of its very success.

III

The second aspect of this problem, the outcome of the Renaissance critique of 'superstitious' worship, sheds further light on the question. Both confessions, by inculcating a more reasoned and conscious obedience to their principles, sought to 'civilize' early modern belief. The churches educated their priests or ministers before sending them into the parishes. When they returned to rural life in a perhaps unfamiliar parish, they at once stood at a cultural and intellectual distance from most or even all of their parishioners.[69] The new style of priest or minister was aware of himself as a professional individual, rather than as one of an organic community; parish religion in the early modern period lost some of its communal, traditional quality.[70] Priests and ministers were, in theory, predisposed to question traditional attitudes to folk religion. Their own educators attacked the belief that words, gestures, shapes drawn on parchment, or anything else could secure spiritual or material graces. The custom of divining the weather, or good or evil fortune, from chance occurrences of various kinds was denounced. This campaign to remould the popular mind clearly forms part of a move towards a more rational outlook on the causes of things in the universe.[71]

Protestant theologians did not immediately take up the Renaissance critique of 'popular religion' insofar as it was popular, rather than Catholic. They struck first and foremost at medieval Catholicism itself, its ideals as well as its debasements and corruptions. However, in the mid-sixteenth century several lines of argument enabled Protestant theologians to move the critique of 'superstitions' on from the stage reached in the later Middle Ages. Preachers and writers such as Johannes Spreter, Augustin Lercheimer or Jakob Heerbrand insisted that no ritual or form of words had power to change the properties of matter, or to instil into objects any qualities that were not there in all species of the same kind at their creation.[72] Therefore the charms of folk magicians, or the spiritual or magical significance ascribed to particular objects at particular times, were futile and meaningless. Words were just words: shapes or letters written on parchment had no power other than to contain a message. Protestants, of course, had no need to cover their condemnations of magical charms so as to protect the consecration of the eucharist or the blessing of 'sacramentals', holy water, bread, herbs, palms, and so forth. On the contrary, they went out of their way to exploit the obvious parallels between Catholic rites and magical spells: they noted the resemblances and condemned both equally.[73]

A second characteristic of Protestant thought was providentialism. Given that late medieval pastoral theologians had taught that misfortune or sudden illness might often arise from the malice of sorcerers or witches,[74] Protestants risked encouraging more, not less, recourse to folk magicians by stripping away ecclesiastical protective magic. They responded that spiritual defences against evil or misfortune were beside the point. Everything that happened proceeded from the judgement and wisdom of a loving God; one should use natural means of protection, and trust to prayer.[75] This message, though anticipated by the late medieval nominalist Martin Plantsch of Tübingen,[76] laid a far more one-sided stress on God's sovereignty than had been customary in the past.

Such extreme providentialism led, eventually, to the decline of the devil as a serious factor in religious thought. It was a small step from dissuading defence against demons, to play down the role of personified evil until it disappeared altogether. Mainstream Protestant theologians wished no such thing. Luther wrote about the presence and power of the devil frequently – too frequently for some humanists.[77] Even Melanchthon, who lacked Luther's gothic near-Manichaean imagination, lectured conventionally on the nature and power of demons.[78] Later in the century, Protestants allowed themselves, to their disadvantage, to be drawn into exorcism contests with their more impressive Catholic brethren.[79] Yet the logic of providentialism tended to set aside, if not demons as such, at least their power to shape events. Reginald Scot's *Discoverie of Witchcraft* reads in many respects like a classic Protestant work: it denounces the ignorance of the old clergy and appeals to religious knowledge and trust in the divine dispensation. However, so rigorously does it exclude the devil from serious consideration that it strays closer to unorthodoxy than most of its counterparts. Some collusive evidence has appeared to link Scot with the Familists.[80] More orthodox in his beliefs, Sir Thomas Browne nevertheless thought the chief harm done by the devil was not physical damage, but the sowing of error – including the error, which Browne thought widespread enough to mention, that the devil did not exist.[81]

Some parts of Thomas Hobbes' *Leviathan* seemed impeccably Protestant in their reasoning. In Book IV, 'Of the Kingdome of Darknesse', Hobbes reinterpreted the Protestant demonological tradition to suit his own unorthodox ideas. He attacked, in terms close to (for example) Heinrich Bullinger's *Decades*, the idea that consecrations, whether of the eucharist or any other cult object, could change the nature of the thing consecrated. He objected that the word 'consecrate' in the Bible meant nothing of the sort.[82] He departed from the traditional view in his doctrine of souls and spirits. As a materialist and a mortalist, Hobbes despised the Aristotelian and Thomist idea of 'separated essences' or 'incorporeal spirits', and not only because belief in such spirits, and especially in souls in purgatory, reinforced the politically divisive authority of the pope.[83] The whole science of 'demonology' he dismissed as derived from wrong-headed ancient philosophy. Possession and lunacy were one and the same thing; most scriptural language concerning possession was figurative. If scripture spoke of 'spirits corporeall (though subtle and invisible)', they played no part in his scheme of things.[84] Hobbes represents an extreme example: yet he shows what could happen when Aristotelian philosophy (largely protected in the Protestant universities of the sixteenth century) was discarded, and the Protestant critique of the traditional religious worldview was taken to its logical conclusion. By the late seventeenth century, the fear of intellectual 'atheism', the fear that intellectuals who took the new philosophies to their logical conclusion would undermine *all* supernatural beliefs, largely replaced the fear of superstition and magic.[85] Many bold thinkers were themselves Protestant clergy. Besides the numerous English sceptics, the Cartesian Balthasar Bekker in his *The Enchanted World* blew open the whole question of spirits and apparitions from within the heart of the Dutch Reformed Church.[86]

Protestant critiques of popular superstitions began from identical standpoints to their Catholic counterparts. Yet the logic of Protestant beliefs about the transcendence of God led inexorably to a different view of the devil, and therefore of superstition itself. Without demonology, wrong religion became less the result of demonic seductions than a product of human folly and ignorance. This attitude to wrong religion both looked backwards to the Renaissance humanists, and foreshadowed the more sweeping critiques of 'superstition' (meaning most traditional religions) made in the Enlightenment.

Roman Catholicism inherited from its late medieval past a campaign against 'vulgar errors' expressed through penitentials, confessional manuals, sermons, and treatises such as *Dives and Pauper*.[87] It brought new weapons to the task, notably the Inquisitions (in Spain and Italy) and diocesan pastoral visitations (nearly everywhere).[88] However, even to scrape the surface of this issue reveals new complexities. In the first place, the Roman Catholic Church of the Counter-reformation had to preserve continuity with its heritage, while purging that heritage of un-Catholic or corrupt elements. The frontier between popular and magisterial Catholicism was marked by a string of difficult cases. In the later Middle Ages, many cults grew up that claimed to ensure certain spiritual benefits, in this world or in the next, for their devotees. Lady Fasts gave protection against sudden death, offerings in honour of St Onofrius protected against demons, the *Bulla Sabbathina* shortened the time Carmelite friars spent in purgatory, and so on.[89] In the early modern period – and indeed before – individual theologians tried to dissuade people from trusting to rites of this sort. However, short of an absolute papal condemnation, or indeed renunciation of the whole idea of the intercession of saints, others could continue to uphold such practices.[90]

Second, some Catholic writers used the argument that special divine favours had been 'delegated' to particular cults, to justify, or at least bring into a disputable grey area, various quasi-magical charms and curative spells. If God had endowed particular saints, or particular sacraments, with special holiness for human benefit, might he not also have given particular places, or particular people, or certain forms of words, other spiritual properties? This sort of reasoning was found in highly reputable and otherwise orthodox Catholic sources such as Hieronymus Llamas and the Jesuit Leonardus Lessius. Rigorous rationalists, who denied any automatic benefits to acts of worship of any kind, may have been in a minority in the late sixteenth and early seventeenth centuries.[91]

Two circumstances encouraged Catholic defenders of the 'magical' power of ritual to press the point further than their late medieval predecessors. First, there was the mission field. Missionaries in Asia and the New World, especially those in central and southern America, struggled with indigenous religions (which they regarded as demonic) like dark-age missionaries in northern Europe.[92] Ultimately, Roman Catholicism would arrive at an accommodating syncretism at variance with its official outlook.[93] In the short term, the pressures of mission provoked eager reporting of miracles, special providences, and dramatic demonstrations of spiritual power. Missionary friars, for instance, reputedly forced devils to carry water or stones for them during the building of monasteries or mission stations.[94] Such stories found their way, via the published reports of the missions,[95] into the works of Martín Delrio or Friedrich Forner as proofs of the spiritual power inherent in Catholicism. Indigenous Americans had been exorcized, or converted to Catholicism, or both, through the power inherent in the sacraments, holy water or the sign of the cross.[96]

The confessional struggle within Europe provided another reason for Catholic writers and preachers temporarily to suspend their rationalism. Propagandists could not resist demonstrating the superiority of their faith by its power to work special miracles, above all miracles of exorcism. Tales were told of possessed people, or even haunted houses, whom Protestant prayer had failed to help, but whose demons had quailed and vanished in the presence of priests or holy objects.[97] On occasions clerics from both creeds were drawn into contests of the power, to exorcize leading in turn to pamphlet controversies over what had actually happened.[98]

These Roman Catholic responses to popular religion may ultimately prove to have been marginal examples: certainly there was little scope for future development. Nevertheless, if Protestantism's logic tended towards providentialism, Catholicism's belief that divine power was delegated downwards into holy rituals and consecrated objects tended to confirm rather than discourage an immanentist, even a 'magical' view of spiritual power. The consequences of this approach were seen in Rome's uneasy relationship with emergent science, and remain today in the official papal recognition of miracles. This outlook would have required preserving elements in late medieval religion that the humanists would certainly have regarded as 'uncivilized'.

IV

The differences between Protestant and Catholic attitudes to dogma and superstition arose not from mere coincidence or circumstances, but from fundamental differences in assumptions. Protestantism believed in an absolutely sovereign transcendent God. The churches on earth carried out his revealed will, but neither institutions nor their teaching had any prerogative access to spiritual power. In any case, the reformed churches right from the start were several, not one. Multiplicity forced Protestants to come to terms with the provisional character of much of what they wrote. Initially, this was only possible because they set scripture apart from every other form of religious writing. They uncoupled it from the continuous hermeneutic tradition within the church, in which medieval theologians had believed. In the short term this made religious pluralism easier to live with. These basic assumptions predisposed the Protestant theologians, ultimately, to adopt an attitude towards religious language and the power of ritual that had obvious affinities with the rationalism of the Renaissance humanists.

Roman Catholicism entered the early modern world with a renewed emphasis on the absolute unity of the church on earth and its teachings, and a conviction – expressed in controversy and confrontation – that it, and it alone, represented the divine dispensation on earth. This outlook tended to dampen down any doubts about the power of human language to express the faith absolutely, and to look for supernatural confirmation of its powers and authority. Yes, Roman Catholicism adopted many of the trappings of the Renaissance: its rhetoric, its educational methods, some of its textual criticism. In some respects the Jesuit tradition followed the Renaissance more enthusiastically than that of the Protestants. This humanist 'civility', however, took shape under the mantle of idealized uniformity, and of studied continuity with many of the traditions of the past. Continuity and uniformity made it difficult for the Catholic Church to respond with any suppleness to the rapidly changing cultural environment of the Counter-reformation centuries.

We have come a long way from books on manners and courtesy. However, what the humanists approved in religion, and contrasted to 'uncivilized' or 'barbarous' religion, was in fact Christianity on the threshold of modernity: religious thought awakening to a sense of the provisional, as opposed to the absolute, character of all human creeds and rituals. Both the Protestant and Catholic traditions laid claim to the mantle of the Renaissance; yet it was ultimately easier for the former to embrace its effects on religion than for the latter, with consequences that can be seen in the development of religious thought up to the present.

Notes

1 N. Elias, *The Civilizing Process: The History of Manners and State Formation and Civilization*, trans. E. Jephcott (Oxford, 1994), 43ff.; Erasmus' original text was entitled *De civilitate morum puerilium* (1st edn, ?1526; certainly 1530; 30 edns by 1536).

2 Elias, *The Civilizing Process*, 65; Giovanni Della Casa, *Galateo*, ed. Saverio Orlando (Milan, 1988); cf. M. P. Becker, *Civility and Society in Western Europe, 1300–1600* (Bloomington, 1988), 29.

3 Elias, *The Civilizing Process*, 60; Friedrich Dedekind, *Grobianus, et Grobiana … Libri tres* (Leiden, 1642).

4 Elias, *The Civilizing Process*, 538 n134; Baltasar Grecián, *Oráculo manual y arte de prudencia*, ed. M. Romera-Navarro (n.p., 1954). On this see H. Phillips, *Church and Culture in Seventeenth-century France* (Cambridge, 1997), 81ff.; on the religious background to instilling 'civility', see Phillips, *Church and Culture*, 77ff. and refs.

5 See e.g. the comment of Francis Hutchinson from 1716 quoted by I. Bostridge, *Witchcraft and its Transformations* (Oxford, 1997), 151.

6 D. Knox, '*Disciplina*: The Monastic and Clerical Origins of European Civility', in J. Monfasani and R. G. Musto (eds) *Renaissance Society and Culture: Essays in Honor of Eugene F. Rice Jr* (Ithaca NY, 1991), 107–35.

7 Elias, *The Civilizing Process*, 83ff.

8 This is the broad interpretation of 'civility' favoured in Becker, *Civility and Society, passim*, though there are others in current use.

9 A charge discussed implicitly by Luther in *Martin Luthers Werke: Kritische Gesamtausgabe* (Weimar, 1883–1948), viii, 53ff.

10 For Erasmus' attacks on theologians, see his *Praise of Folly*, in *Collected Works of Erasmus* (Toronto, 1974–), xxvii (1986), 127ff.

11 L.-E. Halkin, *Erasmus: A Critical Biography*, trans. J. Tonkin (Oxford, 1993), 133, 177, based on P. S. and H. M. Allen (eds) *Opus epistolarum Desiderii Erasmi*, iv (Oxford, 1922), 118. See also *Collected Works of Erasmus*, vii. 126–7.

12 Erasmus [and others], *Adagia, id est: prouerbiorum, paroemiarum et parabolarum omnium, quae apud graecos, latinos, hebraeos, arabas, &c. in vsu fuerunt, collectio absolutissima*, ed. J. J. Grynaeus ([Frankfurt], 1643), 31; modern translation in *Collected Works of Erasmus*, xxi (Toronto, 1982), 240–1. The passage quoted was excised by Paolo Manuzio in his expurgated *Adagia* (Rome, 1575).

13 For Pier Antonio Bandini's reminiscences, see P. McNair, *Peter Martyr in Italy: An Anatomy of Apostasy* (Oxford, 1967).

14 See ch. iii, entitled 'The *Theologia Platonica* in the Religious Thought of the German Humanists', in L. W Spitz, *Luther and German Humanism* (Aldershot, 1996), esp. ch. iii, 124ff. (chapters are separately paginated).

15 Spitz, *Luther and German Humanism*, ii. 48; cf. with the seventeenth-century French *libertins*, as in Phillips, *Church and Culture*, 237.

16 Becker, *Civility and Society*, xv; cf. *ibid.*, 54–7.

17 Becker, *Civility and Society*, 160 n23, and refs; L. W. Spitz, *The Religious Renaissance of the German Humanists* (Cambridge MA, 1963), 137–9.

18 Becker, *Civility and Society*, 14, with refs at 160 n23; Francesco Novati (ed.) *Epistolario di Coluccio Salutati* (4 vols; Rome, 1891–1911), II, 303–4; Eugenio Garin, *Italian Humanism: Philosophy and Civic Life in the Renaissance*, trans. P Munz (New York, 1965), 28; R. G. Witt, *Hercules at the Crossroads: The Life, Works, and Thought of Coluccio Salutati* (Durham NC, 1983).

19 See e.g. Erasmus' *Praise of Folly*, in *Collected Works of Erasmus*, xxvii, 144–5; *The Colloquies of Erasmus*, ed. and trans. C. R. Thompson (Chicago, 1965), esp. *Rash Vows* (4ff.), *The Shipwreck* (138 ff.), *A Pilgrimage for Religion's Sake* (285 ff.).

20 Defining the boundaries between superstition and religion forms the main issue in St Thomas Aquinas, *Summa theologica*, iia, iiae, qq. 92–6, and in a large expository and occasional literature based on these questions.

21 The whole rhetorical structure of Erasmus' *Praise of Folly* is based on the premise that Folly earns the blame (or credit) for people's superstitions: see 40–1, as in note 10 above.

22 See Spitz, *Luther and German Humanism*, ch. iv, 109; ch. v, 209.

23 See Luther's *De servo arbitrio*, as trans. in E. G. Rupp (ed.) *Luther and Erasmus: Free Will and Salvation* (1969) 105–9; on humanist scepticism, see Becker, *Civility and Society*, 58.

24 See P. M. Hayden-Roy, *The Inner World and the Outer World: A Biography of Sebastian Franck* (Renaissance and Baroque Studies and Texts, 7: New York, 1994); R. E. McLaughlin, *Caspar Schwenckfeld, Reluctant Radical: His Life to 1540* (New Haven, 1986); S. Zweig, *Ein Gewissen gegen die Gewalt, Castellio gegen Calvin* (Frankfurt am Main, 1979).

25 See C. W. Marsh, *The Family of Love in English Society, 1550–1630* (Cambridge, 1994); but cf. K. Thomas, *Religion and the Decline of Magic: Studies in Popular Beliefs in Sixteenth and Seventeenth Century England* (1971), 322.

26 Phillips, *Church and Culture*, 230 and refs.

27 W Dilthey, 'The Interpretation and Analysis of Man', in L. W. Spitz (ed.) *The Reformation: Basic Interpretations* (2nd edn, Lexington, 1972), 18.

28 See e.g. Spitz, *Luther and German Humanism*, ch. ix.

29 Becker, *Civility and Society, passim* but esp. 140–2.

30 Note the phrase 'the debt of interchanging neighbourhood', which was used in the *Golden Legend* to describe one of the reasons for reverencing the saints: E. Duffy, *The Stripping of the Altars: Traditional Religion in England 1400–1580* (New Haven, 1992), 160–70.

31 See Becker, *Civility and Society*, 62, for the decline of the idea of vicarious holiness; see also *ibid.*, 71, 182.

32 See H. Scheible (ed.) *Melanchthons Briefwechsel: Kritische und kommentierte Gesamtausgabe* (1977–), vol. T2 [Texte 255–520] (Stuttgart and Bad Cannstatt, 1995), nos. 268 (T2, 57–8), 342 (T2, 178); see also H. Scheible, 'Melanchthon, Philipp (1497–1560)', in *Theologische Realenzyklopaedie*, xxii, 373.23–6; and cf. *Briefwechsel* 432, T2, 365.1–9.

33 See S. Kusukawa, *The Transformation of Natural Philosophy: The Case of Philip Melanchthon* (Cambridge, 1995), 188–9; cf. E. Cameron, 'Philipp Melanchthon: Image and Substance', *Journal of Ecclesiastical History* 48/4(1997): 705–22, esp. 712.

34 B. Tolley, *Pastors and Parishioners in Württemberg during the Late Reformation 1581–1621* (Stanford, 1995), 10–11, 24ff.

35 K. Maag, *Seminary or University? The Genevan Academy and Reformed Higher Education, 1560–1620* (Aldershot, 1995), 24ff., 186ff.

36 On the Genevan academy, see G. Lewis, 'The Genevan Academy', in A. Pettegree, A. Duke and G. Lewis (eds) *Calvinism in Europe 1540–1620* (Cambridge, 1994). On refugee religious culture, see H. A. Oberman, *The Reformation: Roots and Ramifications*, trans. A. C. Gow (Edinburgh, 1994), 218ff.

37 Maag, *Seminary or University?*, 129–40; see also O. P. Grell and B. Scribner (eds) *Tolerance and Intolerance in the European Reformation* (Cambridge, 1996), 115.

38 Maag, *Seminary or University?*, 168.

39 *Letters of John Johnston c.1565–1611 and Robert Howie c.1565–1645*, ed. J. K. Cameron (Edinburgh, 1963), xviiiff.; Grell and Scribner (eds) *Tolerance and Intolerance*, 116.

40 See e.g. Tolley, *Pastors and Parishioners*, 10–11.

41 G. Strauss, *Luther's House of Learning: Indoctrination of the Young in the German Reformation* (Baltimore, 1978), *passim*.

42 For the diversity of early German catechisms, see F. Cohrs, *Die evangelischen Katechismusversuche vor Luthers Enchiridion* (2 vols, Berlin, 1900–2), *passim*; Strauss, *Luther's House of Learning*, 164–5.

43 A. Cochrane, *Reformed Confessions of the Sixteenth Century* (1966), 305–31; K. Barth, *The Heidelberg Catechism for Today*, trans. S. C. Guthrie (Richmond VA, 1964), 12, 22ff.

44 R. Kolb, *Confessing the Faith: Reformers define the Church, 1530–1580* (St Louis, 1991); G. Strauss, 'The Mental World of a Saxon Pastor', in P. N. Brooks (ed.) *Reformation Principle and Practice: Essays in Honour of A. G. Dickens* (1980), 164–7.

45 For Knox, see *The Works of John Knox*, ed. D. Laing (6 vols, Edinburgh, 1854–64), IV, 26. For English catechisms see I. Green, *The Christian's ABC* (Oxford, 1996), *passim*, but esp. 45–92, and 51 for an estimate of numbers.

46 Calvin, *Institutes*, IV. i. 10–16.
47 Thomas Hobbes, *Leviathan*, ed. C. B. Macpherson (Harmondsworth, 1968), 711.
48 A. Scaglione, *The Liberal Arts and the Jesuit College System* (Amsterdam, 1986), 58–9.
49 Scaglione, *Liberal Arts*, 71–2; cf. A. Schindling, *Humanistische Hochschule and freie Reichsstadt* (Wiesbaden, 1977); L. Junod and H. Meylan, *L'Académie de Lausanne au XVIème siècle* (Lausanne, 1947), 11–17.
50 Scaglione, *Liberal Arts*, 78–9.
51 *Ibid.*, 98–109.
52 *Ibid.*, 86.
53 *Ibid.*, 84; cf. F. Cesareo, 'Quest for Identity: The Ideals of Jesuit Education in the Sixteenth Century', in C. Chapple, *The Jesuit Tradition in Education and Missions: A 450-year Perspective* (London, 1993), 17–29.
54 Scaglione, *Liberal Arts*, 84, 95. See the claim from a Jesuit lecturer in the Philippines quoted by J. O'Hare, 'Jesuit Education in America', in Chapple, *The Jesuit Tradition*, 147–8, that 'not only is Jesuit education the finest system of education ever devised by the mind of man, it is the finest that ever could be devised by the mind of man'.
55 See the Simon–Bossuet debate in Phillips, *Church and Culture*, 126ff.
56 Scaglione, *Liberal Arts*, 90–1.
57 See C. B. Schmitt, Q. Skinner and E. Kessler (eds) *The Cambridge History of Renaissance Philosophy* (Cambridge, 1988), 512ff., 606ff.
58 Phillips, *Church and Culture*, 89.
59 Scaglione, *Liberal Arts*, 97–8.
60 See C. H. Lohr, 'Les Jésuites et l'aristotélisme du XVIème siècle', in L. Giard (ed.) *Les Jésuites à la Renaissance* (Paris, 1995), 79–91, esp. his comment that metaphysics in the Jesuit college resembled a body of systematic doctrine rather than an exposé of Aristotle as such.
61 Phillips, *Church and Culture*, 163ff.
62 Originally entitled *Catechismus ad parochos* (Rome, 1566); later *Catechismus Romanus*. On pre-1566 Catholic catechisms, see *Theologische Realenzyklopaedie*, xvii/5, article 'Katechismus' (Berlin, 1988), 729ff.
63 Petrus Canisius, *Summa doctrinae christianae* (Vienna, 1556), *Catechismus minimus* (Ingolstadt, 1556), and *Catechismus minor* (Cologne, 1558); Scaglione, *Liberal Arts*, 84.
64 From the preface to *Catéchisme du Concile de Trente* (Paris, 1969), 3.
65 Becker, *Civility and Society*, 83.
66 R. I. Bradley, *The Roman Catechism in the Catechetical Tradition of the Church* (Lanham MD, 1990), 3.
67 *Catechism of the Catholic Church* (1994).
68 See M. J. Walsh (ed.) *Commentary on the Catechism of the Catholic Church* (1994), esp. 2–3; J.-B. Metz and E. Schillebeeckx (eds) *World Catechism or Inculturation?* (Edinburgh, 1989).
69 Tolley, *Pastors and Parishioners*, 5ff.; cf. Phillips, *Church and Culture*, 298.
70 For communal versus individual religion in the Counter-reformation, see M. R. Forster, *The Counter-Reformation in the Villages* (Ithaca NY, 1992).
71 On the early modern critique of superstition, see e.g. S. Clark, *Thinking with Demons: The Idea of Witchcraft in Early Modern Europe* (Oxford, 1997), 472–88; cf. E. Cameron, 'For Reasoned Faith or Embattled Creed? Religion for the People in Early Modern Europe', *Transactions of the Royal Historical Society*, 6th series, VIII(1998): 165–87.

72 Johannes Spreter, *Ein Kurtzer Bericht, was von den Abgoetterischen Saegen and Beschweren zuehalten* (Basel, 1543), sigs Aiir–v , Aiii r–v; Augustin Lercheimer, *Ein Christlich Bedencken und Erinnerung von Zauberey*, in *Theatrum de veneficis* (Frankfurt am Main, 1586), 289; Jacobus Heerbrandus, *De magia disputatio* (Tübingen, 1570), 12.

73 Spreter, *Kurtzer Bericht*, sig. Aiiiv; Lercheimer, *Christlich Bedencken*, 289–90; Heerbrandus, *De magia disputatio*, 13–15; Johann Georg Godelmann, *Tractatus de magis, veneficis et lamiis* (Frankfurt, 1601), 55–8; Antonius Praetorius, *Gründlicher Bericht von Zauberey* (Frankfurt, 1629), 63–5.

74 Johannes Nider, *Formicarius*, republished as *De visionibus ac revelationibus* (Helmstedt, 1692), book 5, ch. 3; Silvestro Mazzolini Prierias, *De strigimagarum demonumnque mirandis libri iii* (Rome, 1521), book 2, ch. 7, sigs bb iiv ff. Cf. E. E. Evans-Pritchard, *Witchcraft, Oracles and Magic among the Azande* (Oxford, 1976), 18.

75 Thomas, *Religion*, 90–103.

76 Martin Plantsch, *Opusculum de sagis maleficis* (Phorce, 1507), sigs a ivr–b ivr.

77 H. A. Oberman, *Luther: Mensch zwischen Gott und Teufel* (Berlin, 1982); see also Oberman, 'Martin Luther: Between the Middle Ages and Modern Times', in Oberman, *The Reformation: Roots and Ramifications*, 56–70.

78 A story told by Melanchthon in his lectures about the illusory resuscitation of a dead musician by demonic magic is reported by Caspar Peucer, *Commentarius, de praecipuis divinationum generibus* (Frankfurt, 1607), 14.

79 See the instances described below, notes 97–8.

80 Reginald Scot, *The Discoverie of Witchcraft* (1584); on Scot's possible links with the Familists, see Clark, *Thinking with Demons*, 543–5.

81 Sir Thomas Browne, *Pseudodoxia epidemica*, in *The Works of Sir Thomas Browne*, ed. C. Sayle (3 vols, Edinburgh, 1927), I, 182–93.

82 Hobbes, *Leviathan*, 633–5.

83 *Ibid.*, 638, 691–2. Cf. H. Bullinger, *The Decades of Henry Bullinger*, trans. 'H. I.' and ed. T. Harding (4 vols, Parker Society; Cambridge, 1849–52), IV, 254–60.

84 Hobbes, *Leviathan*, 657–64. See R. Tuck, 'The "Christian Atheism" of Thomas Hobbes', in M. Hunter and D. Wootton (eds) *Atheism from the Reformation to the Enlightenment* (Oxford, 1992), 111–30.

85 Thomas, *Religion*, 309; see N. Smith, 'The Charge of Atheism and the Language of Radical Speculation, 1640–1660', in Hunter and Wootton, *Atheism*, 159–81; J. Redwood, *Reason, Ridicule and Religion: The Age of Enlightenment in England, 1660–1750* (1976), 29ff.

86 Balthasar Bekker, *De betoverde weereld* (Amsterdam, 1691–3); editions appeared in German, French, and English; A. Jelsma, 'The Devil and Protestantism', in A. Jelsma, *Frontiers of the Reformation* (Aldershot, 1998), 25–39.

87 *Dives and Pauper*, ed. P. H. Barnum (Early English Text Society OS 275, 280; 2 vols, Oxford, 1976–80), exposition of the First Commandment, chs 31–50. Nikolaus von Dinkelsbühl, 'Ain Tractat von den zehen Poten', in K. Baumann (ed.) *Aberglaube für Laien* (Quellen und Forschungen zur europaeischen Ethnologie, 6, 2 vols, Würzburg, 1991), II, 503–50.

88 M. R. O'Neil, 'Magical Healing, Love Magic and the Inquisition in Late Sixteenth-century Modena', in S. Haliczer (ed.) *Inquisition and Society in Early Modern Europe* (1987), 88–114; M. R O'Neil, '*Sacerdote ovvero strione*: Ecclesiastical and Superstitious Remedies in 16th Century Italy', in S. Kaplan (ed.) *Understanding Popular Culture* (Berlin, 1984), 53–83; U. Mazzone and A. Turchini, *I visiti pastorali: Analisi di una fonte* (Bologna, 1985).

89 *Dives and Pauper*, book I, ch. 42, i, 172–3; Nider, *De visionibus ac revelationibus*, 420ff.; Emanuele do Valle de Moura, *De incantationibus seu ensalmis opusculum Primum* ... (Evora, 1620), fol. 9v–p. 13.

90 Valle de Moura reports different views on the *Bulla Sabbathina: De incantationibus*, 12ff., citing Fr Thomas de Jesus, *De antiquitate et sanctitate ordinis carmilitani*, book 2, ch. 1.

91 Valle de Moura, *De incantationibus*, 29ff., with refs to Nicolaus Serarius, *Commentarii in sacros Bibliorum libros, Josuae, Judicum, Ruth, Tobiae* ... (Paris, 1611), on Tobit, ch. 8; and to Francisco Valles, *De iis quae scripta sunt physice in libris sacris, sive de sacra pbilosophia liber singularis* ([Geneva], 1595), ch. 28; see de Moura's discussion of Llamas and Lessius, in *De incantationibus*, 65 ff.; also Martinus Delrio SJ, *Disquisitionum Magicarum Libri Sex*, 3 vols (Lyon, 1599–1600), I, 37–42, on *saludadores*.

92 V. I. J. Flint, *The Rise of Magic in Early Medieval Europe* (Oxford, 1991); A. Murray, 'Missionaries and Magic in Dark-Age Europe', *Past and Present* 136(1992): 186–205.

93 Jacques Lafaye, *Quetzalcoatl and Guadalupe*, trans. B. Keen (Chicago, 1976); N. S. Davidson, *The Counter-reformation* (Oxford, 1987), 70ff.

94 Valle de Moura, *De incantationibus*, fol. 5r, with refs to Joannes dos Santos, *Ethiopia Oriental* (Evora, 1609), and [Diego] Ortiz, *Compendium summarum*.

95 Accounts used to this effect include: Luis Frois, *Brevis Iapaniae insulae descriptio* (Cologne, 1582); Pedro de Cieza de Leon, *Cronica del Peru* (Seville, 1553, and subsequently), part I, ch. 118.

96 Delrio, *Disquisitionum*, III, 237ff., 247ff., 263ff., 284ff.; Friedrich Forner, *Panoplia armaturae Dei* (Ingolstadt, 1626), 141, 148–9, 255, 262ff.

97 Delrio, *Disquisitionum*, II, 75ff., III, 285; Forner, *Panoplia*, 98–9, 268–9.

98 E.g. the 'Miracle at Laon' of 1566, in D. P. Walker, *Unclean Spirits* (London, 1981), 19–28; or Peter Canisius' exorcism of Anna von Bernhausen at Altötting, in Martin Eisengrein, *Unser liebe Fraw zu Aten Oetting* (Ingolstadt, 1571), and Johannes Marbach, *Von Mirackeln und Wunderzeichen* (Strasbourg, 1571), as analysed by Philip Soergel.

RENAISSANCE READINGS

Readers who wish to pursue the secondary literature on particular topics raised by the essays in this volume will find useful references in the endnotes to each of the chapters. But one of the pleasures of the study of the Renaissance is the ready availability of a wide array of primary sources in translation. Here I provide a sampling. *Ad fontes!*

Documentary sources

Domenico Scandella Known as Menocchio: His Trials before the Inquisition (1583–1599), ed. Andrea Del Col and trans. John A. and Anne C. Tedeschi. Binghamton: Medieval and Renaissance Texts and Studies, 1996.

The English Renaissance: An Anthology of Sources and Documents, ed. Kate Aughterson. London: Routledge, 1998.

Life and Death in a Venetian Convent: The Chronicle and Necrology of Corpus Domini, 1395–1436, trans. Daniel E. Bornstein. Chicago: University of Chicago Press, 2000.

The Society of Renaissance Florence: A Documentary Study, ed. Gene A. Brucker. Toronto: University of Toronto Press, 1998.

Two Memoirs of Renaissance Florence: The Diaries of Buonaccorso Pitti and Gregorio Dati, ed. Gene A. Brucker. Prospects Heights IL: Waveland Press, 1991.

Venice: A Documentary History, 1450–1630, eds David Chambers, Jennifer Fletcher and Brian Pullan. Toronto: University of Toronto Press, 2001.

Renaissance texts: humanism, literature, religion, philosophy and science

Individual authors

Alberti, Leon Battista, *The Family in Renaissance Florence*, translation and introduction by Renée Neu Watkins. Columbia: University of South Carolina Press, 1969.

——*On Painting*, trans. Cecil Grayson, introduction by Martin Kemp. London: Penguin, 1991.

Aretino, Pietro, *The Marescalco (Il Marescalco)*, trans. with an introduction and notes by Leonard G. Sbrocchi and J. Douglas Campbell. Ottawa: Dovehouse Editions, 1987.

Ariosto, Ludovico, *Orlando Furioso*, trans. Guido Waldman. Oxford: Oxford University Press, 1998.

Boccaccio, Giovanni, *The Decameron*, trans. G. H. McWilliam. London: Penguin, 1995.

Bodin, Jean, *Colloquium of the Seven about Secrets of the Sublime*, trans. Marion L. Daniels Kuntz. Princeton: Princeton University Press, 1975.

——*Method for the Easy Comprehension of History*, trans. Beatrice Reynolds. New York: Norton, 1969.

Bracciolini, Poggio, *Two Renaissance Book Hunters: The Letters of Poggius Bracciolini to Nicolaus de Niccolis*, trans. Phyllis Walter Goodhart Gordan. New York: Columbia University Press, 1991.

Bruni, Leonardo, *History of the Florentine People*, vol. 1, ed. and trans. James Hankins. Cambridge MA: Harvard University Press, 2001.

Castiglione, Baldassare, *The Book of the Courtier*, trans. George Anthony Bull. London: Penguin, 1987.

Catherine of Siena, *The Dialogue of St Catherine of Siena*. Pittsburgh: Harry Plantinga, 1995.

Cellini, Benvenuto, *The Autobiography*, trans. George Anthony Bull. New York: Penguin, 1998.

Cereta, Laura, *Collected Letters of a Renaissance Feminist*, ed. Diana M. Robin. Chicago: University of Chicago Press, 1997.

Cervantes [Saavedra], Miguel de, *The Adventures of Don Quixote*, trans. John M. Cohen. London: Penguin, 1965.

Compagni, Dino, *Dino Compagni's Chronicle of Florence*, trans. Daniel E. Bornstein. Philadelphia: University of Pennsylvania Press, 1986.

Della Casa, Giovanni, *Galateo: A Renaissance Treatise on Manners*, trans. Konrad Eisenbichler and Kenneth R. Bartlett. Toronto: Center for Reformation and Renaissance Studies, 1994.

Christine de Pizan, *The Book of the City of Ladies*, trans. Rosalind Brown-Grant. London: Penguin, 2000.

Dante [Alighieri], *The Divine Comedy* – many translations readily available.

Da Vinci, Leonardo, *The Notebooks of Leonardo da Vinci*, ed. and trans. Irma A. Richter. Oxford: Oxford University Press, 1998.

Bernal Diaz [del Castillo], *The Conquest of New Spain*, trans. J. M. Cohen. Harmondsworth: Penguin, 1963.

Erasmus, Desiderius, *The Praise of Folly*, trans. Betty Radice. London: Penguin, 1994.

Ficino, Marsilio, *Platonic Theology*, vol. 1, eds William R. Bowen and James Hankins. Cambridge MA: Harvard University Press, 2001.

——*Three Books on Life*, eds John R. Clark and Carol V. Kaske. Binghamton: Medieval and Renaissance Texts and Studies, 1989.

Fonte, Moderata, *The Worth of Women: Wherein Is Clearly Revealed Their Nobility and Their Superiority to Men*, trans. Virginia Cox. Chicago: University of Chicago Press, 1997.

Franco, Veronica, *Poems and Selected Letters*, ed. Margaret F. Rosenthal and trans. Ann Rosalind Jones. Chicago: University of Chicago Press, 1998.

Galileo Galilei, *Dialogue Concerning the Two Chief World Systems, Ptolemaic & Copernican*, trans. Stillman Drake, with a foreword by Albert Einstein. Berkeley: University of California Press, 1967.

——*The Galileo Affair: A Documentary History*, ed. and trans. Maurice A. Finocchiaro. Berkeley: University of California, 1989.

Guicciardini, Francesco, *The History of Italy*, ed. and trans. Sidney Alexander. Princeton: Princeton University Press, 1984.

——*Maxims and Reflections of a Renaissance Statesman (Ricordi)*, trans. Mario Domandi with an introduction by Nicolai Rubinstein. New York: Harper & Row, 1965.

Ignatius of Loyola, *Personal Writings: Reminiscences, Spiritual Diary, Select Letters including the Text of the Spiritual Exercises*, trans. Philip Endean and Joseph A. Munitz. London: Penguin, 1996.

Landucci, Luca, *A Florentine Diary from 1450 to 1516*, trans. Alice de Rosen Jervis. London: J. M. Dent and New York: Dutton, 1927.

Las Casas, Bartolomé de, *A Short Account of the Destruction of the Indies*, ed. and trans. Nigel Griffen with an introduction by Anthony Pagden. London: Penguin, 1992.

Machiavelli, Niccolò, *Discourses on Livy*, trans. Harvey C. Mansfield and Nathan Tarcov. Chicago: University of Chicago Press, 1996.

——*Florentine Histories*, trans. Harvey C. Mansfield and Laura Banfield. Princeton: Princeton University Press, 1990.

——*The Mandragola (The Mandrake)*, trans. Mera J. Flaumenhaft. Prospect Heights IL: Waveland Press, 1981.

——*The Prince* – many translations readily available.

Marinella, Lucrezia, *The Nobility and Excellence of Women, and the Defects and Vices of Men*, trans. Anne Dunhill. Chicago: University of Chicago Press, 1999.

Michelangelo [Buonarotti], *The Complete Poems of Michelangelo*, trans. John Frederick Nims. Chicago: University of Chicago Press, 1998.

Montaigne, *The Complete Essays of Montaigne*, trans. Donald M. Frame. Stanford: Stanford University Press, 1989.

More, Thomas, *Utopia*, ed. and trans. David Wootton. Indianapolis: Hackett, 1999.

Petrarch [Petrarca, Francesco], *Petrarch's Secret: Or the Soul's Conflict with Passion: Three Dialogues between Himself and St. Augustine*, trans. William H. Draper. Westport: Hyperion Press, 1978.

——*Selections from the Canzoniere and Other Works*, ed. and trans. Mark Musa. Oxford: Oxford University Press, 1999.

Pico della Mirandola, Giovanni, *Oration on the Dignity of Man*, trans. A. Robert Caponigri with an introduction by Russell Kirk. Washington: Regnery Publishing, 1996.

Poliziano, Angelo, *Stanze of Angelo Poliziano*, trans. David Quint. University Park: Pennsylvania State University Press, 1993.

Polo, Marco, *The Travels of Marco Polo*, trans. Ronald E. Latham. New York: Penguin, 1992.

Rabelais, François, *Gargantua and Pantagruel*, trans. J. M. Cohen. New York: Penguin, 1983.

Shakespeare, William, *The Norton Shakespeare*, eds Stephen Greenblatt, Walter Cohen, Jean E. Howard, Katharine Eisaman Maus and Andrew Gurr. New York: Norton, 1997. For individual works, the Arden editions are excellent, but readers have a wide range of choices of formats and publishers.

Teresa of Avila, *The Life of St Teresa of Avila by Herself*, ed. J. M. Cohen. Harmondsworth: Penguin, 1957.

Valla, Lorenzo, *The Treatise of Lorenzo Valla on the Donation of Constantine*, trans. Christopher B. Coleman. Toronto: University of Toronto Press, 1993.

Vasari, Giorgio, *Lives of the Artists*, trans. George Bull. New York: Penguin, 1987.

Vespasiano da Bisticci, *The Vespasiano Memoirs: Lives of Illustrious Men of the Fifteenth Century*, trans. William George and Emily Waters. Toronto: University of Toronto Press, 1997.

Vespucci, Amerigo, *Letters from a New World: Amerigo Vespucci's Discovery of America*, ed. Luciano Formisano, trans. David Jacobson. New York: Marsilio, 1992. Also includes letters from Columbus and Las Casas.

Anthologies

The Catholic Reformation: Savonarola to Ignatius Loyola: Reform in the Church, 1495–1540, ed. John C. Olin. New York: Fordham University Press, 1993. Selections of works by Girolamo Savonarola, John Colet, Egidio da Viterbo, Erasmus, Gasparo Contarini, Lefèvre d'Etaples, St Ignatius and others as well as selected documents.

The Civilization of the Italian Renaissance, ed. Kenneth R. Bartlett. Lexington: D. C. Heath and Company, 1992. Selections by, among others, Giovanni Villani, Boccaccio, Bruni, Salutati, Poggio Bracciolini, Isotta Nogarola, Ficino, Poliziano, Francesco Barbaro, Alberti, Laura Cereta, Brunelleschi, Isabelle d'Este, Aenaeas Silvius Piccolomini and Lorenzo Valla.

The Earthly Republic: Italian Humanists on Government and Society, ed. Benjamin G. Kohl and Ronald G. Witt. Philadelphia: University of Pennsylvania Press, 1978. Selections of works by Francesco Petrarca, Coluccio Salutati, Leonardo Bruni, Francesco Barbaro and Angelo Poliziano.

The Renaissance Philosophy of Man: Petrarca, Valla, Ficino, Pico, Pomponazzi, Vives, eds Paul Oskar Kristeller, John Herman Randall and Ernst Cassirer. Chicago: University of Chicago Press, 1948. Selections of works by Francesco Petrarca, Lorenzo Valla, Marsilio Ficino, Pietro Pompanazzi and Juan Luis Vives.

INDEX